D0223821

Choral Conducting

FOCUS ON COMMUNICATION

Harold A. Decker

Colleen J. Kirk

WAVELAND
PRESS, INC.
Prospect Heights, Illinois

For information about this book, write or call:

Waveland Press, Inc.
P.O. Box 400
Prospect Heights, Illinois 60070
(847) 634-0081

Copyright © 1988 by Harold A. Decker and Colleen J. Kirk
1995 reissued by Waveland Press, Inc.

ISBN 0-88133-876-1

Printed in the United States of America

7   6   5   4   3   2

To the many students
from whom we have learned

Contents

Preface

This book is designed to provide direction and guidance for college students of choral conducting, and to stimulate the practicing conductor who is receptive to alternative approaches to choral development and problem solving. It is the result of professional experience in guiding choral conductors who share this art with singers and audiences.

The authors recognize the importance of using quality repertoire to achieve skill in artistry and communication. They further recognize that development of effectiveness in choral conducting depends on laboratory experience that provides singers' response to conducting. For these reasons, the text includes a section of musical selections representing the several periods of choral composition entitled Music for Class Study and Conducting.

The musical selections used as illustrations and material for study are available from the publishers, as well as in the collection designed for class use in coordination with the text.

Conducting teachers seeking an effective framework for the progress of their students will find useful projects and assignments in the Appendix. They will also find guides for establishing an effective choral laboratory situation (singers who respond to the student conductors' developing skill in communication). Appendix material provides additional annotated repertory suggestions and language pronunciation guides.

The authors believe that two explanations are important:

Musical selections included for illustration and practice are representative of repertory that has endured the test of time through various periods of choral art. While the transient nature of "popular" selections makes their inclusion inadvisable, principles of effective communication can be applied to choral music of any style.

Principles of singing and vocal development have optimal effect upon performance of music in which nuance is dependent upon vocal control. When a microphone is used by a developing singer, the voice is not challenged to achieve its full potential. Its development may even be arrested.

This book is not intended as a substitute for in-depth writings in the area of choral music history. The authors make no attempt to rewrite scholarly resources that contribute significantly to the understanding of those who would delve into all useful writings. For this reason, we have included a selected bibliography.

Definitions of terms used in this text appear in the Glossary.

The writers gratefully acknowledge the following:

For permission to reprint octavo music selections: Mark Foster Music Company, Champaign, Illinois; National Music Publishers, Tustin, California; Carus Verlag, Stuttgart, Germany; Chantry Music Press, Springfield, Ohio.

For drawings, illustrations, and music engraving: Barbara Brinson; William Jay Colle III; Stephen Ten Eyck; Charles McConnell.

For permission to include concert programs: Doreen Rao; Stephen Rosolack; John Silantien.

For compiling listings of repertory: Monte Atkinson; Jameson Marvin; Doreen Rao.

For typing and other technical assistance: Shirley Hicks; David Bradley.

Music publications are frequently out-of-print. Conductors are asked to refer to a current edition of *Choral Music in Print* for listing of publishers when ordering copies of the recommended music in Chapter 7 and Appendix D. You will find this available to you at retail stores and in music libraries. Also available directly from Musicdata, Inc., P.O. Box 48010, Philadelphia, PA 19144, tel. (215) 842-0555.

Harold A. Decker
Colleen J. Kirk

Prologue

The Importance of Communication

Music has long been respected for its power to convey feeling, to create or alter mood, to appeal to our spirit, and to unify humankind. Music can reflect much about the life, feelings, and interests of our ancestors and all who lived before us. It can also tell us about our society and the era in which we live. Through the creation and re-creation of music, we can tell others about ourselves.

Music, a temporal art, is more effectively perceived during the period of time devoted to its performance. The artistic beauty of music is conveyed through sound; it must be *heard* if it is to achieve its potential as an art form. A composition depends heavily upon the quality of performance for its ability to reach an audience. The composer communicates with an audience through performers. Conversely, an audience depends upon the performers' skills in communication for enjoyment and understanding.

Communication has been defined as a giving and receiving of information, signals, or messages by talk, gestures, or writing. To communicate, then, is to impart, to share, to pass along, or to make common; to give or interchange thoughts, feelings, information, or the like, by writing or speaking.[1]

The choral experience is an avenue that is unique for communication. Because of the group dynamic, a conductor's role is that of catalyst and facilitator. Both singing group and audience are dependent upon the conductor's skills and artistry.

Conducting presents musical opportunities and challenges for communication. As illustrated in Figure P-1, a solo performer is concerned with imparting *directly* to an audience the artistic intentions and messages of composers. By contrast, conductors are faced with a formidable and complicated assignment. They must first share perceptions of a composer's intentions with the musicians who combine to form the instrument (chorus, instrumental ensemble, or both).

---

[1]*Random House Dictionary.*

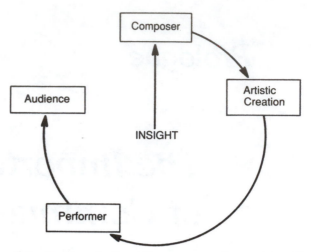

Figure P-1   Communication: Composer-performer(s)-audience.

After rehearsing, conductor and ensemble will have as their common goal an artistic communication with an audience (Figure P-2).

To illuminate the composer's intentions and to share them with an audience, the conductor must assume responsibility for communication. He or she recognizes the essential tools of study (perceiving); direction giving and explanation (verbalizing); gestures (picturing); and guides to stimulate improvement and to inspire artistry (writing). These tools are skills that can be developed. All are important and can be made increasingly effective through rehearsals, where each tool can be used. The conductor also considers the effectiveness of each tool utilized in communicating with an audience.

Conducting, like playing an instrument or singing, depends on practice to develop skill. The function of conducting is communication. In re-creating choral music there are, then, four essential factors: the composer, the conductor, the choir, and the listener.

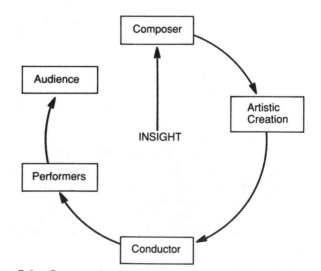

Figure P-2   Communication: Composer-conductor-performers-audience.

THE CONDUCTOR

The role of a conductor is many-faceted. It demands integrity, sensitivity, creativity, and thought. The successful conductor of a pre-professional choral group recognizes this challenge and assumes responsibilities as an interpreter of music, a teacher of skills, an organizer of experiences, a self-motivated learner, and a sensitive human being.

Interpreter of Music

The conductor is responsible, with the members of the choir, to seek out the composer's intent through investigation of historical perspective, as well as through analysis; and to faithfully re-create the music while adding appropriate personal interpretation. The conductor first researches the music exhaustively. Intensive study results in response to the music; the conductor seems to *become* the music both physically and emotionally. Movements and facial expression reflect the timing, the flow, and the dramatic expression of text and music.

To facilitate communication, the conductor's gestures must be clear and unencumbered by extraneous movements that confuse the singers. Control of gesture must be mastered; gestures that distract the attention of the listeners are inappropriate. The conductor's function is to aid the choir in performance as an ensemble in order that the audience may concentrate upon the music.

A conductor's every movement must be prepared—whether it be an indication for a breath and the beginning of sound, a release of sound, an accent, or a fermata. A conductor responds to the music dynamically by developing phrase lines and by indicating tempo and expression. The conductor's total body is involved, but without excessive movements. Posture, face, and eyes reflect alertness, understanding, feelings, and intentions. Like an actor or an orator, the conductor gives the lines importance to bring out the drama of the text. He or she gives shape to the music, works toward dramatic climactic points, and translates notation into an artistic entity. From the first preparatory gesture through the final release of sound, there is continuity of contrasting expression that gives vitality to the music.

Making music is more than entertainment: It is a life-enriching expression. The marvelous thing about music making is the ever-present capability for reflecting human feelings, whether they be serious or frivolous, happy or sad, grieving or exulting, worshipful or playful, loving or spiteful. The very rhythm, color, richness, and patterns of life can be expressed in music.

The variety of music available for performance presents a conductor with an ever-increasing challenge. From an expanding acquaintance with composers' works, the conductor is able to choose repertory through which he or she can most effectively communicate expressive ideas; share insights into composers' intentions; and satisfy the audience aesthetically through complementary programming.

Teacher of Skills

Conductors of all pre-professional choral groups must communicate as teachers with student singers who are in the process of vocal and musical development. Effective teachers will themselves be skilled in their use and control of the voice and in their ability to guide the emerging voices of choristers. They will be thorough musicians who care to share and who are secure in the teaching-learning process. Skill development involves ever-increasing understanding in teachers and in students.

Repertory provides an important key in the development of skills and understanding needed by singers. Repertory should be selected for its capability to permit, and to assist in, the development of vocal and musical skills. Since music has reflected Western culture for more than 400 years, the conductor can choose from a wealth of resources to develop communication and skills. The process should build gradually and intelligently, in an ever-widening and deepening spiral.

A conductor's responsibility begins with recognizing the relationship between expressive characteristics and the skills needed for notational translations. Every attempt at music making, including music reading, will be put into *phrase context* as soon as possible. Reading pitches, intervals, and rhythms is extremely important, but without an awareness of how these elements relate to a work of art, the possibility for exciting performance will be limited.

An effective conductor demonstrates understanding of the capabilities of singers; their readiness for growth; and the veritable "storehouse" of musical repertory from which to select appropriate compositions. If a conductor is perceptive and adroit in this selection, singers will be excited by the widening of musical horizons and the growth in their skills.

Some conductors are disheartened by singers' lack of responsiveness to or outright disapproval of their repertory choices. It is important to recognize and remember that inexperienced choristers have a limited acquaintance with repertory and an equally limited perspective regarding skills that will be needed for performance. The conductor has a serious responsibility for developing insight into these needs, and for discovering ways to communicate these understandings to students.

Organizer of Experiences

The conductor who recognizes the value and importance of music accepts responsibility for organizing experiences that contribute to musical growth and enjoyment. A sage once phrased the philosophy of the choral conductor in these terms: "Think not of the musician as a special kind of person: think of each person as a special kind of musician."

The objectives of the choral conductor-teacher include

1. Guiding students in their development of a love for music.
2. Teaching students to appreciate music as an art.
3. Guiding students in their ability to read and interpret musical notation and symbols.
4. Leading students in their response to music as they work together toward a common goal.

A conductor can inspire students to make music an important segment of their lives for as long as they live.

Community support for music is important for the choral ensemble and the community. In addition to presenting formal concerts, choral ensembles can perform for luncheon or banquet audiences, or for parents and teachers at a meeting. For such informal occasions, a good policy is to perform more complicated or "serious" music first, and "lighter" works, such as arrangements of folksongs or spirituals, later. This programming can help ensure the respect of, and enjoyment by, an audience; it can also provide opportunities for the audience and the singers to grow musically.

Self-motivated Learner

The variety of music provides the choral conductor with unlimited possibilities for growth. The attitude toward exploration, research, and learning is vital to the conductor, the singers, and the audience. Conductors-in-training can easily become accustomed to fulfilling assignments that have been carefully outlined. Such assignments are merely guides or beginnings. Conductors who recognize their own potential for growth will enjoy exploring musical scores. They broaden their understanding by thinking in terms of the beauty and special appeal of the work; appropriateness of a composition for the choir's ability and for its placement in a program; and potential for communication with audiences.

The conductor who becomes a self-motivated learner never loses the fascination with discovery. The more he or she learns, the more effective and satisfying can be the contribution to communication.

Sensitive Human Being

Since all people are capable of emotional response, it is possible for the conductor to become increasingly sensitive. The conductor who develops an understanding of the diverse interests of others is better able to recognize and respond to those interests. He or she acknowledges the potential of music as a common language and becomes increasingly aware that music carries emotional qualities and evokes human response in a unique way. The conductor accepts the responsibility for broadening horizons for all with whom he or she communicates. A conductor is challenged to guide choir members in an ever-increasing awareness of their responsibilities in the process of music making. As conductor and singers become fully cognizant of their potential for communication, the result will be a more exciting level of performance.

Chapter 1

Relating Gesture to Musical Expression

A conductor must have a complete understanding of the composer's intention. Without this, there is no significant or important message to communicate. Assuming that a clear, artistic message has been discovered and researched, the conductor must develop skills essential for communicating through gesture.

The Random House Dictionary of the English Language defines *gesture* thus:

> Movement of the body, head, arms, hands or face that is expressive of an idea, opinion, emotion.

This definition reveals the potential for communication that the conductor can develop.

The purpose of this chapter is to assist conductors in their continuing growth through progressive exercises in gesture communication. Gesture is the physical means by which a conductor *pictures* music to performers in a group. Through gesture, facial expression, and verbal communication with singers, a choral conductor brings to life a musical score. Clarity of gesture depends on control developed through intelligent practice. While the fledgling conductor begins his or her practice by developing habits that will ensure that the meter pattern becomes clear "automatically," it is important that practice of patterns be related to music itself as soon as possible. The expressive conductor is one who has developed physical and mental coordination. Only then can the emotional aspect of music be communicated effectively through gesture.

The function of gesture is many-faceted. It can indicate

Meter and tempo.
Subdivisions of meter.
Character of music: marcato, staccato, legato, leggiero, portato.
Timing and character of cues: entrances, releases, and preparation for an ensuing musical event

Rhythmic configurations (through timing): syncopation, accent, stopping of sound.

Fermata and its release.

Activation of rests and phrase endings that serve to facilitate continuity of movement.

Shapes of phrases: stress or negation of emphasis, crescendo–diminuendo, sound–silence.

Feeling of movement and vitality throughout sustained passages.

Reinforcement of vocal sound: reminders to singers of the required degrees of support and depth appropriate for musical interpretation.

Amount of sound desired from the choir.

Proportion of sound required from various sections of the choir (balance).

Two independent ideas (through use of left hand as well as right).

Drama indicated by the score.

Relationships of vocal and instrumental portions of the music wherever appropriate.

The responsibility of a conductor is complicated and awesome. The development of technique for effective communication through gesture necessitates careful analysis and practice. Since choral compositions differ greatly, each demands gesture practice. The improvement of gesture can be facilitated by use of a video recorder. This invaluable audiovisual aid is beneficial in several ways:

1. The monitor can provide instant "feedback" during individual practice.
2. Following conducting practice, the tape can be replayed for careful scrutiny as many times as desired.
3. A videotaped excerpt can be replayed at a slower speed for more minute analysis.
4. Following a choral "laboratory" performance (during which singers respond to the conductor whose performance is recorded on videotape), the conductor is able to
   a. Observe and analyze his or her own conducting repeatedly and at different speeds while observing the singers' response both visually and aurally.
   b. Assess the effectiveness of verbal and visual communication with the choral ensemble.
   c. Listen to the choral ensemble to hear any aspects that escaped his or her attention or that were missed during the conducting experience.

Concentrating (with eyes closed) upon each aspect of sound and interpretation during replays of the tape can sharpen aural perception. As the conductor listens critically to sounds and imperfections that escaped notice earlier, he or she is able to hear more acutely during ensuing conducting experiences. Aural acuity does not just happen; it can be developed and refined through concentrated effort.

Just as the gymnast practices to gain control of both large and small muscles, the conductor practices to develop control over placement of gesture, use of the arm, and communication through wrist, hand, and fingers.

POSTURE

To be understood clearly, the conductor finds an erect posture and a commanding stance of primary importance. Choral sound is affected by a conductor's body language. When the conductor's shoulders are tense, the group may sound tight or pinched. When the conductor's posture is not erect, it cannot remind the singers to maintain the posture necessary to support the vocal sound. Body weight should be distributed evenly on both feet, placed slightly apart. If balanced properly on the balls of the feet, with knees unlocked, the conductor will be able to involve the entire body in conveying, with varying degrees of subtlety, the reminders needed for vocal support, line extension and shape, accent and emphasis.

While physical readiness is essential, excessive body movement such as swaying, weaving, or "bobbing" can distract from communication. The stance of a conductor is erect rather than leaning toward or "into" his instrument, the choir. Shoulders are back and chest erect. The conductor's awareness of drawing sound *from* singers or of bringing the sound *to* the conductor and other listeners is important. A conductor who constantly bends toward the chorus diminishes possibilities for communication as well as for sound projection.

Position of Arm and Hand

A conductor who works on hand position will find that problems of arm position are minimized. The hand is an extension of the arm; messages are communicated through the fingertips. The hand is centered directly in front of the body so that singers can clearly see preparatory indications, the point of a downbeat, and the conductor's facial expression (Figure 1-1).

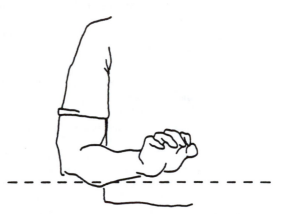

Figure 1-1   Position of arm and hand.

The hand does not turn with each arm movement. The palm remains down (toward the floor); fingers are slightly apart and curved just a bit while they remain directed toward the singers at all times (Figure 1-2). Excessive flexing of the wrist causes the hand to break the line of communication with singers.

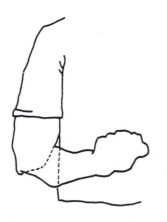

(a)   (b)

Figure 1-2   Position of hand.

The upper arm (shoulder to elbow) is close to the body but not "glued" next to it. The arm should form no more than a 45-degree angle with the body and should extend forward slightly (Figure 1-3). In this basic position the forearm and hand can be centered and elbow movement minimized. The elbow should not move up and down; such movement distracts from the focus on the fingertips.

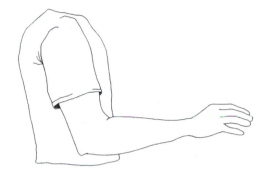

Figure 1-3   Position of hand and arm (side view).

RIGHT HAND GESTURE MOVEMENT

In describing the basics of conducting technique, it is customary to think in terms of *Takt* or *beat*. Meter patterns are pictured through placement of these units. Just as each measure has within it a certain number of beats, each beat has aspects of both up and down direction and feeling. To be intelligible the beat must have a discernible *ictus (point)*. The importance of gesture motion and control in leaving a beat point cannot be overemphasized. The timing of movement from any beat point represents not only the second half of a beat, but also preparation for the next beat. (See Figure 1-4.)

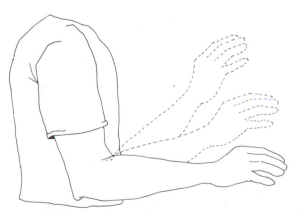

Figure 1-4   Right hand gesture movement.

Through the character of the upward direction or movement from the beat point, singers are prepared for the following beat. It may be observed that the downward direction of a beat is the preparation for a rebound or upward motion, and vice versa. (See Figure 1-5.)

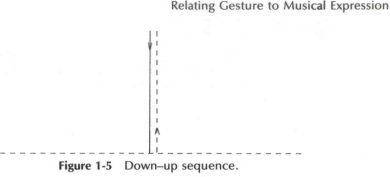

Figure 1-5   Down–up sequence.

Exercise 1

Practice the down–up sequence of a *1* pattern in marcato style:

> Conduct the vertical pattern from upper to lower extremes of the imagined space frame; repeat several times at moderate tempo.
>
> Reverse direction: Begin the vertical pattern at the imaginary line; move in an upward direction to prepare for the *down* beat.

Appropriate preparation for each musical event is really more important than the event itself. How the beat point is marked communicates the character of the music. If the desired musical result is to be marcato, the beat point must be clear (marked) and the rebound from the beat point moderately quick and deliberate. Control of the upward motion representing the second half of the beat is just as important as point clarity.

Repeat all steps outlined in Exercise 1, using (1) full arm with hand extended (no wrist motion); (2) vertical hand movement through wrist motion (no movement of the full arm or fingers); (3) well-defined vertical movement of fingers only (no movement of arm or wrist). Practice each of these means of communication until you achieve clarity and confidence.

CHARACTER AND STYLE OF GESTURE COMMUNICATION

Practice in conducting meter patterns is beneficial if it is associated with the character and style of music. Following is a list of terms used most frequently to differentiate style or character of music.

1. *Marcato:* Strongly accented; marchlike; emphasized
2. *Staccato:* Detached; short; crisp
3. *Legato:* Smooth; flowing; connected; no perceptible interruption between the notes
4. *Leggiero:* Light; graceful; dancelike
5. *Portato:* Moderately stressed; somewhat detached; a manner of performance midway between legato and staccato

A conductor considers the following three variables in determining gestures for each style:

1. Weight of the *ictus* (beat point)
2. Speed and character of rebound and reflex away from the ictus
3. Momentum or motion that connects the beats

In a *marcato* gesture, the ictus is clearly defined by a moderate degree of weight given to it and through a quick rebound from the beat points. The hand or the baton may be used as an extension of the arm; wrist motion should be minimized.

A *staccato* gesture differs from the marcato gesture in that it must convey lightness and separation. The ictus is proportionally lighter than in the marcato gesture; a quick rebound from each beat point is stopped immediately after it is begun. This stopping interrupts momentum and permits the appearance of space between beats. The staccato gesture is a motion of the hand controlled almost entirely by the wrist; arm movement is minimized.

Legato gesture is dependent upon a controlled connection *between* beat points. Both ictus and rebound are minimized in response to continuous momentum. This results in a flowing, horizontal feeling. The full arm is employed to convey legato; wrist motion is minimized, and the hand functions as an extension of the arm. The conductor seems to *pull* between beat points—actually drawing sound from the singers.

Leggiero gesture portrays a flowing momentum between beat points. To achieve this, the conductor lessens the weight of the ictus and the sharpness of the rebound in contrast to either marcato or staccato gesture indications. There is little wrist motion; phrase shaping is accomplished in large part by the forearm in order that the music have the desired lilt.

Portato indicates a character of articulation between legato and staccato. Though somewhat marked, the note durations are separated slightly.

Marcato Practice

The reader may now assume the proper posture (Figure 1-6) and explore communicating the character and timing of a marcato duple pattern.

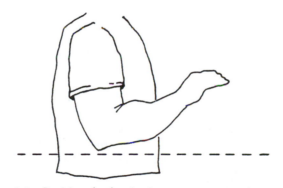

Figure 1-6   Position for beginning marcato practice exercise.

Exercise 2

Be sure the body weight is evenly distributed on both feet, slightly apart, and that there is a feeling of reaching into oneself as though preparing to sing.

Note: In all work toward perfection of patterns and timing, a beginning conductor will find it helpful to observe the result on a monitor. When that is not possible, a mirror can help.

After you have made certain that posture is erect, the following will be useful:

> Think of an imaginary horizontal line drawn in front of the body at approximately waist height (Figure 1-7). This line may vary with respect to distance from the body: The farther the line is from the conductor's body and in the direction of the choir, the more conducive it will be to a high level of dynamic intensity; the closer the line is to the conductor's body, the more effective it will be to communicate a *piano* or *pianissimo* singing. The imaginary line may be drawn at a slightly higher level to call attention to a *piano* or *pianissimo* dynamic level.

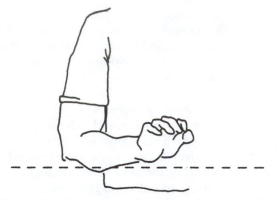

Figure 1-7 Placement of imaginary horizontal line.

After determining placement of an imaginary horizontal line, you are ready to practice conducting a duple pattern in marcato style (Figure 1-8).

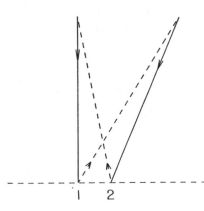

Figure 1-8 Duple pattern in marcato style.

Exercise 3

To begin this practice exercise, think of the imaginary line placed appropriately for *mezzo forte* communication. Careful scrutiny of the diagram will reveal the necessity for beginning right hand movement from a point approximately ten inches above an imaginary line.

1. Experiment with the placement of each beat on a line and directly in front of the body. Use only the right hand to describe the pattern. There are three reasons for this: First, a pattern is outlined more clearly by one hand. Second, the left hand is most effective when it functions independently and indicates aspects of the music that the right hand cannot show. Third, habits of *parroting* and *mirroring* right hand gesture with the left hand are difficult to overcome.
2. Count aloud while practicing the pattern at moderate speed: 1 + 2 + (speak *one-and-two-and*). Be sure that the rebound from a beat point is a clear, well-timed preparation for the next beat point.
3. While maintaining the marcato character, increase speed of the pattern gradually from moderate tempo to fast, to very fast, and then into a *1* pattern in which the point is made by an immediate spring from the point on the line. Be sure to continue prestissimo counting 1 + 2 +.
4. Recheck posture and gesture placement.
5. Repeat the exercise, being careful to review guides for arm and hand position (Figure 1-9). Check that
   a. Forearm functions directly in front of the body (avoiding a position to the right of center) so that it is in unmistakable communication with the singers.
   b. Elbow is close to the body and is not raised with the beats.

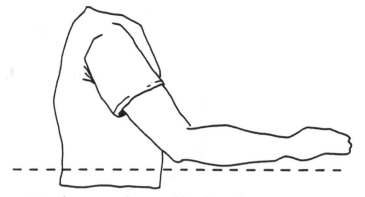

Figure 1-9 Placement of arm and hand in relation to imaginary line (side view).

    c. Wrist and fingers do not flex or droop. The hand position appears relaxed. The palm is down (toward the floor), and the fingers are extended though not rigid. Fingers are neither crammed together nor stretched far apart. Notice that communication from the conductor *flows* directly through the arm, hand, and fingers to the singers.

6. Repeat the exercise; increase speed. Notice that as speed is increased, gesture size may decrease slightly to facilitate fluency and clarity.
7. Repeat the exercise, beginning with a faster speed; gradually slow the tempo. Notice that as speed is decreased, gesture size may increase slightly to control tempo.
8. Repeat all steps in this exercise until you have established a feeling of confidence in control of the marcato duple meter indication.

Staccato Practice

Staccato indications necessitate control of wrist movement. To develop effective use of the wrist, practice controlling wrist movement (deliberate down–up repeatedly) without any arm movement. The following suggestions will prove useful.

1. Grasp the right arm firmly just above the wrist with the left hand.
2. Adapt the marcato 2 pattern for clean, crisp beats by using the wrist and lower arm muscles (no movement of upper arm).
3. Be sure that the *up* motion is as strong and marked as is the *down* motion.
4. Use a baton or a pencil as an extension of the hand. Permit the baton to be held lightly between the thumb and the first two fingers. Position a music stand at waist height and proceed to tap (with staccato character in mind) the rhythmic beats of a basic duple pattern.
5. Minimize the distance of the rebound from each beat so that the taps are activated by the wrist rather than the arm. Listen carefully to make certain the taps of the baton on a music stand are uniform in volume and intensity of sound.

After experimenting with wrist control necessary for effective staccato indication, the conductor will wish to recheck posture and stance. Practice the duple pattern (Exercise 3) in staccato character, beginning at a moderate tempo. Count (1 + 2 +). Increase speed gradually as suggested for practice of the duple pattern in marcato.

Legato Practice

Legato gesture is dependent upon *connecting* beat points. When communication of a smooth, flowing line is desired, the conductor works to minimize the emphasis placed upon the beat point itself (particularly across bar lines within a phrase), and to draw steadily and smoothly from each beat point. The more the gesture resembles the desired musical effect, the greater will be the clarity of communication between conductor and singers. A legato duple pattern will thus be less angular and more rounded, with less emphasis upon the beat point. That point can be clarified by control and timing of the pull from its placement on the imaginary line (Figure 1-10).

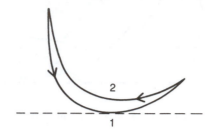

Figure 1-10 Duple pattern in legato style.

Recheck posture and stance. Practice communicating duple feeling through the pattern in legato character beginning at a moderate tempo. Feel a smooth pull from the point where the gesture meets the imaginary horizontal line. This feeling should help the conductor literally draw sound from singers and extend phrases across bar lines.

Having practiced repeatedly a duple pattern in marcato, staccato, and legato styles, one becomes cognizant of a basic difference in the appropriateness of these styles to convey musical intentions. It will now be helpful to practice in succession four or eight measures of the duple pattern in each style: marcato, staccato, legato. Keep tempo constant at about ♩ = 60. Observe that the horizontal flow of a legato pattern can be more clearly indicated if the upward distance covered by the second beat is minimized. This can keep the depth of *one* from becoming too great for legato communication.

In marcato and legato styles, the hand is an extension of the arm; wrist motion should be kept to a minimum. In staccato style, arm movement is minimized and controlled; sharp motion of the hand conveys crispness. If the desired musical effect is to be staccato, a rebound from the beat point should be quick and delicate. There is also a difference in the use of the arm: Whereas marcato communication is dependent upon use of the forearm with minimal movement of the wrist, staccato communication is more effective through a minimizing of arm movement and employment of controlled wrist movement, which can facilitate fast and delicate rebounding from the beat point.

Leggiero and Portato Character

Expressing leggiero and portato through gesture requires sensitivity to the relationship of marcato, staccato, and legato styles. There must be a feeling of the music's being ongoing, and a sensitivity to phrasing and nuance. Since the character of music marked *portato* differs subtly from that which bears *legato* or *staccato* indications, and since leggiero is between staccato and legato, it may be unnecessary to practice these gesture styles independently. Ability to express either portato or leggiero will result from mastery of the relationships of marcato, staccato, and legato gestures. Each may be practiced as it is appropriate in the context of a musical composition.

METER AND TEMPO

Meter is indicated by conducting patterns that are universally understood by musicians. Meters are duple, triple, or a combination thereof. The tempo of music is controlled by the speed and the timing of gestures indicating these patterns. As each meter pattern is introduced and illustrated, it should be practiced in various tempos and styles of gesture.

Duple Meter

Patterns for duple meter communication include the basic 2 ($\frac{2}{2}$, ¢ ,$\frac{2}{4}$,$\frac{2}{8}$) and the basic 4 ($\frac{4}{4}$, C ,$\frac{4}{2}$,$\frac{4}{8}$). The pattern for the basic 2 has already been introduced. The pattern for indicating the division of a measure into 4 counts is illustrated in Figure 1-11. Practice conducting the 4 pattern in marcato, staccato, and legato styles at various dynamic levels.

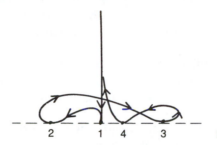

  2   1   4   3   **Figure 1-11**   Duple pattern for 4 counts.

Duple meter indications may be interpreted through either a 2 pattern or a 4 pattern. Determination of the pattern is based on tempo. If the tempo is slow, the 4 pattern may be more appropriate. If the tempo is fast, the 2 pattern may a better choice. Whenever the 2 pattern is possible, it will probably facilitate music making. A change from the 2 pattern into the 4 pattern (or subdivided 2) is advisable when greater control is needed for a rallentando or a ritard.

Practice conducting the 4 pattern in a moderately slow tempo for four measures. Continue the 4 pattern while gradually increasing speed over four measures; change to the 2 pattern for four measures. Continue the 2 pattern while gradually increasing speed over four measures; change to the 1 pattern *fortissimo* for four measures.

Repeat the entire exercise *pianissimo* until you no longer need to concentrate on the pattern.

Triple Meter

The pattern for triple meter ($\frac{3}{4}$,$\frac{3}{2}$,$\frac{3}{8}$) is illustrated in Figure 1-12.

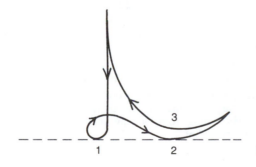

  1   2   **Figure 1-12**   Pattern for triple meter.

In marcato style, the vertical aspects of the conducting pattern will be more apparent.

In legato style, the horizontal character of gesture should predominate. The depth of 1 and the height of 3 should be minimized, while the length of 2 should be stressed appropriately to emphasize breadth and musical flow.

Practice conducting the *3* pattern in marcato, staccato, and legato styles at various dynamic levels and at different tempos.

PREPARATORY GESTURE

The preparation is invariably in the direction of the beat preceding the one on which sound is to begin. If sound begins on a beat, the preparation is the *preceding* beat. When sound begins on a note that is one-half or less of the beat's duration, the preparatory gesture is the beat itself. It is essential that the preparatory indication convey *tempo, mood*, and *dynamic level* desired; therefore, the conductor must establish the tempo and the dynamic level firmly in his or her mind before giving the preparatory gesture. It is helpful to count aloud while practicing.

Practice indicating breath intake in various tempos. Remind yourself that it is essential to breathe as you give this indication. Using the basic duple pattern, think first of sound beginning on count *1* with the preceding breath indication given in the direction of count *2*. After a feeling of security has been established, think of sound beginning on count *2* so that preparation will begin from a point slightly above the imaginary line at waist height. For this event, the preparatory indication will be a dropping of the hand (as for count *1*) to prepare singers with breath for an entrance or a beginning of sound on count *2*.

Well-timed preparations are essential for the intake of breath (which ensures a unified and secure beginning of sound) and for precise releases of sound that may entail placement of final consonants. Until a conductor and singers are secure with the timing of a single beat as preparation, the conductor may need to give an additional beat or two. When such steadying of tempo is advisable, the conductor should firmly establish the habit of breathing *with* singers at the appropriate moment.

Practice of Sound Preparation

Think of music having a $\frac{4}{4}$ meter signature.

Imagine sound beginning on count *1* following a breath preparation on count *4*. Practice repeatedly indicating both the intake of breath (well timed and directly in front of the body) and the gesture necessary to activate the sound.

Imagine sound beginning on count *3* following a breath preparation in the direction of count *2*. Practice repeatedly indicating both the intake of breath (well timed and toward the conductor's left) and the point of the sound's beginning. In this exercise, be sure the ictus indicating the beginning of sound is near the center of the body. Follow this with a continuing movement to the right before changing direction for count *4*.

Imagine the beginning of sound on count *4* with the breath preparation on count *3* (to the conductor's right). Practice until security is established.

Imagine that sound is to begin on count *2*. Placing the hand about six inches above the imaginary line, breathe as you drop the hand on count *1*. Continue the gesture pattern rebounding from the line and moving in tempo to the left to indicate sound beginning on count *2*.

THE FERMATA

To indicate a fermata, be sure that the elbow remains down (slightly away from but relatively close to the body); the palm is down; and the wrist and fingers are not flexing or drooping. Begin to practice the duple pattern legato and at

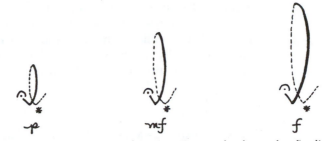

Figure 1-13 Direction of preparation and release for finality.

a moderate tempo. Gradually decrease the speed to slow, to very slow, and finally into a fermata. The fermata should be placed directly in front of the body and moderately high (slightly above the imaginary line drawn at the waist) regardless of where in the measure it occurs. Intensity throughout the duration of the fermata can be maintained by a slight movement or pull in an upward direction. Release of a fermata may be accomplished in one of several ways.

First, if a feeling of finality is desired, the preparation for release can be a slight increase in the speed of the upward motion followed immediately (in the faster speed) by a change to downward direction, with a slight rebound from the imaginary line. The firmness of, or distance covered by, the rebound relates to the size and the intensity of sound being released. (See Figure 1-13.)

Second, if music continues after a fermata, the release preparation is a tiny loop made so that the baton or the fingertips can continue with the next beat gracefully and without undue loss of time. (See Figure 1-14.) Guidelines for direction of releases are as follows:

1. When ensuing beat is to the right, a fermata release will be to the left.
2. When ensuing beat or preparation is to the left or down, a fermata release will move first in an upward direction.
3. When ensuing beat or preparation is up, a fermata release will be toward the conductor's right.

Third, if there is to be no interruption of sound following a fermata, its release will be accomplished merely by changing direction and resuming the tempo.

Through timing and change in direction, the loop can show where the sound ends and resumes. Anticipate the ceasing of sound at the point of line intersection (*). The loop, when properly timed, serves as preparation to help ensure a well-timed release of sound. When it is desirable to have silence for a moment or two after the sound's release, the gesture can cease at the line inter-

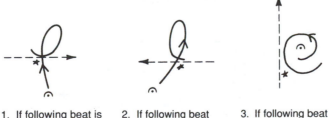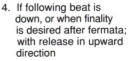

1. If following beat is to the right
2. If following beat is to the left or up
3. If following beat is up
4. If following beat is down, or when finality is desired after fermata; with release in upward direction

Figure 1-14 Directions of preparation and release when music follows the fermata.

section and resume in the direction, spirit, and tempo indicating a new breath preparation (preparatory beat). This should be in the opposite direction from that which will indicate the next sound. Direction chosen to release the sound is determined by the music that follows the fermata. A conductor thus maintains the continuity of the music through choice of the most logical direction.

Fermata Practice

Recheck posture, stance, gesture placement, elbow, wrist, hand.

Repeat the legato duple exercise from intake of breath indication at moderate tempo, through four measures in tempo, followed by two measures decreasing in speed, and ending with a fermata. Practice releasing the fermata as illustrated in Figure 1-13. Release the fermata at both *ff* and *p* intensity levels. Continue until you feel secure and the image projected on video screen or mirror indicates clarity of communication.

Practice the legato triple exercise from intake of breath on count *3*. Conduct four measures in moderate tempo, followed by two measures decreasing in speed into fermata on count *1*. Release the fermata at both *ff* and *p* intensity levels. (See Figure 1-13.)

Practice repeatedly the releasing of sound in various directions as illustrated in Figures 1-13 and 1-14. Imagine a fermata placed on a particular count of a measure so that the ensuing breath preparation will be shown in various directions that might be desirable in a *4* pattern. Practice releases at various volume levels.

Practice conducting the fermata in the following examples of notation:

1. When music continues after a *caesura* (//):

   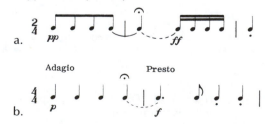

2. When it is followed by a rest:

3. When the music continues a *tempo*:

4. When the dynamic level changes:

5. Supplementary examples:

The practice here does not include all types of fermatas, but mastery of these patterns will help in working out the subtle demands of any musical score. Fermata releases can be treated in any way that ensures continuity of the music.

ASSOCIATION OF GESTURE PRACTICE AND MUSIC

Along with practice of patterns (in different tempos and styles), the conductor should work with actual music and text. In-class practice sessions for beginning conductors can include a pianist playing well-known tunes that suggest different meters and thus call for specific patterns. Examples are "Anchors Aweigh," "The Stars and Stripes Forever," "America the Beautiful," "Ode to Joy," "America," "Silent Night," "My Bonnie Lies Over the Ocean," as well as familiar hymn tunes and chorales. A musically sensitive accompanist can encourage phrase shaping, dynamic inflection, slowing at cadences, and other appropriate responses. If an accompanist is not available, carefully chosen recordings of familiar carols or folksongs can be useful.

As soon as security with patterns and phrasing is achieved, the conductor should see if singers respond to the gestures. This experience permits the conductor to lead the group (rather than follow the pianist or the recording). Singers will be most helpful to the conductor if they are careful to sing *exactly* as the conductor's gesture pictures the music.

Two selections from Music for Class Study and Conducting (at the back of this book) are especially useful for beginning conductors when they are ready to experience singers' response to their gestures:

Musica est Dei donum optimi (p. 258)

In moderate tempo, conduct Voice I, using first the 4 and then the 2 patterns.
Practice indicating intake of breath, showing phrasing, and cuing releases.
Conduct Voices I and II singing together. Use first the 4 and then the 2 patterns.
Conduct all four voices singing together.

Musica vivat aeterna (p. 247)

Conduct each voice separately using the 3 pattern.
Practice indicating breath intake, phrasing, and releases.
Conduct Voices I and III singing together.
Conduct all three voices singing together.

Selections included in Music for Class Study and Conducting are grouped according to difficulty of challenges presented. (See Appendix B for other conducting repertory in Group I.)

TIMING AND CHARACTER OF CUES

One of the critical aspects of conducting is timing. Cues include timing of breath preparation for a vocal entrance; timing of a rebound from the Takt (or beat) to indicate musical style or character; timing of a release as it relates to the following section; and timing of a pause to activate syncopation.

Breath preparation must be timed so that a singer is encouraged to breathe in the tempo of the music, and the desired musical style and dynamic intensity are clearly visible.

As stated previously, the conductor should breathe with singers as though he or she were going to sing with them. If the conductor can coordinate the gesture with his or her own physical and vocal readiness, then timing of clear, precise vocal entrances is simpler.

The conductor must be careful to only *prepare* to make the vocal entrance. If the conductor actually sings with the ensemble, his or her ability to hear the singers will be diminished. The conductor is aware of both the sound that he or she hopes to hear, and the actual sound the group is producing. Conductors who habitually sing along during rehearsals will be disappointed when they hear recordings of their ensembles. There may be inaccuracies that escaped their attention, because they listened more to their own voices than to the group.

In the ongoing context of music, the release of a phrase ending and preparedness for the beginning of the next phrase may be the same indication. Timing may not permit two distinctly different signals. The conductor must think carefully about placement of a final consonant. Is breath needed following the consonant? How much of the final count of the phrase is required for the breath? Can this be indicated through timing of rebound from the beat point without interrupting the communication of style? Repeated practice in slow motion will be required before such indications can be perfected.

Every movement in conducting serves as preparation for the ensuing musical event (entrance, release, emphasis or accent, fermata). Each must be planned carefully to ensure the readiness and security of the musicians.

SUBDIVISIONS OF METER

Basic patterns may be varied to indicate subdivisions of beats when greater control is desired in slow or slowing tempos. A subdivided *2* pattern is illustrated in Figure 1-15. This pattern is very similar to the *4* pattern. Although a subdivided *2* pattern may become a *4* pattern (marcato or staccato), the *linear* character needed to describe the flow of music can be established in legato passages by the subdivision illustrated in Figure 1-16. When tempo is very slow, a pattern subdividing *4* into *8* is helpful. Practice conducting a subdivided *4* pattern that indicates *8* beats in a measure (Figure 1-17). Subdivisions can be helpful in rallentando control. Conversely, in a prestissimo passage, a conducting pattern indicating *1* in each measure can facilitate musical expression.

A subdivided *3* pattern is illustrated in Figure 1-18.

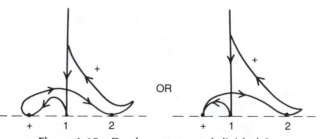

Figure 1-15   Duple pattern: subdivided 2.

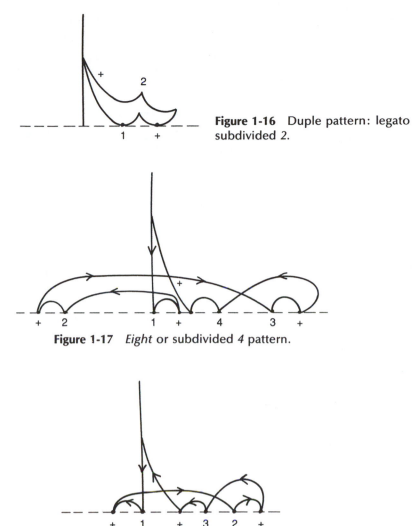

Figure 1-16 Duple pattern: legato subdivided *2*.

Figure 1-17 *Eight* or subdivided *4* pattern.

Figure 1-18 Subdivided *3* pattern.

The appropriateness of subdivisions is determined by tempo. Subdivisions in slow tempos can help ensure greater control. When subdivisions are appropriate, the direction of subdivision placement is *opposite* (or away from) the direction for the following beat.

Conducting patterns that involve subdivisions are more clearly understood when the subdivisions are smaller than the primary beats in the measure. This principle becomes increasingly important as the number of subdivisions is increased. In slower tempos, the conductor may wish to interpret music in $\frac{9}{8}$ and $\frac{12}{8}$ through patterns that delineate triple subdivisions (Figure 1-19). As the number of subdivisions increases, gestures may become cluttered, and the need for minimizing the subdivisions becomes even more critical.

Patterns for compound meter configuration using *6* as the numerator $(\frac{6}{8}, \frac{6}{4})$ depend on the primary and secondary emphases within the measure. A $\frac{6}{8}$ meter signature often indicates a basic duple feeling (*2*) with a subdivision (or *prolation*) of *3*. When the primary meter feeling is duple and the pulsing subdivision provides a triple feeling within the duple framework, the basic pattern is similar to the one used for $\frac{2}{4}$, $\frac{2}{2}$, or $\frac{2}{8}$. The duple pattern with triple prolation is indicated in Figure 1-20.

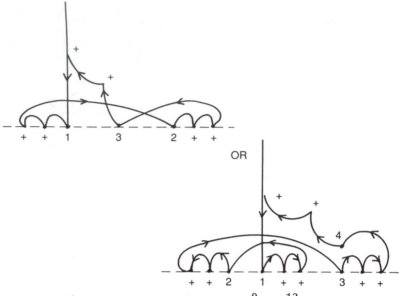

Figure 1-19   Triple subdivisions: $\frac{9}{8}$ and $\frac{12}{8}$ meter.

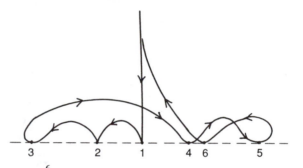

Figure 1-20 $\frac{6}{8}$ meter: duple pattern indicating triple prolation.

Progression to the second primary count *(4)* is emphasized with a change in direction. This pattern is employed when the tempo is slow enough to make conducting of subdivisions possible. When the tempo is faster and the conducting of subdivisions becomes cumbersome, the basic *2* pattern may be conveyed in gesture, and singers must feel the subdivisions along with the conductor. Often, the *2* pattern will permit more graceful and flowing communication of the musical line. Whenever the *6* pattern is used, care must be taken that *2, 3, 5,* and *6* are not heavily stressed.

A $\frac{3}{2}$ or $\frac{3}{4}$ meter signature indicates that each of the three beats can be divided into two. Notice that this pattern is really the subdivided *3* (Figure 1-21). This pattern is useful in portraying a *hemiola*—a triple feeling extended over two measures in triple meter. Hemiola note values appear in a relationship of *3 = 2*:

$$\frac{6}{4}\ \ \delta. \quad \delta. \ | \ \delta \quad \delta \quad \delta \ | \qquad \text{or} \qquad \frac{3}{4}\ \ \delta. \ | \ \delta \quad \delta | \delta \quad \delta \ |$$

Whenever tempo is slow and subdivisions are appropriate, indication of a secondary pulse should be smaller than that of the primary ones. Sometimes it is clearer *not* to conduct subdivisions.

Compound meter signatures that indicate a combination of duple and tri-

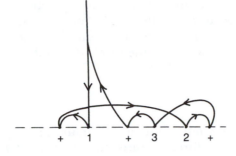

Figure 1-21 Triple meter pattern with subdivisions.

ple patterns within a measure ($\frac{5}{4},\frac{5}{8},\frac{7}{4},\frac{7}{8}$) require careful analysis of primary and secondary emphases. When the upper number is *5*, the conductor must determine whether the feeling is *2* plus *3*, or *3* plus *2* (Figures 1-22 and 1-23). In either instance, the gesture's directional change can help ensure clarity of duple versus triple divisions within the measure.

When the numerator is *7*, the conductor experiments with groupings of *2* and *3*. Choices may be duple–triple *(2 + 2 + 3)*; triple–duple *(3 + 2 + 2)*; or duple–triple–duple *(2 + 3 + 2)*.

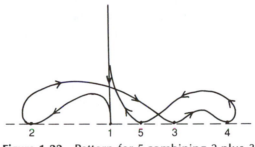

Figure 1-22 Pattern for *5* combining *2* plus *3*.

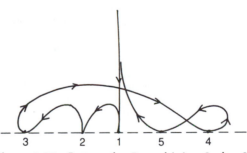

Figure 1-23 Pattern for *5* combining *3* plus *2*.

Additional Gesture Practice

Expressive conducting depends largely upon conveying clear meter patterns that describe phrases, indicate character of articulation (marcato, staccato, legato), and show levels of intensity or volume. Conductors are encouraged to practice each meter pattern illustrated. Practice should include determining marcato, staccato, or legato character, and volume levels. When the conductor is secure with each pattern, he or she may arrange the patterns in sequence: four measures each of *2, 3, 4,* and *6* (in both patterns that reflect the contrasting duple–triple relationships). This sequential exercise may be practiced both forward and backward. After repeated practice, patterns for *5, 7, 8, 9,* and *12* may be added to the sequence. These exercises should be practiced in each conducting gesture style and at various dynamic levels. Mastery of the patterns will allow you to work out the subtle demands of any musical score.

LEFT HAND GESTURE

The conductor's left hand can communicate expression that the right hand can't, or can reinforce gestures the right hand makes. Functions of the left hand include dynamic shadings, phrase shaping, cues for entrances of various parts, and preparation for release of sound. Communication through the left hand requires just as much practice as does communication through the right hand.

Duplication of right hand gestures by the left hand should be avoided in most instances. "Parroting" of the right hand pattern can present a cluttered appearance that minimizes communication. After independent control of the right hand has been established, left hand gesturing can be learned without having to break a habit.

During practice sessions in front of the video camera/monitor or the mirror, conductors should practice right and left hand communication. The two should be practiced separately before an attempt is made to coordinate them. Guides and exercises for use and control of the left hand follow.

1. Keeping in mind the position for the right hand—centered directly in front of the body—practice placing the left hand slightly to the left of body center and on the plane established by the imaginary horizontal line at waist height. Fingers will be slightly apart, outstretched, and slightly curved, with the palm down toward the floor. The wrist will be relaxed but not limp. The hand should appear as an extension of the arm (Figure 1-24).
    a. Turn the hand over slowly until the palm is in an upward position without turning a full 180 degrees. There should be no change in finger or wrist position (Figures 1-25 and 1-26).
    b. Slowly, as though indicating an extended, controlled diminuendo, return the hand to its original, palm-down position (Figures 1-27 and 1-28).
    c. Lower the left hand to its relaxed and "normal" position at your side in preparation for continuing with the right hand only.
    d. Repeat the exercise, thinking of timing an extended crescendo and an extended diminuendo. Turn the palm slowly from downward to upward position and then from upward to downward position. Be careful not to change finger and wrist positions. Repeat the slow rotation of the hand until its control is smooth and comfortable.

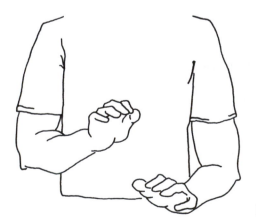

Figure 1-24 Placement of the left hand.

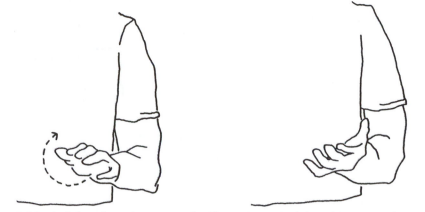

Figure 1-25   Left hand turning upward.   **Figure 1-26**   Left hand in upward position.

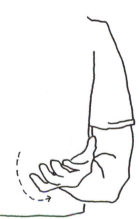
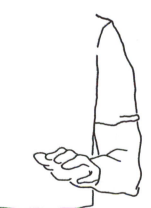

Figure 1-27   Left hand turning downward.   **Figure 1-28**   Left hand in palm-down position.

    e.   Lower the left hand to the position at your side in preparation for continuing of conducting with right hand only (Figure 1-29).

    f.   Repeat the exercise and add a slight and slow movement upward and toward the body center at an angle that moves gradually from 45 degrees to 90 degrees to call attention to an extended crescendo indication (Figure 1-30).

    g.   At the peak of the crescendo, turn the palm down slowly while reversing the upward motion and returning the hand to the position from which it began the crescendo, thus indicating a diminuendo (Figure 1-31).

2.   To reinforce steady growth in intensity, the left hand may be placed well below the imaginary line to begin portraying a gradual rise through a controlled, upward movement. For this indication, the fingers may be outstretched and slightly apart. At the beginning of this maneuver the palm may be open toward the body. As the hand rises, it will move from the left side of the body toward the center (Figure 1-32). As the hand rises, the palm may turn slightly in an upward direction—not more than 45 degrees. Movement of the hand should be apportioned so that the peak of intensity growth is observed when the hand is not more than twelve inches above the imaginary line. Avoid having either hand at a maximum height that gives the appearance of a wild or an uncontrolled gesture. As the hand is raised gradually, be sure the left shoulder remains down and relaxed.

3.   To portray music in a smooth-flowing horizontal line or to indicate a carryover of a phrase that may be broken by singers' breathing, the left hand may be extended to the conductor's left and placed slightly below the level of the imaginary line. The palm should be down toward the floor. Move the hand slowly and evenly to the right until it has passed the center of the body (Figure 1-33). While practicing this exercise, think of the point of possible phrase-fracture exactly in front of the body. By so doing, the

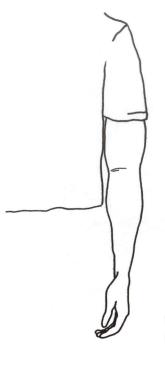

Figure 1-29 Left hand in relaxed, normal position.

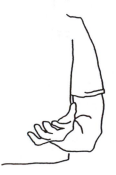

Figure 1-30 Left hand at peak of crescendo.

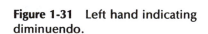

Figure 1-31 Left hand indicating diminuendo.

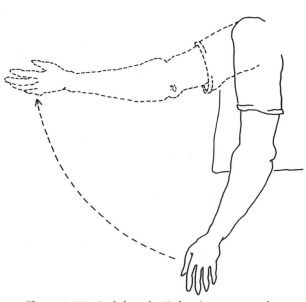

Figure 1-32 Left hand reinforcing crescendo.

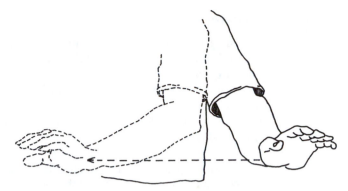

Figure 1-33   Left hand indicating phrase carryover.

slow movement from the conductor's left up to the center of the body will serve as a reminder that breath should not be taken at the anticipated point.

4.   To reinforce a *piano* or a *pianissimo* indicated through right hand gesture, the left hand may be placed fairly close to the body, slightly to the conductor's left of center and with the palm forming a 45-degree angle with the floor (Figure 1-34). This indication may be either slightly above or slightly below the waist line. Its actual position may vary with the music being performed. The video camera/monitor can help the conductor determine its most effective placement for any specific communication.

5.   To time a section's intake of breath and point of entry, extend the left hand so that it is slightly above the imaginary line and the palm forms a 45-degree angle with the floor (Figure 1-35).

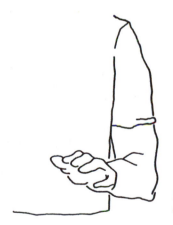

Figure 1-34   Left hand reinforcing *piano* or *pianissimo*.

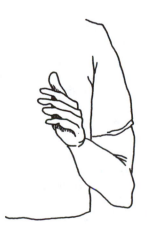

Figure 1-35   Section's intake of breath.

Exercise 4

Establish a tempo in any given meter by counting aloud. Imagine a sectional entry on *1*; indicate breath intake by moving in an upward direction on the preceding count. As the hand begins its ascent, the palm may be turned upward gradually. Follow this breath indication with a downward motion exactly to where sound is to be heard. Repeat this exercise to indicate breaths on other counts of the measure until the beginning of sound has been assured on every possible count.

6. To time a section's (or the full choir's) release of sound, extend the left hand slightly above the imaginary line so that the palm forms a 90-degree angle with the floor (Figure 1-36).

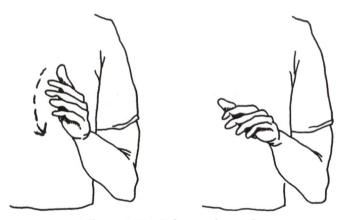

Figure 1-36   Release of sound.

7. To prepare for release of sound more obviously, the hand or a combination of hand and arm may be used. The greater the volume or intensity of sound, the larger will be the preparation and motion indicating a release. When reinforcement is appropriate, the left hand may time and execute releases the way the right hand releases a fermata. Extending the palm to form a 90-degree angle with the floor, anticipate the release of sound on a given measure count. The preparatory upward motion and tiny loop must be timed so that a warning precedes the actual point or moment when sound should cease. In this way, singers can be prepared to release sound together.

8. Since it is not recommended that the left hand resume a conducting pattern after a release, the direction of a left hand cutoff is usually inconsequential. It is important, however, that cues and releases be well controlled in timing and in position, so that they are effective.

Exercise 5

Establish a tempo in any meter by counting aloud. Practice releasing a choir section's sound by lifting the hand or fingers on a predetermined count of the measure, and then on a predetermined second half of a measure count. Preparation for release in an upward direction or movement of hand will be down. When only fingers are utilized for a release, only fingers need indicate preparation.

Repeat this practice until sound has been released by an upward "flick" of the fingers on every possible measure count and second half-count. To improve dexterity, practice a section's release of sound by moving the hand or fingers downward on a predetermined count of a measure, and then on a predetermined second half of a measure count. Preparation for release in a downward direction will be up.

Repeat this practice until sound has been released by a downward hand movement or flick of the fingers on every possible measure count and second half-count.

Practice of these basic gestures without any movement of the right hand can result in secure control of the left hand. When effective left hand communication has been established, one can attempt to coordinate both hands.

FACIAL EXPRESSION

Communication of mood and spirit can be effectively achieved through body alertness and facial expression. The timing of a glance and eye contact are extremely important. The increase and decrease of musical tension depend on the combination of eyes, face, right and left hand gestures, and body language.

Practice "conducting" a selection using only body alertness and facial expression. You can first experiment by "conducting" recorded selections or familiar music performed by an expressive pianist in the conducting class. Then you may try practicing facial expression in front of a video camera/monitor or a mirror. While thinking of pattern and phrasing necessary to interpret a selection, you can communicate the rise and fall of intensity through eyes and facial muscles. The excitement or feeling of relaxation in the music can be conveyed to the singers without gesture.

The facial expression advocated here is *not* the mouthing of words. A conductor's habitual formation of text syllables can be confusing to singers, especially when voice parts are assigned different words.

Following practice of facial expression alone, the conductor can combine it with hand and arm gestures. Expressiveness in conducting is the result of intelligent practice coupled with thorough mastery of the score. Additional suggestions for conducting practice appear in Chapter 3 and Appendix A.

Chapter 2

Preparing for Music Making: Score Study

One of the most enjoyable and challenging aspects of a conductor's many responsibilities is the preparation of a musical score. When musical knowledge and research are combined with imagination and musical instincts, the conductor, identifying with the composer and learning about the performance practices of a specific period, becomes increasingly compatible with musical structure. A conductor who merely attempts to imitate recordings or performances by other conductors is denied these opportunities and will not reap the full benefits of music making. Communicating the composer's intent or conveying the music's spirit will be impossible.

Through exhaustive study of a musical score the conductor becomes intimately acquainted with the style characteristics of a composer, and learns useful information about performance practices of the historical period.

Since historical perspective is pertinent to present-day performance, the following kinds of information should be gathered to assist a conductor's preparation:

> The number of singers and instrumentalists likely to have performed the work
>
> The probable acoustics of chapel, cathedral, chamber, courtyard, salon, or concert hall for which the performance was intended
>
> Facts concerning background and source of text (biblical, liturgical, poetic); author or poet; context and placement within a religious service if text is from scripture or liturgy; context within a major work if it is excerpted

When studying an edition published during, for example, the Renaissance or the Baroque, the conductor refers to the original manuscript. Accuracy of notation, clefs, chromatic alterations (*musica ficta*), mensural signs, meter and tempo relationships, text underlay, and part assignments (instrumental and vocal) can be checked. If manuscript or microfilm is not available, collected editions of the composer's works may be found in many college and urban libraries.

Historical awareness gives the conductor's interpretation authenticity and conviction. Understanding of the composer's intent heightens choir members' interest as well as that of the listeners. The following overview relating to historical awareness may prove helpful to a conductor's preparation of the music.

ESTABLISHING HISTORICAL PERSPECTIVE FOR SCORE STUDY

The Renaissance (ca. 1430–1580)

The music of every age, like painting and other forms of artistic expression, reflects the mores, the beliefs, and the character of people. All art is a mirror of life in the epoch in which it was conceived. The religious concept of the Middle Ages was that people live only to prepare themselves for the life to come after death. Music of that time reflected strict supervision and the ritualized existence of man, and it was not until the birth of the Renaissance that new vistas opened. These gave hope and rebirth to the ancient Greek concept of personal worth and fulfillment in life on earth. The largest body of choral music representing a single period was composed during the Renaissance.

The first music designated specifically for chorus dates from the Gothic period, the early years of the fifteenth century, when vocal composition evolved from complex melodic and rhythmic formulae of the Middle Ages. With the music of Guillaume Dufay (ca. 1400–1474) and John Dunstable (ca. 1380–1453), the foundations were laid for our Western harmonic concept of music based on thirds and sixths, combined with expressive ideas of consonance and dissonance. The music of Josquin des Prés (1440–1521), composed on these musical premises, brought the early Netherlands School to its peak in the High Renaissance at the turn of the sixteenth century. Some of the most beautiful, most sonorous music of the Renaissance was composed by Josquin and his contemporaries, such as Alexander Agricola (1446–1516), Heinrich Isaac (1450–1517), Jean Mouton (1459–1522), Pierre de la Rue (1460–1518), and Clement Janequin (1485–1560).

The rise of the city-states in Northern Italy gave impetus to the concept of the power and dignity of humankind, and there developed an importance of the secular versus the sacred. Leaders such as Lorenzo de Medici in Florence vied with the popes in the sponsorship of great artists like Michelangelo and his contemporaries. Lorenzo the Magnificent, as he was called, brought the famous Netherlands musician, Heinrich Isaac, to his Italian court. Isaac was subsequently called to Rome and then to Innsbruck and Vienna, where he spent the rest of his life as court composer to Emperor Maximilian I. Josquin also spent many of his early years in the service of papal and ducal chapels in Italy, but he eventually returned to his home in Burgundy, where he became extremely influential as both composer and teacher. Although music had been and still was regarded as a science rather than an art, the Josquin School added to this very highly organized music a warmth and a sonority heretofore unheard.

Music in the High Renaissance. Choral composition about the beginning of the sixteenth century exemplified characteristics that can be identified with the High Renaissance:

Textures were polyphonic and linear, with highly developed, imitative counterpoint.
Forms included secular canons, rondeaux, and chansons, as well as liturgical music, motets, masses, and psalm-settings.
Motivic development and repeated thematic material provided a unifying element to the form.

Overlapping phrases gave continuity to prescribed lines of prose texts from the liturgy. Word painting, or representative music, illustrated or symbolized the text.

A variety of textures was attained by contrasting high and low vocal registers, passages of block chords in the midst of polyphony, alternating emotional intensity with complete serenity, and pairing voices, usually in thirds or sixths.

These and other characteristics of the High Renaissance may be observed in an excerpt from Josquin's *Ave Maria, gratia plena* (Example 2-1).

Sacred Music of the Late Renaissance (1550–1580). In the latter half of the sixteenth century, Netherlands composers continued to make their way to the palaces and chapels of Italy. This migration had a stimulating effect on Italian composers and made Italy the center of musical culture. Orlando di Lasso (1532–1594), Philippe de Monte (1521–1603), and Giovanni Pierluigi da Palestrina (1525–1594) stand out in this period as masters of the polyphonic art. Di Lasso held a musical post at the court of Albert V in Munich for thirty-eight years; De Monte was *maestro di cappella* for the court of Maximilian II in Vienna from 1568 until his death; and Palestrina spent most of his life in the service of Pope Julius III in Rome.

Orlando di Lasso composed more than two thousand works in various forms, both sacred and secular; De Monte's motets number more than three thousand; he composed twenty-four masses, and his secular music includes over twelve hundred books of *madrigale, chansons, villanelle,* and *madrigale spiri-*

Example 2-1 (a) Repeated thematic material; (b) overlapping phrases; (c) word painting; (d) contrasting textures: (e) block chords versus polyphonic section; (f) pairing of voices. (Excerpt from "Ave Maria, gratia plena"—Josquin des Prés.)

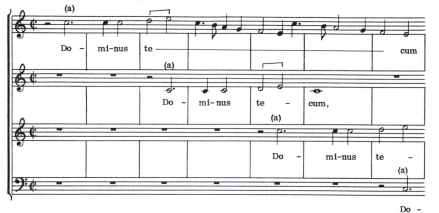

tuale. His motets and masses have been compared favorably to those of Palestrina for their refinement and sincerity. Palestrina's writing, more conservative than that of di Lasso, influenced the compositional style of church music, even into the nineteenth century.

Microrhythms in the Music of Orlando di Lasso.   At the Bavarian court in Munich, di Lasso was blessed with excellent singers and instrumentalists. Liturgical music of the fifteenth and sixteenth centuries favored plainchant reference with linear polyphonic concepts based on the ecclesiastical modes. Speech patterns from these biblical-liturgical texts resulted in juxtaposition of duple–triple relationships referred to as microrhythms. A conductor's awareness of this polyrhythm in the context of polyphony is important.

Di Lasso's motet *Jubilate Deo* is an example of the independent rhythms with which singers should be familiar in performance of polyphonic music. Modern editions with bar lines tend to inhibit the grouping of speech rhythms and musical motifs inherent in Renaissance music. A comparison of music with and without bar lines is seen in Examples 2-2 and 2-3. In the first example, (1) bar lines obviously do not coincide with natural speech stresses (*DE-o, O-mnis, TER-ra*); (2) the groupings of *Jubilate Deo* and *omnis terra* into rhythmic segments is not apparent in Example 2-2 as it is in Example 2-3; (3) one observes the duple–triple relationships (microrhythms) in Example 2-3.[1]

Council of Trent (1545–1563).   The Council of Trent was established to restore dignity and meaning to the Catholic Service, at a time when there had

[1]For further discussion of this subject, read the article by John Haberlen, "Micro-rhythm: The Key to Vitalizing Renaissance Music," *The Choral Journal*, XIII, no. 3 (November 1972), 11–14.

Example 2-2 *Jubilate Deo* (with bar lines).

⌐ = duple meter
△ = triple meter

Example 2-3 *Jubilate Deo* (without bar lines, with indications of microrhythms).

been increasing degeneration and secularization. The results, which took twenty years to achieve, were that certain extraneous, secularized portions of the service were abolished, and the complicated polyphony that made text impossible to understand was forbidden.

Polyphony itself was not abolished, but only the style of writing that was close to Palestrina's was sanctioned. Characteristics of this "Palestrina style" include predominantly stepwise melodies resulting in smoothly curved melodic lines and beautiful sound; regular rhythms; frequent homophonic passages with text coming together in all parts; less chromatic, more diatonic harmony; and emphasis on the ethical rather than the aesthetic purpose of music in a service of worship.

Agnus Dei—Palestrina.   The score for Palestrina's *Agnus Dei* reveals many characteristics of the new ideal in church music. Stanley Hill's edition[2]

[2]See Music for Class Study and Conducting, p. 260.

includes a plainchant setting of the text to prepare the choir for the smoothly curved lines of the motet that follows. The choir's mastery of this flowing, non-metrical melody is the first step to understanding Palestrina's style. Other factors of the motet to be considered by a conductor include the following:

> The imitative, diatonic lines, ascending in SA parts and descending in the ATB, continue to the conclusion of phrase 1 in m. 11.
>
> The imitative lines in the second phrase (*qui tollis peccata mundi*) proceed tonally, T–S–A followed by B in exact repetition. (Note the diatonic progressions that follow each descending interval of a fourth.)
>
> The pairing of AT voices in mm. 12–13 lends grace and forward movement to the lines.
>
> The continued forward movement is propelled in mm. 16–23, when, each time a cadence is expected, the bass part enters in "dovetail" fashion to avoid the cadence and to move the lines forward.
>
> In the final phrase (mm. 28–41) *miserere nobis* begins in T, is completed by S, and then repeated in A; again in "paired thirds," there is a second theme in the two alto parts, which is repeated in T and B; the phrase continues to move in ascending fashion as S and B rise in tenths with the second theme; a final statement of *miserere nobis* appears in T (m. 38); the rising tenths are repeated in AB, and the final cadence is stressed by the presence of two suspensions and a major third (Picardy third).

Except for somber religious services, such as the Tenebre Good Friday observance and others at Passiontime, sacred choral music was accompanied by instruments or by an organ playing basic harmonies. One notable exception to this practice occurred in the Sistine Chapel at the Vatican, where singing *a cappella* was traditional. Palestrina composed liturgical music for use in the Cappella Giulia as well as for the Sistine Chapel, and since Cappella Giulia is known to have contained an organ, there is no reason to suppose that his music was not sung there with organ accompaniment.

Palestrina's pupil and successor at the papal chapel was Giovanni Maria Nanino (1545–1607). Felice Anerio (1560–1614), a pupil of Giovanni, followed him in this capacity and carried on the Palestrina tradition that served as a model for composers of church music for over four centuries.

Spanish Composers of the Roman School.   One of the prominent composers influenced by the Roman School of Palestrina was Tomas Luis Victoria (ca. 1549–1611), who spent many years in Rome before returning to Spain. Victoria's motets and masses are less austere than those of Palestrina; a typical example of his warmth and expressivity is found in the Christmas motet *O magnum mysterium*.

Three additional Spanish composers of sacred music in the Renaissance are of significance. Cristóbal Morales (ca. 1500–1553) spent fifteen years of his early adult life as a student and priest in Rome, then returned to Spain as choirmaster in Toledo and Málaga until his death. His motets are masterpieces of the polyphonic style. Francisco Guerrero (1528–1599) of Seville composed sacred music with folklike flavor, and combined it with Spanish folk instruments. Late in the century, Philippe Rogier (1560–1596), a transplanted Netherlander, was brought to Spain as a singer in the Royal Chapel of Philip II. Rogier's polychoral compositions are text oriented and expressive, and have special rhythmic interest. His style was transitional, with frequent interpolations of rhythmic homophonic passages in contrast to polyphony.

Sacred Music in England.   In spite of ideological struggles and oppression in the early part of the sixteenth century, important advancements were made in English church music through the works of such composers as John Fayrfax (ca. 1464–1545) and John Taverner (ca. 1495–1545). Around 1550

Christopher Tye (ca. 1500–1573) and Thomas Tallis (ca. 1505–1585) were the leading composers.

Tallis and his pupil, William Byrd (1543–1623), composed music for both Catholic and Protestant services. Tallis served under four royal monarchs, including Henry VIII, who broke away from the Catholic Church and established the Church of England with the Act of Supremacy (1534), Edward VI, Henry's successor, and the short-lived "Bloody" Mary, who reestablished Catholicism. Before his death Tallis also provided Protestant service music for Queen Elizabeth I, who reestablished the Church of England in 1558. Tallis's setting of *Lamentations* and his extraordinary forty-voice, polychoral motet for eight choirs, *Spem in alium*, rank high in the annals of sacred music. William Byrd, Tallis's successor and a devout Catholic, also wrote for the Protestant service. His three Masses and numerous Latin motets are among his finest music.

Byrd introduced the verse anthem, which was later developed by his pupil, Orlando Gibbons (1583–1625). This form anticipated the seventeenth-century Baroque *solo-tutti* principle by alternating the instrumentally accompanied solo voice with full choir. Gibbons and Thomas Morley (1557–1602) both contributed a wealth of sacred music. John Wilbye (1574–1638) and Thomas Weelkes (ca. 1575–1623), best known for their English madrigals, also composed motets of distinction.

The term *motet* had a slightly different meaning in Renaissance England from the meaning it had on the Continent. Morley not only described it as "a song made for the church either upon some hymn or Anthem or such like," but also went on to include with it "all grave and sober musicke."[3] Orlando Gibbons published a volume entitled *Madrigals and Motets for 5 Voices*, in which it is difficult to distinguish the sacred from the secular. Martin Peerson (ca. 1580–1650) gave the title of *Mottects* (early English spelling) *or Grave Chamber Music* to his collection of vocal music in 1630. Frequently there was a mixture of sacred and secular subjects in a single publication. Byrd's *Psalms, Songs, and Sonnets* and his *Psalms, Sonnets, and Songs of Sadness and Piety* are typical examples.

Word Painting in Music of William Byrd. A master of word painting in both Latin and English, William Byrd made this concept central in musical composition. He wrote in his Dedication and Foreword to the *Gradualia*:

> There is such a profound and hidden power in these words that to one thinking of things divine and diligently and earnestly pondering them, all the fittest numbers occur as if of themselves and freely offer themselves to the mind which is not indolent or inert.[4]

Byrd's mastery of text–music relationships and his unique musical style place him with the great masters of music of any period. Renaissance text painting, as evidenced in the works of William Byrd, have the following characteristics:[5]

Rhythmic patterns of musical settings that correspond to speech patterns
The tempo of music in keeping with the mood of the text
Musical illustrations where the direction of the melody corresponds with the sense of

---

[3]Thomas Morley, *A Plaine and Easie Introduction to Practicall Musique* (1597). New York: Da Capo Press, 1969.

[4]E. H. Fellowes, ed., *William Byrd: Complete Works*, Vols. II and III (London: Stainer-Bell, 1937–38).

[5]Comments based on an article by Walter Gray, "Some Aspects of Word-Treatment in the Music of William Byrd," *The Musical Quarterly*, 55 (1969), 45–64.

the text (examples: an ascending melody on the text *heaven* and a descending line for *earth*, music that imitates a bird singing or a cock crowing)

Musical translations that transfer the meaning or emotional content of the text into a musical "symbol" (example: the use of four tones in succession to symbolize a cross, skipping from a lower tone to a higher one [vertical representation] and then crossing horizontally with two tones moving diatonically at a slightly lower level of pitch [horizontal representation], such as C-A-E-F)

Musical imagery—the use of a minor or Phrygian mode to convey sorrow or sadness and Lydian or Mixolydian to indicate joy and happiness

Musical synonym—a melodic, rhythmic, or harmonic device that gives special meaning to the text; a unique harmony or rhythmic stress on an important word that the composer wishes to emphasize or give it special consideration.

Such concepts in the minds of composers had also been apparent in the earlier music of Josquin and his school; these principles reached maturity in the sacred and secular works of William Byrd.

Tone Quality in Renaissance Choirs.   The conductor should be aware that Renaissance choirs consisted entirely of boys and men, or men alone. A concept of appropriate tone is influenced by this fact. The quality of boys' unchanged voices is approximated by adolescent voices that have little or no vibrato and sing with a light voice production. Women's voices may produce such a quality if the singers are not permitted to oversing and if they control the rate and size of vibrato. Since the quality of the mature male alto would also have been in the mind of the Renaissance composer, an air of authenticity is given when male falsettists are added to the alto section when performing this music today.[6] Many baritones and some high tenors sing freely in the *falsetto* range, and, combined with female altos, their voices add sonority and depth to the overall tone quality.

Secular Music: Flemish, Italian, and Spanish Composers.   Besides being responsible for writing music for liturgical services, the Renaissance composer was also expected to furnish secular musical entertainment for the royal household. Secular forms of the early Renaissance in the Netherlands, like sacred music, consisted primarily of polyphony and were highly developed by Isaac, Josquin, and Janequin. In the hands of their successors, the popular French chanson turned to a more homophonic texture in the music of Claude Sermisy (ca. 1490–1562), Pierre Certon (ca. 1510–1572), and Clément Janequin (ca. 1485–1560). Janequin is remembered chiefly for his "program" chansons, like "Le chant des oiseaux," where he imitates the songs of birds, and "La bataille," which portrays the sounds and sights of a famous battle at Marignano.

Although the madrigal originated as a literary form in Italy, it was first developed in its musical context by Netherlands composers brought to Italy as *maestri di cappella* for ducal chapels. Some of the most notable were Jacob Arcadelt (1505–1557), Philippe Verdelot (1500–1565), and Adrien Willaert (1485–1562). The madrigal was based at first on the popular *frottola*, essentially chordal in style with three or four parts, the lower ones usually played by instruments.

Andrea Gabrieli (1510–1586), Cipriano de Rore (1516–1565), Orlando di Lasso, Philippe de Monte, and Giovanni Pierluigi da Palestrina all contributed to the artistic development of the madrigal. De Monte and Palestrina composed *madrigale spirituale* for family devotions.

Other secular forms of this period include the *villanella* and *villancico*, the

---

[6]For further information, read a fascinating article by Robert Garretson, "The Falsettists," *The Choral Journal*, XXIV, no. 1 (September 1983), 5–7.

canzonetta, and song-dance forms like the *balletto*, made famous by Giovanni Gastoldi (d. 1622). The Italian madrigal developed into a highly artistic form with five or six parts written in contrasting polyphonic-homophonic textures. In the latter half of the sixteenth century it became highly imitative as well.

Many compositions by Spanish composers are still unpublished. There are two composers whose works are particularly deserving of performance because of their unique qualities. They are Juan Vasquez (ca. 1500–ca. 1560), who wrote Italian madrigals as well as Spanish *villancicas*, a popular form of the period that resembles the Italian *frottola*; and Mateo Flecha (ca. 1520–1591), who composed Spanish and Latin *ensaladas*, a type of *quodlibet*, or medley, with humorous subject matter in which folk instruments are sometimes imitated in the midst of sacred texts.

Luca Marenzio (1553–1599), Giaches de Wert (1535–1596), Carlo Gesualdo (1560–1613), and Claudio Monteverdi (1567–1643) brought the Italian madrigal to its height in the last years of the century. They greatly influenced the English Madrigal School, which flourished at the beginning of the seventeenth century.

The Golden Age of the English Madrigal.   An obscure chorister at St. Paul's Cathedral in London, Nicolas Yonge (d. 1619), was largely responsible for popularizing madrigals in England. In 1588 he published his *Musica Transalpina*, a collection of Italian madrigals that had been "Englished" for home use. Yonge's collection popularized madrigal singing to the point that a gentleman of quality was expected to be able to sight-read a madrigal part that had been passed to him after dinner. Amateur composers wrote their own lyrics, and wealthy merchants hired professional musicians to provide the music for use in their manor houses. Many of these composers are known primarily for their madrigals: Orlando Gibbons, Thomas Morley, John Wilbye, Thomas Weelkes, John Dowland (1563–1626), John Farmer (1565–1605), Thomas Campion (1567–1620), Francis Pilkington (1562–1638), Thomas Tomkins (1573–1656), and John Hilton (1599–1657) are representative of an even greater number. *Madrigal* in England became a generic term, used loosely to apply to all secular vocal forms such as the Ayre, the Sonet, the Ballett, and even the English consort songs of Dowland, Campion, and Pilkington.

A typical Ayre may be examined in a work by John Hilton (1599–1657), a graduate of Cambridge University, who later became organist at St. Margaret's, Westminster, London. He composed numerous rounds and catches as well as a set of *Ayres* called *Fa-la-las for 3 Voices* (1627). "You Lovers That Have Loves Astray" is taken from this volume.[7] Certain Renaissance compositional techniques can be discovered in this example.

> Contrasting polyphonic-homophonic writing (mm. 1–2 followed by mm. 3–8, first ending; mm. 8–10³ followed by mm. 10⁴–12³; and so forth.
>
> Meter relationship of $\frac{2}{2}{:}\frac{3}{4}$ (2:3) at m. 15   ($\circ = \bar{d}.$).
>
> *Fa-la-la* refrain, related to the Italian *balletto*, a song-dance form, indicates a highly rhythmic rendition with an accentuation of consonants in the performance of these nonsense syllables.
>
> Repetition of phrases, indicating a softer, lighter treatment the second time.
>
> Modal tonality with lowered seventh (Aeolian) on descending passages, raised third (Picardy third) at cadence points.
>
> Suggestions of word painting: implications of "straying" with the imitative writing in mm. 3–8, faster notes with text "quick music best" in mm. 8–10, sudden shift to major triad on "best" in m. 10.
>
> Text and music ignore the bar line in mm. 12–13.

[7]See Music for Class Study and Conducting, p. 248.

The Consort Song. Chests of viols and recorders as well as keyboard instruments were not uncommon in homes of the rising middle class of Elizabethan England. The consort song was probably derived from the Italian word *concerto*, meaning to combine voices with instruments. In the hands of John Dowland, consort songs were usually composed for solo voice with lute accompaniment. Some of Dowland's partbooks, however, include three additional vocal lines, indicating that in performance a quartet of voices may also sing, with parts doubled by recorders or viols, or both. This practice was not unique in that secular music had been sung with accompanying instruments throughout the Renaissance. Such a vocal-instrumental performance may be applied to a madrigal by Francis Pilkington, "Rest Sweet Nymphs,"[8] a typical consort song with possibilities for contrasts in texture and sonority when sung and played in the traditional manner. The procedure and choice of instrumental consorts are optional:[9]

> Verse 1—Voices sing *a cappella*.
> Verse 2—Soprano part sung, with lower strings doubling ATB.
> Verse 3—Strings play all parts without voices.
> Verse 4—Voices and strings sing and play together.
> (Harpsichord plays with instruments.)

The "orchestrating" of each verse and the refrain heightens musical interest and is in accord with the performance practice of the period.

Italian Secular Music at the Close of the Century. A madrigal based on a solo from his opera *Arianna* reveals Monteverdi's expressive, adventurous style, typical of the late Renaissance in Italy. In "Lasciatemi morire," one observes characteristic imitative polyphony with several new elements of *secunda prattica* present:

> Frequent chromaticism and dissonance for expressive purposes
> Repeated notes in declamatory style, which serve to emphasize the drama of the text and implement the forward movement of the phrase
> A repetition of phrases that provides unity and form to the music
> General emphasis upon speech rhythms in a dramatic context

Monteverdi's impact upon English madrigalists is apparent in the works of John Wilbye and Thomas Weelkes in particular. Their sonorities and word painting favor the dramatic expressiveness of the Italian late Renaissance.

Other influential composers from Italy in this period include Alessandro Striggio (1535–1595) of Mantua and Florence, a personal friend of Orlando di Lasso, who composed some of the first madrigal comedies and several programmatic madrigals, one of which describes a hunting episode (*La caccia*) with dogs barking, horses galloping, and foxes running. His son, a poet and author, wrote the libretto for Monteverdi's opera *Orfeo*. The father also composed a 22-part motet for a royal wedding at the Bavarian court, where Orlando di Lasso was Master of the Chapel. Luzzasco Luzzaschi (1545–1607) of Ferraro, teacher of Gesualdo, composed elegant madrigals in a very sophisticated style. Orazzio Vecchi (1550–1605) of Modena, wrote delightful *canzonettas* and a madrigal comedy, *L'Amfiparnasso.* Andriano Banchieri (1567–1634) of Bologna also composed madrigals and a very humorous madrigal comedy, *Festino*, which has frequent contemporary performances.

[8]See Music for Class Study and Conducting, p. 265.
[9]Ernest H. Meyer, "Concerted Instrumental Music," in *The New Oxford History of Music*, IV (London: Oxford University Press, 1968), p. 551.

Observations on Performance of Renaissance Music. A historical perspective on musical development during the Renaissance and an examination of representative composers and their compositional techniques lead to certain conclusions about choral performance, especially as related to the following:

Polyphony and Balance

It is important that each voice part has its own personality—independent, yet aware that it is a part of an ensemble. The balance of parts is equal, in order to give integrity to each melodic line.

Rhythm and Tempo

Since sixteenth-century music was printed in partbooks without bar lines, the singer looks for rhythmic patterns that may begin any place within a given phrase; therefore, when reading from modern notation, he or she must ignore the given time signature and bar lines. Tempos are not so quick that any detail is sacrificed, but they must not lag; they are linked to the rate of human pulse.

The Use of Instruments with Voices

Consorts of instruments were employed to give interest and to provide contrasts in texture in performance of secular music. As a general rule, sacred music was accompanied by the organ in church services (except during Holy Week); instrumental doubling (*colla parte*) was added at church festival periods.

Melody and Harmony

Diatonic or chromatic lines are sung in legato fashion.

Skips are most often separated to bring out their special significance, especially large skips.

Faster notes are performed lightly and clearly so as not to obscure other lines.

Syncopated notes approached from above are sung smoothly; ascending intervals larger than a second are accented; notes tied across bar lines are given no accent and should be sung as if no bar lines were there.

Suspensions should be "leaned into" and then the resolution moved into smoothly, without stress.

Each phrase maintains its integrity with firmness to the end; there is a building of tension in an ascending line, and a relaxation as it descends; each line has a focal point to which it moves and from which it flows away.

Harmony in this period was based on the ecclesiastical modes, usually transposed, but recognizable by special intervals identified with each; triads are not related so much to the tonic as they are to each other; cadences seldom have a dominant-tonic relationship but often a plagal one (IV-I) or Phrygian (with minor second and seventh); a slight increase in sonority is appropriate at final cadences.

Dynamics

There are no crescendos or diminuendos as such in sixteenth-century music; intensification and relaxation of lines, an awareness of text stress and lack of stress are evident but no sudden accents or sforzato are evident.

Volume of tone, both loud and soft, should be kept within limits; *forte* music should maintain a good quality and *piano* should have intensity.

Forte and *piano* are used only to contrast complete sections and are never applied suddenly within a phrase.

Contrasts in dynamics are built into the music by adding to the number of voice parts, thus increasing the sonority.

Text-Music Relationships

The music expresses the mood of the text as well as its speech rhythms; balance varies slightly according to the importance of each part.

The Renaissance–Baroque Transitional Period

The Venetian School at San Marco. The Venetian School was established during the Renaissance (in 1524) by Adrien Willaert, Flemish pupil of the Josquin School. He made effective use of the spatial and echo effects of *coro spezzati* before polychoral music became a trademark of Baroque composition. Willaert initiated the practices of doubling voice parts with instruments, and substituting instruments for voices. Giovanni Gabrieli extended the practice even further by providing instruments with independent music. The combining of voices with independent instrumental writing was called *stile concertato*.

Word painting was particularly apparent in the works of Venetian composers. It was first evident in the madrigals of Cipriano de Rore, and then later in sacred motets by Giovanni Gabrieli and Monteverdi. These composers exploited progressive elements in the treatment of dissonance and rhythm in their attempts to relate music to text, resulting in a frequent use of augmented and chromatic intervals and irregular rhythms. These were radical departures from earlier Renaissance practices.

Claudio Monteverdi and the Vespers of 1610. Monteverdi adopted the venturous spirit of the Venetian School and applied it to all musical forms of the period. In his *Vespers of 1610*, he included not only a setting of the "Vespers for the Blessed Virgin Mary" but also two *Magnificat* settings and several motets for solo voices with *basso continuo*. Various sections of the *Vespers* are set for multiple choirs, solo voices, independent instrumental parts, and *basso continuo*. The first *Magnificat* is in *stile concertato* style, but the second, no doubt designed for a less formal service, is in the earlier polyphonic style (*prima prattica*). The concerted settings provide contrasts in textures and sonorities heretofore unattained in sacred music.

Composers in Northern Europe. The late years of the Renaissance in the north were illuminated by four composers influenced by the Venetian School; their music reveals extraordinary foresight and inventiveness. These composers are

Jacob Handl (1550–1591), of Slavic origin, also known by his Latin name, Jacobus Gallus. He was a composer of masses and motets of exquisite beauty and sonority.

Hans Leo Hassler (1564–1612), a personal friend of Giovanni Gabrieli, whom he met when they were both pupils of the elder Andrea Gabrieli. Hassler's masses and motets for double choir are unique and rich in sonorities. His secular works, of a more homophonic texture, include madrigals and German polyphonic Lieder.

Leonard Lechner (1553–1606), a prolific German composer, trained in the Munich chapel under Orlando di Lasso, is noted for his setting of the *Joannispassion* in Renaissance polyphonic style, a milestone in development of the German Passion oratorio. Lechner also composed several books of German Lieder in three to five parts as well as masses, motets, and numerous settings of the Magnificat.

Mikolaj Zielenski (d. 1615), a Polish composer of brilliant Venetian-style motets in *concertato* style. His setting of the Magnificat was performed at the Chopin Centenary observance in Poland (1910).

The Baroque Era (1580–1770)

The Council of Trent influenced composers of sacred music to write in a homophonic rather than in the traditional polyphonic style, so that the sung liturgical text could be understood. With the advent of the new music proffered by Monteverdi and others, monadic and homophonic musical concepts were increasingly evident. Independent use of instruments with voices became the norm. In both sacred and secular writing a polarity between soprano and bass lines developed as did a predilection for major-minor tonalities. These characteristics resulted in decreased reliance on ecclesiastical modes and an emphasis on tonal harmony; utilization of the circle of fifths and major-minor key relationships prevailed. Polychoral music and *cori spezzati* (multiple choirs positioned spatially) were conceived during the Renaissance in Italian cathedrals. This practice and Baroque concepts of concerted music utilizing *solo-tutti* performance were developed by Andrea and Giovanni Gabrieli at the Cathedral of San Marco. These Venetian practices were expanded and enriched by Heinrich Schütz (1585–1672) in the Saxon Court of Dresden. The Italian *concertato* style combined with German dramatic elements became basic features of German Baroque performance.

The Early Baroque Period in Northern Europe.   Jan Pieterszoon Sweelinck (1562–1621), Dutch organist and composer, was the teacher of many prominent North German musicians. His psalm settings and motets are among the finest examples of Netherlands polyphony. Samuel Scheidt (1587–1654) was one of Sweelinck's most famous pupils. Scheidt was an outstanding organist and one of the finest German composers of chorale-based motets. Michael Praetorius (1571–1621), composer and theorist, was the author of *Syntaga Musicum* (1610), a chief source of information on Renaissance instruments and performance practices. His settings of carols and chorales from *Musae Sionae* are of particular interest. Melchior Franck (1579–1639) composed madrigals and motets in the nonmetrical, irregular text rhythms of the period. Johann Hermann Schein (1586–1630), with his friend Schütz, introduced Germany to the new Italian monodic and *concertato* styles. Schein was a predecessor of J. S. Bach at the Leipzig Thomasschule; his motets are outstanding examples of lyrical beauty combined with Baroque expressivity.

Heinrich Schütz (1585–1672), also known as Henricus Saggitarius.   Schütz became a student of Giovanni Gabrieli in 1609. He remained in Venice for three years, before returning to Kassel after Giovanni's death in 1612. He later returned to Italy for additional study with Monteverdi. Schütz's solid German theoretical background is apparent in his writing, but his years in Italy changed the direction of his composition and provided him with tools that made him one of the outstanding figures of the Baroque.

Schütz's first publication on his return to Germany was a book of madrigals (1611) in the Italian style of Gabrieli and Monteverdi. In 1619 he produced the polychoral settings of the *Psalms of David*, composed in the Venetian *concertato* style with two, three, and four choirs and instruments. In the preface of the latter collection, Schütz gives specific instructions for the performance of his concerted works. They are as follows, in abbreviated form.

> With only one *continuo* player, the organ is registered softer or louder in order to balance with the *favorita* singers (soloists) and the *capella* (full chorus).
>
> Only one *continuo* instrument is needed for multiple choirs when performing in a single area. If the choirs are separated in various parts of the building, it is necessary to provide one for each choir. In this case, contrasting instruments should be used. Lute, chamber organ, and harpsichord are recommended.
>
> With solo singers the bass line should be doubled by cello or bassoon, or both; with full chorus a violone (double bass) or a bass trombone should be added.
>
> *Favorita* singers are essential to a performance, but the full chorus (also called *ripieno*) may be omitted and the parts played by instruments, or the parts may be sung, accompanied by instruments (*colla parte*). An alternative is provided when outer parts are too high or too low for vocal ranges, in which case they may be played by instruments, and only the inner parts sung. *Ripieno* parts may be sung a *cappella*, or more than one upper part may be sung and the remaining parts played by instruments.

With multiple choirs, voice parts may be doubled by instruments (*colla parte*); a second choir may imitate the first (echo), with the parts performed by instruments; or, if no organ or *continuo* instrument is available, a chorus may sing without *continuo*, with instruments doubling the parts.

When choruses are doubled by instruments, or when instruments play both choir parts without voices singing, contrasting families of instruments are used, chosen from strings, woodwinds, or brass. Bright versus dark sonorities are recommended.

When instruments double voices, they should "tint" voice parts, not overpower them.

Choruses doubled by instruments should be separated from each other acoustically. That is, if there are two choirs, each with instruments *colla parte*, the instruments doubling Choir I should be placed in proximity to Choir II, and vice versa (Figure 2-1).

Favorita soloists should be encouraged to ornament their parts in alternation, not at the same time.

Music should be sung at a moderate tempo so that the text can be understood easily, declaimed intelligently, and perceived.[10]

Figure 2-1 Positioning of Choirs I and II with instruments.

Schütz's compositions, not unlike Monteverdi's, frequently reflect the old Renaissance style (*stile antica*) as well as the new *concertato* style. All of Schütz's works bear the stamp of his own originality. Paul Henry Lang appraises Schütz's contribution as follows:

> Schütz was not only the greatest musician of his period but was one of the outstanding creative geniuses in music history. Like some of his compatriots, he was profoundly inspired by Italian music of the early Baroque and transplanted monody, polychoral writing, and *concerto* manner to Germany; but the spiritual roots of his art are deeply set in German soil.[11]

Schütz's choral writings were few in the area of secular music, but his madrigals are among his most sensitive and challenging music. His contribution to sacred music runs the gamut from chorale settings in the *Becker Psalter* and his concerted music for solo voices, *Kleine geistliche Chor Musik*, to his two *Magnificat*s, the *Psalms of David*, and *Sinfoniae Sacrae*. In addition he composed oratorio and passion settings that are major contributions to the development of these forms.

Christoph Bernhard (1628–1692), a pupil of Schütz and a bass soloist in his Dresden choir, revealed the composer's concern for dramatic renditions of his music. Bernhard reported that Schütz gave his choir instructions that when expressing words of joy or rage "the voices must be strong, courageous, and

---

[10]For further, more detailed information read George J. Buelow, "A Schütz Reader, Documents of Performance Practice," *American Choral Review*, XIII, no. 4 (October 1985). Also Wilhelm Ehmann's preface to Heinrich Schütz's "Psalms of David" (1619), *Neue Ausgabe sämtlicher Werke*, Vol. 24 (Kassel: Bärenreiter, 1969).

[11]Paul Henry Lang, *History of Music in Western Civilization* (New York: W. W. Norton & Co., Inc., 1941), p. 397.

hardy." He cautioned the soloists not to ornament such lines and not to sing them legato. On the other hand, "sad or gentle words" should be sung with a lighter tone quality, legato, at a softer dynamic level, and even at a slower tempo. When expressing the effect of "joy or rage" a faster tempo is appropriate.[12]

These instructions reveal to the conductor that the music of Schütz is not stiff and formal; rather, it portrays vivid contrasts in mood and is drama oriented and text oriented in performance.

Italian Composers of the Early Baroque.   A number of Italian composers were producing works in *stile nuovo* early in the seventeenth century. Some of the notable ones concentrated on writing operas, but a few experimented with sacred and secular choral forms in the new idiom. Ludovico da Viadana (1560–1627) of Mantua and Venice was one of the first to compose for solo voice with *basso continuo* in his *Cento concerti* (1602). His innovative *concertato* style is said to have had influence on Monteverdi's *Vespers of 1610*. He also composed motets, psalm-settings, masses, and *Magnificats*. Giovanni Croce (1560–1609), *maestro di cappella* at San Marco in Venice (1603), composed both secular and sacred music, some in the old polyphonic style and some for multiple choirs in the style of Andrea Gabrieli. Baldassare Donato (1530–1603), also of Venice and San Marco, was known for his writing of madrigals as well as motets.

Alessandro Grandi (d. 1630), born in Sicily, became a student of Giovanni Gabrieli and was highly regarded as a composer of masses and motets in *concertato* style; his motets for solo voices and *continuo* became extremely popular in Germany and quite possibly served as a model for Schütz's compositions in this form. In Grandi's *Peace Today Descends from Heaven (Hodie nobis de coeli)*,[13] for example, we find many characteristics of early Baroque practice:

> Voice parts may be performed by two solo voices or a two-part choir (SA or TB).
>
> The *basso continuo* may be played by any bass instrument (cello, bassoon, trombone); it is an independent, integral part of the composition with considerable musical interest.
>
> The form is unified by imitation of phrase lines, melodic sequences, and repeated "alleluias" in the refrain.
>
> The music is tonal with modal inflections that add interest and vitality to the work.
>
> The faster eighth notes in the "alleluias" lend excitement and forward motion to the music; the contrasting meter relationship (2:3) and the pairing of voices singing consecutive, diatonic thirds create a climax at the end of each verse.
>
> Word painting is evident in the sequential descent of the phrase "peace has descended on us from Heaven" (*nobis de coelo pax vera descendit*); the trumpetlike pronouncement "is made known to me" (*facti sunt mihi*) is emphasized by repeated notes (mm. 27–29).

The Baroque Cantata and Oratorio in Italy.   By the mid-seventeenth century there were efforts to project the drama of opera into sacred composition. The first attempt was made by Emilio di Cavalieri (ca. 1550–1602), a nobleman in Rome, who combined a morality play with music. This new form had little effect until Giacomo Carissimi (1605–1674) composed four short oratorios in Latin, based on dramatic episodes from the Old Testament. *Jephte* is Carissimi's masterpiece, a work in monodic style having recitatives, solos, and a variety of choruses, all with independent instrumental accompaniments. The concluding

[12]For a complete discussion of Christoph Bernhard's recommendations for performance of Schütz's music, see preface to Arthur Mendel's edition of *The Christmas Story* (New York: G. Schirmer, 1949), p. vii.

[13]See Music for Class Study and Conducting, p. 271.

chorus of six parts, "Plorate filii Israel," is a typical example of Carissimi's sonorities and expressive style.

Alessandro Scarlatti (1654–1725), a pupil of Carissimi, became the founder of the Neapolitan School. Although known primarily as a composer of opera, Scarlatti also wrote over two hundred masses, several books of *Concerti sacri*, and motets for solo voice and chorus with two violins, viola, and organ *continuo*. In addition, his secular music includes madrigals, *serenatas*, and nearly eight hundred solo cantatas. His lyrical "Italian aria" style influenced many composers of the period.

Antonio Caldara (1670–1736), born in Italy, was known both as a cellist and as a composer. After many years as a practicing musician in Italy, he went to Vienna to become assistant choirmaster to Johann Joseph Fux (1660–1741), Austrian composer and theorist. Caldara composed thirty-two oratorios in addition to masses, cantatas, and madrigals. The Italian lyrical style dominates his music.

The Court of Louis XIV at Versailles. Conductors must seek the spirit of an age to fully understand its music. Seventeenth-century Western civilization was characterized by world exploration and extraordinary expansion. Powerful monarchs reigned over some of the most lavish courts in history. With the elegance that was part of court life came the chamber cantata and the dance suites—both important features of extravagant musical entertainments. Courts throughout Europe vied for the finest maestros and for the most talented singers and instrumentalists, in spite of the fact that musical activity was often curtailed or interrupted by wars and frequent fighting between princedoms. Louis XIV was particularly noted for surrounding himself with talented instrumentalists and singers under the leadership of Jean-Baptiste Lully (1632–1687). The musical style and inventiveness of this composer influenced compositional practice and musical performance throughout Europe during the latter half of the seventeenth century.

French Composers Contemporary with Lully. Three significant French composers of this period are of special interest to the choral conductor. Marc-Antoine Charpentier (1636–1704), who many believe was even more talented and innovative than Lully, is known especially for his tuneful, folklike Christmas mass, *Messe de minuit*. All of Charpentier's masses and motets were composed for chorus with instruments, usually strings, oboes or trumpets or both, keyboard, and percussion. Michel-Richard De Lalande (1657–1726), noted Parisian organist and composer, also followed in this tradition; he was *maitre-de-chapelle* for many years at Sainte-Chapelle. His compositions include forty-five excellent motets for voices and instruments that are still rewarding in performance.

Guillaume Bouzinac, about whom little personal data is available, was associated with the cathedral at Grenoble early in the seventeenth century. His few existing motets are unique in their free, dramatic expressiveness. Although no instrumental parts are indicated, organ and *basso continuo* were probably employed in performance.

The Court of Charles II in England. Lully's music in Versailles had special influence on the English court of Charles II, who had lived much of his youth in exile at the French court. When he was brought back to become king of England, he insisted on bringing with him twenty-four French instrumentalists who had been trained in the Lully tradition. These men were placed in the hands of Henry Purcell (ca. 1659–1695), who was the appointed master of the

Chapel Royal. Purcell combined strings with voices in the French tradition when he composed English verse anthems, a form that he inherited from Byrd and Gibbons. The French dance rhythms, the bowing traditions, the practice of playing *notes inegales*,[14] and the exaggerated rhythms of the French overture were all absorbed into Purcell's style. George Frideric Handel (1685–1759) took Purcell's elegant court style, with its French influence and its unique command of the English language, and combined it with his own Teutonic-Italianate background.

Before moving on to Handel's music, there are two contemporaries of Purcell who are important to consider. They are John Blow (1648–1708), Purcell's teacher, predecessor, and successor at Westminster Abbey, and Pelham Humfrey (1647–1708), a member of the Chapel Royal and a friend of Purcell. Blow composed several anthems and an "Ode for St. Cecilia's Day" that are especially delightful in performance. Humfrey composed numerous anthems and a noteworthy setting of the Anglican service. Although he died quite young, Humfrey was very knowledgeable about French performance practices and is said to have influenced Purcell's writing.

Handel and the Late Baroque in England. George Frideric Handel was born and educated in Germany, and had his early professional experience as a church organist and an opera harpsichordist there. At the age of twenty-one he left his opera position and journeyed to Italy. After three years of successfully playing keyboard concerts and composing opera and oratorio (which he presented in leading Italian musical centers), Handel was invited back to Germany to become *Kapellmeister* for the Elector of Hanover. Soon after that engagement, he was called to England to write and produce Italian opera. It was in England that Handel found a permanent home. His former employer in Germany was brought to England to become King George II, and Handel was asked to compose music for his coronation and that of his consort, Queen Caroline. These monarchs remained Handel's close friends and supporters throughout his career.

Handel was truly a cosmopolitan composer. From the *Chandos Anthems* through the *Coronation Anthems*, to his later oratorios, elements of his musical composition were drawn from Monteverdi and Carissimi, from Henry Purcell, and even from Friedrich Wilhelm Zachau (1663–1712), his first German teacher. Handel's oratorios reflect his years of writing Italian opera; a sense of drama and the importance of text are observed in all his choral music. German contrapuntal skills are apparent in his great choral fugues; flowing melodies and sonorities reminiscent of Italian polychoral music appear frequently. His choral writing and his choice of instruments are closely allied; clearly articulated rhythms and text-music relationships reflect Handel's sensitivity to dramatic elements.

Baroque Conventions in the Music of Handel. Handel's music has universal qualities that combine German training in form and counterpoint, Italian leanings toward flowing melody and dramatic expression, and English choral traditions. His sensitivity to English text grew as he became increasingly familiar with the language and as he absorbed word treatment in the music of Purcell and others. Handel, with Johann Sebastian Bach (1685–1750), brought music of the Baroque era to its zenith. His compositional objectives were quite different from those of Bach, however. As a musician representing English roy-

---

[14]See the article entitled "Notes inegales" in *The New Grove Dictionary of Music and Musicians*, XIII (London: Macmillan, 1980), pp. 420–25.

alty, Handel was affected by the aesthetic concepts of pomp and splendor conceived in the music of Gabrieli and the Venetians at the beginning of the Baroque. Bach was a musician of the Lutheran Church. Also schooled in German musical traditions and with universal concepts, he dedicated his music solely "to the glory of God."[15]

Combining a knowledge of Baroque compositional traditions with an awareness of Handel's motivations for composing music, a conductor will view his choral music with certain expectations.

> The *basso continuo* and accompanying keyboard instruments (organ, harpsichord) deserve attention as moving forces of tonal harmony and structural development.
>
> Of equal importance to the bass line is that of the soprano; except in fugal writing, the inner parts (alto, tenor) are less individual in character and are subordinate to the outer voices.
>
> Courtly elegance is apparent; reference to Baroque dance forms and their meter signatures (*minuet, allemande, sarabande, gigue, passacaglia, chaconne, courante*) are important in establishing appropriate tempos.[16]
>
> Music is related to the dramatic significance of text; emotional implications of text are expressed through speech rhythms and harmonic colorings in vocal and instrumental parts.
>
> Melodic ornamentation is employed for expressive purposes, most often in solo lines and in instrumental parts. The appoggiatura and the cadential trill are traditional in performance. There are source readings on the subject, with which the alert conductor will become familiar. Robert Donington[17] and Thurston Dart[18] are particularly helpful.
>
> Performance of choral music with instruments requires a special knowledge of Baroque bowing and articulation.[19] The ability to realize a *continuo* part from a figured bass is also essential.[20]
>
> Notation of Baroque rhythms is in many respects unique; copyists used a type of shorthand that is interpreted according to practices of the period.

Baroque rhythmic characteristics and illustrations from Handel's choral music follow.

> Overdotting is a feature of slow or moderately fast tempos; to clarify dotted rhythms, a small space will occur between the dotted note and the sixteenth note that follows. This "decay" of the dotted note results in precise articulation (Example 2-4).
>
> Paired notes also tend to decay, with second note treated staccato (Example 2-5).
>
> Articulated rhythms are frequently contrasted with *sostenuto* passages (Example 2-6).
>
> Predominant rhythms are assimilated into all parts; dotted rhythms are changed to triplets when triplet rhythm prevails in accompaniment (Example 2-7).
>
> Eighth notes are sung as sixteenths to agree with predominant dotted-eighth, sixteenth-note rhythm in orchestra parts (Example 2-8).
>
> Dotted rests do not appear in Baroque manuscripts; a figure such as ♩ ♩ ♩. ♪ is played ♩. ♪ ♩. ♪ (Example 2-9).
>
> Altered notations of instrumental parts are duplicated in voice parts (Example 2-10).
>
> French rhythmic conventions relating to successive eighth notes (*notes inegales*)[21] applicable to music of Henry Purcell (Example 2-11).

---

[15]Bach inscribed his sacred music scores with the letters J.J., representing the Latin words *Jesu, juva* ("Jesus, help") at the beginning, and at the end, S.D.G., *Soli Deo gloria* ("Only to God be glory").

[16]Thurston Dart, *The Interpretation of Music* (New York: Harper & Row, Pub., 1954), p. 84.

[17]Robert Donington, *A Performer's Guide to Baroque Music* (London: Faber & Faber, 1978), pp. 181–190, 195–203.

[18]Dart, *The Interpretation of Music*, p. 85.

[19]Ibid., p. 92.

[20]Franck Thomas Arnold, *The Art of Accompaniment from a Thorough-Bass*, 2 vols. (New York: Dover, 1965).

[21]Read article on "Notes inegales" in *The New Grove Dictionary of Music and Musicians*.

Melodic conventions[22] observed in solo arias may be applied to chorus parts as observed in a quasi-recitative chorus (Example 2-12).[23]

a. *Land* is sung as two quarter notes, with the appoggiatura coming on the beat: .

b. *Felt* is sung as two eighth notes, with the appoggiatura coming on the beat: .

c. *Dark* is sung as two eighth notes, with the appoggiatura coming on the beat: .

d. Even if notated as a quarter note on b, it would be sung as written here, as two eighth notes with the e repeated.

e. *Darkness*, originally notated as two quarter notes, may be sung with passing note, as in parenthesis.

f. Final chords in *continuo*, written originally on first and second beats of the measure, are conventionally played after the voice part concludes.

Hemiola, frequently occurring in triple meter, results in three beats to a measure ($\frac{3}{4}$) expanded to three beats covering *two* measures ($\frac{3}{2}$); a hemiola usually occurs at cadence points but sometimes may be observed within a phrase (Example 2-13).[24]

Example 2-4 Space between dotted eighth and sixteenth in opening chorus from *Saul*. (See "How Excellent Thy Name" in Music for Class Study and Conducting.)

Example 2-5 Execution of paired notes (*Saul*—G. F. Handel).

[22]Donington, *A Performer's Guide to Baroque Music*, pp. 160–63.

[23]See "And He Sent a Thick Darkness" in Music for Class Study and Conducting.

[24]This example of hemiola may seem to give an unnatural stress to the text. The importance of placing stress on *their*, however, cannot be questioned; this stress and the rising inflection of the soprano line on *among* combine to make this alteration of the rhythm effective in performance.

Example 2-6 Contrasting rhythmic-*sostenuto* passage (*Saul*—G. F. Handel).

Example 2-7 Assimilation of dotted rhythms into prevailing triplet rhythm (*Israel in Egypt*—G. F. Handel).

Example 2-8 Assimilation of vocal dotted eighth, sixteenth-note rhythm with string parts (*Saul*—G. F. Handel).

Example 2-9 Implied dotted rest in Baroque notation (*Messiah*—G. F. Handel).

Example 2-10 Altered rhythm of vocal part corresponds with introduction by flute in orchestral part (*Israel in Egypt*—G. F. Handel). See "But As for His People" in Music for Class Study and Conducting.

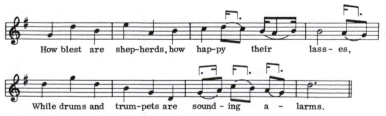

Example 2-11 Application of notes inegales to soprano part in chorus "How Blest Are Shepherds" (*King Arthur*—Purcell).

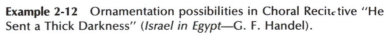

Example 2-12 Ornamentation possibilities in Choral Recitative "He Sent a Thick Darkness" (*Israel in Egypt*—G. F. Handel).

Example 2-13 Cadence requiring shift of rhythmic stress (hemiola), "But As for His People" (*Israel in Egypt*—G. F. Handel). See Music for Class Study and Conducting.

Tone Quality and Balance in Baroque Performance. *Stile nuovo*, initiated by Monteverdi and his contemporaries, emphasized the polarity of voices. This remained as a fundamental principle throughout the period. The soprano and bass lines predominate; the inner parts are less prominent and serve as "fillers" in the tonal harmony. Unchanged boys' voices continued to provide the upper parts in sacred choral music, while female singers began to appear as soloists and as members of secular vocal ensembles.

In polychoral performances, instruments doubled voice parts, substituted for individual parts, or even replaced choirs. With solo voices, the bass line was traditionally played by cello, bassoon, or trombone; with chorus rather than soloists, the violone or a double bass was added an octave lower. Strings and flutes (more commonly, recorders) were assigned a cello on the bass line, while oboes called for a bassoon. The bass trombone was associated with higher brass, and the alto and tenor trombones, or their predecessors the sackbuts, traditionally doubled the three lowest parts in a choral fugue. Handel added extra bassoons to the bass and extra oboes to the soprano line when choruses were augmented.

Handel combined his opera soloists with boys and men from the Chapel Royal in oratorio performances. His melismatic writing demands an easy, flexible, and facile vocal production (*bel canto*) with bright, clear tempos that facilitate the singing of traditional ornamentation and long melismatic passages. There was no concept that a chorus was "accompanied" by instruments; rather, there was an equality of sound between them. Clarity and transparency of texture are ideals sought in Baroque performances.

Johann Sebastian Bach and the Late Baroque Period in Germany. While Handel was associated with Italian opera and English court music, Bach was employed by officials of small German princedoms and a city-state; he was both a *Kapellmeister* and a court musician. His final and longest appointment was that of cantor at the Thomasschule in Leipzig. In addition to his responsibilities as organist and music director of two major Lutheran churches and teacher in the Thomasschule, he was assigned to meet the musical needs for the court of Prince Leopold of Anholt. During his twenty-seven years in Leipzig, he composed most of his sacred music and wrote several secular cantatas. His chorale settings, many of them incorporated into his cantatas, motets, and Passion settings, are models of expressive harmonization and musical inventiveness.[25] The Mass in B Minor and the Passion settings of the gospels of St. Matthew and St.

[25]See Bach chorales in Music for Class Study and Conducting, p. 268.

John are musical legacies of such universality that they are still widely performed in the third century after his death.

Bach's Contemporaries in Germany.   Johann Pachelbel (1653–1706) had an influence on Bach as a young composer. His music combines Venetian polychoral concepts with a strict contrapuntal background. His finest works are chorale-based polychoral motets.

Georg Philipp Telemann (1681–1767) was a prolific composer and was highly esteemed as Musical Director of the City of Hamburg. He composed twelve series of motets for the church year, nearly three thousand motets, forty-four Passion settings, and numerous secular cantatas and occasional works for chorus and instruments.

Carl Heinrich Graun (1699–1765) also received high acclaim during Bach's lifetime. His Passion oratorio, *Der Tod Jesu*, was performed annually for nearly a century in Germany. His style was influenced by the new *Empfindsamer Stil* (espoused by Carl Philipp Emanuel Bach and others), which exaggerated the emotional elements of text and music.

Franz Tunder (1614–1667) preceded Bach, but his cantatas in chorale-variation form served as a model for Bach's Cantata No. 4 BWV, *Christ lag in Todesbanden*. Tunder was Buxtehude's immediate predecessor in the north German city of Lübeck.

Antonio Vivaldi (1675–1741) is an important Italian composer who also had some influence on the music of J. S. Bach. He is famous for both instrumental and vocal music composed for orphaned girls at the *Ospedale della Pietà* in Venice. There Vivaldi gained an international reputation for the high quality of the girls' singing and playing. Vivaldi's themes were woven into Bach's keyboard works, and both Bach and Handel introduced the Italian *siciliano*, a shepherd's folk-dance form employed by Vivaldi, into their major works. This Italian form is found in the alto solo "Erbarme dich" from Bach's *Passion According to St. Matthew* and in the instrumental "Pastoral Symphony" from Handel's *Messiah*. Vivaldi employed the *siciliano* rhythm most effectively in the soprano solo "Domine Deus" from his setting of *Gloria*.

Dietrich Buxtehude (1637–1707) was an inspiration to the youthful Bach. The successor to Franz Tunder at the Marienkirche in Lübeck, Buxtehude instituted his celebrated *Abendmusik*, during which he performed organ music and Advent cantatas for voices and instruments. He is a worthy predecessor of Bach in the development of the German cantata form.

The German Pre-Classic Period.   Even during the elder Bach's lifetime, there was a reaction to the "heaviness of polyphony." The French *rococo* or *galant* style was the art of the aristocratic world. Music began to emphasize pleasantness and beauty in contrast to Baroque grandeur and impressiveness, and the broad, homogeneous approach of the French and English courts gave way to an emphasis on *Empfindsamkeit* (sensitivity), which sought to impart feeling through every musical detail. An accepted "Doctrine of Affections" carried this to an extreme by establishing musical motifs to represent emotions.

Johann Joachim Quantz (1697–1773) was both a composer and an author. He wrote an instruction book on playing the flute that is one of the most important sources of information on performance practice in the Baroque period.[26] Along with the elder Bach's sons, Johann Christian (1735–1782) and Carl Philipp Emanuel (1714–1788), Quantz was a leader in the *Empfindsamer Stil* (sensitive style) movement. Quantz had this to say on the subject:

[26]J. J. Quantz, *Versuch einer Anweisung, die Flöte traversiere zu spielen* (1752) (*Essay on How to Play the Flute*), trans. Edward J. Rielly (New York: Schirmer Books, 1975).

Musical interpretation can be compared with the interpretation of an orator. Orator and musician have in common the intention of mastering the hearts . . . of putting the listener now in this, now in that affection.[27]

Carl Philipp Emanuel Bach was a choral composer of the pre-Classic, rococo, *Empfindsamer Stil* period. An excerpt from his oratorio *Die Israeliten in der Wüste (The Israelites in Egypt)* is the chorus "Anthem of Thanksgiving."[28] The setting is in the Promised Land after the Jews had crossed the Red Sea with Moses, their leader. Surging of parted waves is represented by a continuous flow of sixteenth notes played by violins in the orchestra. The strictly homophonic writing with sudden harmonic shifts is an example of the composer's effort to project realism and a heightened emotion into his music.

Paul Henry Lang evaluates the composition of Bach's second son in the following way:

[He was] the outstanding master of the late *rococo* of pre-Classical times, a master who triumphed over the weaknesses of the art and atmosphere of his own period.[29]

The Mannheim School and the New Dynamics.   Under leadership provided by Johann Stamitz (1717–1757), the Mannheim Orchestra initiated the use of crescendo and diminuendo in performance. Niccolo Jomelli (1714–1774), Italian composer-conductor, is credited with originating this new expressive device. There are frequent admonitions in the Classic period to regard a separated p————f as a gradual increase (*crescendo*) and f————p as a gradual decrease in sound (*diminuendo*); this was the first time in history that the terms actually appeared. Although the "echo effects" of the Baroque period continued to be observed, the p followed by f and the f followed by p in the works of Haydn and Mozart are frequently interpreted as crescendo and diminuendo in keeping with this principle initiated by the Mannheim School.

The Classic Period (1770–1830)

The *Empfindsamer Stil* movement led to excesses and sentimentality in performance and resulted in reactions on the part of critics and composers who strove for a more rationalistic approach to artistic expression. This reaction culminated in establishing certain characteristics of a new Classic era. Lang describes the aspirations of the period as follows:

Composers sought for a noble, refined, courtly style which was thought to represent middle-class elegance as opposed to the extravagant excesses of the old art of the aristocracy. . . . Men returned to the idea of beauty of classical antiquity. This new humanism focused its attention once more on man and nature, but not with the passionate and soul-stirring vehemence of the Baroque nor the playful superficiality of the Rococo.[30]

Haydn and Mozart.   The late eighteenth century and the early years of the nineteenth constituted the time of "enlightened absolutism." During this

[27]Frederick Dorian, *The History of Music in Performance* (New York: W. W. Norton & Co., Inc., 1966), p. 139.

[28]See Music for Class Study and Conducting, p. 297.

[29]Lang, *Music in Western Civilization*, p. 957.

[30]Ibid., pp. 622–23.

period rulers placed all their weight and resources behind scientific and artistic endeavors. They commissioned musical works to enhance the reputation of the state and their own dignity as rulers. It was a period of unrest and experimentation in science as well as in music, and it led to a search for strict formal structure and closed forms. As a result, the sonata form was developed by Franz Joseph Haydn (1732–1809) and Wolfgang Amadeus Mozart (1756–1791). At the castle of the Esterhazy in Eisenach, Haydn applied this form that he had developed in his symphonies and keyboard sonatas to his last six masses. He organized the Kyrie and Gloria into an exposition, development, and recapitulation. He followed the same procedure in the longer Credo, also constructing it into three sections. Finally, he shaped the Sanctus-Benedictus and Agnus Dei into a third sonata form.[31]

One of the first major choral works composed for a nonprofessional chorus was Haydn's oratorio *The Creation*. During his middle period the composer traveled to England, where he experienced an enthusiastic reception for his symphonic music. While in London he attended the famous memorial performance of Handel's *Messiah* at Westminster Abbey (1794). Instrumental and choral forces on this occasion, unlike the limited forces employed during Handel's lifetime, consisted of a gigantic chorus and orchestra. In spite of this overblown performance, Haydn was so moved by the music that he returned to Austria determined to emulate the "master." He began almost immediately to compose a work of large dimensions, and *The Creation* had its first performance in 1798. An English libretto, which had been presented to Haydn in London, consisted of material from the first chapter of Genesis combined with excerpts from writings of Milton. The English text was set to music side by side with a German text translated by Haydn's friend, Baron von Swieten. The first edition was printed in both German and English. A conductor should examine this first English edition before using one of the often awkward translations taken from the original German.[32]

Mozart's masses and other liturgical works are Classic in style, but the Requiem reverts to more conventional Baroque practices. The melodic lines reflect ideals of classical beauty and require little "interpretation." It was Mozart's wish to keep the tempo and the dynamics he indicated intact. A conductor should approach the music of Mozart with simplicity and elegance; he or she should strive for legato lines, phrase shaping, forward rhythmic movement, harmonic drive, dynamic sensitivity, and rhythmic clarity. Slower tempos may be enhanced by an exaggeration of dotted rhythms and an element of rubato in the treatment of melodic lines, yet with a steady bass. An enlightening quotation from a letter written by young Mozart to his father gives some insight into the Classic rubato:

> No one seems to understand the *tempo rubato* in an Adagio, namely, that the left hand does not know anything about it.[33]

The Romantic Era (1830–1900)

The Romantic period provided a change from the Classic emphasis on individual expression to a search for an effective expression for all mankind. Beetho-

[31]H. C. Robbins-Landon, *Haydn: Chronicle and Works*, Vol. IV (Bloomington, Ind.: Indiana University Press, 1977).
[32]Read Nicholas Temperley's article on Haydn's libretto for *The Creation* in *Music in Eighteenth Century England*, ed. Christopher Hogwood and Richard Luckett (Cambridge: Cambridge University Press, 1983).
[33]Dorian, *The History of Music in Performance*, p. 188.

ven's performances of the Ninth Symphony and the *Missa Solemnis* were signs of the times. The *Sturm und Drang* principle of the early Romantic period was a form of extreme sentimentalism and personal expressiveness that emphasized dramatic and passionate elements in music. Similar to the earlier attitude of the *Empfindsamer Stil* advocates who reacted against Baroque music, the Romantics were no longer satisfied with Classic formality and poise. They sought to express extreme emotions with a predilection toward fantasy, completely liberated from conventional forms and concepts.

Mendelssohn and Schumann.   Certain works by Felix Mendelssohn (1808–1847) and Robert Schumann (1810–1856) are examples of the Romantic predilection for fantasy. Choral/orchestral works of this nature include Mendelssohn's *The First Walpurgis Night,* based on a text by Goethe concerned with Druid priests and the supernatural, and Schumann's *Paradise and the Peri,* another subject of fantasy. The atmosphere of the supernatural is enhanced by weird orchestration, sudden dynamic contrasts, changing rhythms, and eerie melodic lines.

Colossal Works for Large Chorus and Orchestra.   Major works calling for huge instrumental and choral forces to be presented in large halls followed Beethoven's Ninth Symphony (1822). The concept of "music for the common man," themes on subjects of fantasy, and the expression of extreme emotions in music permeate these compositions. After composing *Symphonie Fantastique* in 1829, Hector Berlioz (1803–1869) conceived his Requiem Mass for a chorus of 1800 and augmented forces of instrumentalists. The orchestra includes a large battery of tympani, cymbals, and French horns in addition to four brass ensembles to be spaced at four corners of the combined ensembles. Berlioz initially conducted the work at the church of Les Invalides in Paris, but he also conceived the possibility of an outdoor performance, as evidenced by the large forces he recommended. He called his massive conception *Grande Messe des Mortes.* The first performance was in 1837.

Shortly before this occasion, Gioacchino Rossini (1792–1868) had composed *Stabat Mater* (1832) in operatic style, overexpressive to present-day taste, yet highly acceptable in his time. Later in the century, Giuseppe Verdi (1813–1901) wrote his *Manzoni* Requiem, dedicated to the famous nineteenth-century writer whom he greatly admired. This work for large chorus, soloists, and symphony orchestra was first presented in 1874. Other composers of works calling for gigantic forces in this period include Franz Liszt (1811–1886) *(Missa solemnis, Hungarian Coronation* Mass, *Christus,* and *The Legend of St. Elizabeth),* Anton Bruckner (1824–1896) (Masses in c, e, and f minor, *Te Deum,* and Requiem Mass), and Gustav Mahler (1860–1911) *(Resurrection* Symphony [II] and *Symphony of a Thousand* [VIII]).

Composers of More Intimate Forms.   Franz Schubert (1797–1828) wrote choral music that relied heavily upon his gift for melody and his own individual qualities of expression. Schubert's frequent employment of *forte-piano (fp)* and *forzando (fz)* indicates the exaggeration of expressive dynamics that became characteristic of Romantic music. Dynamic phrase development and sudden contrasts are important in the interpretation of Schubert's masses as well as his Lieder and quartets.

Gabriel Fauré (1845–1924) found his personal expression in the music of the past and based his Requiem on medieval plainchant references. His music is both lyrical and dramatic. In the Requiem, his major work, the ominous presence of fate and eternity is present in the Introit and Kyrie and, even more dramatically, in the "Libera me." These episodes are contrasted sharply with the lyrical Offertorium, the ethereal soprano solo, "Pie Jesu," and the treble-dominated "In paradisum." Dynamic and textural contrasts are indigenous to the Romantic style of both Schubert and Fauré.

Johannes Brahms (1833–1897) was probably the most prominent composer of choral music in the Romantic era. He, unlike other composers of this period, based nearly all his music on traditional forms. He did not, however, accept the traditional form of the Requiem Mass. On the contrary, he selected portions of scripture that stirred his own imagination and expressed his own personal philosophy in *Ein deutsches Requiem*. He chose verses from both the New and the Old Testaments, and he dedicated the work not to a single person but to all mankind; he preferred the title "A Human Requiem." In contrast to Schubert, the songwriter, Brahms was an expert contrapuntalist; his employment of traditional forms is apparent in the motets, in the *Liebeslieder*, and in an *a cappella* work for double chorus, *Deutsche Fest und Gedenksprüche*. Many of these characteristics may also be observed in his motet with organ accompaniment, *Lass dich nur nichts nicht dauren*:[34]

The organ accompaniment provides independent musical interest throughout, especially in the introduction and in two quasi-ritornello interludes.

Chromatic harmony reveals a predominance of secondary seventh chords, and there is an avoidance of strong cadential feeling until the final coda.

There are long archlike, extended phrases with overlapping cadences, reminiscent of Josquin and Palestrina, yet freer and more personally expressive.

There appear frequent contrapuntal devices such as the canon, sequences, and other means of melodic imitation.

There is a close relationship between text and music, particularly in regard to mood and texture.

Russian Choral Music of the Romantic Period.   Some of the most significant choral music of nineteenth-century Russia is that of the Russian Orthodox Church. Features of this large segment of musical repertory include

Slow-moving, sustained openings with *divisi* parts followed by a fast-moving response, such as an "Alleluia."

A wide range of vocal tessitura, from high soprano to *basso profundo*, with a second bass part duplicating the written bass line an octave lower.

A preponderance of modal harmony with changing sonorities and rich chordal structures.

Textures that are mainly homophonic and that tend to be thick with parts *divisi*.

The use of liturgical chant within the framework of a motet.

Occasional polyphony with only three or four voice-parts.

Frequent four-part music for male voices.

The principal composers of Russian Orthodox music include Dmitri Bortniansky (1751–1825), Piotr Ilyich Tchaikovsky (1840–1893), César Cui (1835–1918), Vassili Kalinnikov (1866–1901), Alexander Gretchaninov (1864–1956), and Sergei Rachmaninov (1873–1943). A wealth of exciting, sonorous music of this genre is yet to be revealed by contemporary research.

Close of the Romantic Era.   This period was an era of personal expression on a large scale, from intimate folksongs and chamber music to choral/orchestral works on a grand scale. As with other transition periods, the groundwork for a new movement in the arts was laid before the old era had ended.

---

[34]See Music for Class Study and Conducting, p. 316.

For example, Monteverdi at the beginning of the seventeenth century composed in the old Renaissance style (*prima prattica*) as well as in the new (*seconda prattica*); *Rococo* and *Empfindsamer* concepts anticipate the Classic and Romantic periods; Beethoven's early works reflect Haydn and Mozart, but his later compositions express the new Romantic spirit.

In the nineteenth century Berlioz and Mahler far exceeded the expectations of the *Sturm and Drang* concepts that motivated Beethoven and his contemporaries. At the close of the century Arnold Schoenberg (1874–1951), steeped in Romantic tradition, first composed "Friede auf Erden" and *Gurre-Lieder,* two works that reached the limits of expression within the bounds of previous harmonic concepts. From here, Schoenberg turned to atonality and the serial techniques that set the stage for twentieth-century musical composition often referred to as representing "The Age of Experimentation."

The Twentieth Century

As we have already mentioned, at the beginning of a new era there are composers who look forward and those who look back. Bach brought the Baroque era to its height with compositional tools of the past. During Bach's time, his own sons and the young Giovanni Battista Pergolesi (1710–1736) composed in a new vein that anticipated the music of Mozart and Haydn. Those composers considered J. S. Bach "old-fashioned."

In the words of Nadia Boulanger, the evolution of compositional styles does not indicate that a "new" style is more or less effective than the old—only that there are new conceptions on the part of some composers.

> The idea of chronology in artistic matters seems quite fallacious to me. There might be a history of oppositions: being tired of going along this road, I take another. That doesn't prove that the first way was bad nor that it was exhausted; the first way doesn't take the course of the second because it isn't the same.[35]

Around the turn of the century, many excellent composers preferred to express themselves in the Romantic idiom, rather than to pursue new roads opened by a few leaders in the new century. Some of these Late Romanticists were influenced by the rise of nationalism and a renewed interest in folk music traditions. Others became engrossed in the possibilities of new melodic, rhythmic, and harmonic exploration.

The Late Romanticists.   Claude Debussy (1862–1918) and Maurice Ravel (1875–1937) were two of the first composers to react to the violent and grandiose self-expressionism of the followers of Richard Wagner. They were influenced by the Impressionist school of painting, by such artists as Degas, Monet, and Renoir, and by the sensitive poetry of Beaudelaire, Verlaine, and Mallarmé. Their music is suggestive rather than bombastic, subtle rather than explicit. Debussy's poetic settings of Charles d'Orleans' *Trois chansons* is an excellent example of the intimate subtleties inherent in Impressionism.

The English Late Romanticists are represented in the music of Edward Elgar (1857–1934), whose mystical setting of *The Dream of Gerontius* is a monumental choral/orchestral work. Elgar also composed numerous part songs and

---

[35]Bruno Monsaingeon, *Mademoiselle: Conversations with Nadia Boulanger,* trans. Robyn Marsack (Manchester, England: Carcenet, 1981), p. 111.

cantatas that reveal his gift for writing beautiful melody and rich vocal sonorities reminiscent of Brahms.

Another British composer of this period was Frederick Delius (1862–1934). He possessed a uniquely individual style that is revealed in large choral works such as *A Mass of Life* and even in his more intimate songs of nature: "Songs at Sunset," "A Song of the High Hills," and "Wanderers Song." Unlike Elgar, who was influenced by Brahms, Delius was influenced by the Romantic works of Beethoven and Berlioz. Like Beethoven's, his choral tessituras are vocally demanding.

The Church of England is indebted to a number of composers who wrote memorable sacred music in this period. Their music remains in the basic repertory of twentieth-century Protestant church choirs. These composers are Hubert H. Parry (1848–1918), Charles Villiers Stanford (1852–1924), and Dr. Charles Wood (1866–1926). Their music is inspiring, worshipful, and dignified, a model to be wished for in some Protestant service music of today. They explored vocal sonorities with double chorus as well as with voices in combination with organ. Although much of their music is challenging to the amateur chorus, these compositions are within the capabilities of experienced singers.

In America, this period is represented by a musician from Yale University, Horatio Parker (1863–1919), who had been trained in Germany. Parker reflected the Romantic spirit in his oratorio, *Hora Novissima*, a major work that offers thrilling choruses and outstanding arias. He was a master contrapuntalist and composed strong, surging melodic lines inspired by the music of Brahms.

Other American composers representing this period include Arthur Foote (1853–1937), Edward MacDowell (1861–1908), Henry Hadley (1871–1937), Daniel Gregory Mason (1873–1953), and Howard Hanson (1896–1981). Some of them portrayed strong feelings for America in their music; others endeavored to reflect European masters.

Twentieth-century Innovators.   Three prominent innovative composers changed the course of music in this century: Arnold Schoenberg (1874–1951), Igor Stravinsky (1882–1971), and Charles Ives (1874–1954). These three initiated trends that may be categorized as Neo-Classic, Neo-Romantic, and, for want of a better term, avant-garde. Schoenberg turned from a late Romanticist into a Neo-Romanticist after he composed "Friede auf Erde" and *Gurre-Lieder;* he then created an alternative style based on twelve-tone serial techniques. This led to such a work as "De profundis," which incorporated *Sprechstimme*, a form of song-speech on "approximate" pitches for dramatic purpose. A work employing the prescribed "tone row" is his "Dreimal tausend Jahre" for orchestra and chorus.

Schoenberg's philosophy regarding music followed that of twentieth-century Expressionism: a reaction against the concepts of French Impressionists who portrayed "impressions" of the "outer world." The new expression was of the subconscious or "inner self"; it constituted a replacement of naturalism and "color technique" with abstractions and distortions not associated with traditional music. A close follower of Schoenberg was Anton Webern (1883–1945), whose two *Cantatas* employed twelve-tone serialism. Webern used voices melodically as if they were instruments, in a pointillistic manner. This technique was a reaction to melodies shaped in standard patterns of four- to eight-measure phrases. Pointillism actually divides words and syllables on separate pitches with little or no relationship to each other. These Schoenberg innovations were imitated by numerous composers who followed him.

Igor Stravinsky was the prime instigator of Neo-Classicism, although he also composed in the twelve-tone serial technique of Schoenberg and reflected his Russian heritage in much of his music. He frequently called upon folk-references and his deeply religious Russian Orthodox faith. With the highly complex rhythms of *Les Noces,* medieval references in his Mass, and terse repetitive melodies of *Symphony of Psalms,* Stravinsky initiated approaches to music that have become basic tools for twentieth-century composers. In addition, he proved in *Canticum Sacrum* that Schoenbergian theories in his hands could result in a musical masterpiece. In his search for musical objectivity, Stravinsky eliminated all forms of sentimentality and nineteenth-century Romanticism. His writings reveal vital rhythms; strong, purposeful melodic lines; and frequent shifts in rhythmic accent. These characteristics keep his music objective and impersonal, even austere at times.

Although Charles Ives, the third innovator, was unaware of Schoenberg's approach, his isolation in New England didn't inhibit his development of new concepts but freed him from traditional rules. Polytonality, atonality, polyharmony, tone clusters, and polyrhythms are all a part of Ives's compositional palette. In "Psalm 67" he juxtaposed two keys between male and female choirs. Polyrhythms characterize the music of "Harvest Home Chorales"; "Psalm 90" contains cluster chords that combine as many as thirty-six notes based on semitone intervals. Some of his music is written without bar lines, with no time signature. In "Like a Sick Eagle," he asked singers to sing quarter tones. Ives's music has had far-reaching influence on twentieth-century composition; his innovative techniques are now almost commonplace. His commitment to uninhibited self-expression has inspired many American composers.

The Rebirth of Nationalism

France—The French Six (Les Six): Of the six composers who were leaders in French reaction to the Impressionists after the first World War, three have made distinguished contributions to choral literature: Darius Milhaud (1892–1974), Arthur Honegger (1892–1955), and Francis Poulenc (1899–1963). Some of Milhaud's work reveals an interest in the serial technique of Schoenberg, yet he was a versatile composer who created forms and music appropriate to the subject matter. "Deux Cités," a work divided into two parts that Milhaud calls a cantata, and "Naissance de Vénus" are both *a cappella* settings. His cantata *Job* is set for choir and chamber orchestra. Of particular interest are his works based on the Hebrew liturgy: "Kaddisch," with organ accompaniment, and "Sabbath Morning Service," for baritone solo, chorus, and organ. Milhaud's unique style is lyrical and rhythmic, with text and music closely related.

Arthur Honegger has created three notable compositions for chorus and orchestra: *Le Roi David, Jeanne d'Arc au bûcher,* and *Cantate de Noël.* These works are conceived dramatically, and all have striking orchestrations. Honegger's melodic lines are simplistic and unadorned, yet closely related to the text. Harmonies are often stark and dissonant, at times polytonal, but always with the purpose of unifying the basic tonality.

Francis Poulenc may be identified as a choral composer, although he wrote music in other genres as well. A large segment of his sacred and secular choral music is unaccompanied. His Lenten and Christmas motets are considered standard repertory for many college and professional choirs. The "Chansons" are also *a cappella,* yet they provide a variety of textural contrasts with frequent alternation of homophony and polyphony, male and female voice parts, and solo-tutti settings. Vocal tessituras are sometimes challenging, and there are frequent changes in rhythm and meter to accommodate the text. Melodies are terse, yet appealing, and harmonies exploit sudden chord changes and are often modal in tonality.

Poulenc's Mass in G, for voices *a cappella*, reveals his familiarity with the beauty of the human voice. His mastery of textural contrasts and his ability to manipulate vocal sonorities are notable in this work. Poulenc's most often performed choral/orchestral works are the *Gloria* and *Stabat Mater*. His penchant for melody and exciting rhythms is present in both of these major works. Numerous other choral works for mixed chorus, for women's voices, and for men also exist.

Czechoslovakia: Anton Dvořák (1841–1904), prominent nineteenth-century composer, instigated interest in Hungarian folk music and began a national movement that was later pursued by Leoš Janáček (1854–1928), a fellow countryman. Dvořák's appealing choral style is found in the "Songs of Nature" and "Six Moravian Lyrics" (arranged for mixed voices by Janáček). His major works for chorus and orchestra brought him fame and fortune in England and on the continent, even in America. Best-known are the *Te Deum, Stabat Mater*, Mass in D, and Requiem. Dvořák is noted for a wealth of melodic invention and rhythmic drive. His style is eclectic and reflects both Wagner and Brahms, yet, at its best, his music has a unique appeal.

Janáček was a prolific composer and a tireless researcher of folk music. Many of his choral works are not yet translated into English. His most important and gratifying work is the *Slavonic*, or *Festival*, Mass. Although he originally set the music to a medieval Slavic text, Janáček himself adapted the liturgical Latin text to the Mass. A dramatic setting, one feature is an effusive Interlude for organ solo. Two works that are published with English translation are a setting of "The Lord's Prayer," for accompanied chorus, and "Lord, Have Mercy Upon Us," for soloists, double chorus, brass, harp, and organ.

Hungary: Béla Bartók (1881–1945) and Zoltán Kodály (1882–1967) together explored the folksongs of their native Hungary, as well as those of Slovakia, Rumania, and Transylvania. Bartók's choral music includes "Hungarian Peasant Songs," "Slovak Folksongs," "Village Scenes" (for women's voices with chamber orchestra), and *Cantata Profana* for chorus, soloists, and full orchestra.

Zoltán Kodály is famous for his method of teaching music fundamentals through choral music. His choral compositions reflect his interest in folk music but span a much wider field than those of Bartók. In addition to his well-known *Te Deum* and *Missa Brevis* (both composed for soloists, chorus, and full orchestra) and his most famous work, *Psalmus Hungaricus* for tenor solo, chorus, and orchestra, Kodály offers a wealth of unaccompanied music for mixed chorus, women's voices, and men's voices. Of particular interest are "Jesus and the Traders," "Evening," "Pictures from the Matra," and "Transylvanian Lament." For men's voices (TBB) he has an appealing trilogy: "The Peacocks," "The Bachelor," and "Soldier's Song," the latter with snare drum and trumpet.

England: Ralph Vaughan Williams (1872–1958) followed the nationalist movement in Great Britain by collecting volumes of English folk melodies, many of which he incorporated into his writings. English Christmas carols were combined into a work for chorus and orchestra entitled "Fantasia on Christmas Carols." Other important choral works with instruments include "Serenade to Music"; "Benedicité," for soprano solo and choir; *Dona nobis pacem* with soprano and baritone soloists; *Toward the Unknown Region; Hodie; Flos campi*, with viola solo; *Sancta Civitas,* for chorus, semichorus, baritone solo, and an antiphonal choir of women's voices; and "Festival Te Deum" with organ or orchestra. Vaughan Williams's unaccompanied works include numerous settings of folksongs ("Springtime of the Year," "Ca' the Yowes," for example), and his outstanding masterpiece for double chorus and soloists *a cappella*, the Mass in G Minor.

Gustav Holst (1874–1934), also a researcher of British folk music, was prolific in his output of choral music. His sacred anthems include "Gird on Thy Sword," "Two Psalms," and "Christmas Day," a setting of four carols for chorus and orchestra. His folksongs for mixed voices include "I Love My Love," "Lullay My Liking," and "Just as the Tide Was Flowing." Works for women's chorus include "Two Eastern Pictures," with harp, "Choruses to Alcestis," with harp and flute, and an eight-part "Ave Maria." For men's voices with brass instruments, he wrote a stunning setting of Walt Whitman's "Dirge for Two Veterans." Additional choruses for mixed voices are included in his settings of the "Choral Hymns from the Rig-Veda." His most important major work is *Hymn of Jesus*, for two choirs, orchestra, piano, and organ.

Postwar Composers in Europe.   Paul Hindemith (1895–1963) was undoubtedly the most important German composer to emerge from postwar Germany. His most significant choral-instrumental works are a setting of Walt Whitman's poem *When Lilacs Last in the Door-yard Bloom'd* (for chorus, soloists, and orchestra) and *Apparebit repentina dies* (for mixed chorus and brass). Probably his most appealing choral works are the intimate "Six Chansons," "Five Songs on Old Texts," and a set of "Madrigals." His style is Neo-Classic with a predominance of linear counterpoint and an emphasis on flowing melodic lines. The resulting harmonic base is often dissonant.

Ernst Křenek (b. 1900), influenced by Arnold Schoenberg, has maintained serial techniques in two *a cappella* works: "The Seasons" for mixed voices and "The Santa Fe Time Table," a setting of names of railroad towns from Albuquerque to Los Angeles. In addition, he composed a collection of "Five Prayers" for women's voices, set to texts by John Donne. Křenek's works reflect both atonal and polychoral approaches to harmonization, with emphasis upon text rhythms.

Hugo Distler (1908–1942) might be termed a Neo-Baroque composer, in that his musical treatment of text emulates that of Heinrich Schütz. A church musician, he incorporates sacred texts in the majority of his music. Some of his most intriguing compositions, however, are settings of secular texts by Eduard Mörike, a nineteenth-century lyric poet, who was second only to Goethe. The *Mörike Lieder* offer a variety of musical treatment in a style that is both unique and vital. These settings incorporate from three to six parts and are for mixed, women's, and men's voices.

A few of the *Mörike Lieder* have been translated into English, but because of the close rhythmic relationship between music and speech in Distler's settings, translation is difficult and the original German is often preferred. Important sacred works by Distler include an unaccompanied Christmas cantata, *Weihnachtsgeschichte* (Christmas Story), containing several beautiful settings of "Lo, How a Rose E'er Blooming," and psalm-settings *Singet dem Herren* and *Lobet den Herren.* The latter are frequently included on American choral programs. Other motet settings include *Singet frisch und wohlgemuth* and *Wachet auf, ruft uns die Stimme. Eine deutsche Choralmesse* and a choral setting of the traditional *Totentanz* are two of his extended *a cappella* works.

Carl Orff (1895–1982) is recognized as one of Germany's most intriguing choral composers. His music may be identified by its rhythmic repetitions and dissonant counterpoint put into old monodic forms. An example may be observed in his treatment of thirteenth-century student poems written in medieval Latin and German found in a Bavarian monastery and popularly known as *Carmina Burana.* Percussion instruments, including two pianos, are prominent in Orff's orchestration. Another work with a similar rhythmic approach is *Catulli Carmina*, a scenic cantata written to Latin texts by the Roman poet Catullus. These works are extremely effective when supported by choreographed dance.

Johann Nepomuk David (1895–1977) and Ernst Pepping (b. 1901) are two composers of considerable stature. Both may be classified as Neo-Classicists in that their works are in traditional forms. David has written secular part songs, sacred motets, and a *Stabat Mater*. Pepping composes mainly for the German Lutheran church service. His numerous psalm-settings and a *Te Deum* are typical examples.

Avant-garde choral music is notated in unconventional patterns and symbols. Although the musical language is not common or familiar, the composer's explanation of his symbolic notation and his directions for performing procedures are usually explicit; meaning becomes increasingly clear through careful study. Steps prescribed for study of scores from any period may be followed generally and modified appropriately for application to the study of twentieth-century music.[36]

Karlheinz Stockhausen (b. 1928) and György Ligeti (b. 1923), two of Europe's most influential composers in the mainstream of twentieth-century writing, are both recognized as leaders in continental avant-garde musical composition.

Stockhausen's *Momente* (for soprano soloist and four choruses, with thirteen instrumentalists and percussion) calls for numerous nonmusical vocal approaches, including laughing, speaking, whispering, screaming, stomping, and clapping. A soprano soloist imitates birdcalls and improvises on given tones (aleatory music). Ligeti's chief choral works are his sixteen-voice *a cappella Lux Aeterna* and a Requiem for two soloists, two choirs, and orchestra. Although born in Hungary, Ligeti has spent his adult life in Austria and Germany, where he has been active as a composer of avant-garde music. In *Lux Aeterna* he divides each voice part into four and, through subtle rhythms in canon, creates a tonal cluster that is wonderfully effective and sonorous. His dissonances are frequently sung *pianissimo*, and the extreme high and low ranges require expert singers. In contrast to the aleatory approach in Stockhausen's music, Ligeti's is meticulously calculated rhythmically and melodically.

Olivier Messiaen (b. 1908) has been identified as the leader of the French avant-garde. His influence on contemporary music has been widespread, and his prominent pupils have become leaders in their own right: Pierre Boulez, Stockhausen, Iannis Xenakis, and others. Messiaen's approach to music is both mystical and religious; he draws on Gregorian chant as well as oriental rhythms. His chamber choral works include *O sacrum convivium* for voices *a cappella* and *Cinq Rechants* for twelve-voice chorus.

French Neo-Classical Composers.   André Jolivet (1905–1974) is best known for instrumental works that he conducted around the world. He and Messiaen led the progressive movement to promote a national French style. Although he wrote a limited number of choral works, *Epithalôme,* for mixed voices *a cappella*, is worth mentioning. In it the textual rhythms and contrasting vocal sonorities are both subtle and sensuous.

Maurice Duruflé (b. 1902) is recognized as a devoted church composer who may be called the successor to Gabriel Fauré with his mystical, sensitive approach to sacred music. Duruflé's Requiem and Mass were composed for soloists, chorus, and orchestra, in a traditional manner. He also composed Four Motets on Gregorian Themes that are frequently performed.

---

[36]For further information on extended vocal technique and avant-garde notation, see Pooler and Pierce's handbook, *New Choral Notation* (New York: Walton Music Corp., 1971).

Swiss Composers.   Ernest Bloch (1880–1959) and Frank Martin (1890–1974) are two Swiss composers with divergent compositional styles. Bloch was a Neo-Romanticist known for his major choral work based on the Hebrew ritual, *Sacred Service (Avodath Hakodesh)* for baritone solo, chorus, and orchestra. Frank Martin was a major choral composer. His best-known compositions are *In terra pax,* a large work for soloists, chorus, and orchestra, and *Golgotha,* a dramatic work also for large forces. Perhaps Martin's most sensitive vocal music is found in his setting of an *a cappella* Mass for double chorus. Numerous other choral works by this composer follow the main line of traditional compositional styles but offer a distinctiveness that is both sensitive and emotional in approach.

Italian Composers.   Luigi Dallapiccola (1904–1975) was one of the twentieth-century Italian composers who gained a place of international leadership in choral music. Probably the most highly respected of the early generation, Dallapiccola employed the Schoenberg twelve-tone serial techniques with strikingly beautiful results. His *Canti di Prigionia* (*Prisoner's Songs*) with two pianos, harp, and percussion and *Canti di Liberazione,* for chorus and orchestra, are high points of musical expressiveness. The *Cori di Michelangelo* for voices *a cappella* should also be mentioned.

Goffredo Petrassi (b. 1904) and Bruno Maderna (1920–1973) are also renowned international composers. Petrassi's choral works include a *Magnificat* (for soprano solo, chorus, and orchestra), "Psalm IX" (for chorus, strings, brass, two pianos, and percussion), and numerous cantatas and small forms for chorus with small groups of instruments. One of his most intriguing secular pieces for mixed chorus is "Nonsense," with text by Edward Lear. Maderna's "Tre liriche greche" is a lovely trilogy for soprano solo, small chorus, and chamber orchestra.

Mario Castelnuovo-Tedesco (1895–1968) spent most of his musical life in America. Besides a sacred Synagogue Service, he composed two delightful works for chorus with guitar solo: "Romancero Gitano" and "Tonadillo on the Name of Andréa Segovia."

Luciano Berio (b. 1925) follows avant-garde trends in twentieth-century composition and espouses extended vocal techniques, inflected recitations, noises, electronic effects, and aleatoric passages in his writing. His *Magnificat* (for mixed voices with two pianos) is mystical in concept, with repetitive pitches and rhythms that rise subtly from extreme *pianissimo* to a striking *fortissimo* at the conclusion.

British Composers.   The popularity of choral singing, both traditionally and currently, can be observed readily in the numerous choral societies, in boys choir schools, and in the frequent performances of choral works from all periods throughout Great Britain. High artistic standards in church music have encouraged many outstanding composers to write sacred music. While the majority of this music follows traditional patterns, there are some exceptions where so-called avant-garde composers have produced sacred works that are performed on a regular basis. One of these exceptions is Paul Patterson (b. 1948), who has written "Kyrie" and "Gloria" for choir and piano. In these settings, the piano requires two players, one at the keyboard and the other manipulating the strings. The score of "Kyrie" calls for string glissandos, strings struck with plastic ruler or soft and hard sticks, and strings plucked in small and large clusters. Singers change the shape of sustained vowels by opening and closing their mouths, vary the width of vibratos, and produce nonvocal sounds, even a scream into the open piano at one point. Special symbols (notated carefully at the beginning of the work) denote a "very high note," the length of a sustained note, and changes of tempo. Aleatoric passages are repeated in all parts at the central climax. Important examples of major works by Patterson are Requiem (for John F. Kennedy) and *Mass of the Sea.* Two amusing secular works, both commissioned for performance by the King's Singers, are "Spare-Parts" and "Time Piece."

John Tavener (b. 1944) is another contemporary British composer who writes in a new twentieth-century idiom. An effective work for two soprano soloists, chorus, and chamber ensemble is his "Introit for March 27." Here he employs aleatoric passages for voices and instruments and writes both lyrical and dramatic passages in keeping with the mood of the text. *The Whale* is a dramatic cantata for narrator, soloists, chorus, and orchestra; it requires large choral forces and employs avant-garde techniques.

Peter Maxwell Davies' (b. 1934) music is a combination of traditional and avant-garde. In his Christmas choral work, *O magnum mysterium,* he alternates Renaissance-like choral settings of the text with instrumental interludes played by a variety of solo wind and string instruments, and with numerous percussionists that perform on Indian cymbals, castanets, snare drums, temple blocks, and handbells. He has also written a set of Five Motets, including one on the text *Veni sancte spiritum,* for mixed voices *a cappella.*

Nicholas Maw is a composer who employs serial techniques but adapts them to music with a tonal center. His very clever "Five Epigrams," settings of texts by Robert Burns, are excellent for chamber chorus *a cappella.* His major works include a Requiem for female choir, soloists, string trio, and string orchestra.

Thea Musgrave is one of the most creative and original composers of our time. She has devoted her energies primarily to major operatic and instrumental works but has also composed shorter works for chorus that merit frequent performances. Her music integrates avant-garde techniques with traditional tonal-centered harmony and contrapuntal invention. Sensitive to the drama of text and speech rhythms in her setting of *Rorate coeli,* she utilizes tone clusters, undulating rhythms, and aleatoric passages that are set beneath traditional hymn-like melodies. Soloists proclaim their lines in quasi-recitative style, and the chorus whispers, shouts, glissandos, and speaks on indefinite pitches (*Sprechstimme*). The opening and closing choral passages for full choir and soloists are reminiscent of Gabrieli polychoral sonorities. Musgrave's writing expresses twentieth-century emotions in the highest artistic sense. An earlier set of compositions showing similar sensitivity to text and music without avant-garde elements is Four Madrigals, for small vocal ensemble *a cappella.*

Sir Benjamin Britten (1913–1976) is outstanding among twentieth-century composers. His *War Requiem* is a monumental work. While his musical style is essentially traditional, in this work he employs polyrhythms, aleatoric passages, polytonality, and dramatic textural contrasts. The score calls for two orchestras; the second is a chamber orchestra that is identified with the tenor and bass soloists. A full orchestra supports the soprano solo and a large chorus. A positive organ accompanies the singing of an antiphonal boys' choir. The text is based on poems by Wilfred Owen interspersed with the traditional Latin of a Requiem Mass. The interested conductor will apprise himself or herself of Britten's complete choral repertory of cantatas, church parables, and smaller choral works. His cantatas call for a few instruments or a chamber orchestra; many of these are effective with organ or piano accompaniment. Britten's numerous shorter works are both accompanied and unaccompanied, sacred and secular. He is not only a prolific composer but also a grateful one, easily accessible to the listener. His style is both eclectic and unique in that he does not consistently employ avant-garde techniques, yet he exploits polyrhythms, modal tonalities, and a variety of sonorities. His music may be described as Neo-Classical, because it is never cluttered or thick in texture. Britten was a master of orchestration who was well aware of the capacity and potential of the human voice.

Sir Michael Tippett (b. 1905) may be considered a Post-Romanticist in his first major choral work, *A Child of Our Time*, based on his own libretto. In this work, Tippett's music is both lyrical and dramatic. Incorporation of his own arrangements of negro spirituals into the body of this work is comparable to the use of chorales in the Bach Passions. His later works follow the mainstream of twentieth-century music, with intricate rhythms, a preponderance of dissonance, and polyphonic textures. An example of a later major work is *The Vision of St. Augustine*, with Latin text, for baritone, chorus, and orchestra. He has also composed a number of shorter choral works, including a setting of "Nunc dimittis" for mixed voices. His musical inspiration for this work comes directly from the text in a very explicit manner; a melisma falls on the word *glory* and a quasi-chant appears with the text of the traditional "Gloria."

Sir William Walton (1902–1980), along with Britten and Tippett, may be considered one of the three pillars of British music in the twentieth century. Walton's primary contribution to choral music is his setting of an Old Testament story, *Belshazzar's Feast*, for baritone solo, chorus, and orchestra. It is without doubt one of the most colorful, dramatic combinations of music and text in modern choral repertory. In addition, Walton has composed *Gloria* and *Te Deum* for large chorus and orchestra and a *Missa Brevis* for double chorus and organ.

Other twentieth-century British composers who have written significant choral music include Herbert Howells (1892–1980), Peter Warlock (1894–1930), Gerald Finzi (1901–1956), Lennox Berkely (b. 1903), Mátyás Seiber (1905–1960), Elizabeth Lutyens (b. 1906), Peter Racine Fricker (b. 1920), Iain Hamilton (b. 1922), Alexander Goehr (b. 1932), Harrison Birtwhistle (b. 1934), William Mathias (b. 1934), and John Rutter (b. 1945).

Scandinavian Composers. Ingvar Lidholm (b. 1921), a leader in the avant-garde group of composers in Sweden, has written serial-based choral music with flowing counterpoint and expressive melodic lines. One of the best examples is a setting of Ezra Pound's "Canto LXXXI" for unaccompanied mixed chorus. His "Summer Evening" is essentially homophonic with quiet, dissonant chords calling for extremely low basses.

Knut Nystedt (b. 1915), writing primarily on Biblical texts, employs frequent tone clusters and free rhythm in his choral settings; *De profundis* is his most popular work and an effective example of his style. Other sacred music includes earlier, more conventional works: "Now Is Christ Risen" for trumpet, chimes, organ, and mixed choir, and "Cry out and Shout" for mixed voices *a cappella*.

Eskil Hemberg (b. 1928) is a prolific choral composer whose works have been performed frequently in the United States. His avant-garde music is highly inventive, yet it incorporates references to classical polyphony. "Signposts," a setting of texts by Dag Hammarskjöld, and *Messa d'oggi* are outstanding examples. In these compositions, Hemberg explores choric speech, tone clusters, free rhythms, whispering, sighing, and *Sprechstimme*.

Bengt Johansson (b. 1914) is a Finnish composer whose outstanding choral compositions include "The Tomb at Akr Çaar," a work for chamber chorus *a cappella* with divided parts in all voices. Solo voices contrast with full polytonal chords moving homophonically. Free rhythms interplay with sustained chords; whispered interjections add a sense of mystery to the Eastern text.

Other Scandinavian choral composers of proven ability are Carl Nielsen (1865–1931) and Bernard Lewkovitch (b. 1927) of Denmark, Joonas Kokkonen (b. 1921) of Finland, and Bo Nilsson (b. 1937) and Sven-Erik Bäck (b. 1919) of Sweden.

Canadian Composers.   Healy Willan (1880–1968) is a significant composer of sacred music. His liturgical motets are plentiful and include "Lo, In the Time Appointed," "Rise Up, My Love, My Fair One," and "I Beheld Her Beautiful As a Dove." Two of Willan's most effective anthem settings are "Isaiah, Mighty Seer" and "Hodie" (a Christmas text).

Other Canadian composers have been active in ferreting out the national folk music and providing excellent settings for chorus. These are R. Murray Schafer (b. 1933), Harry Somers (b. 1925), Robert Fleming (1921–1976), and Derek Healey (b. 1936).

Polish Composers.   Witold Lutoslawski (b. 1913) has composed music that is definitely Polish, yet uniquely his own. He was influenced by serial music and aleatoric practices, yet his imaginative application of these contemporary techniques makes them subservient to his own musical conception. Of significance to the choral repertory is his setting of *Trois poemes d'Henri Michaux* for chorus, winds, percussion, two pianos, and harp (requiring that two conductors read from separate scores).

Krzysztof Penderecki (b. 1933) is a world leader in twentieth-century avant-garde composition. His works are noted for their sonorities, and they make use of shouting, hissing, calling, and other avant-garde techniques. The chorus is asked to tap and stomp feet as well as to proceed from given pitches to nonpitch extremes of their voices. His *Passion According to St. Luke* is his most famous choral/orchestral work. It calls for three mixed choruses, a chorus of children, and orchestra; there are also three soloists and a narrator. Also of significance are "Psalms of David" for chorus, two pianos, harp, celesta, four double basses, and percussion; and *Stabat Mater,* for three choirs *a cappella,* taken from the *Passion* and frequently performed separately. An *Agnus Dei* and a setting of the *Magnificat* are unaccompanied works for mixed voices.

South American Composers.   Hector Villa-Lobos (1887–1959) was a prominent Brazilian composer whose rhythmic, folk-based native melodies are reflected in large choral-instrumental works such as *Cantos V*. His smaller choral works include "Mass to St. Sebastian," "Ave Maria," both *a cappella*; "Nonetto," with woodwinds, celesta, harp, percussion; and "Quatuor" with flute, harp, and percussion.

Alberto Ginastera (b. 1916) is an Argentinian composer best known to choral conductors for his unaccompanied "Lamentations of Jeremiah" and a major choral/orchestral work, *Psalm 150*.

Luis Antonio Ramirez, a Puerto Rican, composed a popular and effective *Misa criolla* for choir, soloists, harpsichord, guitars, and percussion.

Carlos Chavez (1899–1978) has written several works for chorus with instruments. *Canto El Sol*, a cantata for chorus and orchestra, is one of his best known.

United States Composers.   Performances of American twentieth-century choral music have been both widespread and limited. Three positive streams of compositional style have emerged, with some composers combining them quite successfully. The first stream includes followers of Igor Stravinsky's Neo-Classic style. These composers have maintained a conservative stance in most instances, employing conventional forms, yet applying the rhythmic and harmonic freedom associated with twentieth-century music. A second stream, the Neo-Romanticists, some of whom involve Schoenberg's serial techniques, also include those inclined toward thicker textures and a more personal expressiveness. The third stream comprises those who write for chorus with electronic tape, microtonal tuning, aleatoric procedures, and for extended vocal techniques in strictly avant-garde, nontraditional performances.

Neo-Classicists: Composers aligned with the Neo-Classic style include such leaders as Aaron Copland, Randall Thompson, and Vincent Persichetti. Copland's "In the Beginning" (for soprano solo and choir *a cappella*) and choruses from *The Tender Land*, Thompson's "Peaceable Kingdom," "Odes to Horace," and "Frostiana," and Persichetti's unaccompanied Mass and "Celebrations" for choir and wind ensemble are all outstanding works that have been widely accepted into the choral repertory. Other prominent composers included in this category are Jack Beeson, Jean Berger, Gordon Binkerd, Elliott Carter, David Diamond, Emma Lou Diemer, Cecil Effinger, Paul Fetler, Irving Fine, Ross Lee Finney, Lukas Foss, Jeanne Fuller, Karl Korte, Burrill Phillips, Normand Lockwood, Daniel Moe, Ned Rorem, Williametta Spencer, Robert Starer, Halsey Stevens, Virgil Thomson, and David Ward-Steinman. Many of their works are included in the repertory lists provided in the Appendix.

Neo-Romanticists: Leaders among the Neo-Romanticists are Samuel Barber, William Schuman, Norman Dello Joio, and Roger Sessions. Barber's "Reincarnations," Schuman's "Carols of Death," Dello Joio's "A Jubilant Song," "Song of the Open Road," and "A Psalm of David," and Sessions's "Three Biblical Choruses" (for choir and chamber orchestra) are already standard choral repertory. They represent only a sampling of the breadth of textures and moods created by American composers writing in this style. Others whose works exhibit similar stylistic traits are Samuel Adler, Dominick Argento, William Bergsma, Boris Blocher, Paul Chihara, Paul Creston, Michael Fink, Edwin Fissinger, Roy Harris, Alan Hovhaness, Ulysses Kay, Gail Kubik, Billy Jim Layton, Peter Menin, Gian Carlo Menotti, Ron Nelson, Elie Siegmeister, Leo Sowerby, Dede Duson, and Kirke Mechem.

Avant-garde: The most frequently performed avant-garde composers who have consistently combined voices with electronic tape and explored vocal potential are Leslie Bassett, Richard Felciano, and Pauline Oliveras. Bassett's "Collect" (for choir and prepared tape) and "Moon Canticles" (an aleatoric composition for choir and cello), Felciano's numerous liturgical choral settings with electronic tape, and Oliveras's "Sound Patterns" (a highly complicated rhythmic composition consisting solely of unpitched sounds) are outstanding examples of these exploratory techniques.

A few highly regarded composers have skillfully incorporated avant-garde techniques into an otherwise basically conservative approach. Representative of these are Daniel Pinkham, Ben Johnston, and Thomas Frederickson. Pinkham's "Christmas Cantata," "Easter Cantata," and "Wedding Cantata" (all combining voices with instruments), "Songs of Departure" for choir and guitar, and several sacred compositions for chorus and tape represent a wide spectrum of sonorities found in his works. Ben Johnston's intriguing *Mass* for choir, eight trombones, jazz bass, and improvised percussion is based on microtonal tuning of voices and instruments. Frederickson's "Impressions," on settings by four twentieth-century poets, dramatically incorporates tone clusters and choric speaking.

Other composers who are producing significant music in this genre are John Biggs, Michael Colgrass, Kenneth Gaburo, Anthony Iannaccone, Andrew Imbrie, Dennis Kam, Karl Kohn, Edwin London, Salvatore Martirano, Brock McElheran, Brent Pierce, and Charles Wuorinen.

Innovations in Twentieth-Century Choral Music

Melody

May be of unpredictable length
Is often not repeated
May be angular, pointillistic, each note becoming significant in itself rather than a part of a phrase or motif

Harmony

Polytonal, with different keys sung or played at once
Atonal, with harmony being incidental and unrelated to horizontal lines
Polyharmonic, with interplay between blocks of harmony assigned to chorus and those suggested for instruments
Chords based on fourths or fifths instead of thirds; *cluster chords* based on seconds
Tone clusters based on minor seconds sounded simultaneously
Polychords with triads built on each other

Rhythm

Free rhythm: no bar lines; no meter; free, as in medieval chant
Nonsymmetrical rhythms
Multirhythms in consecutive measures
Complex kinetic rhythms
Syncopation and jazz rhythms

Texture

Pervasive dissonance: dissonant counterpoint; dissonant chords and intervals
Nontonal elements: clapping, stomping, nonsense syllables
Choric speech
Aleatoric music for both voices and instruments
Electronic music, tape and other sound devices with chorus

Sonority

Choice of instruments according to timbre
Frequent use of percussion instruments
Folk instruments combined with voices
Serial music

Tonality

Frequent reference to ecclesiastical and medieval modes
Dissolution of tonality-atonality
Whole-tone and pentatonic scales
Far-Eastern scales
Microtuning

PROCEDURES FOR SCORE ANALYSIS

Score study will vary in scope and approach with each musical composition. After researching the composer and the characteristics of his period, the next step is to seek an overall impression of the composition by playing or reading the complete score from beginning to end. Doing this, the conductor endeavors to sense overall form and principal divisions within the composition. Consistent with a *Gestalt* approach, he or she will proceed as follows:

1. Number the measures.
2. Read through the music, marking major sections and cadence points.
3. Look for places where text and music reinforce each other to achieve dynamic climax.
4. Note contrasting musical textures throughout the composition.
5. Read the music a second time from beginning to end; identify phrase lengths and indicate the number of measures in each; note harmonic or modal functions.
6. Read the text as an entity apart from the music; make a literal translation if written in a language unfamiliar to the singers.
7. Reinforce the composer's dynamic markings to indicate more clearly where the tension building and relaxation occur within phrase structures (*arsis-thesis*); keep in mind all text-music stress relationships.
8. Note dynamic indications for dramatic effect in the music; indicate degrees of intensity within crescendos and diminuendos as they relate to contour of phrases.

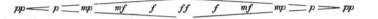

9. Determine appropriate tempos and meter relationships by consulting the composer's manuscript or collected works.
10. Examine melodic repetitions and development, interplay of voice parts with instrumental parts (*colla parte* or accompaniment).
11. Devise a system for color-coding thematic and formal development of the music. (Such markings of the score clarify at a glance the internal relationships of melodic-thematic material as each is introduced, extended, and developed in sequence, in repetition, or in both).
12. Sing each vocal line aloud and mark phrasing of each voice-part:
    a. Full breath at ends of phrases and at dramatic points = ǀ .
    b. Half-breath to clarify meaning of text within a phrase = ᾽.
    c. No breath taken, but phrased to indicate comma when important to meaning = (᾽).
    d. *Staggered* breathing (breathing not apparent to listeners), used in long phrases (characteristic of music from the Romantic period). Indicate by drawing extended phrase line over entire phrase. This marking serves to remind chorus members to breathe while singing on a vowel rather than between words or syllables. An alternative suggestion regarding this marking can be the assignment of exact places for portions of the chorus to breathe at different points within the extended phrase.
13. Clarify articulations: Mark agogic text stresses $\left(\bar{\rho}\right)$ or accents $\left(\acute{\rho}\right)$ to be emphasized in the vocal line; indicate negation of stress where appropriate $\left(\breve{\rho}\right)$; indicate staccato $\left(\dot{\rho}\right)$, portato $\left(\dot{\bar{\rho}}\right)$, or *note-pairing* treatment $\left(\sqcup \ \sqcup\right)$.
14. Play keyboard accompaniment and observe relationships to voice-parts and instrumental lines.
15. Read through each instrumental part separately; check and mark phrasings, dynamics, tonguing, bowing, and other articulations; prepare to offer suggestions for *continuo* realization or accompaniment.
16. Mark the placement of final consonants where timing is critical to phrase endings, diction, thematic clarity, or musical continuity.
17. Identify problems concerning diction: pronunciation, enunciation, prolongation of vowels, proportionate sounds of diphthongs and triphthongs.
18. Construct a skeletal outline to reinforce formal conceptualization and to assist in memorization (see Example of Score Study, p. 90).
19. Invent rhythmic and tonal exercises that will stimulate the learning process in rehearsal.

Examples of analyses suggested for implementation of these steps can be observed in the two models that follow. Since music of each historical period requires a unique approach to score study and performance practices, an example from each period is included in Chapter 3.

SCORE ANALYSIS MODELS

I

Title: *Tenebrae factae sunt*[37]

Composer: Marc Antonio Ingegneri (1545–1592). Ingegneri was choirmaster at the cathedral in Cremona and a teacher of Claudio Monteverdi. He composed twenty-seven *Responsorio* for Holy Week; these were long attributed to Palestrina. This motet, based on music found in Haberl's complete edition of Palestrina's works (1894), reflects the Venetian influence of Cipriano de Rore and Giovanni Gabrieli rather than the Roman style of Palestrina.

Description (source): A motet composed for the *Tenebrae* Service during Holy Week

Formal Design: Through-composed; *Introduction A B C*

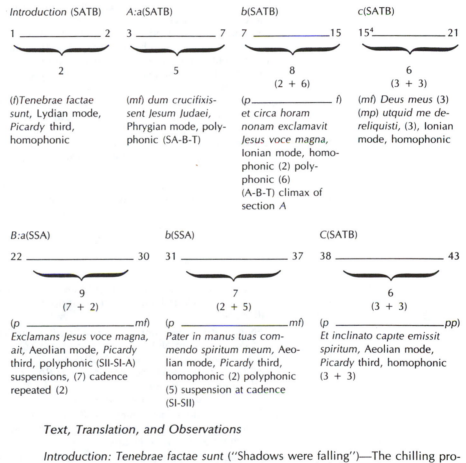

Introduction (SATB)

1 _____ 2

2

(f)Tenebrae factae sunt, Lydian mode, Picardy third, homophonic

A:a(SATB)

3 _____ 7

5

(mf) dum crucifixissent Jesum Judaei, Phrygian mode, polyphonic (SA-B-T)

b(SATB)

7 _____ 15

8
(2 + 6)

(p _____ f) et circa horam nonam exclamavit Jesus voce magna, Ionian mode, homophonic (2) polyphonic (6) (A-B-T) climax of section A

c(SATB)

15⁴ _____ 21

6
(3 + 3)

(mf) Deus meus (3) (mp) utquid me dereliquisti, (3), Ionian mode, homophonic

B:a(SSA)

22 _____ 30

9
(7 + 2)

(p _____ mf) Exclamans Jesus voce magna, ait, Aeolian mode, Picardy third, polyphonic (SII-SI-A) suspensions, (7) cadence repeated (2)

b(SSA)

31 _____ 37

7
(2 + 5)

(p _____ mf) Pater in manus tuas commendo spiritum meum, Aeolian mode, Picardy third, homophonic (2) polyphonic (5) suspension at cadence (SI-SII)

C(SATB)

38 _____ 43

6
(3 + 3)

(p _____ pp) Et inclinato capite emissit spiritum, Aeolian mode, Picardy third, homophonic (3 + 3)

Text, Translation, and Observations

Introduction: Tenebrae factae sunt ("Shadows were falling")—The chilling pronouncement that shadows and darkness surrounded those who stood at the foot of the cross is depicted awesomely in the descending lines of the opening phrase. The original mensural sign, $\frac{3}{1}$, relates proportionally as 3:2 with the signature $\frac{4}{4}$ (originally ¢), which follows in m. 3.

A—a: dum crucifixissent Jesum Judaei ("while Jesus of Judea was crucified")—Each voice part outlines the shape of a cross as the first two notes ascend and the three notes that follow "cross" over them. The eighth-note passing tones in A-S-T parts are of special importance and should be given full rhythmic value as they move upward independently. The close-knit polyphony merges into homophony as the principal character of this dramatic episode is pre-

---

[37]See copy of the music in Music for Class Study and Conducting, p. 254.

sented. The Lydian mode of the opening measures now reverts to the more somber Phrygian with the introduction of an A-flat, and a Picardy third makes the cadence even more special.

b: *et circum horam nonam exclamavit Jesus voce magna* ("and about the ninth hour Jesus cried out in a loud voice")—From a quiet beginning of repeated notes, the phrase rises to the motet's first climax at *voce magna*. Note the imitation between B and A as the parts descend while T and S begin an ascent polyphonically. The first S-T suspension occurs on the word *Jesus*, and the second, also between S and T, leads into the cadence; they bring to the phrase an emotional intensity that is compounded by movement into the Ionian mode when an E-flat is introduced.

c: *Deus meus, utquid me de reliquisti?* ("My God, why hast Thou forsaken me?")—Continuing the tension and concern, the alto ornaments the word *meus* with feeling as the lines descend again in sadness and dejection.

B—a: A repetition of text (unusual in a polyphonic setting) follows with a complete change of texture. Only the treble voices sing: *exclamans Jesus voce magna, ait:* ("Jesus cried out in a loud voice, saying:")—A second time the voices rise to a climax on *magna*; the cadence is repeated for emphasis. On the way to this second climax we observe canonic imitation between the two soprano parts followed by a tonal imitation in the A. Movement toward the cadence is engendered by melismas in both soprano parts on *magna*; tension is apparent in the suspension between the upper parts at the cadence, and a reaction of awesome fear is felt in the repetition that follows, totally stark and unadorned.

b: *Pater in manus tuas commendo spiritum meum* ("Father, into Thy hands I commend my spirit")—The trusting yet awesome quality of *ait* is carried over into this phrase as Jesus makes this simple statement. The music flows homophonically on a very even keel, with a hint of imitation found only on *commendo*, between A and SI; there is a sensitive suspension with the resolution on *meum*.

c: The final phrase *Et inclinato capite, emisit spiritum* ("And, bowing His head, He gave up the spirit"), is dramatic yet simple. Descending a full octave in the soprano and nearly an octave in all parts but the bass, Christ's death on the cross, painted graphically by many Renaissance artists, is revealed here in a masterpiece of tone painting.

Guide for Score Marking

To observe more clearly the relationship of note values and melismas to syllabic stress in the text, underline or use a felt-tip marker. Stressed syllables are capitalized here:

TEN-e-brae FAC-tae sunt, dum cru-ci-fix-IS-sent JE-sum Ju-DAE-i:
et CIR-ca HO-ram NO-nam ex-cla-MA-vit JE-sus VO-ce MAG-na:
DE-us ME-us, utquid me de-re-li-QUI-sti?
Ex-CLA-mans JE-sus VO-ce MAG-na, A-it: PA-ter in MAN-us TU-as com-MEN-do SPI-ri-tum ME-um.
Et in-cli-NA-to CA-pi-te e-MI-sit SPI-ri-tum.

Mark major sections of the motet (A-B-C); mark phrases by indicating number of measures within each phrase (with subdivisions in parentheses) below the staff where each phrase begins.

With broad-tip felt pen or pencil line, mark all polyphonic entrances and imitative melodic lines; underline or color imitated notations.

Encircle all suspensions.

II

Title: "But As for His People"[38]

Composer: George Frideric Handel

---

[38]See copy in *Music for Class Study and Conducting*, p. 258; for further examples of Score Study see Chapter 3, pp. 82–102.

Source: *Israel in Egypt,* an oratorio concerned with the flight of the Israelites from Egypt into the Promised Land.

Formal Design:

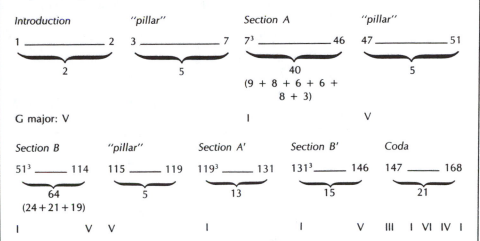

Text:

    A: But as for His people, He led them forth like sheep;
    B: But as for His people, He brought them out with silver and gold.
 A'B': But as for His people, He led them forth like sheep; He brought them out with silver and gold.
 Coda: There was not one feeble person among their tribes.

Observations

Mm. 1–46: After a brief, two-measure orchestral statement in the dominant (V) and two repetitions of the same phrase by the chorus, the soprano presents the *A* theme in the tonic G major; the theme is immediately echoed in the orchestral accompaniment. This pastoral melody expresses the Israelites' naïve trust in God as they are led by Moses out of Egypt into the Promised Land.

Mm. 47–114: The four-measure choral introduction is presented a second time, like a "pillar," again in the dominant, and leads into the *B* theme in the tonic G. The second theme is quasi-fugal and flows forward smoothly, giving a feeling of a procession moving through the wilderness. A brief development section occurs in mm. 75–115.

Mm. 115–146: The four-measure "pillar" is repeated, and an abbreviated statement of the *A* theme returns before a final stretto-like reiteration of the *B* theme is presented (mm. 113³–146).

Mm. 147–168: The chorus concludes with a 22-measure coda, a firm, homophonic statement repeated sequentially a step higher and then reinforced with a slight variation. Each phrase concludes with an emphatic hemiola, which is repeated by the orchestra in the final two measures.

Guide for Score Marking.   Devise color code to highlight thematic entrances and repetitions.

Mm. 3–8: Indicate "pillars" with horizontal brackets (⌐‾‾‾¬).
Mm. 8–47: Indicate important entrances and cues with vertical brackets (⊏).
M. 7: Indicate sixteenth-note pickup (as notated in accompaniment, bar 11)

   above staff in parentheses at each recurrence of *A* theme (⅞ ♪) .
Mm. 17–26, 35–47: Bracket themes in orchestral interludes (⌐‾‾‾¬).
Mm. 30, 36, 40, 44, 125, 129: Insert dynamics where sustained notes diminish as important themes enter.
Mm. 27, 33: Note "link" (lower dynamic level) in parentheses.

Mm. 51, 54, 61, 69: Bracket *B* theme and imitative entrances.

Mm. 52–115, 131–144: Indicate rising lines, characteristic of *B* theme, which propel forward motion of the phrase.

Mm. 71–74, 110–114, 147–166: Indicate in parentheses preliminary, central, and final climax points.

Mm. 74–80: Write in dynamics where change of texture indicates a diminuendo leading into the bass entrance with *B* theme: (*mf*).

M. 95: Indicate beginning of stretto that leads to central climax at m. 114.

Mm. 113–114: Indicate *piu ritard* leading into final statement of the "pillar."

M. 146: Indicate a definite "break" at the end of the *B'* theme, with a crescendo from *forte* to *fortissimo* on the dominant chord which proceeds to the beginning of the coda; insert eighth rest to indicate consonant placement.

Mm. 147–149, 153–155: Write in accents ($\overset{>}{\rho}$) over stressed notes of repeated chords in *Coda*.

Mm. 150–151, 156–157, 164–165, 166–167: Indicate hemiole in choral and instrumental parts: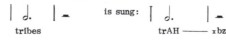

Explanation of Text Markings; Diction Treatment

1. *People:* Avoid stress on unaccented syllable (m. 4). Example: ♩ ♩ ♪
   peo-ple

2. *Sheep, forth:* Place final consonants on the rest at the bar line (mm. 14–15, 30–31).

3. *Gold* (m. 56): If followed by a new phrase and there is no printed rest, place an inserted eighth rest on the beat preceding the new phrase; because the *l* is a "pitch" consonant, it receives one-half beat; the final consonant, *d*, is pronounced on an inserted rest. Example:

   $\left.\right.$ is sung: $\left.\right.$
   gold, He   gOH—l d, He

   M. 65: If followed by a rest, the *l* is placed on an inserted eighth note before the rest; the final *d* is pronounced on the printed rest. Example:

   is sung:
   gold   gOH - l d

   M. 74: If *gold* is a quarter note and is followed by a new phrase beginning, it is sung as an eighth note and an eighth rest; the final consonants get proportionately less value so that the half note that follows is not late. Example:

   is sung:
   gold, He   gOH - l d, He

4. *Out* (m. 70): If a dotted half note is followed by a new phrase, sustain the *AH* two beats, give the diphthong *oo* an eighth-note value, and place the final *t* on an inserted eighth rest. Example:

   is sung:
   out,   He   Ah — oo t, He

5. *Tribes* (m. 158): If a half note ends the phrase and a new one begins on the following beat, sustain *trAH* for one and one-half beats and place an inserted rest on the last half of the second beat. Example:

   is sung:
   tribes, not   trAH - ɪbz, not

   M. 166: If a dotted half note ends the phrase and a new phrase follows, the *trAH* is held for two and one-half beats and the diphthong "glide" is placed with the *bz* on the following rest. Example:

   is sung:
   tribes   trAH ——— ɪbz

Example 2-14   Score Marked for Rehearsal

HOW EXCELLENT THY NAME/
HALLELUJAH!

For S. A. T. B. and Organ or Piano

G. F. HANDEL

Edited by Hugh Chandler

Example 2-14 (*cont.*)

Attácca

Example 2-14 (*cont.*)

45
[sost. f]
- jah, Hal-le - lu-jah, Hal-le - lu-jah. Hal - le - lu - jah, Hal - le - lu -
- jah, Hal-le - lu-jah, Hal-le - lu-jah, Hal - le - lu-jah, Hal - le - lu -
- jah, Hal-le - lu-jah, Hal-le - lu-jah, Hal - le - lu-jah, Hal - le - lu -
Hal-le - lu-jah, Hal-le - lu-jah, Hal - le - lu - jah, Hal - le - lu -
49
[mf]
- jah, . . Hal-le-lu-jah, Hal - le - lu - jah, Hal le-lu-jah, . . .
- jah, Hal-le - lu - jah, Hal - le - lu - jah, Hal -
- jah, Hal-le - lu - jah, Hal-le-lu-jah, . .
[f]
- jah, Hal le - lu - jah,
53
. . . . . . Hal - le - lu - jah, ... Hal - le - lu - jah, Hal - le - lu -
- le - lu - jah, AH. . . . . Hal-le-lu -
. . . . . . Hal - le - lu - jah, Hal - le - lu - jah, ... Hal-le-lu -
Hal - le - lu - jah, ... Hal - le - lu -

Example 2-14 (*cont.*)

Chapter 3

Creating Music with the Choral Instrument

The goal of a conductor's skill development is to bring to life the beauty and nuance of a composer's intentions. Practice in score study, in gesture clarity and control, and in rehearsal planning can contribute to increasingly effective communication between conductor and singers. The conductor who becomes an artist in choral music making is relentless in developing skills essential for communication. Basic understandings are broadened and deepened through each experience with selected repertory. This chapter focuses on nine compositions chosen from choral literature representing various style periods of composition. Rehearsal challenges posed by the nine selections range from those quite easily met to those that are more complex.

For each work there is a guide to facilitate rehearsal preparation through analysis of the formal design and the harmonic scheme, or both; observations on style; steps (questions) that may assist the developing conductor in gesture practice; and an outline for an initial presentation to a choral ensemble. A copy of each musical score presented in this chapter may be found in the collection of music at the back of this textbook, Music for Class Study and Conducting. An appropriate page number follows each title.

Much of the guide is meant to help young conductors develop habits necessary for thorough rehearsal preparation. Relatively advanced choral conductors who have developed these habits may not need to observe all the steps proposed for practice, although a review may prove useful. Experience and understanding will guide the conductor in selecting essential steps and eliminating (or subordinating) those of lesser importance.

Conductors who engage in intensive research will do well to remind themselves that the purpose of research is not so much to impart knowledge to the choir as to enhance the conductor's own understanding, stimulate imagination, and assist in recreating the composer's musical and aesthetic concepts. Bits of information will increase the choir's understanding if presented at opportune moments, but musicological lectures do not generally belong in a rehearsal where music making has top priority. Upon completion of research, conductors ask themselves: How can I best relate the results of my research, score study, and musical understanding to my choir? Answers may include the following: by the clarity and meaning of gesture in conducting; by well-conceived rehearsal procedures; by sharing relevant insights about the composer and his or her music; and by personal involvement in all aspects of the text and music.

Practical Suggestions

1. In approaching any of the choral selections presented in this chapter, a conductor is advised to
   a. Become familiar with text and, if necessary, with the translation.
   b. Number measures in the musical score.
   c. Analyze and mark the score following suggestions offered in Chapter 2.
   d. Practice gesture (style, timing of breath and releases of sound, expressive nuance).
   e. Outline the initial presentation to a choral group.
2. Progress will be accelerated when the conductor practices gesture in front of the video camera. After a score is memorized, the conductor can observe his or her gesture as well as facial and body-stance communication. Before a score is memorized, practice can be recorded on tape, then studied and criticized between practice trials. (Suggestions for effective use of videotaping appear in Appendix B.)
3. In anticipation of the initial rehearsal of a work, a copy of the score marked by the conductor may be made available to choir members as a model for their individual score marking. Such a procedure facilitates all rehearsing and contributes substantially to learning during a rehearsal.
4. The initial rehearsal of a work can influence markedly the speed with which that work is learned and polished. A planned presentation ensures steady progress in learning and avoids stumbling blocks.
5. During rehearsals, the conductor's creativity in planning and in unfolding aspects of the music contributes to singers' enjoyment and learning.
6. In the examples that follow, abbreviations are used consistently:

   m. = measure.

   mm. = measures.

   Arabic numbers mark measures in sequence.

   Exponents following a measure number refer to a specific count within that measure.

   Alphabet letters refer to keys or to Soprano (S), Alto (A), Tenor (T), or Bass (B) voices.

   Roman numerals denote chords within a specific key; when coupled with letters representing voices, they indicate the range expectation (SI, SII, AI, AII).

EXAMPLES OF SCORE STUDY: REHEARSAL PRESENTATION GUIDES

I

Title: *Musica est Dei donum optimi* (p. 258)

Composer: Orlando di Lasso (1532–1594)

Formal Design:

1 ———————— 8	9 ———————— 16	17 ———————— 24
8(3½ + 2½ + 2)	8(3½ + 2½ + 2)	8(3½ + 4½)
I V I V I I	V I V I I	V I V I
Voices 1-2-3-4	Same	Same
enter every 2 mm		

Text: Same   Same

　　Musica est Dei
　　　donum optimi,
　　Musica Dei donum

Translation:

　　Music is a gift
　　　of the highest God,
　　Music, a gift of God

Observations

1. A canon for four equal voices, the melody is repeated three times and cadences V-I at eight-measure intervals. Each voice enters after two measures (mm. 1-3-5-7).
2. Each phrase is divided into two segments; the first segment is 3½ measures, the second 4½ measures.
3. The text is fully stated in the first segment; in the second it is *musica Dei donum, Dei donum.*
4. The final repetition is treated as an extended authentic cadence with a suspension.
5. After all four voices enter, the second section segment is divided into two short segments (2½ + 2), each containing a V-I cadence.
6. Each entrance of a new voice should be heard slightly more prominently than the voices already singing.
7. A subtle crescendo-diminuendo at each suspension is called for, and the overall phrase shape (3½ + 4½) results in a feeling of *arsis-thesis.*

Conducting Practice.   Have you

1. Sung this canon theme and
    a. Identified phrasing and breath points?
    b. Marked in the score types of breath desired at each point?
    c. Observed dynamic contour of the canon's melody?
    d. Determined that the most encouraging and descriptive pattern to guide the grace of the musical line will be a slow, subdivided 2? (4 can ensure greater control during the familiarizing process.)
2. Practiced conducting the theme by using the subdivided 2 pattern and describing phrase shapes through
    a. Increases in and relaxation of intensity?
    b. Appropriate covering of space to denote suspensions and sustaining sound across indicated bar lines?
3. Noted the need to use the beat itself as an impetus for entrances that occur on the second half of a beat when employing the 2 pattern?
4. Practiced giving breath preparations and inviting each voice part to enter (two-measure intervals) by gesture preparation and well-timed glance?
5. Practiced a graceful and subtle subdivision in m. 24?

Rehearsal Presentation

1. All sing the theme (Voice I) on *IAH.*
2. Repeat for security of pitches and rhythms.
3. Divide singers into two groups: Still on *IAH,* first group sing Voice I and second group sing Voice II (repeat as necessary).
4. Divide singers into three groups: On *IAH,* Voices I, II, and III enter appropriately.
5. Divide singers into four groups: Sing canon (on *IAH*) in its entirety.
6. Present Latin text:
    a. Speak and have chorus repeat text by phrases—
        Musica est Dei donum optimi
        Musica Dei donum, Dei donum
    b. Sing Voice I in unison (Latin).

7. Sing entire canon (four parts) on Latin text. (If singers are young and inexperienced, it may be necessary to repeat certain steps or to insert intermediate steps, such as: Voices I and II together, and Voices I, II, and III together.)

II

Title: *Musica vivat aeterna* (p. 247)

Formal Design:

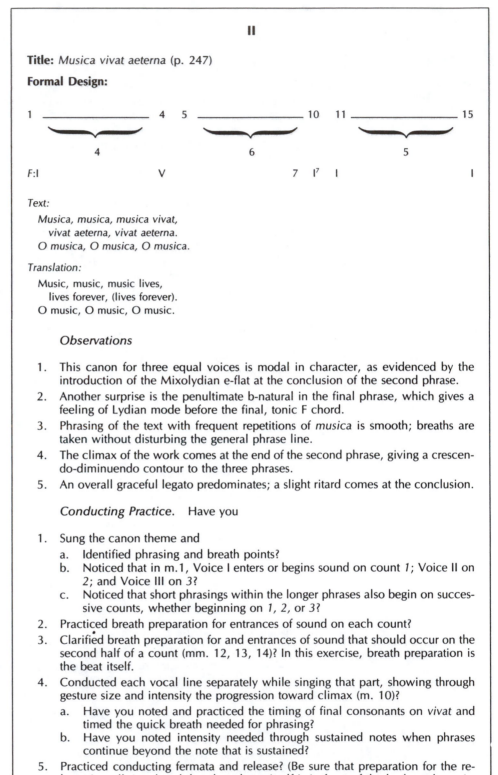

Text:

> Musica, musica, musica vivat,
> vivat aeterna, vivat aeterna.
> O musica, O musica, O musica.

Translation:

> Music, music, music lives,
> lives forever, (lives forever).
> O music, O music, O music.

Observations

1. This canon for three equal voices is modal in character, as evidenced by the introduction of the Mixolydian e-flat at the conclusion of the second phrase.
2. Another surprise is the penultimate b-natural in the final phrase, which gives a feeling of Lydian mode before the final, tonic F chord.
3. Phrasing of the text with frequent repetitions of *musica* is smooth; breaths are taken without disturbing the general phrase line.
4. The climax of the work comes at the end of the second phrase, giving a crescendo-diminuendo contour to the three phrases.
5. An overall graceful legato predominates; a slight ritard comes at the conclusion.

Conducting Practice.   Have you

1. Sung the canon theme and
   a. Identified phrasing and breath points?
   b. Noticed that in m.1, Voice I enters or begins sound on count *1*; Voice II on *2*; and Voice III on *3*?
   c. Noticed that short phrasings within the longer phrases also begin on successive counts, whether beginning on *1, 2,* or *3*?
2. Practiced breath preparation for entrances of sound on each count?
3. Clarified breath preparation for and entrances of sound that should occur on the second half of a count (mm. 12, 13, 14)? In this exercise, breath preparation is the beat itself.
4. Conducted each vocal line separately while singing that part, showing through gesture size and intensity the progression toward climax (m. 10)?
   a. Have you noted and practiced the timing of final consonants on *vivat* and timed the quick breath needed for phrasing?
   b. Have you noted intensity needed through sustained notes when phrases continue beyond the note that is sustained?
5. Practiced conducting fermata and release? (Be sure that preparation for the release is well timed and that the release itself is in front of the body and consistent with mood and spirit established.)

6. Conducted Voices I and II together? (Prepare as many entrance cues as possible, being careful to maintain the forward motion of the music.)

7. Conducted Voices II and III together? (Prepare as many entrance cues as possible, being careful not to interrupt the forward flow of the music.)

8. Conducted all three voices? (Prepare initial entrances with breath and cue glances. Be aware of as many phrase beginnings as possible.)

9. Increased complexity by conducting the entire work twice? (Think of beginning the repetition by having those singers who have been singing Voice III change quickly to sing Voice I. Those who sang Voice I the first time may sing Voice II, while those who sang Voice II sing Voice III. Practice cuing these voice entries appropriately with awareness of the assigned change in part.

    At the conclusion of the second time the work is sung, think of adding a rallentando in m. 14. Try subdividing the third count of m. 14 before the fermata.)

10. Noticed the relationship of a dynamic development to the rising intensity of the line and the relaxation felt in the final phrase?

11. Practiced shaping this in gesture?

12. Practiced all of this repeatedly until it is firmly in mind and under gesture control so that the interpretation can project the musical feeling?

Rehearsal Presentation

1. See suggestions for *Musica est Dei donum optimi.*

2. Note similarities between the two canons; adapt the steps for presentation of *Musica est Dei donum optimi* to a similar plan for presentation of *Musica vivat aeternam.*

III

Title: *Agnus Dei* (p. 260)

Composer: Giovanni Pierluigi da Palestrina (1525–1594)

Source: An excerpt from one of ten responsorial masses written for the Duke of Mantua

Formal Design: Through-composed, with overlapping cadences

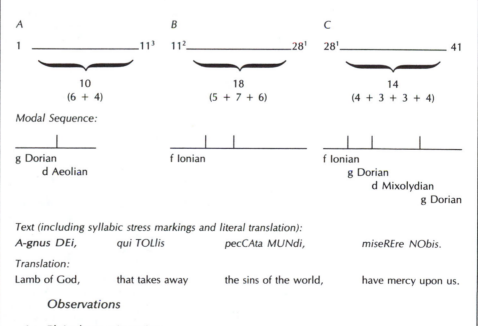

Modal Sequence:

g Dorian
 d Aeolian

f Ionian

f Ionian
 g Dorian
  d Mixolydian
   g Dorian

Text (including syllabic stress markings and literal translation):
A-gnus DEi,   qui TOLlis   pecCAta MUNdi,   miseREre NObis.

Translation:
Lamb of God,   that takes away   the sins of the world,   have mercy upon us.

Observations

1. Plainchant orientation

    a.   Divided into three sections (*a b c*)
    b.   Text also in three sections (*A B C*)

2. Dorian mode is utilized with e-natural (raised sixth degree); altered e-flats are found in mm. 31 (AII) and 38 (B). Picardy third at conclusion.

3. Cadences
    a.   Coincide with textual divisions.
    b.   Overlap throughout (mm. 6, 11, 16, 21, 28, 32, 35, and 38).
    c.   Are anticipated by suspensions that give emotional expression to text.

4. Unity is derived from imitative melodic lines that overlap. In this way sectionalization is avoided and a feeling of "flow" is maintained.
    a.   Phrase 1: In mm. 1–6, ascending four tones (d-a-c-d) of AI are imitated in S while descending diatonic four tones (g-f-e-d) of AII are imitated in T and B. In mm. 7–11, AII repeats rising line of AI (mm. 1–2) in Aeolian mode (d-e-d-a) while B repeats descending diatonic line of AII (mm. 1–2), with an ornamental turn on the fourth pitch (d-c-b$^\flat$-g-a).
    b.   Phrase 2: In mm. 11–28, thematic material is introduced in AII, with T entering similarly; in mm. 12^4–16^1, the theme is established in S (c-d-a-b$^\flat$-c-g-b$^\flat$-a-g-f) and repeated verbatim in B (mm. 16^3–20^1). At the cadence (mm. 22–23), AI begins the theme again, and it is imitated immediately by B, which then leads on to the cadence (mm. 27–28) and to Phrase 3.
    c.   Phrase 3: In mm. 28–41, the "shaping" of *miserere* in the music is indicative of the composer's sensitivity to the text. With a climax of the motive on the third syllable (*mi-se-RE-re*), he follows through with the opening statement in T (mm. 28–29), then in S (mm. 29–30), and again in AII (mm. 32–33). Of particular interest is the final statement of this motive in T (mm. 38–41) at the conclusion. One will also observe contrasting movement in the descending line of AI and AII (mm. 29–30) and similarly in T and B (mm. 32–33). Also noteworthy are suspensions (mm. 31, 34, 37, 40), which heighten the emotional quality of *miserere nobis* at each repetition.

5. Relationships of plainchant reference and musical setting are
    a.   Flowing lines reflected in legato singing
    b.   Repetition of melodic segments that give momentum and unity to music and text
    c.   Similarity of text-music relationships

6. These observations result in an understanding of the horizontal concept of polyphony and a recognition of the need to employ conducting gestures that are conducive to
    a.   Forward movement of melodic lines.
    b.   Sensitivity to dissonance-consonance relationships.
    c.   Entrances and rise and fall of motives and phrases.
    d.   Textual stresses that are within the horizontal flow of the music and not accented vertically.

7. Macro–micro rhythms and duple–triple relationships
    a.   The macro basis of the tactus is observed in AI at the beginning of *Agnus Dei.* The duple "inner pulse," or microrhythm, is felt as a quarter-note beat:

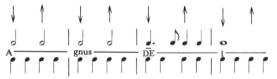

    b.   This arrangement is altered, however, when we observe A II:

       The syllabic stress of *A-gnus DEi,* coming on the unstressed portion of a duple beat requires a shift to a triple division.
    c.   Alternations can be pursued by analyzing the Bass part from its beginning. Bar lines (or tactus indications) do not always coincide with the text stresses:

(mm. 4–7)

A – gnus DE – i   A – gnus DE – i

(mm. 8⁴–11)

A – gnus DE ——————————— i ——————

(mm. 16–20)

qui   TOL – lis pec – CA – ta MUN——————— di

d. Alternation of stress requires a subtle agogic treatment that does not imply an accent in the general sense, but rather a slight pressure on the note as it moves forward in the musical line. The result is an undulating polyrhythm within the polyphony.

e. The conductor will readily understand the importance of underlining the stressed syllables of the text and asking choir members to do likewise. The Renaissance singer was not impeded by bar lines and was totally familiar with Latin pronunciation, the basis for the composer's musical setting.

Conducting Practice.   Have you

1. Conducted *Agnus Dei* plainsong chant to which reference is made? (In conducting chant, indications of note groupings of two or three in irregular order are depicted by the hand's drawing in an upward direction from a subtle ictus on the first note of each group.)

2. Determined that the flow of Palestrina's setting, with its relationships of movement in the various vocal lines, can best be depicted *sempre legato e tranquillo* through a slow 2 pattern with much attention to "drawing from" the ictus?

3. Practiced conducting each line while singing the part on *IOO* and noting entrances that occur on a beat as well as those that occur in response to the beat—on the second half of a count?

4. Practiced conducting each line again, singing text and noting through subtle gesture indications the word or syllable stress suggested by text?

5. Assessed "picturing" of each line's shape?

6. Practiced conducting
   a. Each line with every other line in succession (S-A I, S-A II, S-T, S-B, A I-A II, A I-T, A I-B, A II-T, A II-B, T-B)?
   b. The three lower lines together?
   c. The three upper lines together?
   d. All parts together?

6. Given careful attention to timing of "invitational" entrance cues?

7. Experimented with timing of ritard and appropriate subdivision to indicate movement in m. 40?

Rehearsal Presentation

1. Sing on *IOO* each phrase of *Agnus Dei* chant. Share appropriate brief explanations of style, place in music history, and themes.

2. All sing A II part on *IOO*. Continue similarly with T and B.

3. Combine A II, T, and B.

4. All sing A I line, then S line, on *IOO*.

5. Combine S and A I.

6. Sing all parts together on *IOO*.

During a second rehearsal on this work:

1. Review chant on *IOO*.
2. Speak text in phrases, being careful to clearly enunciate and enjoy each syllable of every word.
3. Sing plainchant reference on text.
4. Repeat for reinforcement.
   a. Sing all parts together on text for Section *A: Agnus Dei.*
   b. Speak text for Section *B* (mm. 11–28): *qui tollis peccata mundi.*
   c. Sing all parts together on Section *B.*
   d. Speak text for Section *C* (mm. 28–41): *miserere nobis.*
   e. Sing all parts together on Section *C.*
5. Sing Section *A* (mm. 1–11) on *IOO*.
6. Sing Section *A* on text: *Agnus Dei.*
7. Speak text for Section *B*, being careful to stress word syllables appropriately: *qui TOL-lis pec-CA-ta MUN-di.*
8. Sing Section *B* (mm. 11–28).
9. Speak text for Section *C* (mm. 28–41): *mi-se-RE-re NO-bis.*
10. Sing Section *C*, all parts together.
11. Sing entire work, all parts together on text.

IV

Title: "Christ Jesus Lay in Death's Strong Bonds" (p. 268)

Composer: Johann Sebastian Bach

Source: Chorale from Cantata No. 4

Formal Design:

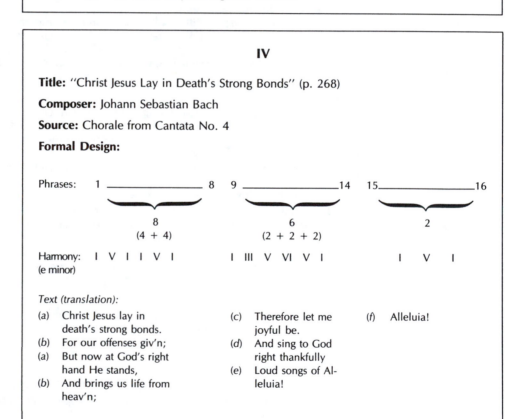

Text (translation):

(a) Christ Jesus lay in death's strong bonds.
(b) For our offenses giv'n;
(a) But now at God's right hand He stands,
(b) And brings us life from heav'n;

(c) Therefore let me joyful be.
(d) And sing to God right thankfully
(e) Loud songs of Al-leluia!

(f) Alleluia!

Observations

1. The text of this chorale was written by Martin Luther, and the original melody was composed in 1524 by his fellow musician and close friend, Johann Walther. Cantata No. 4 is one of Bach's early cantatas in which the chorale is employed as a *cantus firmus* in each movement.
2. In this final statement of the cantata, the form of the chorale itself is based on the form of the text (*a b a b c d e b*). The first musical phrase is repeated (4 + 4), and the next six measures (2 + 2 + 2) form an arch that rises and

falls. The closing musical statement of two measures repeats the final segment of the first phrase.

3. Fermatas are placed traditionally at the close of phrases in a congregational chorale of Lutheran origin. Their duration varies with harmonic function. In this chorale, the second and fourth fermatas, occurring on tonic chords (mm. 4 and 8), require sustaining for a period of time longer than that given the first and third fermatas, harmonized on the dominant (mm. 2 and 6). There is a feeling of continuity in each repetition of the four-measure phrase.

4. After the repeat, there is again a feeling of continuity from m. 9 to m. 14, as each two-measure segment contributes to the six-measure arch. Fermatas are treated as subtle tenutos here. The longer fermata is reserved for the final syllable of the first *Alleluia*, which occurs on a deceptive cadence (m. 14). A feeling of propulsion requires intensity on this chord as it leads to the final suspension and cadence.

5. The tempo of the chorale is responsive to the emotion evoked by the preceding cantata movements. One is moved to rejoice in Christ's resurrection rather than to feel intense sorrow because of His crucifixion. For this reason, a somber tempo seems inappropriate. On the other hand, a fast tempo lacks a necessary feeling of concern.

6. Attention should be given to repeating the vowel (without stopping the flow of tone) when successive eighth notes occur on a single syllable.

7. The final *Alleluia* is sung broadly and firmly with a strong rallentando and a final fermata.

Conducting Practice.   Have you

1. Studied relationship of text to musical phrasing and fermata lengths?
2. Practiced conducting the chorale melody with attention to
   a. Eighth-note pulse?
   b. Breath preparation for vocal entrance on count 4?
   c. Fermata in front of body on count 3 with release in direction of count 3?
   d. Continuing of phrase flow *a tempo* beginning on count 4?
3. Practiced repeating Section A?
4. Utilized count 4 in m. 8 to prepare vocal entrance of Section B? (Release may be upward in the direction of 4 as pictured on page 18.)
5. Observed that in m. 14 the fermata over the half note may be approached by a slight rallentando?
6. Practiced a confident, joyful expression of *Alleluia* (final two measures), slowing appropriately in strong conclusion of this intensely moving cantata?
7. Practiced release of final fermata in spirit and mood recreated?

Rehearsal Presentation

1. All parts sing S (melody) line with text.
2. All parts sing B line on neutral syllable *dOO*.
3. Sing S and B together (T with, A with B) on *dOO*.
4. All parts sing A line on *dOO*.
5. S and T sing T part.
6. Sing A and T together (B with A, S with T).
7. Sing all parts (S, A, T, B) together (still on *dOO*).
8. Sing again, articulating the eighth-note pulse on *dOO* (two eighth notes for each quarter-note value). Observe descending passing tones in descending bass line (m.1), ascending part (m. 1) and descending A (m. 2), and so on. Keep steady pulse and give eighth notes full value.
9. Read text aloud slowly, once for meaning, once with attention to extending vowel sounds and articulating consonants.
10. Sing entire chorale with text, giving attention to repeating the vowel on each passing tone.
11. Concentrate on phrase concepts (4 + 4; 6; 2). Take "half-breaths" [= ,] to observe commas in middle of phrases; "full breaths" [= ı] at ends of phrases.

Suggestions for Subsequent Rehearsals

Singing on unified vowels that are given full rhythmic value is essential. To emphasize this, it is important to practice singing the *inner pulse* (repeated eighth notes) on all word syllables. This procedure helps to relate exactly the coinciding and moving eighth notes that should be clearly articulated in a legato framework. The final step of the rehearsal should be a singing of the chorale that approximates its performance.

V

Title: "How Excellent Thy Name/Hallelujah!" (p. 289)

Composer: George Frideric Handel (1685–1759)

Source: Successive positioning of two independent choruses from the opening scene of *Saul*. This scene depicts the return of David, victorious in battle against Goliath and the Philistines.

Formal Design:

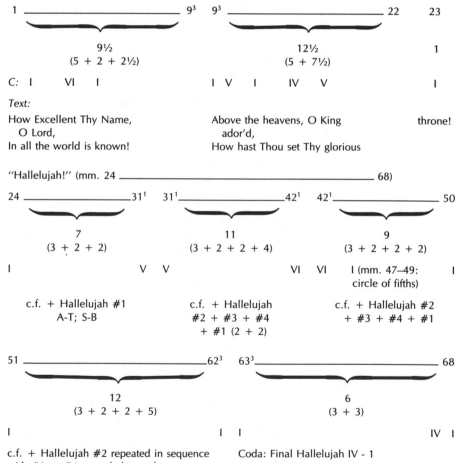

"How Excellent Thy Name" (mm. 1 _____ 23)

1 _____ 9³	9³ _____ 22	23
9½ (5 + 2 + 2½)	12½ (5 + 7½)	1
C: I VI I	I V I IV V	I

Text:

How Excellent Thy Name, O Lord, In all the world is known!	Above the heavens, O King ador'd, How hast Thou set Thy glorious	throne!

"Hallelujah!" (mm. 24 _____ 68)

24 _____ 31¹	31¹ _____ 42¹	42¹ _____ 50
7 (3 + 2 + 2)	11 (3 + 2 + 2 + 4)	9 (3 + 2 + 2 + 2)
I V V	VI VI	I (mm. 47–49: circle of fifths) I
c.f. + Hallelujah #1 A-T; S-B	c.f. + Hallelujah #2 + #3 + #4 + #1 (2 + 2)	c.f. + Hallelujah #2 + #3 + #4 + #1

51 _____ 62³	63³ _____ 68
12 (3 + 2 + 2 + 5)	6 (3 + 3)
I I I	IV I
c.f. + Hallelujah #2 repeated in sequence with #1 + #4 extended to cadence	Coda: Final Hallelujah IV - 1

Observations
"How Excellent Thy Name"

1. The opening strains in the orchestra are trumpetlike as they outline a C major tonic chord.

2. Strings play diatonic melismas leading to a deceptive cadence before A and S enter on a rising melody consisting of three imitative segments (a b c). Segments a and b are stated first, followed by imitative entrances in T and B. After a repetition of a and b (S-A-B-T), the c segment is imitated (S-A-T) and leads into the final cadence of the introduction to the "Hallelujah" section. All voices come together at the climactic full cadence. (See Example 2-14.)

"Hallelujah!"

3. A *cantus firmus* forms the chief unifying element of this chorus:

Hal - le - lu - jah,   Hal-le-lu - jah

4. The *cantus firmus* melody is first introduced by unison B and T (mm. 1–4). It is repeated in T (mm. 8–11); then in A (mm. 19–22); and finally in B line (mm. 28–31).

5. Between the *cantus firmus* statements are contrasting series of *Hallelujah* statements.

6. A coda concludes the chorus.

Conducting Practice. (*Note:* Steps suggested for practice in gesture communication are detailed in relation to specific measures in sequence.) Have you

1. Numbered measures consecutively (1–68)?
2. Checked tempo marking?
3. Established a mental framework for *maestoso* beginning?
4. (m. 1) Prepared strong beat for instrumental beginning and turned attention immediately to voices for their beginning?
5. (m. 2) Practiced left hand's holding of half note and a clear release with consonant placement on count *3?*
6. (mm. 2, 3) Conducted instrumental parts?
7. (m. 4) Prepared voices for entrance on count *2?*
8. (m. 6) Practiced left hand's holding of half note and a clear release with consonant placement on count *3* (as in m. 2)?
9. (m. 10) Considered contrasting style of beat articulation (more legato) and dynamic level in preparation for the rise in intensity dictated by the line's progression upward? (Style of beat articulation should help prevent or avoid tendency to sing eighth notes too staccato.)
10. (m. 10) Practiced timing of count *3* that serves as preparation for A entrance on the second half of count *3?*
11. (mm. 12, 13, 14) Practiced timing of count *1* that serves as preparation for entrance on second half of count *1?*
12. (m. 15) Practiced timing of cues
    a. T on count *2?*
    b. B on count *3?*
    c. A on count *3½?*
13. (m. 16) Practiced cue for T on count *1?* (Use left hand to sustain A; release on m. 17, count *1.*)
14. (m. 17) Practiced cuing S and B on count *1?*
15. (m. 18) Practiced sustaining S-T-B with left hand through count *1* and releasing on count *2?*
16. (m. 18) Practiced cuing A on count *1* and S on count *3?*
17. (m. 19) Practiced use of left hand to sustain and release A?
18. (m. 19) Practiced cuing B on count *1* and T on count *3?*
19. (m. 20) Practiced showing increase in intensity throughout measure while cuing B on count *2* and A on count *3?*
20. (mm. 21, 22, 23) Practiced helping S sustain intensity by use of left hand while cuing T on count *1?*
21. (m. 22) Practiced maintaining majestic character throughout?

a. Cued T change of note on *3* by a glance preceding count *3* and by a definite indication of *3* in gesture?

b. Turned eyes to other parts immediately and given strong indication of count *4*?

22. (m. 23) Practiced sustaining whole note by use of both hands and releasing sound on count *1* following the whole note?

23. (m. 24: *Hallelujah*) Practiced pausing momentarily after release of sound in m. 23 and preparing with right hand movement in upward direction for beginning of Hallelujah *a tempo giusto*?

a. Cued vocal entrance?

b. Given attention to instrumental parts?

24. (m. 27) Practiced using left hand to sustain and release B part?

a. Cued A and T on count *2* for their entrance on count *2½*?

25. (mm. 28, 29) Practiced communicating two-note groupings of eighth notes?

a. Become aware of the need to energize sixteenth-note groupings in forward movement?

b. Used left hand to make certain that quarter notes are not shortened?

26. (m. 30) Practiced preparing on count *4½* for T entrance on m. 31 count *1*?

27. (m. 32) Practiced preparing on count *1* for S and A entrances on count *1½*?

28. (mm. 34, 35) Practiced sustaining quarter note on count *4* with left hand and releasing on count *1* of succeeding measure?

29. (m. 36) Practiced preparing vocal entry on count *1*?

30. (mm. 38, 39) Practiced sustaining quarter note with left hand and releasing on count *2*? This release serves as preparation for entrances of S, A, and B. T entrance may be cued with glance on count *3*.

31. (m. 40) Practiced sustaining quarter note with left hand and permitting its release to serve as preparation for entrance of all voices on count *2½* ?

32. (m. 41) Practiced preparing on count *4½* for *forte* entrance and statement of the *cantus firmus* in A part?

33. (m. 42) Attempted to control balance of S-T duet in relation to A *cantus firmus*?

34. (m. 45) Practiced sustaining quarter note (count *1* with left hand and releasing on count *2*, as preparation for entry on count *2½* ?

35. (m. 45) Practiced sustaining quarter note (count *4*) with left hand and releasing on count *1* of m. 46?

36. (m. 46) Practiced giving a definite *2*, as preparation for entries on count *2½* ?

37. (m. 46) Practiced sustaining the quarter note (count *4*) with left hand and releasing on m. 24, count *1*, as preparation for entries on count *2*?

38. (m. 49) Practiced sustaining and indicating crescendo with left hand through half note in S line while giving definite *2* as preparation for A and T entries on count *2½*?

39. (m. 50) Practiced using left hand to stretch quarter-note duration and indicate release on count *2*?

40. (m. 50) Practiced preparing B on count *4* for statement of *cantus firmus*, which begins in m. 51 on count *1*?

41. (m. 51) Practiced turning attention immediately after B entrance to prepare S for their entrance on count *2*, and then A on count *3* for their entrance on count *4*?

42. (m. 52) Practiced preparing T on count *1* for their entrance on count *1½*, and encouraging A to enunciate (articulate) two eighth notes evenly on count *4*?

43. (m. 53) Practiced encouraging A to reenter on count *4* (*AH* vowel)?

44. (m. 55) Practiced using left hand to remind B and S to stretch quarter notes through count *1* and to release on count *2*, as preparation for S and B reentry on count *2½*?

45. (m. 56) Practiced reminding singers through gesture to make quarter notes as broad as possible without slowing tempo?

46. (mm. 58, 59) Practiced using left hand to sustain B note while giving definite *2* as preparation for reentry of S-A-T on count *2½*?

47. (mm. 60, 61) Practiced portraying a stretch of the first quarter note followed by (ʼ)? Counts *2, 3, 4* are broad without slowing tempo.

48. (m. 62) Practiced using left hand to sustain intensity through half note and to reinforce complete release on count *3*? (Following clear release on count *3* at *forte* level, cease conducting gesture and count silently on fourth beat.)

49. (m. 63) Practiced continuing the silent counting on *1* and *2* while preparing on count *2½* in Adagio tempo for entrances on count *3*?

50. (m. 64) Practiced using left hand to sustain vitality throughout duration of the note—especially across the bar line?

51. (m. 65) Practiced continuing the sustaining with left hand through counts *1* and *2* and showing clearly with right hand gesture the beginning of the syllable on count *3*? (Sustaining of intensity should be reinforced with the left hand throughout the half note on counts *3* and *4*.)

52. (mm. 66, 67) Practiced sustaining intensity with the left hand while conducting instrumental parts with the right hand?

53. (m. 68) Practiced sustaining intensity with both hands (notice that length of sound in this measure is doubled) and releasing final sound with both hands? (This release can be accomplished by moving in upward direction clearly on final count as preparation for a strong and definite release in downward direction on the double bar.)

Rehearsal Presentation. (Steps 1–6 may be accomplished in the first rehearsal and steps 7–22 in the second, if desired.)

1. Sing entire work using neutral syllable for mm. 1–23; use the *Hallelujah* text for remainder of the work.

2. Count-sing on eighth-note pulse mm. 1–23. Be careful to continue counting *sotto voce* on all rests.

3. m. 8: Ad-lib on *IAH* to clarify harmonies.

4. m. 19: B and T slowly on *IAH*. Beginning m. 19, ad-lib to end of m. 23.

5. Count-sing again on eighth-note pulse mm. 1–23.

6. Repeat mm. 1–23 on text.

7. *Hallelujah!*
   a. All sing on text the *cantus firmus* found in B part, mm. 24–27.
   b. All sing on text the *cantus firmus* found in T part, mm. 31–34.
   c. All sing on text the *cantus firmus* found in A part, mm. 42–45.
   d. All sing on text the *cantus firmus* found in B part, mm. 51–55.

8. Delineate notation for the five *Hallelujah* settings:

9. Mark repetitions of these figures in both choral and instrumental parts.

10. In slow tempo sing on *dAHt* duets (A-T, S-B) found in mm. 27–31; sing #2 as if the second eighth note of each slurred group were a sixteenth note followed by a sixteenth rest.

11. SATB sing together mm. 24–31; give strong second beat before AT and SB entrances.

12. Continue with S-A duet in mm. 32–34; sing #3 with the first three eighth notes staccato; repeat the AH on each sixteenth note as in vocalizing (not *hAH*). Phrase sixteenth notes in groups of eight after the first sixteenth note. *Caution:* This is to provide forward movement, and the phrasing is very slight; keep tempo steady. Repeat SA, adding T.

13. Continue in slow tempo with all parts mm. 34–35; sing #4 as if it were written:

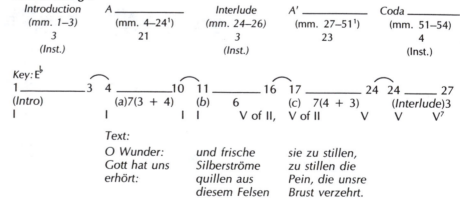

14. Sing on *dAH* mm. 36–38 (#5), with S making slight rest on dot, as if it were written:

15. Sing on *dAHt* mm. 38–41 (slow tempo): S-B (as in #2), then A-T (A as in S, #5).

16. Sing on *dAHt* m. 41 TB (with strong second beat), then S-T mm. 42–45; repeat mm. 41–45 with SATB.

17. Sing on *dAHt* mm. 45–50[1], in slow tempo with all parts, SATB (see #4).

18. Sing on *dAHt* mm. 51–56[1] in the following order: T, ST, AT, SAT, SATB. Refer to articulation in #3 (STA), #1 and #2 (B).

19. Relate mm. 56[2]–58[1] to mm. 47[2]–49[1]; sing on *dAHt* mm. 56–62; continue on *dAHt* with mm. 63–68.

20. Repeat m. 51 to the end in a quicker tempo, singing on *dAHt*.

21. Sing entire *Hallelujah* section (mm. 24–68) up to tempo, with *cantus firmus* singing text and all other parts on *dAHt*.

22. Review entire *Hallelujah* section *a tempo*, all singing text.

VI

Title: "O Wunder! Gott hat uns erhört" (Anthem of Thanksgiving; p. 297)

Composer: Carl Philipp Emanuel Bach (1714–1788)

Source: The chorus is taken from one of two oratorios composed by C.P.E. Bach. The work has been edited and arranged for performance with piano accompaniment by Richard Brewer. Translation of the text in German has been paraphrased by the editor. Instrumental parts are available from the publisher.

Formal Design:

Introduction	A	Interlude	A'	Coda
(mm. 1–3)	(mm. 4–24[1])	(mm. 24–26)	(mm. 27–51[1])	(mm. 51–54)
3	21	3	23	4
(Inst.)		(Inst.)		(Inst.)

Key: E♭

1 _____ 3   4 _____ 10   11 _____ 16   17 _____ 24   24 _____ 27
(Intro)   (a)7(3 + 4)   (b)   6   (c) 7(4 + 3)   (Interlude)3
I   I   I   I   V of II,   V of II   V   V   V[7]

Text:

O Wunder: und frische   sie zu stillen,
Gott hat uns   Silberströme   zu stillen die
erhört: quillen aus   Pein, die unsre
                diesem Felsen   Brust verzehrt.

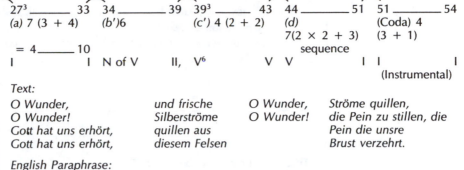

```
27³ _____ 33  34 _____ 39  39³ _____ 43  44 _____ 51  51 _____ 54
(a) 7 (3 + 4)    (b')6            (c') 4 (2 + 2)   (d)              (Coda) 4
                                                  7(2 × 2 + 3)     (3 + 1)
   = 4_____ 10                                     sequence
 I                    I  N of V       II, V⁶     V  V           I  I              I
                                                                        (Instrumental)
```

Text:

O Wunder,	und frische	O Wunder,	Ströme quillen,
O Wunder!	Silberströme	O Wunder!	die Pein zu stillen, die
Gott hat uns erhört,	quillen aus		Pein die unsre
Gott hat uns erhört,	diesem Felsen		Brust verzehrt.

English Paraphrase:

Thanksgiving! Thanksgiving! God has blessed our land.
Fresh silver streams flow forth in fullness,
God's great bounty, the bounty of everlasting grace.

Literal translation of German:

O Wonder! God has heard us now and fresh silvery streams are springing from the hard rocks, coming down to heal the pain that consumes our hearts.

Observations

1. Clearly defined phrases.
2. Simple binary form, which gives unity and balance to this early Classic composition.
3. Sensitive relationship of German text to music. (See literal translation.)
4. Striking dissonance m. 42.

Conducting Practice.   Have you

1. Established tempo and character of conducting gesture? (*Note:* In establishing Allegro tempo for music of the Classic period, notes of shortest duration are to be considered.)
2. Practiced breath preparation on *3* for vocal entrances on count 3½ (mm. 4, 5, 18, 27, 28, 45)?
3. Practiced breath preparation on *3* for vocal entrances on count *1* (mm. 6, 8, 16, 29, 31, 43)?
4. Practiced breath preparation on *2* for vocal phrase beginnings on count 3 (mm. 10, 33, 41)?
5. Practiced all phrase beginnings with gesture size appropriate for desired dynamic levels?
6. Practiced left hand indications for continuing intensity through half notes and dotted half notes (where intensity might diminish inappropriately and phrase lines sound broken or interrupted; mm. 11, 12, 13, 14, 17, 21, 22, 34, 35, 36, 38, 40, 42, 44, 46, 48, 49, 50)?
7. Practiced showing awareness of punctuation (catch breath) in m. 39 (count 2½) in preparation for continuing line on count 3)?
8. Checked gesture portraying phrase shapes, appropriate dynamic relationships, and well-timed releases (mm. 5, 6, 8, 10, 16, 18, 24, 28, 29, 31, 33, 41, 43, 45, 51)?
9. Practiced conducting entire work, including instrumental interludes?

Rehearsal Presentation

1. Read entire anthem on neutral syllable *dAHt*.
2. Count-sing with attention to dynamic levels.
3. Read again on *dAHt* with attention to phrasing and dynamic levels.
4. If English text is desired, speak text (omit steps 5–8).
5. If German text is preferred, speak text in rhythm of the music; follow this with singing of each short section (mm. 4–10, 10–16, 17–24).
6. Sing on German text from beginning to m. 24.

7. Since text is repeated beginning in m. 27, speak *B* section on text mm. 27–51.
8. Sing *B* section on text.
9. Sing entire work on text, with instrumental accompaniment.

VII

Title: "Luci care, luci belle" (p. 312)

Composer: Wolfgang Amadeus Mozart (1756–1791)

Description or Source: Originally a nocturne for two sopranos and bass, with three bassett horns or two B-flat clarinets and bass clarinet. Instrumental parts may also be played on two violins and cello. Instrumental parts double voice parts (SAB in this edition).

Formal Design: *A B B*

1 _____ 8^3	8^4 _____ 16 (repeated)
(*mp–mf*) 8 (1½ + 2 + 2 + 2½)	(*mf–f*) 8 (1½ + 2 + 2 + 2½)
Key of F: I V I V I	I VI II I IV V I

Text:

Luci care, luci belle,   Se per vói sospíro e móro,
  cári lúmi, a-máte stélle,   ídol mío, mío bel tesóro,
  dáte cálma a quésto córe,   →   fórza e sólo del Dío d'amóre,
  dáte cálma a quésto córe!   →   fórza e sol del Dío d'amóre.

Translation:

Lovely evening stars, beautiful and clear,   If I long for you and die,
  Lovely evening lights, lovely stars, calm,   Idol mine, my lovely treasure,
  Oh calm this heart of mine,   Silent and strong from the God of love.
  Oh calm this heart of mine!   Silent and strong from the God of love.

Observations

1. Tempo is Allegretto; melodies are graceful, dancelike.
2. Two balanced, eight-measure phrases (*AB*) with *B* section repeated (*ABB*).
3. Appoggiaturas in mm. 4, 5, 12, 13 are played and sung as two sixteenth notes on the beat.
4. Paired eighth notes sung and played with slight emphasis on the first, with diminuendo on the second ($\overset{\frown}{\flat\ \flat}$) , played and sung in graceful manner.
5. Bass line often in tenths with soprano. Soprano and alto lines often in thirds.
6. Dynamic development of each phrase leads to penultimate chord of cadence.

Conducting Practice.   Have you

1. Practiced preparations for entrances on fourth beat in both eight-measure phrases?
2. Practiced mm. 4 and 6 where breath is taken after second beat? Also mm. 12 and 14?
3. Practiced altering the size and the intensity of your beat to develop slight crescendos in the *A* section (*mp–mf*) and larger ones in Section *B* (*mf–f*)?
4. Practiced a graceful, dancelike, yet legato, conducting gesture?

5. Researched the Italian text and practiced pronunciation in preparation for teaching?

Rehearsal Presentation

1. Sensitive accompanist plays piano score, which is exact reduction of vocal and instrumental parts. Choir members watch scores and discover phrasing scheme by conducting (*4 pattern*) as piano part is performed. Note playing of appoggiaturas, evenly divided and on the beat (not before).
2. Repeat procedure; singers conduct and raise left hands to indicate points where one phrase ends and another begins.
3. Choir members sing own parts on *IAH* while pianist again plays instrumental reduction.
4. Sing again on *IAH*, with special attention to phrase shaping as dynamics indicate.
5. When the music is fairly well learned, Italian text may be added with the following steps:
   a. Conductor speaks pattern for first phrase.
   b. Choir members repeat and then sing the first phrase.
   c. Conductor speaks pattern for second phrase.
   d. Choir members repeat and then sing that phrase.
   e. Repeat this procedure throughout *A* section.
   f. Sing all of *A* section before introducing Italian for *B* section in the same manner.
   g. After each phrase of *B* section has been sung, choir may sing the entire composition in Italian.

VIII

Title: *Let Nothing Cause You Anguish* (p. 316)
    (Lass dich nur nichts nicht dauren)

Composer: Johannes Brahms (1833–1897)

Description or Source: This motet with organ accompaniment is one of the many studies which Brahms composed as an exercise in developing his contrapuntal technique; the result is a short masterpiece.

Formal Design: *Introduction-A-Interlude-B-Interlude-A-Coda*

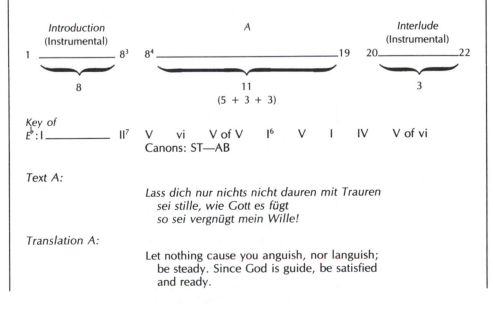

Text A:

    Lass dich nur nichts nicht dauren mit Trauren
      sei stille, wie Gott es fügt
      so sei vergnügt mein Wille!

Translation A:

    Let nothing cause you anguish, nor languish;
      be steady. Since God is guide, be satisfied
      and ready.

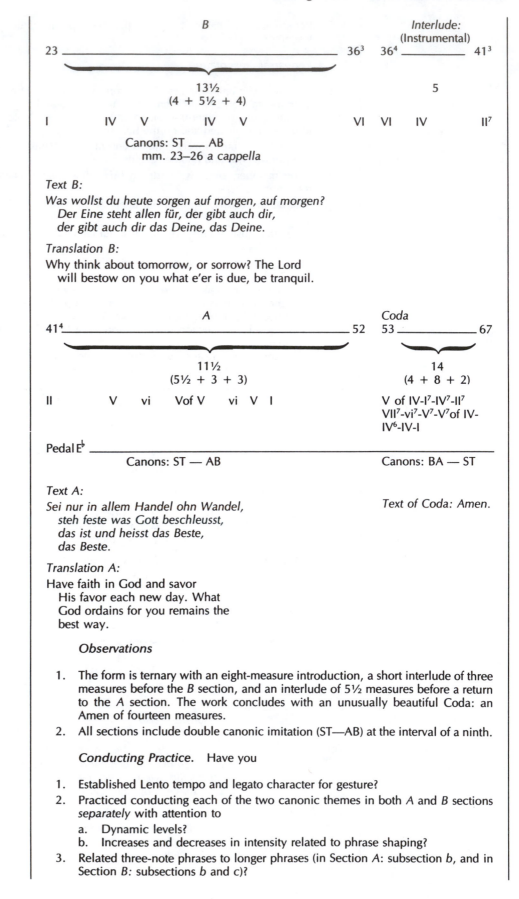

B   *Interlude:*
                                                           (Instrumental)
23 _____ 36³   36⁴ _____ 41³

                    13½   5
              (4 + 5½ + 4)

I   IV   V   IV   V   VI   VI   IV   II⁷

     Canons: ST ___ AB
       mm. 23–26 *a cappella*

Text B:

Was wollst du heute sorgen auf morgen, auf morgen?
  Der Eine steht allen für, der gibt auch dir,
  der gibt auch dir das Deine, das Deine.

Translation B:

Why think about tomorrow, or sorrow? The Lord
  will bestow on you what e'er is due, be tranquil.

A   *Coda*
41⁴ _____ 52   53 _____ 67

                    11½   14
              (5½ + 3 + 3)   (4 + 8 + 2)

II   V   vi   Vof V   vi   V   I   V of IV-I⁷-IV⁷-II⁷
                                                  VII⁷-vi⁷-V⁷-V⁷of IV-
                                                  IV⁶-IV-I

Pedal E♭ _____
     Canons: ST — AB   Canons: BA — ST

Text A:

Sei nur in allem Handel ohn Wandel,   *Text of Coda: Amen.*
  steh feste was Gott beschleusst,
  das ist und heisst das Beste,
  das Beste.

Translation A:

Have faith in God and savor
  His favor each new day. What
  God ordains for you remains the
  best way.

Observations

1. The form is ternary with an eight-measure introduction, a short interlude of three measures before the *B* section, and an interlude of 5½ measures before a return to the *A* section. The work concludes with an unusually beautiful Coda: an Amen of fourteen measures.
2. All sections include double canonic imitation (ST—AB) at the interval of a ninth.

Conducting Practice.   Have you

1. Established Lento tempo and legato character for gesture?
2. Practiced conducting each of the two canonic themes in both *A* and *B* sections *separately* with attention to
   a. Dynamic levels?
   b. Increases and decreases in intensity related to phrase shaping?
3. Related three-note phrases to longer phrases (in Section *A:* subsection *b,* and in Section *B:* subsections *b* and *c*)?

4. Practiced conducting all parts together from the beginning through m. 52 until
   a. All entrances are well timed?
   b. Dynamic levels, crescendos, and diminuendos are clearly described in gesture?
   c. Left hand communicates appropriate independent reminders for phrase shaping, dynamic levels, entrances and releases?
5. Practiced conducting the Coda:
   a. Bass and alto lines together?
   b. Soprano and tenor lines together?
   c. All parts together, with special attention to suspensions and resolutions in relation to shaping of phrases and the overall contour of the Coda?
   d. Left hand communication to reinforce timing and intensity of crescendo-diminuendo in m. 66?
6. Practiced conducting entire motet?

Rehearsal Presentation

1. All voices sing canonic themes of *A* section on *IOO:*
   a. Soprano line, mm. 8–19
   b. Tenor line, mm. 9–19
   c. Alto line, mm. 10–19
   d. Bass line, mm. 11–19
2. Become aware of relationships of lines in *A* section:
   a. S-T sing S line, mm. 8–19.
   b. A-B sing A line, mm. 10–19.
   c. Combine S-A lines (S-T on S line, A-B on B line).
   d. S-T sing own lines, mm. 8–19.
   e. A-B sing own lines, mm. 10–19.
   f. Combine T-B lines, mm. 11–19 (S-T on T line, A-B on B line).
3. Beginning with Introduction, sing all parts on *IAH* through m. 19.
4. Beginning in m. 41 (return of *A* section), sing all parts on *IAH* through m. 52.
5. On *IOO,* read Coda:
   a. Combine B-A lines.
   b. Combine S-T lines.
6. On text, combine all parts, with careful attention to suspensions and resolutions. Note harmonic movement to consonance and expressive quality of dissonance.
7. On *IOO,* follow steps 1 and 2, becoming acquainted with canonic themes in *B* section (mm. 22–36).
8. Beginning with Introduction, sing all parts on *IAH* through m. 52; sing Coda on text: *Amen.*

Suggestions for Second Rehearsal

1. Review on neutral syllable *IAH* mm. 8–52; sing text for Coda.
2. If German text is to be sung, begin work on diction with Section *A:*
   a. Speak and repeat German poetry for each phrase.
   b. All sing S line in German text.
   c. All sing A line in German text.
   d. Sing all parts using German text.
3. Present German diction for Section *B*, following steps in suggestion 2.
4. Present German diction for Section *C*, following steps in suggestion 2.
5. Beginning with Introduction, sing entire motet, using German text.

IX

Title: Sanctus-Benedictus from *Mass* (p. 358)

Composer: Ben Johnston (b. 1926)

Description or Source: *Mass* is for mixed voices, trombones (or organ), jazz drummer, and pizzicato double bass. It is to be performed with *modified just-tuning*: in d minor with third, fourth, and seventh degrees of scale lowered one-third tone, and second and fifth degrees raised one-tenth tone.

Formal Design: *A B C A B C Coda*

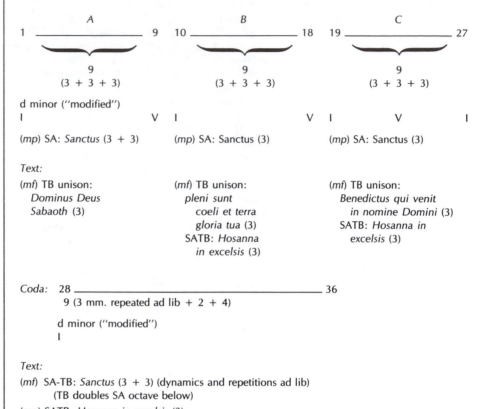

d minor ("modified")

I   V   I   V   I   V   I

(*mp*) SA: *Sanctus* (3 + 3)   (*mp*) SA: Sanctus (3)   (*mp*) SA: Sanctus (3)

Text:

(*mf*) TB unison: (*mf*) TB unison: (*mf*) TB unison:
  Dominus Deus   *pleni sunt*   *Benedictus qui venit*
  Sabaoth (3)   *coeli et terra*   *in nomine Domini* (3)
                                                gloria tua (3)   SATB: *Hosanna in*
                                          SATB: *Hosanna*   *excelsis* (3)
                                              in excelsis (3)

Coda: 28 _____ 36
                  9 (3 mm. repeated ad lib + 2 + 4)

                  d minor ("modified")
                  I

Text:

(*mf*) SA-TB: *Sanctus* (3 + 3) (dynamics and repetitions ad lib)
        (TB doubles SA octave below)
(*mp*) SATB: *Hosanna in excelsis* (3)
a niente, instruments to the end (3)

Observations

1. Instruments: Trombones (or organ) sustaining open fifth continuously throughout; double bass repeating three-measure phrase pizzicato throughout; brushes on snare drum are played ad lib in jazz style.
2. Section *A*: The first six measures serve as an introduction and are repeated chantlike (3 + 3). TB enter in unison, singing second line of the liturgical text as they introduce the principal melodic interest. Trombones sustain, dronelike, an empty d chord (without a third) and the pizzicato bass repeats a three-measure phrase to the cadence at close of section C. The music creates an atmosphere of chantlike reverence.
3. Section *B*: Continuing of the repetitive *Sanctus* in treble voices for three measures; B and T, again in unison, reenter in m. 13 and continue the principal theme. A four-part (SATB) *Hosanna in excelsis* completes the second section.
4. Section *C*: Continued repetitions of three measure phrase on *Sanctus* (SA); unison TB concludes the principal theme with *Benedictus qui venit in nomine Domini*. A four-part (SATB) *Hosanna in excelsis* completes the third section.
5. Coda: The opening *Sanctus* is doubled an octave below by male voices; the three-measure phrase is repeated several times ad lib (each repetition to be sung at a different dynamic level), leading into the final *Hosanna in excelsis* with a cadence in d minor. Instruments sustain or repeat the tonic d *a niente*.
6. Dynamics outline:

mm. 1 _____ 9;   10 __ 18; 19 __ 27;   28 _____ 30   31 _____ 36
(mp) _____ (f)   (mp) __ (f) __ (mp) __ (f)   (mf __ (f) __ (mf) __ (mp)   (mp) __ (a niente)

Conducting Practice.   Have you

1. Practiced the composer's *modified just-tuning* of the d minor scale until you can hear and demonstrate it?
2. Considered an appropriate tempo that will create a "chantlike" atmosphere, reflect the meaning and the mood of the text, and make it possible to sing three-measure phrases on one breath?
3. Indicated on your score types of breaths to be taken:
   a. Full breaths = ı
   b. Half-breaths = ,
4. Practiced conducting gestures that are legato yet rhythmically precise, that clearly reveal preparations for
   a. Accent on second syllable of *Sanc-TUS* (in first two measures of each three-measure phrase)?
   b. Syncopation on third beat of m. 3?
   c. Release of final quarter note at end of phrase?
5. Practiced well-timed gestures
   a. For entrances of TB when primary melody enters?
   b. For syncopated tutti rhythms at varied dynamic levels? (Compare mm. 16–18 and 25–27 with mm. 31–33.)
6. Observed dynamic development of each phrase? (Refer to Dynamics Outline in Observations.)

Rehearsal Presentation

1. Ear training in preparation for singing Johnston's "Sanctus-Benedictus":
   a. Establish perfect unison and octave (no beats).
   b. SA move one half step higher as TB remain firmly on unison pitch.
   c. TB move slowly to semitone higher pitch of SA (eight slow counts); tune carefully.
   d. Begin again with perfect octave; TB move directly one half step higher.
   e. SA proceed to raise the pitch slowly (eight counts) to semitone matching TB.
   f. Follow same procedure as above, only stop halfway (at the quarter tone) and then move up to semitone.
   g. Finally, move up and back a third-tone, then a tenth-tone.
   h. After the quarter tone, third-tone, and tenth-tone are clearly delineated, divide the choir into SSA-TBB, each singing a major triad; then proceed in the same fashion as in b–f.
   i. Practice slowly ascending and descending on d minor scale, using the following altered intervals (*modified just-tuning*):

D   +E   7+F   7+G   +A   B♭   7+C   D

Key to symbols: + raises pitch one tenth-tone
                 7 lowers pitch a quarter tone
                 7+ lowers pitch one third-tone

2. After intonation is clearly in mind and d minor scale is practiced, proceed as follows with Latin text:
   a. All parts sing S opening line (mm. 1–3); concentrate on tuning, phrasing, accents, and exact timing of final quarter note (final *s* of *Sanctus* pronounced sharply, but lightly, on rest).
   b. After S line is established, B and A parts practice A line with same attention to detail; but both lines together.
   c. All parts sing mm. 28–30, varying dynamics on repetitions.
   d. SA sing *Hosanna in excelsis* (mm. 16–18); TB sing same phrase (making certain that unison pitch on -san- is "tuned"); all parts together.

e. SA sing mm. 25–27; TB sing mm. 25–27; all parts sing.
f. ST sing final *Hosanna in excelsis* (tune fourths carefully) on mm. 31–33; AB sing mm. 31–33 (tune fifths carefully); all parts sing final *Hosanna*; and so on.
g. SATB sing *Coda* (mm. 28–33).
h. TB sing *Dominus Deus Sabaoth* (mm. 7–9).
i. SATB sing entire first phrase (mm. 1–9).
j. TB sing *pleni sunt coeli et in terra gloria tua* (mm. 13–15). Do not let breaths disturb the phrase line.
k. SATB sing mm. 10–18.
l. TB sing mm. 22–27; SATB sing mm. 22–27.
m. SATB sing mm. 19–27.
n. Sing entire *Sanctus-Benedictus*, observing dynamics, phrasing, accents, tuning and balance, with chantlike, flowing lines.

Chapter 4

The Rehearsal: Aesthetic Performance

A productive rehearsal is both educationally rewarding and aesthetically satisfying. If choral singers are to experience these goals, they must be able to recognize their own progress or accomplishment within a rehearsal; they must feel that they have learned something, improved their ability to express ideas musically, and been a part of artistic expression.

Aesthetic satisfaction in performance does not just happen—it is a result of careful planning. Every rehearsal should contain "high points" of musical attainment. Too often, aesthetic highs are thought of only in terms of a public performance. Although choral rehearsals are often viewed merely as preparation for performances, rehearsals, too, can be enjoyable and exciting for singers if they are properly planned. To accomplish this, conductors must recognize the importance of aesthetic satisfactions as reinforcement to the singers.

Planning for a choral rehearsal that is aesthetically rewarding involves several important factors:

1. Choice of literature
   a. The quality of repertory determines in large measure the quality of artistic accomplishment and aesthetic response. Choose repertory of excellent quality.
   b. A musical selection must be appropriate for a particular group in its technical demands, in the degree of challenge it presents, and in its aesthetic qualities. Consider appropriateness of repertory.
   c. Each musical selection should contribute to the musical understanding of singers. Plan for musical growth through repertory.

2. Contrast and repetition
   a. In the order or sequence of a rehearsal. Strategic placement of concentrated work and satisfying "performance" can enhance pleasure in rehearsal. These should be balanced so that singers have a feeling of accomplishment and satisfaction. An effective lift in a rehearsal can be provided by contrasts in key-feeling as well as by variations in meter, tempo, and mood of selections being rehearsed.
   b. In the styles of composition represented in a rehearsal. Contrasting styles and harmonic textures can contribute perceptibly to artistic excitement during a rehearsal

and to development of musical understandings: historical, theoretical, and aesthetic.

3. Thorough knowledge of scores and mastery of the rehearsal plan. The study of each score develops in the conductor's mind ideas and appropriate technical devices to be utilized in a rehearsal. Some effective techniques are presented in Chapters 2 and 3.

4. Recognition of the direction that learning takes. Learning proceeds from crudeness to mastery. Just as the portrait painter first sketches the whole of his or her masterpiece in rough form and then works to perfect details, so the conductor should guide the singers through an exploration of the composition so that a reasonably clear image of the work is grasped.

   The character of a selection must be evident to the choral group if singers are to maintain interest in it. Interest is heightened by exploration of both text and music, with emphasis upon the relationship between the two. From this point of recognition of the whole, a conductor may begin to refine the various parts critical to effective performance. After a chorus becomes aware of a composer's intention, the members will be ready to engage in detail work necessary for performance.

5. Timing. Acute sensitivity to the movement of a rehearsal begins during rehearsal planning. The conductor then directs his or her attention during each rehearsal to subtle cues that can be "caught" from the singers: Evidences of excitement, satisfaction, boredom, or fatigue are usually reflected in facial expressions, posture, and attentiveness. These signs motivate a conductor's decision about continuing specific work or making a change in activity or focus. A conductor can develop sensitivity to the choral instrument when he or she becomes aware of its importance.

RESPONSIBILITIES OF THE CONDUCTOR

A successful or aesthetically satisfying rehearsal results from the conductor's fulfillment of certain responsibilities. These include careful planning for the rehearsal, which entails formulating objectives, determining content, and planning the rehearsal's length, order, and shape. The conductor develops sensitivity during the rehearsal by continually improving the acuity of his or her ear, and by concentrating on development of aural and visual awareness and responsiveness in singers.

Rehearsal planning is comparable to an artistic creation. After setting forth specific objectives and selecting the repertory, a conductor considers the rehearsal shape or format, which has an effective introduction (beginning), a planned contrast, a climax, and a conclusion. The conductor plans with utmost care the way to work on each musical selection.

The effectiveness of the actual rehearsal is dependent upon the rehearsal plan itself and upon the sensitive behavior of the conductor during rehearsal. The conductor's sense of timing or "pacing" is critical. He or she must

1. Develop a feeling for timing; learn when to encourage the group to move and when to allow time for relaxation of the drive. A momentary contemplation of the beauty of even a short, musically expressive idea can be satisfying and can serve as a strong motivator.

2. Be able to select for immediate focus what is necessary to advance the performance level. This implies acute listening at all times.

3. Be adept and perceptive in balancing verbal directions with singing or musical work and performance. The conductor need not share verbally everything discovered about the music. Much of his or her musical understanding can be effectively communicated through appropriate and sensitive gesture and eye contact.

Rehearsal Planning

Goals for a choral ensemble should determine the content of rehearsals. Although the focus or emphasis may vary according to the maturity level of the group, the specific work to be accomplished, and the proximity of a performance, a rehearsal should usually include

1. Physical readiness.
2. Vocalization: a concentration upon development of sound through work on breath management, vowel unification, range extension, vocal flexibility, control of sustained sound, articulation, pronunciation, control of dynamic intensity and contrasts, and flexibility and alertness in following the conductor's gestures.
3. Aural training: a concentration upon development of the ability to *hear* and to sing in tune and in balance with other voices.
4. Mental sharpening: a concentration upon ability to think during the rehearsal span.

Each vocal exercise may satisfy one or more of these specific objectives. There should also be

1. Visual training: a concentration upon association of ear and eye (sight reading, or the translation of notation into sound).
2. Further work on musical selections in various stages of performance preparation. Music chosen for any given rehearsal should represent contrasting musical textures, styles, moods, tempos, and keys or modes.

The number of selections in any single rehearsal may vary, but in an hour's rehearsal most choruses can make progress on three to five different compositions and thus avoid the boredom that could result from devoting too long a period to work on a single selection.

Rehearsal Objectives. Rehearsal objectives are as essential to the effectiveness of a rehearsal as are destinations to be visited by the traveler planning a vacation. Rehearsal objectives should be formulated with care and should reflect goals such as improvement of vocal skills, enhancement of aural and visual skills, growth in expressive sensitivity, and advancement toward performance of musical selections. Most important among all rehearsal goals is a musical objective: Choristers will derive satisfaction and enjoyment from singing musically.

Specific rehearsal objectives are necessary to guide and shape the satisfying rehearsal. Specific objectives may be considered to be *principal* or *secondary* according to the needs, goals, readiness, and maturity level of a chorus. Specific rehearsal objectives permit a conductor to apportion and control time utilized in the rehearsal, to develop and maintain momentum, and thus to further progress toward musical and learning goals.

Specific rehearsal objectives become more compelling when stated in terms of desired behavior. The following examples of rehearsal objectives incorporate exercises mentioned in other chapters, and make reference to selected musical compositions that appear in the accompanying choral collection.

Singers will

Demonstrate good posture for singing.

Demonstrate proper breath management.

Balance EE and OO vowel sounds during vocalization.

Articulate on *tAH* dotted quarter–eighth note and dotted eighth–sixteenth note figures by stopping the sound on the dot to make that dot the impetus for and energizer of the short note.

Extend the resonant *mm* into each pure vowel sound in sequence—m-EE, m-EH, m-AH, m-O, m-OO—without audible emphasis on the vowels.

Experience chord changes: major–minor–diminished–minor–major–augmented–major.

Follow a conductor's gesture and control breath flow with vitality as conductor indicates crescendo and diminuendo gradually and smoothly through sixteen counts.

Improve rhythmic articulation in "Propter magnam gloriam tuam" (from *Gloria*) by Vivaldi.*

Experience the feeling for duple–triple–duple meter relationships in "Rest Sweet Nymphs" by Francis Pilkington.*

Control and shape flowing lines in *Agnus Dei* by Palestrina.*

Heighten awareness of double canon formal structure employed in *Let Nothing Cause You Anguish* by Johannes Brahms.*

In this same composition, relate short three-note phrases to longer phrase lines (see particularly mm. 12–19).

Enjoy "performance" of "Duetto buffo di due gatti" (Comic Duet for Two Cats) by Gioacchino Rossini.*

Rehearsal Length. Time is a primary consideration in planning a rehearsal. Time set aside for the rehearsal or any part thereof may vary with the maturity levels of groups. Physical and vocal maturation determine the singers' "attention span," or the length of time in which productive work can be accomplished. There should be sufficient time to ensure maximum accomplishment. However, a rehearsal should not be so long that loss of interest may result in or from vocal or physical fatigue. Extended rehearsals for mature singers should include appropriate and well-timed breaks for vocal rest and "recuperation." It is helpful to singers if there is an alternation of sitting and standing within a rehearsal.

Rehearsal Order. It is imperative that all rehearsals begin on time. When singers expect a prompt beginning, they are more apt to be on time. Conversely, when rehearsals begin late, singers soon make allowance for this and excuse their own tardiness with a rationalization that "the conductor never starts on time."

Begin a rehearsal with vocalization and proceed to the most exacting work while the singers are most alert and "fresh." However, vocalization need not be planned exclusively for the beginning of a rehearsal. Pertinent exercises (vocal, rhythmic, harmonic) related directly to specific problems in a given work may be inserted immediately before or during the rehearsal of that selection.

Effective rehearsal of a musical composition should follow the developmental process: from crudeness to precision. When presented with a "new" or unfamiliar work, the choral group should first be given an opportunity to sing *through* the selection to discover its general character. The conductor will be well advised to limit the amount of exacting or detailed work during early rehearsals of any musical selection.

Carefully guided marking of scores by choir members should follow. Score marking precedes detailed work and enhances the choir members' perception of the shape and inner relationships of a composition. Obviously, any inaccuracies in the edition should be corrected. The score marking also includes delineation of phrasing, indications of breathing points (sectional and individual), pitch helps, special guides to the relationship of parts, and reinforcing of dynamic contrasts and relationships. (See Chapter 2.)

The initial approach to work on a selection is determined by the texture of the music. In some cases, a work can be read in its entirety on a neutral syllable. In other instances, the rehearsal of a single line can be productive. If the work is fugal, it will be effective to have the entire chorus sing the fugal subject and then the countersubject. Often the singing of one part as it relates

---

*See Music for Class Study and Conducting.

to other parts can be helpful and illustrative with a humming or *pianissimo* accompaniment for the section that has been assigned more prominent melodic interest. Expressive reading of the text (poetry) may best establish the mood and feeling for lyricism. The conductor must choose the most effective approach to a selection. Above all, approaches to any work should be planned thoughtfully to ensure maximum progress and understanding, and to provide refreshing changes of pace.

Sight reading is often placed effectively about midway through a rehearsal. Since the ability of singers to read music at sight can be perfected only through guided and consistent practice, there should be some opportunity to practice sight reading during each rehearsal. Material selected for sight reading should be well chosen so that it is appropriately challenging to the singers. Since sight reading is a skill that can be developed, it is most important that singers feel gratified in their efforts. For the desired growth to take place, the conductor must increase gradually the difficulty or complexity of the challenge, being very careful that singers experience success rather than frustration in their efforts. A sensitive and perceptive approach by the conductor encourages singers to enjoy and to look forward to further experiences in sight reading.

Strategic placement of listening to an artistic performance via recorded example may provide needed motivation, particularly when choral music will eventually be performed with instrumental parts.

Polishing of a work nearing performance stage can provide a welcome change or contrast within a rehearsal. When working on details of a segment within a selection, it is beneficial and rewarding to singers if the section is put back into the context of a larger whole before proceeding to other detailed work or to another musical composition.

Reinforcement is crucial. When detailed or intensive work has been accomplished on a particular selection, that selection should be included in the next rehearsal so that the accomplishment can be reinforced. The lapse of too much time between rehearsals on a particular work may result in regression in the performance level attained.

There should be a high point in the rehearsal. The interest and involvement of singers should be guided skillfully as through a crescendo of intensity toward this musical climax.

The rehearsal should end with "performance" of a work the singers know, enjoy, and perform artistically. The culminating of a rehearsal in a high moment of satisfaction related to performance can ensure positive motivation in the singers and a desire to return for the next rehearsal.

Rehearsal Shaping. The actual shaping of a rehearsal can be accomplished through specific steps. List selections to be rehearsed and outline results to be obtained through their rehearsal. Consider placement of selections for contrast in rehearsal, in terms of the type of work to be accomplished (such as rhythmic clarity, linear shaping, harmonic clarity, polishing, and sight reading); or mood, key or tonality, tempo, and style. Choose as a final composition one that will assure a feeling of satisfaction and accomplishment.

Select vocalises that accomplish specified objectives and prepare singers physically, mentally, aurally, and vocally at the outset of a rehearsal. Vocalises can also provide an appropriate beginning for work on specific music placed later in the rehearsal. A vocalise can give a rhythmic, melodic, or harmonic introduction to a selection to be rehearsed. When this is the case, rehearsal of the music itself reinforces skill development approached through exercises.

A successful rehearsal is dependent upon basic and consistent behavior on the part of a conductor. The crucial element is the conductor's ear. What he or she *actually* hears during the rehearsal must be carefully and continuously measured against what he or she *wants* to hear. It is the conductor's aural perception that actually moves a rehearsal forward. The cue for each next step is based on this perception.

Improving Aural Acuity

A conductor can consciously and relentlessly train his or her ear. The ability to hear should improve consistently throughout one's experience as a musician. The acuity of the conductor's ear is the most influential determinant of aural perception in members of a choral group. The conductor's listening powers and attitudes are readily reflected by the singers as they develop listening habits.

In the process of consciously training their own ears during rehearsals, conductors can expect improvement. At first they will have difficulty hearing any specific aspects of the sound. They will be aware that the choir is singing, but will find the vocal efforts melded in such a manner that they are not easily distinguished. Conductors must focus upon each aspect of the sound, and follow a single vocal line while several lines are being sung. They must listen specifically for vowel unification, clarity of consonants, harmonic balance, specific intonation problems both horizontally and vertically, and each important performance ingredient in its turn. They must attend to the music both vertically and horizontally, although at first this will require separate concentrated efforts. The conductor's ear rarely comprehends everything at once, but with careful concentration, and through repeated efforts, each conductor will improve the ability to hear more aspects of the music simultaneously and to diagnose problems accurately.

Rehearsal Principles

As the conductor develops the ability to hear what the singers are actually projecting, he or she assumes the responsibility for leadership in effecting change. The following principles should be kept in mind:

1. Verbal directions and vocal patterns must be clear and concise.
   a. When giving directions, look at the group. Eye contact is as important as the verbal message.
   b. If a correction is to be made, be ready to give further direction immediately upon stopping the group's singing. Improved pacing results from concentrated effort.
   c. Be careful not to talk too much! Extended verbal comments and unnecessary repetitions of directions can result in a loss of rehearsal momentum and singers' interest.
2. When indicating a starting point, give explicit directions. If rehearsal letters or numbers are not present, give in order the page, the system (brace of staves), the measure, and the count. This order enables singers to follow the direction as it is given and conserves valuable rehearsal time.
3. If the group has been stopped and asked to repeat a section or a phrase, the singers deserve to know what to do to ensure improvement. Repetition alone seldom hastens the desired result.
4. Singers should not be asked to work on too many aspects of the music at one time. The maturity of the group will influence the conductor's judgment. Most singers can remember and act upon only one or two suggestions at a time. When those corrections or improvements have been made, chorus members will be receptive to one or two further directions.
5. Encourage development of pitch memory by asking singers to remember and return to pitches. Ask singers to *remember* or *think of* and then *hum* the pitches at a given point. If they are unable to hum those pitches correctly, the accurate pitches can be

repeated from the keyboard or pitch pipe. Development of tonal memory is essential to a musician!

6. Utilize word pictures or clear analogies that can advance the understanding for and sensitivity to a desired mood or feeling that is to be conveyed through a musical phrase.

7. Choose techniques carefully. Suggestions for preventing or overcoming problems encountered frequently by choral groups include the following:

   a. If the tempo is fast or words are a problem, replace the text with a neutral syllable temporarily. This reduces the complexity of the challenge, provides a means of clarifying rhythmic patterns and pitch intervals, and enhances the overview of the music. Choice of neutral syllable should be determined in response to the character of a musical passage: *dOOt* or *dEEt* can effect rhythmic precision; *lOO* or *lAH* can be helpful in more legato sections; and *bum* or *pum* (with a minimum of time devoted to the vowel sound and an almost instantaneous progression to the *m*) permits singers to experience the relationship of rhythmic figures that differ from part to part. This technique is especially useful when the text is in a language unfamiliar to singers.

   b. An illustrated observation of the inner pulse relationship to the rhythmic pattern can yield important rewards. Singers can tap pulse with one hand (while holding music copy in the other) and can articulate the rhythmic patterns precisely on a neutral syllable such as *tAH* or *tEE*.

   c. Exaggerated staccato singing with either the text or a neutral syllable can contribute substantially to a feeling for rhythmic clarity.

   d. To improve rhythmic accuracy after rehearsing of a selection is well under way, the singing of parts on measure counts and their subdivisions can be helpful (see pages 145–47).

   e. In slow-moving, legato sections in which singers experience difficulty feeling pulse, word syllables may be divided into the appropriate number of eighth notes (for example, My-hy cou-hun-tree-hee ti-hi-his of thee-hee).

   f. To achieve long, flowing, continuous phrases, sing the entire phrase on one *mAH*; then use a *lAH* on each note without letting the consonants interrupt the stream of vocal sound.

   g. To increase the feeling of vitality in sustained singing, have singers pulse the notes of longer duration by singing the entire phrase on quarter or eighth notes.

   h. To convey the idea that dynamics are really the quality of the music and not an effect to be superimposed, dynamics should be approached from the initial reading of the composition as they relate to phrasing.

   i. When the group sings under pitch on a soft passage, ask singers to sing the phrase loudly; then, feeling just as much energy and support, sing the phrase again with only a small fraction of the sound.

   j. In polyphonic sections, let all singers become familiar with each line and realize both the lines' independence and their interrelationships. This can be achieved both aurally and visually. While the conductor may wish to avoid lengthy lectures, he or she can guide the singers in their discoveries during the rehearsal and make appropriate observations that will clarify or reinforce their discoveries.

   k. In fugal sections, isolate the theme or themes. Be sure singers are familiar with a theme before trying to decorate or vary it.

8. No rehearsal plan should be restrictive. There should always be a possibility for spontaneous creativity. If conditions during a rehearsal provide a stimulus for more productive work in an unexpected direction, the sensitive conductor will digress from the rehearsal plan and take advantage of an opportunity to pursue another avenue.

Long-Range Planning

Long-range goals can result in rehearsal planning that ensures growth and progress in goal-directed and sequenced rehearsals. A conductor first identifies goals for the choral ensemble under his or her direction. He or she considers advancing musical skills of singers (vocal, aural, and visual); providing experiences with choral literature that can open doors to further musical understanding; and preparing for public performance repertory that is exciting and pleasurable for both singers and audiences.

A conductor is well advised to compose an extensive list of musical selections that are appropriate for a particular ensemble. The list should include works through which choir members can be guided in their understanding of the music—its ability to convey a mood, its structural elements, and its style. The conductor will then examine the list for breadth, depth, and completeness. From this list, performance programs can be planned. These public programs or concerts should be spaced in such a way that adequate time can be devoted to their preparation, while still allowing the choral ensemble time for a broad acquaintance with repertory selections that are not to be included on performance programs. Limiting the choir to repertory that is to be polished and performed publicly can hinder maximum musical growth.

When a program date has been determined, it is well to plot rehearsals back from that date to ensure adequate preparation time. If some of the program selections are more difficult than others, or if more time is needed for the choir to feel "comfortable" with the music, those selections can be introduced earlier than others. The conductor must be realistic in planning preparation time, and should sketch out the work to be accomplished and the time to be allocated in each rehearsal leading up to performance. Adjustments may need to be made in the extended preparation schedule, but a long-range plan can contribute substantially to the comfort and the quality of program preparation.

If instrumentalists are to be included among performing forces for a particular program, it is imperative that the choral ensemble have adequate rehearsal time scheduled with those instrumentalists. Ideally, the first rehearsal of combined forces will take place when the chorus has the music learned but has not yet begun polishing. This gives all performers a feeling for the desired texture and balance. Prior to this first rehearsal of combined forces, it is advisable for the conductor to schedule at least one rehearsal with the instrumental ensemble alone. This way, instrumentalists can be assisted in matters of phrasing and interpretation while valuable rehearsal time is conserved and utilized for more productive work during the combined rehearsal. As a result of the early scheduling of this first combined rehearsal, the conductor will be better able to assess the number of such rehearsals required to bring the work up to the desired performance level. For professional instrumentalists, a final dress rehearsal with all forces present should suffice.

Rehearsals with Instruments

Music that involves both choral and instrumental timbres requires special preparation and rehearsal planning. A conductor will find it advisable to follow several suggestions.

Check all parts (vocal and instrumental) for agreement on rehearsal letters or numbers. If markings are different, re-mark for rehearsal convenience. Study the score meticulously to ascertain relationships of instrumental parts to each other and to vocal parts; and melodic interest in instrumental parts. (Whenever bowings are called for, mark parts ahead of rehearsal time. If knowledge of bowings is insufficient, consult a reputable authority.)

Be sure choral parts are secure before attempting to combine voices with instruments. Rehearse instruments alone before combining instruments and voices.

Observe principles of efficient rehearsal procedure. Be sure to begin rehearsal on time, conduct with clearly defined gesture, keep steady tempo, time preparatory indication with care, be aware of balance among musical lines, give attention to cues and appropriate encouragement of solo lines, make verbal instruction clear and concise, and end rehearsal on time. Whenever possible, schedule at least two full rehearsals when voices and instruments are to be combined.

When rehearsal time is limited, conduct the entire work or an entire movement so that all performers experience continuity before concentrating on specific sections or problems. Some difficulties can be self-correcting after the all-encompassing musical idea has been grasped by performers. After isolating and working on specific problems, put those sections back into the context of the music for reinforcement and continuity.

In planning for rehearsals of extended works in which certain instruments are utilized in only a few of the movements or sections (for example, trumpets and tympani), rehearse first the parts of the music in which *all* instruments are needed. Rehearse in succession the movments in which the greater number of instrumentalists perform. Whenever instrumentalists (or soloists) have completed rehearsal of all music in which they perform, dismiss those musicians. The final rehearsal combining instruments and voices should move logically from the beginning to the end of the work.

FOCUS IN REHEARSAL PLANNING

Principal and secondary objectives for a rehearsal are determined in response to the maturity level of chorus members.

Children's Choirs

A major concern in the children's chorus is with the development of attitudes of aesthetic singing—attitudes toward music. There must be developed a feeling for phrases and a recognition of a pleasing sound. Basic to this achievement is a primary emphasis upon *hearing*—the development of the ear. If the child is to learn to listen, a favorable climate for listening must be established and maintained. A teacher or a director of a children's chorus keeps this objective uppermost in his or her thinking and guides students in their listening. In each rehearsal, attention is focused upon listening for movement, rhythmic patterns, melody, exact intervals, and harmony—but not simultaneously. Children can be guided to sing a melodic line expressively and in tune.

A secondary emphasis in the children's chorus rehearsal is upon the development of the voice. There should be exercises to ensure flexibility and reasonable extension of the range. In young children, range is limited. Care must be taken to avoid repertory that calls for vocal tessitura exceeding range capability achieved. The children's chorus will usually be able to sing selections for treble voices within the staff. To ensure each child's singing throughout the voice range, it is advisable that he or she not be assigned to sing the same vocal part consistently, but be given experience singing each part at some time during a rehearsal. This will ensure full range development, and help all singers learn the music thoroughly. It may also avoid an unfortunate connotation of a second part's being less important or desirable than the upper soprano line.

Young voices must not be pushed; demands for a big sound can be injurious. Singing that is neither restricting nor constricted will result in vocal freedom essential for fluidity of expression. On the other hand, singing should be projected, natural, and animated. This might be described as controlled enthusiasm on the part of singers. It is important to relate diction to speech. However, since many children have not developed clear speech habits, the conductor will need to plan in the rehearsal for exercises that assist children to speak words clearly.

In selecting repertory for the children's chorus, a conductor should consider that music of superior quality facilitates vocal and musical growth. Also, a repertory of folksongs and uncomplicated composed songs can be expressed effectively through the clear sound of young, treble voices. A variety of music in a rehearsal can contribute to musical development of singers. (See Appendix D.) There should be both *a cappella* and accompanied works; songs that lend themselves to satisfying unison performance through which all singers express the melodic ideas as artistically as possible; contrapuntal music (rounds and canons) to assist in the development of vocal independence; and literature that is homophonic and through which children can develop the ability to sing harmony in tune and in balance.

The greater part of the children's choir rehearsal should be devoted to singing the music and to listening for those aspects of the music designated by the conductor. Some games or drills involving hearing and singing specific intervals and rhythmic patterns can contribute substantially to musical growth. (See Chapter 6.)

Each rehearsal of the children's chorus should provide an opportunity for the chorus to sing at least one song at sight. When music chosen for reading is within the chorus members' range and capability, young singers can feel genuine success in singing it for the first time. When rehearsals begin and end with musical activities in which chorus members feel confident, the children associate rehearsals with the joy of singing. Everything that is sung—from the simplest, shortest phrase through entire musical compositions—should be performed with attention to artistic phrasing and an awareness of the feeling or mood indicated by text and musical setting. (See Chapters 3 and 6.)

Adolescent Choirs

As voices begin to change, the emphasis will be upon gaining control of the "new" voice. During this period of vocal change, singers can be divided into choruses of treble voices and groups of changing and changed voices. In these arrangements, the conductor will be able to focus attention upon the vocal development of each group of adolescents encountering similar problems. That portion of a rehearsal which focuses upon development of the voice is especially important when singers are less experienced and are learning vocal control.

During the period of vocal change, selection of appropriate repertory is crucial. The quality of the musical settings may be of secondary importance, because the primary emphasis must be upon selecting or arranging music so that the various vocal lines fit the limited ranges of the particular groups. Choral directors who are adept in arranging and rearranging the music can accommodate the changing voice. Singing parts accurately while voices are in a state of flux becomes a primary focus of rehearsals. Boys whose voices are changing can become fascinated with their sound and vocal development. Solid, basic harmonies sung well in tune can be an exciting source of personal satisfaction for those undergoing vocal change.

Rehearsals for adolescent choruses should be planned with consideration for the short attention spans characteristic of this age. After about forty-five minutes, the effectiveness of the rehearsal will diminish perceptibly. During a rehearsal of adolescent singers, the focus upon musical activity must change frequently. Cues for this needed change can be observed readily in the singers and can prompt the conductor to alternate physical movement and listening with the singing itself. Enjoyment of participation in singing is a continuing primary objective.

Adult Choirs

In choirs of more advanced singers, the primary emphasis is usually upon repertory. Progress toward goals of continuing vocal, aural, and musical development can be furthered through work on thoughtfully selected repertory. This does not imply that vocalization is unnecessary. Rehearsal time utilized for vocalization can be productive in the continuing development of singers' ears and choral instruments. The proportion of rehearsal time planned for vocalization may diminish as singers become more advanced and better able to control their individual vocal artistry. The purpose of technical development is to perform and express musical ideas artistically. As singers advance, work on technique can be related continually to the music itself. The literature can and should provide motivation for the development of technique that is necessary for its artistic performance. (See Chapter 3.)

Church Choir Rehearsals: Special Considerations

Unique among choirs are those that have direct responsibilities to services of worship—the church choirs. The primary focus of each choir is upon contributing in an artistic way to a well-planned and coordinated service of worship. Church choirs are continually preparing music for a performance that is imminent: services of worship occur weekly. And many church choirs comprise persons of various ages as well as disparate musical backgrounds and vocal capabilities.

Each of these conditions creates special responsibilities for the church choir director. To achieve maximum effectiveness, he or she must exercise a high degree of organizational ability. The director must

> Develop a broad knowledge of sacred repertory with special consideration for the text.
> Engage in a never-ending search for music that can be an effective part of a service of worship, with concern for both music and text.
> Consult well in advance with the clergyman who has a plan for the nonmusical portion of the service of worship.
> Select the most appropriate music that can fit into and enhance a particular service.
> Plan rehearsals in such a manner that he or she is ahead constantly. This includes polishing selections for the most immediate service of worship; working on music that will be a part of the following week's service; and introducing (reading) the music for services two and three weeks hence.

The church choir director must be aware of the need to use time advantageously. The musical result depends on planning a rehearsal carefully, beginning promptly, generating momentum effectively, and pacing rehearsals sensitively.

Communication skills are essential for a successful church choir director. These will permit him or her to attract singers to the choir; inspire the singers to give their best efforts; and articulate and clarify the function of the church choir as it relates to the service of worship.

The concept of expressing prayer and praise through music *for* a congregation differs from the more frequent concept of preparing a concert and performing *to* an audience. The appropriate focus within the setting of worship can be a most effective motivating factor.

Church choir members usually feel the need for some socializing. Unless provision is made for this, the socializing need may manifest itself through distracting behavior during the rehearsal or a feeling that the choir rehearsal atmosphere is cold and impersonal. The astute church choir director will organize the choir through officers or responsible members who can arrange for social opportunities following rehearsals or during breaks in long rehearsals.

The church choir director will realize a marvelous opportunity to build a sensitive instrument that can perform fine sacred choral repertory in an effective setting. The best possible repertory, selected for its appropriateness in relation to the message and the mood of each service, can enhance the experience. A form suggested for collecting and conserving information especially useful to the church choir director appears in Appendix B.

MODELS FOR REHEARSAL PLANNING

The format selected for a written rehearsal plan should reflect the type of rehearsal, the maturity of singers, and the experience of the conductor. Two suggested models follow. A novice conductor will find it advantageous to adopt a format similar to Model I to facilitate planning. An experienced conductor who plans a rehearsal for more capable singers will discover that his or her written plan can be comparatively succinct, as illustrated by Model II. The first of the two models is one that can be beneficial for the relatively inexperienced conductor who plans a rehearsal for adolescent singers. The second model can be adapted for church choir rehearsals of adult singers.

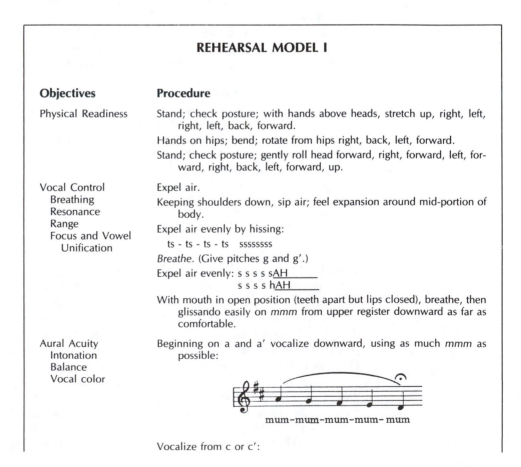

REHEARSAL MODEL I

Objectives	Procedure
Physical Readiness	Stand; check posture; with hands above heads, stretch up, right, left, right, left, back, forward. Hands on hips; bend; rotate from hips right, back, left, forward. Stand; check posture; gently roll head forward, right, forward, left, forward, right, back, left, forward, up.

Vocal Control
  Breathing
  Resonance
  Range
  Focus and Vowel
    Unification
	Expel air.
	Keeping shoulders down, sip air; feel expansion around mid-portion of body.
	Expel air evenly by hissing:
	  ts - ts - ts - ts sssssss
	Breathe. (Give pitches g and g'.)
	Expel air evenly: s s s s sAH_____
	           s s s s hAH_____
	With mouth in open position (teeth apart but lips closed), breathe, then glissando easily on *mmm* from upper register downward as far as comfortable.

Aural Acuity
  Intonation
  Balance
  Vocal color
	Beginning on a and a' vocalize downward, using as much *mmm* as possible:

mum-mum-mum-mum-mum

Vocalize from c or c':

Objectives (cont.)   **Procedure** (cont.)

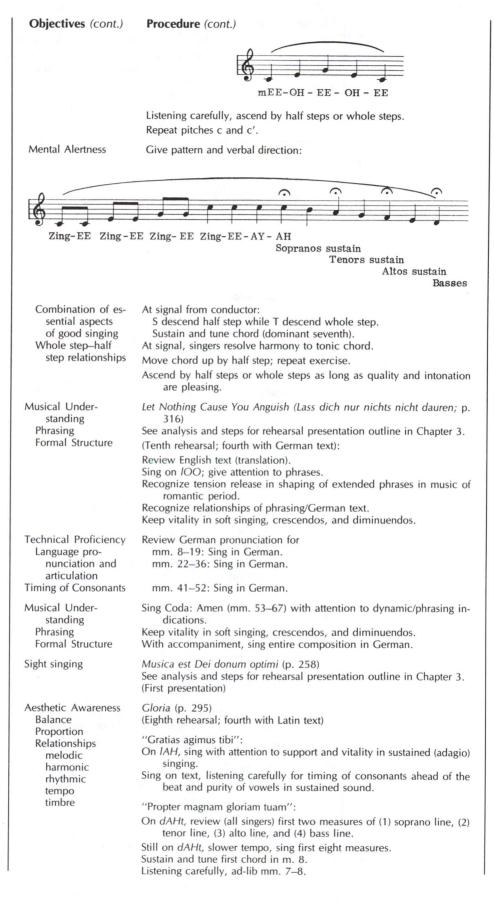

mEE – OH – EE – OH – EE

Listening carefully, ascend by half steps or whole steps.
Repeat pitches c and c'.

Mental Alertness   Give pattern and verbal direction:

Zing-EE Zing-EE Zing- EE Zing-EE-AY- AH

Sopranos sustain
Tenors sustain
Altos sustain
Basses

Combination of es-
sential aspects
of good singing
Whole step–half
step relationships

At signal from conductor:
  S descend half step while T descend whole step.
  Sustain and tune chord (dominant seventh).
At signal, singers resolve harmony to tonic chord.
Move chord up by half step; repeat exercise.
Ascend by half steps or whole steps as long as quality and intonation
  are pleasing.

Musical Under-
standing
Phrasing
Formal Structure

Let Nothing Cause You Anguish (*Lass dich nur nichts nicht dauren*; p.
  316)
See analysis and steps for rehearsal presentation outline in Chapter 3.
(Tenth rehearsal; fourth with German text):
Review English text (translation).
Sing on *lOO*; give attention to phrases.
Recognize tension release in shaping of extended phrases in music of
  romantic period.
Recognize relationships of phrasing/German text.
Keep vitality in soft singing, crescendos, and diminuendos.

Technical Proficiency
Language pro-
nunciation and
articulation
Timing of Consonants

Review German pronunciation for
  mm. 8–19: Sing in German.
  mm. 22–36: Sing in German.

  mm. 41–52: Sing in German.

Musical Under-
standing
Phrasing
Formal Structure

Sing Coda: Amen (mm. 53–67) with attention to dynamic/phrasing in-
  dications.
Keep vitality in soft singing, crescendos, and diminuendos.
With accompaniment, sing entire composition in German.

Sight singing

Musica est Dei donum optimi (p. 258)
See analysis and steps for rehearsal presentation outline in Chapter 3.
(First presentation)

Aesthetic Awareness
Balance
Proportion
Relationships
  melodic
  harmonic
  rhythmic
  tempo
  timbre

Gloria (p. 295)
(Eighth rehearsal; fourth with Latin text)

"Gratias agimus tibi":
On *lAH*, sing with attention to support and vitality in sustained (adagio)
  singing.
Sing on text, listening carefully for timing of consonants ahead of the
  beat and purity of vowels in sustained sound.

"Propter magnam gloriam tuam":
On *dAHt*, review (all singers) first two measures of (1) soprano line, (2)
  tenor line, (3) alto line, and (4) bass line.
Still on *dAHt*, slower tempo, sing first eight measures.
Sustain and tune first chord in m. 8.
Listening carefully, ad-lib mm. 7–8.

Objectives *(cont.)*   **Procedure** *(cont.)*

Begin m. 8—S and B to m. 12; A and T to end.

Begin m. 12—B and S to end; A and S to end.

From beginning (still on *dAHt* at slow tempo) sing parts and *listen for* each entrance and clarity of all moving parts.

Sing on text at slower tempo.

Begin with "Gratias agimus tibi" and continue through "Propter magnam gloriam tuam" with attention to proper tempo relationships.

REHEARSAL MODEL II

Vocalization

Stand, stretch, turn to right, massage shoulders of neighbor in front; "chops" along spine.

Turn 180 degrees; massage shoulders of neighbor; "chops."

Basses and Altos on c and c'; Tenors and Sopranos on c' and c''.

Listening carefully, and following director's indication, B and A ascend diatonically on *IAH* while T and S descend diatonically on *IAH*. Sustain octave and breathe.

Repeat tonic pitch; B and A descend chromatically while T and S ascend chromatically. Tune each pitch; hold final pitch.

Pitches for chord; d, a, f♯', d''.

On *dOH*, prepare with breath as for *ff*; begin *pp*; crescendo over 8 counts; diminish over 8 counts.

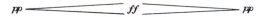

Raise pitch a half step and repeat on *dEE*, crescendoing over 10 counts and diminishing over 10 counts.

Raise pitch a half step and repeat on *dAH*, crescendoing over 12 counts and diminishing over 12 counts.

"Jesu, Priceless Treasure" (first verse as prayer response): Music for Class Study and Conducting, p. 116

On *dAHt*, sing on eighth-note pulse.

Feeling eighth-note pulse, sing as written on *lOO*; listen carefully; bring out moving parts.

Sing *a cappella* on text.

"Anthem of Thanksgiving" (second anthem for next Sunday's service—second rehearsal): Music for Class Study and Conducting, p. 297.

Suggestions for rehearsal procedure appear in Chapter 3, page 94.

"How Excellent Thy Name/Hallelujah!" (principal anthem for next Sunday—third rehearsal): Music for Class Study and Conducting, p. 289.

Suggestions for rehearsal procedure appear in Chapter 3, page 90.

"Let Nothing Cause You Anguish" (for service one week ahead—second rehearsal): Music for Class Study and Conducting, p. 316.

Suggestions for rehearsal procedure appear in Chapter 3, page 97.

"The Lord to Me a Shepherd Is" (for service two weeks ahead—if time permits): Music for Class Study and Conducting, p. 346

> Read on neutral syllables: *dAHt* for eighth notes and *dEEt* for sixteenth notes. For all notes longer than eighth notes, sing on eighth-note pulse. Repeat if advisable.

> Sing on text.

"How Excellent Thy Name/Hallelujah!"

> Review as if in performance.

Chapter 5

Developing the Choral Instrument

Instrumentalists who perform in a high school band or orchestra have usually received several years of training with a private teacher. Many instrumentalists continue lessons while participating in ensembles. This is rarely true with a choral singer. Since voices do not reach a maturity level to warrant serious study until age sixteen to eighteen, the majority of youthful singers receive basic training and establish their singing habits under the guidance of a choral director. For this reason, directors of choirs comprising children and youth bear a tremendous responsibility for their future singing. They need to be well qualified to provide developing singers with competent instruction. Conductors who have not studied singing with an experienced voice teacher are rarely qualified to accept this responsibility.

The suggestions that follow are not a substitute for private singing instruction. A singer with basic skills will find here a methodology evolved through years of experience in working with young voices. This methodology will prove helpful to the inexperienced conductor and provide a stimulus to others by clarifying the vocal process as it is applied to the choral instrument. A practical approach with few technical terms is effective in teaching vocal principles to amateur choirs with limited rehearsal time. The procedures in this chapter need to be adapted wisely to the age group and the previous singing experience of each ensemble. The director may be assured that the result of his or her efforts will be commensurate with an understanding of vocal principles. Although a conductor's singing voice may serve to illustrate a desirable tone quality for a choir, such an example is not a substitute for understanding the teaching process or for the ability to hear and recognize vocal problems and to solve them effectively.

The singing voice is a musical instrument with controllable pitch, duration, intensity, and timbre. Unlike instruments for which one tone quality is considered to be ideal, the human voice is capable of producing a variety of tone colors through vowels, consonants, changes of timbre, and other expressive sounds derived from text. The singer, whether singing alone or with an ensemble, expresses not only music but also drama and poetry. Pablo Casals, one of the world's great cellists, said:

> . . . each musician must learn to play, on the one hand, as if he were a soloist, and on the other, with the constant awareness of being an indispensable part of a team.

Through teamwork a well-trained ensemble singer contributes to a greater musical entity; a singer may realize the capability to offer much more of herself or himself, both emotionally and vocally, as a choir member than as a soloist.

Singing may be likened to playing an instrument, and many of the fundamentals are similar. Each shares the following elements: a generator, a vibrator, a resonator, and an articulator. A French horn player supplies breath to generate a tone, his lips serve as a vibrator, the bore and bell of the instrument become resonators, and the valves and the tongue provide articulators. Singing requires the same components: Wind, supplied by the lungs, supported and managed by the intercostal muscles and the diaphragm, acts as a generator; the vocal folds (also called vocal cords) act as vibrator; the nasopharynx, mouth, and larynx serve as resonators; and the tongue, soft and hard palates, lips, and teeth all serve as articulators. A choral conductor's awareness of these basic elements and their proper functioning in the singing process is essential to developing a choral instrument that will produce beautiful music. Let us consider the elements in more detail as we relate them to principles of choral development and suggest methods of procedure.

THE PHYSIOLOGY OF THE SINGING PROCESS

Breath Management

The term breath *management* is more accurate than breath *control,* since it implies freedom rather than restriction in initiating and supplying breath for singing. The student's first step is to inhale and exhale efficiently. Both actions are controlled consciously at first; later, after practice, they become automatic. Breath management is not limited to respiration, however; the singer becomes aware of a breath connection from the initial beginning of the tone (phonation) to the completion of a musical phrase. Such a breath connection demands a posture that readies the vocal instrument for singing. The body is erect and alert but not tense, the throat and articulators are free to move, and the breathing apparatus is relaxed but operable from the center of the body.

The coordination of breath intake and phonation and the awareness of a breath connection are the first steps in developing a proper relationship between the breath generator and the larynx vibrator (vocal folds) for the singer. After establishing posture, the student is ready to concentrate on diaphragmatic-intercostal breathing. Exercises to develop the process without phonation can be minimal: Five minutes, three or four times a day, will be sufficient to master lower, intercostal breathing. Members of the choir may be encouraged to do this on their own. Little progress will be made until the raising of chest and shoulders in the act of breathing is eliminated.

Breathing that allows for expansion of the lower back ribs provides ample space for the diaphragm to function freely and give support to the tone. As breath is exhaled, the ribs will resist as long as possible the tendency to collapse. It is important that abdominal muscles not be tensed during respiration. The chest remains comfortably high and in place with shoulders relaxed. An illustration showing the position of lungs, sternum (center of the chest), lower ribs, intercostal muscles, and diaphragm is seen in Figure 5-1.

Phonation

The act of uttering vocal sounds is called *phonation;* it is the coordination between breath and the vocal folds located in the larynx. A balance of breath pressure, with firmness but not tension in the larynx, is necessary. A proper breath lowers the larynx into a position where the breath flow causes the vocal folds to vibrate freely. A sustained note preceded by several repeated staccato tones will aid the beginning singer in sensing the breath connection and proper phonation. From open vowels (**AH** and **OH**), the singer will progress to closed vowels. He or she will develop an awareness of a vowel stream, when each vowel progresses smoothly from one to the other, maintaining the breath connection.

The basic vowels in English are **AH, AY, EE, OH,** and **OO**. Although there are intermediate variations, these are referred to as *pure* vowels and compare closely to the five vowels in Latin, the parent language of English. For this reason the singing of Latin motets aids in developing a pleasing tone quality.[1] Elimination of intermediate vowels and the near-absence of diphthongs in Latin pronunciation provide an opportunity for a choir to place full concentration on pure vowels that we refer to as the *vowel stream.*

Taking a proper breath causes the larynx to lower itself into a position where the breath flow activates vibration of the vocal folds; a yawn-sigh exercise can help establish this coordination. A gentle half-yawn lowers the larynx on inhalation; the sigh gives the necessary feeling of pouring the breath into the tone (breath flow) without tension. At first the beginner may establish this coor-

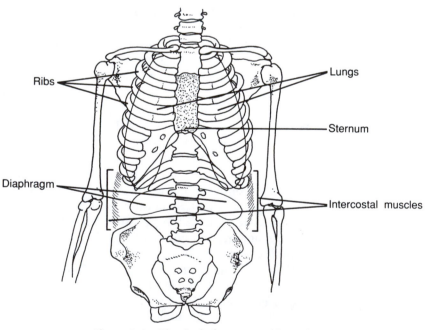

Figure 5-1   Physical elements of breathing.

[1]See Appendix C for a guide to Latin pronunciation.

dination more easily by using the speaking voice. Beginning on a comfortable high pitch, let the voice descend portamento as it speaks with some abandon: "Wh**AH**———t-a be**OO**-tiful day." Sighing on a descending **AH** vowel, keep the speaking voice light and clear in quality and avoid breathiness. When this concept feels comfortable, the singer may repeat the exercise with descending pitches. He or she may begin again on high, light tones (in falsetto range) after a proper breath, and descend portamento to the lower range, ending with a clear, sustained tone on **AH**. This coordination of breath with the larynx is a basic approach to proper phonation.

After sensing the breath flow and a lower position of the larynx, the yawn-sigh concept, the singer may extend this coordination by adding staccato exercises to establish firmness (not tension) in the larynx. He may produce four staccato tones on a random pitch slightly above speaking level using an open vowel, **AH** or **OH**. The staccato tones are followed by a sustained tone on a designated pitch. After freedom and coordination between breath and tone are established in the speaking voice, the concept may be carried into exercises on definite pitches. Alternating the open vowels **OH** and **AH** with minimal jaw movement can be helpful. Suggested exercises appear in the final section of this chapter.

As clear, open, free tones are experienced on staccato repetitions followed by sustained **OH** or **AH**, a student progresses to closed vowels, **EE** and **AY**, keeping in mind the breath connection and developing a sense of the vowel stream. Confidence in singing higher tones will grow as these exercises are combined with employment of lighter texture in the upper range. Practicing yawn-sigh exercises on descending portamentos, arpeggios, and scale passages will encourage this. During practice sessions it is important that there be frequent reference to proper posture, the breath connection, and enunciation. The singer endeavors to sense tone flowing on breath, yet avoiding breathiness.

Resonance and Amplification

Most voice teachers agree that the nasopharynx (area behind and above the soft palate), the mouth, and the throat are the chief resonators for the human voice. (See Figure 5-2.) While one does not want to hear unnaturally "mature" sounds coming from youthful singers, high school choirs improve tone quality when members carry the *half-yawn* feeling into pronunciation of the **AH** and **OH** vowels. (It should be mentioned that the **OO** progresses from the **OH** vowel and should maintain a feeling of openness.)

Encouragement in the employment of resonators in the act of singing may be found through the speaking voice and through the *hum*. Such familiar parallels as "speaking from the stage or pulpit" or "calling to a friend from a distance" will encourage more resonant tone. A comfortably spoken *m-hmm*, as in an affirmative reply, will provide a feeling of vibration in the lips and bone structure of the face (*masque*). The facial area in front of the nasopharynx vibrates sympathetically when humming without tension. Pitch consonants **m** and **n** are aids to this sensation when sung preceding a vowel. For example, the singing of **n**AH on an ascending-descending arpeggio encourages this feeling of resonance in the upper range. A raised soft palate (half-yawn without tension) combined with a sensation of space in the area of the nasopharynx helps to maintain the ringing quality.

Development of falsetto in the male voice is important in freeing and amplifying higher tones. An **EE** or **AY** vowel sung with rounded lips in the falsetto register can usually be produced without effort (with a proper breath connection). Exercises consisting of descending five-tone scales, from falsetto into full

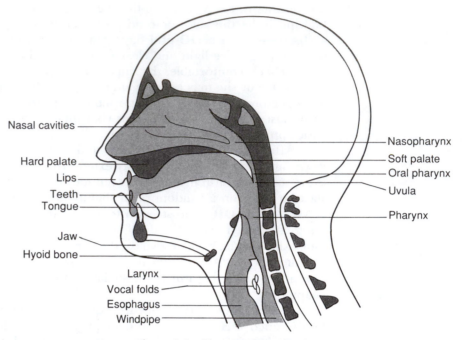

Nasal cavities

Hard palate
Lips
Teeth
Tongue

Jaw
Hyoid bone

Larynx
Vocal folds
Esophagus
Windpipe

Nasopharynx
Soft palate
Oral pharynx
Uvula

Pharynx

Figure 5-2   The vocal mechanism.

voice, may be difficult for a voice in the changing process, but when practiced without forcing, the adjustment becomes easier.[2] The male voice will soon be able to mix the light and heavy registers without a "break." Frequent practice of such exercises will give confidence to both basses and tenors as their vocal ranges are extended.

The speaking voice can encourage resonance in the middle and low ranges. Reciting a text, choir members concentrate on well-enunciated vowels with crisp, clearly pronounced consonants. They may then sing the words in rhythm on a single, sustained pitch. This is especially helpful in eliminating breathiness in lower ranges of bass and alto voices.

Space in the mouth, without forcing the jaw down, is necessary for singing the open vowels (**AH, OH,** and **OO**). Directing the flow of breath to the hard palate increases oral resonance. The tongue remains comfortably on the floor of the mouth when singing open vowels; it is raised in the center and forward (out of the throat) for closed vowels (**EE** and **AY**). It is important that the director remind choir members frequently to check posture and to practice proper breath management and phonation while directing attention to resonation. Improper balance of these elements and the resulting tension will cause forcing of tone and a feeling of fatigue in the throat.

DICTION

Diction in singing requires clarity of both enunciation and articulation. The American Heritage Dictionary of the English language defines these terms as follows:

> *Articulation* refers rather broadly to sound (clarity) and flow (coherence and organization) of speech, whereas *enunciation* refers to sound judged principally on the basis of distinctness of pronunciation.

[2]William A. C. Zerffi, "Male and Female Voices," *A.M.A. Archives of Otolaryngology* (July, 1956), p. 9.

The choral conductor works with a choir for clarity of consonants and purity of vowels, but combines this with an insistence on proper word stress and word groupings so that the meaning and the understanding of the text are communicated. Metaphors and word pictures are also important tools in establishing articulation and enunciation.

Uniform pronunciation of vowels coupled with rhythmic timing of diphthongs and consonants is basic to ensemble diction. It is imperative that a conductor make a detailed mental or written (if necessary) analysis of each word and syllable to be sung. First he or she identifies basic primary vowel sounds and determines the portion of the note value to be allowed for each; then he or she concentrates on timing diphthongs and consonants. The conductor apportions time values accurately in such a way that singers are guided in their placement of the second vowel sound of a diphthong or a clear, well-articulated consonant. This placement usually involves eighth- or sixteenth-note values. An important guiding principle relates to tempo: The faster the tempo, the larger will be the proportional time value needed for clarity. The slower the tempo, the smaller will be the fraction of a beat required for placement of the second sound of diphthong or of a consonant.

The choral director who seeks to develop excellence in ensemble singing will find it necessary to master essentials of diction. He or she will refer frequently to a reliable dictionary for accurate meaning and exact pronunciation of words and will teach singers to maintain the integrity of each vowel without anticipating vowel changes or consonant placement.

Vowels: Phonetic Spelling

A concept of vowel uniformity is basic for establishing choral blend. Vowel uniformity must be combined with sameness of pitch in each voice part. After basic vowels are produced consistently, the conductor proceeds to discover various intermediate vowels in text. He or she will isolate the vowel sound within each syllable and insist that the choir listen for uniform pronunciation as singers sustain the vowel on a single pitch or chord.

In order to maintain beauty of tone and vocal freedom, singers will modify vowels as they proceed into the upper range of the voice. For example, in the high range, an **EE** vowel will be modified to **IH** (short *i* as in *hit*), **AY** to **EH** (as in *met*), and **AH** to **UH** or **AU** (as in *taught*). A diagram of the Vowel Triangle illustrates evolution of the vowel stream from a closed **EE** through an open **AH** to the **OO**. (See Figure 5-3.)

Although the International Phonetic Alphabet (IPA) offers symbols for exact sounds in all languages, a simplified version of phonetic spelling may be a more practical approach for teaching the average choir. Concepts of vowel and diphthong pronunciation will be improved as the choir observes and practices each primary and secondary vowel sound illustrated on the Vowel Triangle diagram (Figure 5-3).

The *Schwa* (ə) and Unaccented Short *i* (ɪ) Vowels

The Vowel Triangle chart includes phonetic spelling, the equivalent International Phonetic Alphabet symbols, and familiar words that illustrate each vowel. There are two vowel sounds in English that are difficult to spell phonetically; it is more effective to refer to them by their phonetic symbols: the **-er** sound in fa-th**er** (ə) and the **de** sound in unaccented syllables of words like **de**-scend (dɪ-sEH-nd) are examples. Treatment of the American **r** is discussed later.

The *schwa,* or neutral vowel (ə), is found in such words as *father* (FAH-

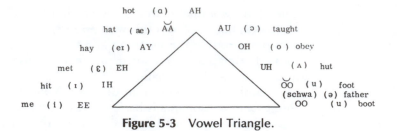

Figure 5-3 Vowel Triangle.

thə), *winter* (wIHn-tə), *ruler* (rOO-lə), *heaven* hEH-vən), *nativity* (nə-tUH-və-tɪ), and *nation* (nAY-shən). The unaccented short **i** (ɪ) vowel is sometimes spelled **y** as in *worthy* (wOǑ-rthɪ). In the dictionary, phonetic spelling should be observed in such words as *demand* (dɪ-mÃAnd), *rejoice* (rɪ-jAUɪs), and *descend* (dɪ-sEHnd).

One may discover from these examples that unaccented syllables in English are usually pronounced with unstressed, modified vowel sounds. There are certain exceptions in singing, however. If the note value for an unaccented syllable is lengthened, or if the syllable is sung on more than one pitch, the stressed vowel pronunciation is preferred (Example 5-1). Frequent reference to a standard dictionary will enlighten a conductor concerning the frequency with which both the *schwa* and the unaccented short **i** vowels are appropriate in English when they approximate the timing of speech.

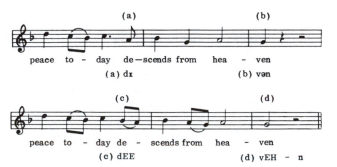

Example 5-1 Pronunciation of long or short vowels:[3] (a) only one short note to a syllable; (b) final, unaccented syllable having shorter note value; (c) more than one note to a syllable; (d) final, unaccented syllable sustained.

Diphthongs

English, unlike the Romance languages, has many speech sounds that begin with one vowel sound and move to another vowel, or semivowel, within the same syllable. Primary vowels in English are **e, a, i, o, u** (and sometimes **y** and **w**). Of these, only the **EE** is pronounced without a semivowel (or glide). The vowels **a, i,** and **o** are diphthongs employing two vowel sounds; they are spelled phonetically: *EH*ɪ, *AH*ɪ, and *OH*oo. The letter **U** is pronounced y**OO** with a glide, or semivowel (**y**) that is pronounced quickly before the **OO**. Other common diphthongs occurring within syllables include **OY**, as in *toy* (tAUɪ) or *boy* (b**AU**ɪ)**,** and **OW**, as in *how* (h**AH**oo). There are a few triphthongs (three sounds in the same syllable). Examples are *fire* (f**AH**ɪə), *yea* (y**EH**ɪ)**,** and *wow* (**ooAHoo**). Examples of diphthongs and triphthongs are given here to emphasize the importance of prolonging the principal vowel sound in singing. The

[3]Example adapted from Alessandro Grandi's *Peace Today Descends from Heaven.* See Music for Class Study and Conducting.

glide, or semivowel, in a diphthong or triphthong, like most consonants, is sung distinctly and quickly at all tempos.

Consonants

Clarity of consonants is important in communication of text. Purity of vowels and legato singing are basic to creation of beautiful sound, but the meaning of text is lost without hearing consonants. Enunciation also has an important bearing on vocal freedom in singing. The singing process is aided when jaw and tongue are not tense but function freely and independently of each other. Calling a choir's attention to similarities in articulation of parallel consonants is helpful. Listed in Figure 5-4 are consonants that employ the same articulators (tongue, lips, soft and hard palates) but differ from each other in that one is given pitch (voiced) and the other, its parallel, is without pitch (voiceless). Exercises to increase singers' awareness of these similarities and differences are included in the developmental exercises provided at the conclusion of this chapter. Consonants without parallels exact more time for pronunciation (except for **r, y,** and **h**). See Figure 5-5.

Since all vowels are sung *on* the beat, voiced (or pitch) consonants **l, m, n,** and **ng** exact a greater proportion of their rhythmic value from the *preceding* pulse than do other voiced consonants. To gain uniformity in enunciation of **l, m, n,** and **ng,** it is necessary to assign specific time values. In a slow tempo these consonants receive a longer time value than in a fast tempo. In contrast, and without exception, unvoiced consonants are sung quickly, like grace notes, when preceding a vowel.

Rhythmic Timing of Consonants and Diphthongs

Basic rules may be applied to obtain clarity of diction without disturbing the vowel flow within a legato phrase. These rules affect timing of consonants and diphthongs.

> Vowels are prolonged without changing and without losing their integrity for as long as possible within the prescribed rhythmic value of a word syllable. The same may be said of the primary vowel in a diphthong.
>
> Vowels are sounded precisely on the rhythmic pulse of the music and on the pitch

Voiced	Unvoiced
b (bad)	**p** (pad)
g (bag)	**c, ck, k, qu** (back)
d (bad)	**t** (bat)
v (very)	**f** (fairy)
j (joke)	**ch, tch** (choke)
gg (eggs)	**x, cks, ks** (extra)
th (then)	**th** (thin)
z (zip)	**s** (sip)
z (azure)	**sh** (shore)
w (wee)	**wh** (wheel)

Figure 5-4   Parallel consonants.

l, m, n, ng, r, y, and **h**

Figure 5-5   Consonants without parallels.

for which the word or the syllable is designated. (Avoid sliding to pitches on pitch consonants.)

Vowels are repeated when singing a *melisma* (without disturbing the continuity of line).

Consonants **l, m, n,** and **ng** (pitch consonants) are sung prior to the vowel that follows and take rhythmic value from the preceding vowel. (See Example 5-2, No. 4.)

Example 5-2 Treatment of consonants, glides, and diphthongs.

Consonants and diphthongs that begin with a semivowel (sometimes called glide), as in the words *few* (fy*OO*), *you* (y*OO*), *refute* (rɪ-fy*OO*—t), *fuse* (fy*OO*—z), are sung as grace notes before the pulse. (See Example 5-2, No. 3.)

Diphthongs in which the first vowel is the primary sound require that the semivowel be treated as if it were a consonant and sung as a grace note immediately preceding the consonant or vowel that follows. (Observe placement of consonants in Example 5-2.)

Such phonetic writing may appear complicated at first glance. After careful scrutiny and practice, conductors will be able to observe and analyze subtle microrhythms in consonants and diphthongs that aid in clarifying diction.

The American *r*[4]

Special treatment of the American **r** is important in singing because of its ugly sound when prolonged. To avoid this problem, a conductor may follow the

---

[4]See Madeleine Marshall, *The Singer's Manual of English Diction* (New York: G. Schirmer, 1953), chaps. 4–6.

general rule of lengthening the vowel that precedes the **r** and minimizing the length of the consonant itself. A few additional reminders:[5]

> Omit the **r** in final syllables of words like *father* (f*AH*-thə), *winter* (w*IH*-ntə), *ever* (*EH*-və).
>
> Flip the **r** (one turn of a trilled **r**) in words or syllables beginning with **thr**: **thr**ough, **thr**ong, **thr**ow; and often between two vowels: fo**r** unto, a**r**e in, hu**rr**ah.
>
> There are no American **r**'s in foreign languages. Latin words that need special attention are glo-**r**i-a, te**r**-ra, a-do-**r**a-mus, Ky-**r**i-e. Each is pronounced with a flipped **r**.

Additional Suggestions for Placement of Consonants

In general, when singing in English, place the final consonant of each syllable within a phrase before the first consonant of the syllable that follows. Employing the phonetic writing recommended, a phrase from a Pilkington madrigal appears as follows:[6]

Rest	sweet	nymphs,	let gol-	den	sleep
r*EH*——stsw*EE*——tn*IH*———mfsl*EH*-tg*OH*——ld*EH*——nsl*EE*——
→	←	⟷ →	↔	←

charm	your	star-	bright—	er	eyes.
pch*AH*———rmɪ*ŎO*———rst*AH*———rbr*AH*———ɪt*UH*-r*AH*——ɪz
→	←	→	→	→ →

Pitch consonants on high notes are sung as their parallel consonants (see Figure 5-4), in keeping with a vocal principle that consonants be articulated lightly when singing in the upper range. Sopranos will find this practice to be particularly helpful in maintaining beauty of tone.

A sustained hum will be improved when sopranos and altos sing an **AH** or **OO** *behind* the hum. Male voices find more resonance when they combine the **mm** with both **ng** and **n** in one sound, while placing lips lightly together without tension.

The final consonant of a phrase is executed rhythmically; it either steals time from the final note when the next phrase begins immediately, or is placed on the rest that follows. The treatment selected is determined by the ensuing phrase. If harmony changes, or if only one part begins the following phrase, all parts release together, placing the final consonant before the end of the phrase. (Members of the choir indicate this in their scores by inserting a rest.) If all parts conclude simultaneously at a rest, the final consonant is placed rhythmically on the rest.

SENSITIVITY TO TEXT

Word and Syllable Stress

A contributor to poor diction is the stressing of unaccented syllables. Frequent practice in reading the text aloud, independent of the musical rhythm, is helpful to both director and choir. An example is found in a chorus from Handel's

---

[5]Since midwestern and western speech tend to prolong the American **r**, these suggestions have been found helpful to choirs from these areas; they do not sound "stilted" when sung in chorus.

[6]See Pilkington, "Rest, Sweet Nymphs" in *Music for Class Study and Conducting,* p. 265.

Saul, where a rising melodic line could easily place too much importance on a weak syllable (Example 5-3).

Example 5-3 Avoiding misplaced word stress.

Care must be taken to stress the lower note of *fainting* and to place less-than-normal emphasis on *ing.* Some stress on the first syllable of *courage* is important in order to alleviate undue emphasis caused by the longer note value on the second syllable.

Another possible error in accenting the wrong syllable can be found in a "Hallelujah" passage from *Saul*[7] in this repeated motive:

Example 5-4 Phrasing of paired notes; avoiding accent on final syllable.

It is very easy to "pounce" on the final syllable each time. By stressing the first note in each pair of notes (*le* and *lu*), by remembering the spoken pronunciation of *hallelujah,* and by "easing up" on *jah,* while giving the note its full eighth-note value, a proper balance will be achieved. With careful, imaginative treatment, the text will be clearly understood and the phrase gracefully performed. Diminuendo indications inserted in choral scores will serve as a reminder.

Text and Structure

In Chapter 3 a more extensive survey of structure, tonal relationships, and melodic development is guided. Importance of an awareness of other parts is mentioned in relation to intonation, diction, and ensemble. Consider how this awareness affects proper balance within the choral ensemble when an imitative figure is presented.

Whenever a phrase or a motive, such as a fugue subject, is reiterated in the music, it is important that this phrase or motive be repeated in exactly the same manner in each part: with the same musical and textual stresses, with the same dynamic levels, and in the same tempo. For this reason a conductor makes it very clear to each part exactly how the phrase or motive is to be performed. It is advisable for all singers to practice the fugal subject in unison. This avoids repetition of identical instructions and also focuses everyone's attention on the musical form and objectives.

A familiar example is Handel's *Messiah* chorus "For unto Us a Child Is Born," where all parts may sing the statement of the subject found in the alto line, since it is in a comfortable range for both high and low voices. The conductor will have worked out musical details (including syllabic stresses, rhythmic values, and dynamics) by marking the score as indicated in Example 5-5.

[7]See Handel's "How Excellent Thy Name" (*Saul*) in Music for Class Study and Conducting, p. 289.

Example 5-5   Marking a fugal subject.

After marking the score, a conductor determines a procedure.

Following a positive entrance with a crisp ''f'' and a short *messa di voce* (< >)
on the opening word *For,* the **r** is flipped lightly between the two vowels (Fo**r** unto).
The phrase proceeds with a slight crescendo to *born* (avoiding a ''w'' before *us*). At
this point, the first of two eighth notes is stressed, and there is a sudden diminuendo
(>) on *born* while **r** (bo**r**n) is minimized and the **n** is voiced at the rest.

The **n** of *unto* takes half the value of the eighth note and the vowel **UH** of *us* gets a
full beat; the **s** is placed lightly on the rest that follows.

The **S** in *a Son* is pronounced precisely (not hissed), and the **n** again gets half the value
of the eighth note. The **s** of *is* is pronounced as **z** and a very slight *schwa* (ə) is inserted
immediately before the **g** of *given* (before the beat).

There is stress on the first syllable of *given* and a diminuendo on the second (>).
A mute **e** (ə) will help establish the diminuendo.

A similar approach to diction and dynamics is taken as the motive is repeated in each
voice part.

Text-Timbre Relationships

A choir's sensitivity to the mood of a text is reflected in the tone color of an
ensemble. A happy madrigal with a *fa-la* refrain is a typical example of a choral
composition identified as having a bright tone quality. Conversely, such bright-
ness of tone is inappropriate for the music and text found in Handel's "For
Sion Lamentations Make." This chorus, from the oratorio *Judas Maccabaeus*,
represents the people of Israel as they lament the death of their leader. Here
the desired tone quality is dark and warm in contrast to that of the madrigal.
In similar manner you may also compare "Deck the Halls" (in $\frac{7}{8}$), a lively, happy
Christmas carol, with the somber "Let Nothing Cause You Anguish" by
Brahms.

Some vocal techniques that are applicable to the creation of bright and
dark tones include the singing of *fa-la-la*s with an exaggerated enunciation of
the **f** and the **l**, formed in the front of the mouth by the lower lip against the
upper front teeth (f**AH**) with tip of the tongue touching the back of the upper
front teeth (l**AH**). Jaw movement should be minimized; the **AH**s will then tend
to be bright and forward; the quality of tone will serve also as a model for the
remaining text.

Although a stimulated imagination is of utmost importance in creating
both mood and tone quality, the vocal approach may enhance the effectiveness.
For a contrasting dark, warm tone appropriate in the Brahms motet, the singers should "round" the lips slightly when singing such words as *anguish, lan-
guish,* and *tranquil*; a broad **AH** is needed when singing *God* and in the

diphthong of *guide* (gAH-ɪd). *Sorrow* expresses true sadness when the primary vowel is pronounced **AU** or **AW** (sAU-rOH), rather than the brighter pronunciation of sAH-rOH. The final *Amen*, repeated several times, should also be "darkened" to express warmth and feeling as it is sung.

Every song text has a predominant mood, even though it may change slightly from phrase to phrase. Moods are reflected in music by means of tempo, tonality, tessitura, and tone quality. Bright, dark, happy, or sad are only a few of many possible emotions that may be reflected in singers' tone quality. Sacred music reflects moods of praise, reverence, and thanksgiving. Other moods are implied in texts that are humorous, joyous, loving, and hating. Such special events as a coronation, a dedication, or an occasion to honor famous men or women also suggest appropriate moods. Sensitivity to the mood of a given text is central to interpretation of choral music.

The Added Dimension: Communication

Since ensemble singing requires beauty of tone, a clearly enunciated text, and sensitivity to appropriate moods, it is important that each singer have an intelligent understanding of and empathy with both texts and music. Whether the text is in English or in another language, each word represents a mental picture that evokes an emotional response. It has been said that "music takes wings when poetry cannot suffice." The importance of excellent diction that encompasses all the aforementioned qualities cannot be overestimated.

Performance is a cooperative venture, a triumvirate if you will: the composer, the performer, and the listener. None is complete without the other two. Choir and conductor together have a responsibility to transmit all the beauty, empathy, and emotion of a composer's music. The singer's goal is to communicate not merely the text and music but also its meaning, drama, passion, beauty, and lyricism.

THE SINGING PROCESS: A SEQUENCE OF DEVELOPMENTAL EXERCISES

Preparation for Singing: Posture and Physical Movement

1. Standing position
   a. Stand with chest erect, shoulders loose and without stiffness, spine straight.
   b. Balance weight equally on the balls of the feet, with feet 6–8 inches apart, one foot slightly ahead of the other, and knees bent imperceptibly to avoid tension.
   c. Loosen neck muscles by rolling head left, forward, right, forward, left several times to overcome stiffness.
   d. Rotate arms; raise shoulders and release with downward motion to loosen muscles and achieve relaxed position. Repeat several times.
   e. Place the base (insides of wrists) of both hands on cheekbones; draw hands slowly down to the bottom of the jaw while jaw drops open and muscles relax under fingertips.
   f. Bounce gently on tiptoes with knees bent slightly, then rest heels lightly on the floor with weight on the balls of both feet.
2. Sitting position
   a. Sit forward on the front 6 inches of chair with feet firmly planted 6–8 inches apart; be prepared to stand at a moment's notice by placing some weight forward on legs and feet.
   b. Keeping spine straight, sit tall, feel neck and head buoyant without tension.
   c. Hold music with arms comfortably forward and perpendicular to the body, so that music and conductor can easily be seen at the same time.

Breathing and Phonation

Now that the body is alert and ready for singing, here are several exercises to develop low, intercostal-diaphragmatic breathing. These will help to avoid high, clavicular, upper-chest breathing, which is contrary to correct singing procedure.

Exercise 1

a. Recheck posture.
b. Expand the intercostal (lower rib) area as breath is taken.
c. Hold the breath for the count of 10.
d. Counting 10, exhale slowly with steady hissing sound until all air has been expelled.
e. Gradually increase the time allowed for step d from 10 to 30 counts as breathing capacity increases.

Exercise 2

a. Instead of taking a slow, deep breath, take a "surprise breath" quickly (without sound). This will promote a reflex action that best adjusts the throat without tension.
b. Gently put lips together and expel air slowly, without a sound, for as long as possible.

(If some singers are still not able to sense the connection with the natural breathing process, a reference to panting like a dog may help. Such an exercise locates the proper area and, if slowed down, establishes the intercostal-diaphragmatic action necessary for breath management.)

Exercise 3

a. Ask singers to blow out four candles in succession.
b. Follow the four breaths immediately with four **AH**s using the same breath connection. These may be sung on a medium pitch, using an imaginary **h** to initiate the sound.
c. Alternate, four times, blowing out a candle and singing **AH.**
d. After two or three alternations, sustain the vowel **AH,** attempting to maintain the connection with the breath (singing on the breath flow).

Exercise 4

After the preceding coordination is established, proceed to the following:

a. Expel as much air as possible while you drop forward from the waist, head down, with arms extending loosely to about knee-level. Silently count 8 slow counts.
b. Without taking a breath, assume an erect singing posture and wait 8 counts.
c. Now let yourself breathe and immediately sing the vowel **EE** for 8 counts (longer if possible) on a low to medium-range pitch.
d. Exhale the remaining breath as you drop forward, assuming the position described in step a. Continue this entire procedure for as long as possible.

Note: At first you may become slightly dizzy, or "hyperventilated," but you will discover a coordination and a feeling that the breathing process is completely separate from your own conscious control. A sense of proper attack with a low position of the larynx will also be derived from this exercise.

When coordination has been established between breath and beginning of sound (proper phonation), the choir may continue with the staccato exercises that follow.

ADDITIONAL EXERCISES

Exercises for Proper Beginning of Sound (Phonation)

To be transposed up and down in the middle range; avoid extreme high range until voice responds with ease. All exercises to be sung in strict rhythm, with minimal jaw movement, and a quick breath on each rest.

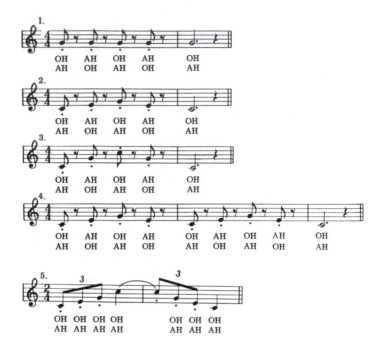

Associating Breath Connection with Vowel Stream

Continue vocalizing in the middle range. In exercises 3 and 4, complete the descending scale of D major.

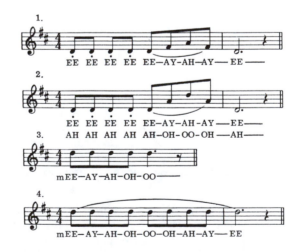

Encouraging Resonation

Exaggerate the voiced consonants, **m** and **ng,** in the syllable *mong* (sung: m**AW**ng). Before singing exercises 3 and 4, speak the *m-hm* as in an affirmative reply. Continue up and down in comfortable range.

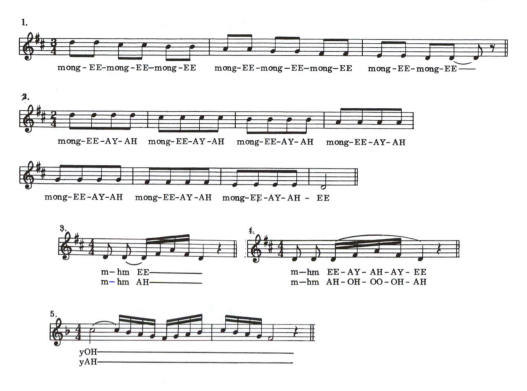

Extending Range

1. Yawn-sigh: Begin without a definite pitch in the high falsetto register with a half-yawn on the vowel **AH;** sigh on a glissando descending to pitches in the lowest register. Repeat from even higher levels several times, with smoothness and continuity.

2. From this sensation of sighing into the tone, sustain the following descending octave arpeggio, keeping the light register until the final note. Continue down by half steps. Sing an **EE** with rounded lips to form the German umlaut **ü**. Sing an **AY** with rounded lips to form the German umlaut **ö**.

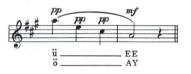

3. The purpose of this exercise is to encourage a covered tone in the transition and in the upper register. Sense a "flipping" into the upper register when singing on **OH** (*pp*) in a light, falsetto tone. The **AH** will then be sung with a mixture of the two registers, keeping a rounded or covered vowel on the highest note.

Developing Vocal Agility

1, 2. Keep vowels firm, yet free. Think a repetition of the vowel on each note of the melisma. Repeat in ascending keys.

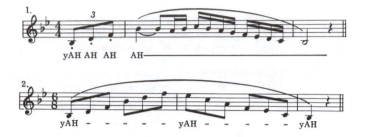

3. Keep rhythm steady; repeat the vowel mentally on each note. Raise by half steps for each repetition. Continue ascent as far as comfortable.

Developing Clarity of Articulation

1. Parallel consonants; to be sung on each note on descending scale in D major. Articulate consonants crisply and distinctly with minimal jaw movement, giving special attention to independent action of tongue and jaw. Complete independence and dexterity of the articulators (tip of tongue, center of tongue, back of tongue, soft palate and lips) are essential for clarity and freedom.

bOH–bAY–bOO–bEE–bAH–bb[8]   pOH–pAY–pOO–pEE–pAH–pp
(Sing firm vowels with loose lips and relaxed jaw.)

gOH–gAY–gOO–gEE–gAH–gg   kOH–kAY–kOO–kEE–kAH–kk
(Sing firm vowels without tension in back of the tongue.)

dOH–dAY–dOO–dEE–dAH–dd   t OH–t AY–t OO–t EE–t AH–t t
(Sing firm vowels with active tip of tongue.)

vOH–vAY–vOO–vEE–vAH–vv   f OH–f AY–f OO–f EE–f AH–ff
(Observe the short, but clear *schwa* vowel at the rest.)

rOH–rAY–rOO–rEE–rAH–rr   rOH–rAY–rOO–rEE–rAH–rr
(Sing flipped **r** until rest; at rest sing a trilled **r**.)

---

[8]Notice that the final consonant is pronounced precisely on the rest.

2. Nonparallel consonants requiring additional time (before the beat) for voicing. Sing on descending D major scale, repeating each syllable sequence; breathe only when needed.

mOH-mAY-mOO-mEE-mAH- mm   mOH-mAY-mOO-mEE-mAH- mm

(Sing with lips lightly together, with humming sensation; keep vowels firm.)

nOH- nAY-nOO- nEE-nAH- nn   nOH-nAY-nOO- nEE-nAH- nn

(Keep tip of tongue active; exaggerate a prolonged **nn**.)

lOH - lAY- lOO - lEE -lAH - ll   lOH -lAY- lOO - lEE -lAH - ll

(With active tip of tongue, prolong **ll**.)

Chapter 6

Developing Musical Skills and Responsiveness

A conductor's ability to communicate musical intentions of composers in an artistic fashion is dependent upon the musical skills and responsiveness of his instrument: the choir. Thus the conductor is concerned with developing the full potential of singers. In addition to consistent work toward vocal beauty and control, a conductor guides singers in their development of acuity of hearing, ability to translate notation into sound, and sensitivity to musical nuance. Capability and sensitivity development can increase satisfaction in future music participation.

One of the exciting aspects of the development of musical talent and potential is that it is never fully accomplished. Any level is only a point on the continuum of development and awareness. The musician has a compelling desire to hear more acutely and to read notation at sight with greater fluency. Both of these capabilities represent skills that can be developed under the guidance of a perceptive and sensitive conductor-teacher. The process can be envisioned as a spiral that has a lifelong effect upon singers' continuing growth and aesthetic enjoyment.

LISTENING

Central to artistic choral performance is habitual, careful listening by singers. O. C. Christiansen observed during the Christiansen Choral School (Chambersburg, Pa., 1947) that "occasional listening can correct problems while habitual listening can prevent them." While singers can be instructed to listen and can be guided in the development of listening habits, their ability to hear is not automatic. Early in their choral experience, singers hear through the ears of a conductor. The focus of the conductor upon single aspects of the group's performance can be shared with singers in such a manner that singers grow in their own ability to hear. Differentiation among tonalities, pitch relationships, intonation, rhythmic relationships, and expressive qualities are the results of a planned growth process.

It will prove helpful here to review a pattern of aural development frequently followed by a conductor and to consider a possible parallel process for singers. The conductor first trains herself or himself to hear sound and intonation in *one* of the vocal lines, by following one part aurally while observing the score. He or she may listen carefully and successively for evenness resulting from proper breath support; color and blend of vowel sounds; exactness of intervals; accuracy of rhythmic figures; clarity of consonants; and shaping of phrases. The process can be repeated for each line in part singing. The conductor may listen *vertically* for chordal intonation and balance of voice parts. Gradually, through this concerted effort, there develops an ability to hear more than one of these aspects simultaneously.

The conductor-teacher follows a similar pattern when guiding singers in developing the ability to hear, by pointing out things like out of tune singing or approximate rhythmic configurations. The singers are guided to hear more acutely and to accept only in-tune intervals and exact rhythms. Singers are asked to listen carefully and to hear intervals (intonation) mentally before they sing a single pitch or line. A conductor can select two parts to be sung together so that singers can attend to their own line in relation to another; this process is repeated, putting various parts together, always with a reminder to listen and to tune carefully. To assist in tuning, singers can be directed to hold notes, such as those contributing to dissonances or approaching a unison, long enough to hear or to feel relationships. This facilitates thinking and singing pitches more accurately and encourages singers to focus on listening.

When a part is out of tune, the conductor asks those singing it to stop singing briefly, listen, and reenter carefully. When rhythmic figures are not exact, the conductor identifies inaccuracies and shares his or her perceptions with singers by employing a technique to improve rhythmic clarity. Examples of techniques will appear later in this chapter.

To encourage listening for and hearing expressive qualities in the music, the conductor-teacher exercises extreme care that all examples, vocal and keyboard, are performed expressively. Notes should never be "banged out" at the keyboard; instead, pitches should be sounded in the character, spirit, mood, tempo, and degree of dynamic intensity suggested by the music that will be sung. This helps to encourage expressive singing. Singers can describe phrases with their hands or with conducting gestures. Part of the group can sing while all other choir members listen intently and critique the performance with regard to expressive qualities. A conductor guides singers in developing their abilities to recognize and control dynamic levels (crescendos, diminuendos) and to relate these abilities to phrasing and to the dramatic events of the music they sing. Expressive recorded examples of music may be played for singers to hear. Singers can be guided in their listening, observing and critiquing expressive qualities in the music heard. Comparisons of two or more recorded examples can be illuminating. Singers may be asked to observe their scores while listening to interpretations that differ in their depiction of expressive nuance. Analysis of these differences can lead to cognition.

EAR TRAINING AND SIGHT SINGING

Aural-visual response has been described as *hearing what one sees, and seeing what one hears*. This goal can be achieved through a consistent and tireless approach to the associating of ear and eye. There are two important keys to success in developing aural-visual awareness in choir members:

1. Ear training–sight singing experiences are most rewarding when they present exactly the appropriate degree of challenge. The goal must be attainable; singers need to experience success in their attempts to *hear* mentally and to translate notation into sound.

2. Ear training–sight singing challenges are most effective when they are presented in a frequently recurring pattern. Guidance in perceptual development and opportunities to read at sight should be a part of *every* rehearsal.

When singers are presented regularly with challenges of the appropriate degree of difficulty, the result will be that the level of intricacy which can be mastered advances continuously. When ear training–sight singing materials are graduated carefully in the degree of challenge that they present, growth in these skills can be encouraged, monitored, and controlled.

In translating notation into sound, two basic goals are melodic (interval) accuracy and rhythmic accuracy. To achieve security in both of these goals, there must be planned and presented a series of interrelated drills (doing or experiencing), explanations (perceiving or relating), repeated practice (reinforcement), and application (the subsuming of skills gained through exercises recalled and utilized in live performance of music). For reinforcement through application, material for drills may be excerpted from sight-singing material or from musical selections to be included later in the rehearsal.

The challenge for a teacher is stimulating: The secret of success will be found in a plan for growth and in the selection of appropriate materials through which that growth can be achieved. Early experiences designed to provide pleasure and to reveal the joys of discovery are ideal.

Consider two patterns that this growth process could take. The choral ensemble might be a group of children who are beginning their choral experience, or a group of adolescents or adults who have engaged in singing through an essentially rote approach over an extended period of time. All these singers enjoy participating in music making; they simply cannot read notation. The approaches appropriate for either of these groups will differ in some aspects from those that might be more effective for the other. The goal for the two groups is the same: that singers understand notation as the means by which sound is symbolized.

Choruses of Children

Before learning ear-eye coordination, small children should enjoy singing and listening to music. In approaching the actual association of ear and eye, a teacher will find it helpful to survey various special aids or approaches and to select the best one. The authors of this book have experienced success through using *solfeggio* (Movable Do system), and they offer examples of its application. Exercises can be devised to demonstrate relationships between solfeggio, numbers attached to degrees of the scale, and pitch letter names.

Pitch Relationships.   Through aural testing, it becomes apparent that human beings differ widely in their innate ability to discriminate pitches. The scale of measurement reveals a range from inability to detect whether pitches are the same or different to an unexplained ability to identify a given pitch with its correct letter name or to produce vocally a specific pitch. When same or different, higher or lower pitch recognition is encouraged at an early age, refinement of pitch relations can proceed systematically. Research has demonstrated that when songs for children are consistently pitched in the keys presented initially, children develop a strong sense of pitch. Asked to sing a particular song without a pitch being sounded, children frequently begin the song in its familiar key. This finding suggests that consistency of key for each song learned could contribute to formation of a base for pitch recognition.

When young children are guided in valuable preparatory experiences, the singing of solfeggio verses (learned by rote) can follow the usual verse or verses (text) in familiar songs. This establishes a firm aural base for later recognition of interval relationships by sound (do ↗ re, re ↗ fa, do ↘ la, do ↘ sol, ti ↗ do). Building upon fluent and consistent use of solfeggio names can provide a foundation for interval recognition. Mention or recognition of a perfect fourth can suggest or recall the pitch relationship between do ↗ fa (fa ↘ do), re ↗ sol (sol ↘ re), mi ↗ la (la ↘ mi), sol ↗ do, (do ↘ sol). Mention of a minor third can stimulate a la ↗ do (do ↘ la), re ↗ fa (fa ↘ re), or mi ↗ sol (sol ↘ mi) relationship recall.

Repeated singing of scales (diatonic, chromatic, whole-tone) can assist singers in discriminating between whole steps and half steps. During vocalization, solfeggio syllables are helpful when utilized in association with the sound and progression of scales, both ascending and descending. Solfeggio can then provide a comfortable tool for transfer when interval exercises are employed and pitch games devised. When scale syllables have been mastered thoroughly in association with their sound relationships, the conductor-teacher can give a *do* or *la* pitch and proceed to dictate intervals to be sung by the children: do ↗ mi; do ↘ la; la ↗ mi; fa ↗ fi.

Interval drills may be practiced in each choral rehearsal. When security has been developed in the singing of intervals on solfeggio syllables, the conductor-teacher may then call for directional change by specific interval size (up a half step, down a whole step, up a major third, down a minor third). In early experiences, the director is careful to allow ample time for singers to think of the requested pitch relationship before giving the hand signal to respond.

Visualizing Interval Relationships.   While aural recognition of intervals can be developed by rote and singers can be trained to identify and sing these intervals as they are called for, this must be considered a preparatory step toward reading notation. Early and frequent association of pitch relationships with their notational representation is essential to the development of reading ability. Diatonic and chromatic scales (ascending and descending) can be notated on chalkboards or presented through an overhead projector. To provide a learning basis for music to be sung and rehearsed, keys and beginning pitches can be changed from rehearsal to rehearsal. Through use of a pointer, singers can learn to respond to the visual stimulus by associating what they have learned through aural and mental realization.

Notation of the diatonic scale will be reinforced by solfeggio syllables, scale degree numbers, and actual pitch letter names beneath or above the corresponding notation (Example 6-1).

1	2	3	4	5	6	7	8	7	6	5	4	3	2	1
do	re	mi	fa	sol	la	ti	do	ti	la	sol	fa	mi	re	do
C	D	E	F	G	A	B	C	B	A	G	F	E	D	C

Example 6-1 Notation of diatonic scale.

While observing this notation, choristers can

1. Sing the scale in its usual sequence (ascending and descending) in each clef.
2. Sing pitches and intervals ad lib as they are indicated by a pointer held by the conductor-teacher or by a member of the group.
3. Observe through relationship to piano keyboard the sequence of whole steps and half steps that occur in any major diatonic scale.
4. Apply this knowledge to the task of placing sharps appropriately within a diatonic major scale begun on D.
5. Rewrite the D major scale, placing two sharps in the key signature for each clef.
6. Notate and sing the relative natural minor scale, being careful to begin on the pitch *b* sung on the solfeggio syllable *lAH*.
7. Repeat the transfer of solfeggio syllables to scales begun in various keys.

Intervals called for through dictation or indicated by pointer may become gradually more complex and the time allowed for thought may be lessened as accuracy increases. Exercises or drills may be accomplished on solfeggio syllables, scale degree numbers, or actual pitch letter names at the discretion of the conductor-teacher. In succeeding lessons or rehearsals, scales should be notated in various keys, both major and minor.

Once singers are secure in reading and singing diatonic scales in various keys, notation of the chromatic scale (ascending and descending to illustrate enharmonic equivalents) can be approached in the same manner. It can be reinforced by solfeggio syllables and by actual pitch letter names; however, scale degree numbers may be more confusing than helpful when used in relation to a scale composed entirely of half steps (Example 6-2).

Example 6-2   Notation of chromatic scale (based on C = *Do*). Enharmonic equivalents for syllables ascending and descending spelled as they sound. Sing ascending scale with syllables of top two lines, then descending with syllables of lower two lines.

Symbolic representation is more effective when related to the piano keyboard. This visual and aural relationship can facilitate understanding of the function of flat and sharp symbols, which may later be extended through double-flat (♭♭) and double-sharp (×) symbols.

Observing scale notation (which can be rewritten for each rehearsal so that it begins on different pitches), choristers can

1. Attend to the relationship of whole steps and half steps in notation and when played on the piano keyboard.
2. Practice singing ascending and descending scales with appropriate syllables, numbers, or pitch letter names.
3. Sing pitches and intervals ad lib as they are indicated by a pointer.
4. Relate through singing chromatic notation those pitches that form the diatonic scale.
5. Discover the function of key signatures by exploring the scale intervals that make up a diatonic major or minor scale on any pitch.

Although early efforts often result in the singing of *approximate* intervals, exact intonation should always be an objective. Mastery of intervals proceeds in a pattern from crudeness to precision. Selected intervals, made more secure through one or more of the suggested approaches, may be observed and reinforced immediately by a sight-singing exercise or by reading phrases contained in music to be rehearsed.

Rhythmic Relationships.   A frequent problem for choral ensembles is an incomplete understanding of rhythmic relationships and the resulting inability to translate symbols into accurate rhythmic figures.

As with visualizing interval relationships, foundations for rhythmic mastery may be related to familiar songs. Dictated rhythms, repeated on *tAH* before the naming of a tune, can be identified by children and can call attention to patterns (Example 6-3).

Example 6-3   Notation of familiar rhythmic patterns.

Introducing Notation.   Following aural identification by the children, rhythmic patterns from familiar songs can be notated on the chalkboard and attention called to the appearance of shorter and longer note symbols. Building upon such an introduction to rhythmic notation, children can be guided to recognize duple or triple meter in familiar songs through a question: Does this song have a *two* or a *three* feeling? Do we *feel* a 1, 2, 3; 1, 2, 3 or a 1, 2; 1, 2 (1 + 2 +) as we listen to this? Following differentiation of meter *feeling* detected through the ear, the appropriate meter symbol can be introduced and illustrated on chalkboard.

The next step is to explain clearly the relationship of note values. Because the eighth-note pulse is vital to rhythmic accuracy, that note value may serve as the basis for experience and later cognition.

Children may be guided in clapping a steady eighth-note pulse while singing a familiar song. They may be shown the visual symbol for the eighth note. Next, they may be guided in clapping quarter notes while singing the same song. The quarter-note symbol may also be displayed, and half of the singers guided in clapping quarter notes while the other singers clap eighth notes. Having experienced the pulse or steady beat in relation to the rhythm of the song, singers will be ready to observe relationships of note durations: ♪ ♪ ♩ ♩ ♩ 𝅝. 𝅘𝅥𝅮𝅘𝅥𝅮 and 𝅘𝅥𝅯𝅘𝅥𝅯 can be added.

The function of the dot can be explored and explained. Symbols for silence (rests) can be introduced. From this point, songs (familiar and unfamiliar) should appear in notation. There can be exercises notated on a chalkboard or projected onto a screen so that the conductor-teacher can monitor the children's performance. These exercises will serve to emphasize note duration relationships (Example 6-4). The conductor-teacher may guide singers to *feel* the eighth-note pulse by directing them to tap eighth notes evenly while singing through each note's duration on *tAH*. Students can sing first the upper line and then the lower; repeat symbols can be explained. Once the tempo is set, an exercise should follow immediately. Instructions can be given on the pitch that

Example 6-4   Note duration relationships (duple meter).

the children imitate. They are rhythmic and indicative of the desired eighth-note pulse:

" on <u>tAH</u>   one-and-two-and-rea – dy-sing-tAH "

After all singers have read the exercise together, one line at a time, the group can be divided and assigned different lines. Singers assigned to read any particular line first may progress to the next line when repeating the exercise; those reading the lower line first may read the upper line during the repetition.

Following this activity, the two groups may be assigned different entry points so that articulation of rhythms will be heard in canon style. The number of divisions of the group can be increased from two to three, four, five, or more until a different group begins each measure. In all attempts to relate note values to each other and to the eighth-note pulse, clarity and rhythmic precision must be emphasized.

While Example 6-4 remains visible on the chalkboard, Example 6-5, notated in triple meter, can be displayed. Articulation of this exercise can be approached in the same way as Example 6-4. The conductor-teacher can establish the eighth-note pulse, and students can read each line on a neutral syllable. When children are secure, the class may be divided and two lines read simultaneously. Finally, the class may be divided further and all three lines read at the same time. Each group of singers may progress to the next line after completing the line assigned first. (Group 1 reads the top line first, then progresses to the middle line followed by the bottom line. Group 2 reads the middle line first, then progresses to the bottom line followed by the top line. Group 3 reads the bottom line first, then the top line, and finally the middle line.)

The conductor-teacher's verbal direction may be at the speed of the quarter note in the tempo desired: (thinking ♩ ♩ ♩), the conductor-teacher says in tempo desired, "On *ti*, speak"; or (thinking ♩ ♩ ♫) the conductor-teacher says in tempo, "On *ti*, 3+ ." In this manner the tempo is set and the eighth-note pulse is established as the model.

Following concentration upon pitch and rhythm, choristers will be ready to relate the two. At this stage of reading development, it is helpful to use the chalkboard or an overhead projector for displaying notation of familiar songs

Example 6-5   Note duration relationships (triple meter).

or phrases that include slight deviations from their usual patterns. Games or contests may be devised to encourage growth in perception. Children may be invited to discover discrepancies in a phrase notated two or three times with slight differences in rhythm or melody. One of the examples may be performed and singers asked to identify that particular notation. Singers may be asked to sing each example exactly as notated. Many possibilities for games and drills will become apparent to an imaginative conductor-teacher.

Choruses of Adolescents or Adults with Minimal Reading Skills

Adolescent or adult singers who have developed dependency upon rote experiences may have learned to read the *text* from the printed copies, and may have attempted to read notation when it is quite basic. However, many singers with beautiful voices totally depend upon an accompanist who reads music and plays each part containing even the slightest difficulty. This is a pattern for many high school choruses and church choirs.

Conductors of these groups frequently resolve to devote time to helping singers improve reading abilities, but they may give in when singers become impatient or when exercises designed to build security are not related to specific problems encountered in a musical selection. Conductors may not be willing or able to devote adequate rehearsal time to developing reading skills.

When asked whether their choruses read fluently, some conductors reply that the pressure of performance allows little or no rehearsal time for work on music reading. However, conductors who plan regularly for reading skill development find that when singers can read fluently at sight, valuable rehearsal time is actually saved for polishing, for interpreting, and for acquainting singers with more literature. Development of sight-singing skill is related directly to the importance that the conductor places upon this goal.

There are similarities between approaches to the development of sight-singing skill in children and those appropriate for adolescents and adults.

1. Security is needed in both pitch and rhythmic relationships.
2. In the associating of ear and eye, an effective sequence is
   a. Singing interval and rhythmic relationships.
   b. Recognizing musical symbols for these relationships in notation.
   c. Translating short excerpts of notation into sound.
   d. Applying a skill learned through exercises to a musical example.
3. In learning pitch and rhythm symbols and relationships, singers should participate in vocal experimentation and physical response to rhythmic stimuli. The ability to identify an interval by name or to answer a question regarding names and time values ascribed to notes and rests is useless without the ability to translate that notation into patterns of sound and silence

Three important differences in approach may be advisable for more advanced singers. First, previous experience with music may make the learning of solfeggio unnecessary and may suggest the use of a different approach to development of security in interval relationships. Second, more extensive background with music will provide wider acquaintance with rhythmic patterns and relationships, which can be utilized in developing rhythmic reading security. And third, since these singers are familiar with printed notation, fewer interval and rhythmic drills may be required. The regular practice of sight-singing music selections of appropriate degrees of challenge will yield appreciable rewards.

Pitch Relationships.   Since interval security is based upon accurate articulation of intervals beginning with whole steps and half steps, vocalization may include the following suggestions for group response.

The conductor may indicate verbally or with hand signals the direction and distance of movement desired from a given pitch. After giving a tonic pitch and indicating the neutral syllable to be used (*mm, lOO, nOO*), the conductor may direct the group to proceed in unison up a whole step, down a half step, up a whole step, at his or her discretion. The left hand may be used with fingers extended and palm turned up or down to indicate the direction to be moved by half steps or whole steps; it may call for movement by whole steps when fingers are closed in fist position. When these directional signals are understood, the gesture calling for movement by a half step or whole step in the direction desired may be displayed first. This gesture may be followed by a movement of the right hand to signal singers when to move.

This same exercise or drill may be accomplished through use of a chord in any position. When the chord is moved up or down by half steps or whole steps, intonation can be checked both vertically and horizontally.

An extension or outgrowth of the pitch movement drill begins with a unison pitch or chord and proceeds to other intervals requested by name: up a perfect fourth, down a minor third, and so on. In this variation, as in the whole-step–half-step exercise, the verbal direction must precede the right hand signal for moving. This provides singers an opportunity to think pitches before singing them.

Another variation can be devised by placing on a chalkboard or projecting on a screen the notation for a scale (ascending and descending). A particular key chosen for the scale may be one that will be encountered by singers in a musical selection to be read at sight or rehearsed. After giving a unison starting pitch and specifying a particular neutral syllable to be used, the conductor may indicate by use of a pointer a succession of pitches to be sung. This practice exercise may move as quickly as singers' capabilities permit. As singers gain security in this drill for ear and eye coordination, the conductor uses this (particularly the chromatic notation) to solve interval problems before they are encountered in music that will then be sung at sight.

Variations on the chord-tuning exercise that assists in developing sensitivity to pitch relationships can also contribute to an awareness of harmony. Early in their choral experiences, singers have probably been guided to tune chords carefully when given a pitch. The sequence of tuning first the octave, then the fifth, and finally the third provides the greatest security for major or minor chord intonation. If additional chord members are to be included, they should be placed and tuned with equal care. When this exercise is associated with its notation written on a chalkboard or projected on a screen, listening for intonation (pitch relationships) can become habitual when reading notation at sight.

Following achievement of interval security developed through familiarity with scale and chord notation, excerpts can be extracted from music to be read at sight. These excerpts may be notated, sung, and then read in the context of more extended musical material.

Rhythmic Relationships. Rhythmic accuracy is preceded by rhythmic awareness. A clear illustration (including experiencing) of the logical way in which note and rest values are related can be followed by exercises.

1. Each section of the choir may be assigned the repeated articulation of a different note value: sixteenth notes, eighth notes, quarter notes, and half notes. These can be articulated on a neutral syllable with each part repeating the pitch of a particular chord member. An order of progression may be prescribed and at a given signal each part can articulate the rhythmic values that are next in sequence (Exercise 1).

Exercise 1 Practice in relating note values.

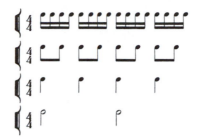

2. To assist in clarifying triple–duple relationships, the conductor-teacher may
    a. Write symbols for rhythmic equivalencies on a chalkboard (Example 6-6). The
        symbol + is articulated *and*.

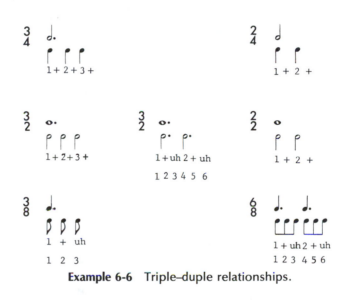

Example 6-6 Triple–duple relationships.

    b. Direct all singers to articulate on neutral syllable *tAH* only the first beat in each
        measure while conductor indicates the triple beat pattern in gesture.
    c. Set a tempo that will permit keeping the eighth-note value constant and conduct
        several measures in each *triple* meter signature notated on the chalkboard.
    d. Call for articulation of three equal note values in each measure.
    e. Call attention to notation for *2* beats in each measure.
    f. Ask singers to return to articulating only the *1* in each measure while conductor
        indicates the *duple* pattern in gesture (being careful to keep tempo for each mea-
        sure in duple meter consistent with that assigned to each measure containing
        triple prolation of corresponding note values).
    g. Call for articulation of two equal note values in each measure.
    h. Repeat this exercise as necessary.
    i. Vary the exercise to illustrate note values remaining constant between measures
        that indicate triple division and those that call for duple division.
3. Building upon skill already developed, singers may practice the following sequence
    and tie various pairs of notes until each change is felt. A change from two groups of
    three notes to three groups of two notes contributes to understanding of a hemiola
    (Exercise 2).

Exercise 2 Tying pairs of notes.

Pairings of notes can be articulated progressively or alternated: A feeling for two beats against three can be developed by practicing a. with d. Assign half of the singers to articulate a. while the others articulate d. Practicing both parts of e. together ($\frac{3}{2}$ and $\frac{6}{4}$) will achieve a similar objective.

A conductor-teacher who devises rhythmic exercises to improve awareness and to develop habits of rhythmic accuracy will find the following guides useful.

All exercises will be more effective when they are accompanied by a visual representation of rhythmic figures to be articulated.
Any skill developed through an exercise will be reinforced if it is used immediately in a musical composition to be read or rehearsed. For example, $\frac{6}{8}$ to $\frac{3}{4}$ alternation occurs in the song "America" from *West Side Story* by Leonard Bernstein.

As singers become increasingly adept at translating notation into sound, they should be provided opportunities to read music during each rehearsal. The music to be read should present appropriate problems of steadily increasing complexity if reading skill development is to be consistent.

There are ways to encourage rhythmic clarity in music that is being read or rehearsed. For example, when reading notation (initially or for improved precision), it is helpful for singers to tap on their knees the steady or underlying meter beats or musical pulse while articulating on a neutral syllable the rhythmic patterns defined by notation symbols in one or more parts. A firm competency in relating underlying pulse to rhythmic patterns must be established.

Feeling for pulse in relation to rhythmic patterns can be encouraged through singers' speaking or singing the staccato pulse: ♩. = ♪ ♪ ♪ and ♩ = ♪♪♪♪ for example. This technique is effective when speaking on a neutral syllable or singing the text with repeated vowel sounds to steady the pulse throughout sustained notes.

Singing vocal lines on a steady flow of numbers and subdivisions representing the measure counts may be effective in clarifying rhythm (the symbol + is articulated *and*):

♪ ♪ ♪ ♪ ♩   ♩
1 + 2 + 3 + 4 +

This technique can be employed in measures where the smallest note is an eighth note. Additional syllables may be integrated for articulation of shorter note values:

$$ \text{♪} \quad \text{♫} \quad \text{♪}. \quad \text{♪} \quad \text{♬} \quad \text{♬} $$

1 + uh 2 (+)uh 3 e + uh 4 e + uh

Of importance equal to that of accurate note articulation is precise counting of rests that constitute silence in music. The steady flow of numbers and subdivisions employed for the notes can be maintained *sotto voce* through practice of silence indicated by rests.

1 + 2 + 3 + (4+) | 1 + 2 + 3 + uh 4 (+) | 1 (+) 2 (+) 3+ (4+)

When vocal lines move at different times, an effective technique for clarifying rhythms is staccato singing of the parts together on a neutral syllable. This will help those who are assigned sustained notes to become aware that the moving notes must assume their proper emphasis. It also helps clarify the rhythms as singers feel pulse carefully in preparation for accurate placement of their staccato notes.

At alternate approach can be provided in music that moves slowly. The syllable *bmm* may be used, with singers proceeding immediately from the consonant *b* to the *mm*. Pitches sustained on the humming sound provide a harmonic framework for moving parts.

AWARENESS OF PHRASING

Musical responsiveness is enhanced by careful phrasing. Phrase schemes differ widely in music from various styles and periods. The formal design of a vocal or choral composition is often associated closely with text; mood and spirit to be communicated are usually responsive to text.

Initial phrase exploration begins with an expressive reading of the text by either the conductor or one of the singers. In some instances it may be possible for the entire ensemble to read the text artistically in unison. An alternative approach is the discovery of *musical* phrases through singing on a neutral syllable appropriate to the mood. A bright, cheery song in a crisp tempo would lend itself to use of *tAH* or *tEE*. More somber, sustained music would be better served by singing on *lOO*, *lOH*, or *lAH*. For marcato style, *dAHt*, *tAHt*, or *dEEt* may be useful.

After the composer's musical intentions have been introduced, phrase similarities and differences may be identified. This observation leads to recognition of form. The text may prove to be reinforcing to the spirit, mood, or style conceived and indicated by the composer.

A feeling of movement is transmitted through the phrase scheme. Contributing to this feeling are tempo, pulse, meter, pattern of rhythmic figures, dynamics, and intensity. The relationship of phrases and movement through them illustrates the contrast of tension and release—the source of vitality, excitement, and satisfaction in music.

To understand phrasing, singers must be guided to experience physical, aural, and cognitive responses to phrase shaping. Early in the singers' experience, the use of hand and arm to depict phrase shapes can be illuminating. These physical representations of the increase and decrease in intensity, the rise and fall of the line, and the general feeling of movement-relaxation (*arsis-thesis*) reveal to singers much about the formal design and the character of the music. This valuable activity can begin with physical descriptions of melodic lines that the singers know and perform well. In this way, the hand and arm provide a physical response to the music—a valuable link between experience and cognition. As the hand shapes the phrase, so the singer is encouraged to shape phrases vocally.

The conductor who guides more advanced choristers will find that physical response to pulse, meter, beat, accent, and phrasing can be encouraged by teaching conducting patterns. Through descriptions of line, flow, and phrasing in hand and arm gestures, the rise and fall of music can be felt. Associating verbal articulation of rhythm with gesture pattern helps in establishing rhythmic security and clarity. It is the experiencing that facilitates cognition.

Finally, singers are guided in marking their scores with exact indications of phrase lengths, shapes, and other musical relationships. Just as the conductor-teacher who has marked the score carefully finds that it enhances learning, so singers discover the shape and the content of music by marking their scores under the conductor-teacher's guidance. Using transparent color codings in marking can make the composer's plan more evident to all who perform the work. To facilitate this aspect of learning, the conductor-teacher may place a copy of his or her marked score and appropriate marking pens where they are accessible to all singers a week prior to rehearsal of the work. Singers may be required to copy these markings into their own scores.

SENSITIVITY TO RELATIONSHIPS

Singers who have learned to listen intently as they sing, and to read notation at sight, will be responsive to a conductor's leadership in further developing sensitivity to tonal, temporal, and textural relationships.

Tonal relationships include pitches, chords, and harmonies. Singers can be guided to sing pitches in patterns prescribed by the conductor during vocalization, and by the composer later in the rehearsal. As singers develop an awareness of pitches within a phrase context, they increase their ability to read phrasewise and to shape phrases vocally. They learn to control development and release of intensity as a result of their awareness of phrase contours.

Temporal relationships have their roots in time. They include tempo, meter, pulse, sound-silence, and all the complex combinations of these that the composer indicates through notation.

Textural relationships are determined by the number of voices or instruments, or both, and by the color of voice, voices, instrument, or instruments in combination. Textural relationships are formed by voices interweaving (polyphony), by a melodic voice or a duet supported by accompanying harmony (homophony), and by the closeness or openness of the harmonic structure. Textures are described as thin (few lines or voice parts), thick (many voice parts), or rich (full chords employing chromaticism). Textures are often associated with vocal colors: bright (voices predominantly in a higher range, moving rapidly, with brighter vowel sounds and generally in major tonality), or dark (voices predominantly in a lower range, moving slowly, and often calling for darker vowel sounds).

COGNITION

The ultimate goal of the conductor-teacher who attempts to develop skills in choristers is cognition. Cognitive response and physical response are interrelated. It is not enough for singers to recognize a whole note, a quarter rest, or an eighth note, and to be able to name those and other symbols appropriately. Singers must be guided in relating these symbol values through an underlying pulse. Experiencing relationships in carefully devised exercises and through consistent use results in the desired understanding.

Cognitive response is the ability of singers to know what they have been led or guided to do (experience). The ability to verbalize any aspect of music notation without being able to translate symbols into sound and sound into symbols does not indicate cognition. A test of cognition is reliable when it follows or summarizes experience. After singers have sung scales, observed and built them by whole-step and half-step relationships at the keyboard and on the chalkboard, and played and sung what they have notated, those singers should be ready to verbalize. They can be expected to illustrate appropriate relationships and to use interval skills effectively when approaching unfamiliar music. Capabilities that can be tested for cognitive response include naming keys from their signatures; building scales in any key indicated by a key signature; relating minor to major through verbalizing or recognizing key signature relationships; verbalizing the whole-step–half-step sequence in any scale; recognizing meter indications and verbalizing their potential effect upon the music; apportioning duration of sound and silence symbols accurately; articulating rhythmic pulse in relation to patterns and figures; reading music at sight; translating notation symbols into sound; and translating sound into notation symbols.

RECAPITULATION

The goal of reading fluently at sight is accomplished through a carefully planned approach. It results from a focus upon association of ear and eye in each rehearsal and selection of reading materials that present the appropriate degree of challenge. Each should be slightly more demanding than the one preceding, and one that can be successfully read.

While choirs of young singers need exercises and reading materials designed to stimulate development of skills in ear-eye coordination, more advanced choirs will respond favorably to the reading of repertory that challenges, reinforces, and builds upon reading skills in each rehearsal. One of our nation's prominent conductors once stated that the true test of musicality (musicianship) is the ability to read at sight.

Chapter 7

Selecting Repertory and Building the Concert Program

> The strains, swelling and dying away with a delicacy quite indescribable, seemed to proceed from one voice. The harmony had the unity of organ diapasons.

So wrote an unidentified critic in the London *Spectator* in 1850 after hearing a concert presented by forty men and boys from the Berlin Dom Chor. Any choral conductor would be overjoyed to receive such a review of a concert. The critique describes the best qualities of choral singing: beauty of tone, sensitive nuance and phrasing, perfection of ensemble, and superb intonation.

An English music critic of the late nineteenth and early twentieth centuries who became a famous composer-conductor was Sir Edward Elgar. He made the following comment at a choral competition in northern England in 1903:

> To get real artistic expression out of a piece of music it is necessary that some real artistic impression shall have moved the maker of it.

These two comments support important elements of a choral program in church, community, secondary school, or college: the selection of music that evokes artistic expression, and the development of choral techniques that make the revealing of that artistic expression possible.

Selection of repertory is a serious responsibility and a source of pleasure for the choral conductor. From a conductor's first experience with developing choirs to his or her association with choirs possessing established techniques, the criteria for selection of appropriate material may well center upon Sir Edward Elgar's statement that a "real artistic impression shall have moved the composer of it."

CRITERIA FOR REPERTORY SELECTION

Since the quantity of choral composition is vast, it is possible to discover repertory that is appropriate for

Vocal and emotional maturity of children, adolescents, and adults.

Attaining teaching-learning objectives, with concern for age level, musical readiness, and rehearsal time available.

Developing artistic potential and musical responsiveness.

Building interesting and engaging concert programs that satisfy philosophical and practical considerations.

Vocal and Emotional Maturity

The human voice grows and matures from early childhood to full development, usually evident in persons between the ages of thirty and forty. During the developmental process, each individual may experience one or two periods of range restriction as well as extension. Repertory for each choral ensemble must be selected with consideration for the particular group of singers. The astute conductor-teacher will listen frequently to children or adolescent choristers to ascertain individual ranges so that each singer may be assigned to the appropriate voice part; examine pitch extremes and tessitura for each of the voice parts in repertory; include musical works that provide the next degree of range and tessitura challenge; increase sustaining power gradually from repertory selected; and nurture continuous development of vocal ease and flexibility through choice of repertory.

A conductor's selection of repertory through which singers can develop as choral musicians is based upon readiness of singers and quality of literature. Since varying degrees of vocal challenge can be discovered in all repertory, the wise conductor selects music that provides a comfortable progression.

Emotional maturity is another important factor. Singers' relating to and understanding of text is important to communication. Interpretation subtleties are dependent upon life experiences. This is particularly true of music chosen from the Romantic period, in which considerable emotional intensity is essential for communication.

Background and musical interests of singers must also be considered when selecting repertory. For example, singers who have experienced only popular or indigenous cultural music cannot function well on a diet that excludes all such repertory. These singers will respond more readily to guidance in familiar music. Their horizons may broaden gradually as they become acquainted with and observe correlations found in other styles of repertory. Singing music in various languages also tends to broaden musical and cultural horizons, particularly if several cultures are represented in members of the ensemble, or if singers are familiar with or studying a language.

Teaching-Learning Objectives

The perceptive conductor of choral music formulates goals and objectives that foster musical growth in the choir. In this book the authors have addressed development of vocal, aural, and cognitive skills that relate directly to performance goals. Recognizing that performance and learning goals can be compatible, the authors believe that choral excellence is dependent upon the conductor's abilities to assess learning readiness; formulate attainable objectives relating to skill development, cognition, and aesthetic responsiveness; teach so that desired skills, understanding, and responsiveness develop consistently; and evaluate progress objectively.

Musical understanding is enhanced through broad and varied experiences with choral repertory. The music of each historical period evokes its own particular set of aesthetic responses. As the conductor acquaints a choir with different musical styles, singers learn to recognize characteristics of the different historical periods and to associate these with music of individual composers. Comparisons are both illuminating and satisfying as developing choral musicians observe relative melodic, harmonic, and rhythmic complexities; identify concepts of texture and structural design; and become increasingly aware of text-music relationships.

Performance and learning goals of choral organizations differ as widely as conductors' philosophies. Two extremes are exploration and artistic performance of music with lasting value through which singers increase both musical understanding and aesthetic satisfaction; and performance of music through which singers find immediate gratification because of its entertainment potential or the relative ease with which it can be learned.

When the former goal has a high priority and the conductor is genuinely concerned with fostering musical growth, the lasting result is rewarding. When there is a lack of compatibility between a conductor's perceptive goals and the musical taste of the choir, a compromise may be necessary. A combination of the two philosophical goals may be a practical solution. A balance may recognize musical maturity and age level through inclusion of some lighter, more entertaining music, while emphasizing long-range educational implications through a broader, more comprehensive repertory.

An important consideration in selecting concert repertory is the amount of rehearsal time available. This factor should not be permitted to inhibit or restrict learning goals; however, it must be given careful thought when selecting concert repertory.

Artistic Potential and Musical Responsiveness

There is in souls a sympathy with sounds; and, as the mind is pitch'd the ear is pleas'd with melting airs, or martial, brisk, or grave: some chord in unison with what we hear, is touch'd within us, and the heart replies.[1]

The human spirit responds to artistic and musical stimuli. Research studies have demonstrated that aesthetic responsiveness and sensitivity can be increased. The conductor who values aesthetic responsiveness will select repertory judiciously. He or she will choose choral literature that can evoke aesthetic responses in varying degrees, and will assess each work to ascertain its potential for aesthetic satisfaction by asking such questions as: Is the text appealing and does the music enhance that appeal? Are melodic, rhythmic, and harmonic components of the music satisfying? Will satisfaction be intensified by repetition? Will the music's formal structure and internal design develop artistic sensitivity in performers? Are the sonorities and the excitement produced by bringing the musical score to life capable of evoking aesthetic responses to beauty?

Trained choristers, as well as singers with less experience, are attracted to choral participation by the quality of repertory. Community choruses that perform choral/orchestral masterworks attract the interest of advanced choral musicians as well as singers who want to develop their talents. Church choirs whose

[1]William Cowper (1731–1800), *The Task: Book VI*, "The Winter Walk at Noon."

repertory consistently combines aesthetic qualities with worship maintain loyal support and commitment from their members.

The question is often asked: "What is meant by *great* or *good* music?" Some define it as that which has lasting quality; that in which elements of aesthetic satisfaction are so inherent in the composer's artistic design that *each* study and performance can bring new insights and discoveries. Examples are Handel's *Messiah,* Bach's Mass in B Minor, and Verdi's Requiem. These and other works of similar quality hold universal appeal for both singers and audiences. Conductors and choirs approaching these works after repeated performances continue to be fascinated by new discoveries and insights. Such music can reflect a composer's genius through exciting relationships of text and texture, tempo and flow, beauty and drama. Whether or not one is capable of singing these masterworks, one questions neither the greatness of the work nor the merit of repeated performance.

In sharp contrast, many popular tunes that offer an immediate appeal to relatively inexperienced musicians and audiences can become dated and grow tiresome with repetition. The conductor-teacher should be careful not to program this music exclusively. When paucity of expressive elements characterizes a given work, or when those elements are relatively undeveloped, the work may not be worth performing.

GUIDES FOR EXAMINING EDITIONS[2]

Musical scholars research composers' works that are currently unavailable for purchase and those that they deem worthy of reediting. Choral conductors searching for repertory must often evaluate a particular edition or compare editions before selecting the one that is more authentic or closer to a composer's intentions. Guidelines that may prove helpful in the study of an edition include the following:

Source

Is the source of manuscript indicated? (Location, catalog number, page or folio, date, manuscript or autograph. Permission from library or owner of manuscript.)

Language

Is the original language included?
Is there a translation if in a foreign language?
Is the source of the literary text indicated?
Is text underlay that is not the composer's underlined or italicized?
If text has been altered, are solutions placed in brackets?

Title

Is original title given?
If taken from a larger work, is its title included or placed in a footnote?

Editorial Markings

Are editorial dynamic markings and tempo suggestions put into brackets or indicated by capital letters? For example: *[accel.],* P for *p.*

---

[2]For further information on editing choral music, refer to Thurston Dart, Walter Emery, and Christopher Morris, *Editing Early Music* (London: Novello and Co., Oxford University Press, Stainer and Bell Ltd., 1963).

Is the original notation indicated in an incipit (also clef, staves, time signature, mensuration)?
Is transposition indicated? Are changes in note values marked clearly?
Are ligatures and coloration shown?
Are changes within the composition footnoted or clearly indicated in notation?
Are missing notes placed in brackets?
Is there a keyboard reduction for rehearsal purposes?
Are editorial slurs and ties indicated by ⌢ and extra extensions by dotted lines?

Printing

Is printing uncrowded?
Is notation clear and large enough to be read easily?

FACILITATING THE SEARCH FOR REPERTORY

The conductor who searches continuously for interesting and useful repertory will be better able to satisfy short-term and long-range requirements. A conductor might consider music performed by other choirs, either live or recorded; also music available for perusal in libraries, in displays and exhibits during professional conventions, in music stores, or upon request from publishers and distributors.

Choral selections performed on convention programs of the American Choral Directors Association (ACDA) and the Music Educators National Conference (MENC) are documented with publication information. Copies of this music may be obtained from the publisher or distributor indicated. Choral conductors who engage in a regular exchange of printed programs with other conductors find this source of information invaluable.

The selection process can be most effective when a conductor has a thorough understanding of his or her objectives and a definition of the word *select:* "To pick out carefully from among many as most suitable."[3] The astute conductor will discover that many more musical compositions must be discarded than are chosen for immediate or eventual use. As the number of gems grows, the conductor will need a systematized means of conserving information. A card file is of value for future reference. (See Appendix A for sample information-gathering format. Both sides of a single file card may be utilized for conservation of information.)

Directors of church choirs might try a slightly different organizational format. By giving priority to information concerning the *text,* a church musician may readily find anthems, motets, introits, and responses especially appropriate for particular seasons of the church year or for reinforcing scriptural, homiletical, or sermon references. (See Appendix B for format useful in conserving church choir repertory information.)

Cards containing repertory information may be cataloged and placed in a reference file. The system adopted should be the one most useful to the conductor. Sections representing *Sacred* and *Secular* may each be subdivided according to voicing: Unison, Treble Voices, Male (changed) Voices, Mixed Voices. As the card file expands, further sectioning may be useful: duplication of information filed under the composer's name (as well as cataloged alphabetically by title); a separation of each major section into style periods, which may be subdivided to accommodate works by various composers; groupings of music appropriate for either small or large ensembles; music for particular seasons

---

[3]*The Random House Dictionary.*

or occasions. Some conductors will provide a special category marked "Music of Top Priority for Future Use."

A time may come when it is beneficial to cross-file by having duplicate cards for some compositions and by arranging these under more than one heading. Cross-filing facilitates decisions. A word of caution is in order: The card file is a means to an end. It is useful when it is individually oriented and when it answers basic questions such as: How does this selection relate to music making? How can this work enhance choir members' knowledge and understanding of music? How can this selection fulfill objectives of concert program building?

CONCERT PROGRAMS: PHILOSOPHICAL AND PRACTICAL CONSIDERATIONS

In selecting repertory for concert programs that interest audiences as well as performers, a conductor-teacher furthers progress toward the goals he or she has established. Conductors of young singers will be more concerned with the learning potential presented by appropriate repertory than with audience appeal. As singers advance in capability and responsiveness, a conductor can choose from literature that accommodates both learning and performance goals.

Encouraging Musical Growth and Understanding

Interest in the chosen repertory will not necessarily be immediate. Many conductor-teachers of college and high school choirs have discovered that singers' first response to music is not always a lasting one. When introduced to a polyphonic motet with Latin text, singers may be tempted to respond negatively simply because the music is different from any experienced previously. The conductor may find it necessary to test his or her powers of persuasion. Singing in Latin has certain developmental potential that makes perseverance worthwhile. Pure (nondiphthong) vowels of Latin encourage beauty of tone and establish diction concepts that can be applied to music sung in other languages. Flowing lines of Renaissance music reinforce essential principles of legato singing and music making. Also, vocal beauty and awareness of tonal balance (when each voice part is of equal melodic importance) encourage unique aesthetic experience.

Providing Aesthetic Satisfaction

If the choir strives for excellence and if the conductor-teacher is enthusiastic and knowledgeable about selections, choir members will discover satisfying relationships in the music and feel that their efforts are amply rewarded. A well-selected concert program—with contrasting moods and with music from various periods and cultures placed in an effective order—provides an audience with imaginative and emotional stimuli. Such a concert program encourages a desirable form of response and meets concert objectives.

The conductor has access to repertory that spans nearly six hundred years. In addition to music by master composers of each age (Dufay and Josquin, Palestrina, Byrd, Morley and Lassus, Monteverdi and Schütz, Bach and Handel, Mozart and Haydn, Schubert, Beethoven, Mendelssohn, Bruckner and Brahms, Debussy and Ravel, Schoenberg and Stravinsky, Barber and Britten, and other musical giants), there are lesser-known composers of worthwhile works. One of the greatest satisfactions for a conductor is sharing discoveries with singers and audiences.

Ensuring Enjoyment of Singers and Audience

A primary source of enthusiasm for concert repertory comes from the conductor who is dedicated to the power of music. A community chorus director may enlist the interest and the support of civic leaders and members of the musical community; a school chorus director may call upon students and interested parents; a church choir director benefits from a committee of choir members and congregation members concerned with music in worship. Members of a group formed to combine moral and emotional support with administrative expertise can foster concert attendance and interest of community, school, and church. These leaders share ideas and responsibilities for implementing proposals and delegating administrative tasks. They may be elected, invited, or appointed. Whether known as officers or boards of directors, these boosters support artistic enterprises and free the conductor to fulfill responsibilities for repertory choices and rehearsal preparation. The conductor willingly accepts suggestions from officers, boosters, and choir members. But it is he or she who must make the final repertory choices to satisfy professional standards and preferences, the long-range purposes and goals of the choir, and the cultural needs of the community.

Both informal and formal concerts are conducive to maintaining high morale of choir members and interest of audiences. When planning and presenting informal programs it is advisable to vary moods and timbres of selections; make use of solos, duets, and small ensembles from within the choir; introduce numbers informally; and involve the audience in singing.

On informal programs it is important that soloists, ensembles, and song leaders all participate in a manner that is consistent with the level of the choir's performance. Verbal comments concerning the program should be brief, positive, and easily heard. They should enhance the listener's enjoyment of the music and not draw attention from it. The director or the members of the choir who announce the program contribute to enjoyment when they present a pleasant attitude of sharing information with the audience.

In contrast to informal programs, a formal concert in an auditorium or a concert hall centers the attention on music rather than on personalities. For a formal concert, carefully written program notes are appropriate; they are designed to assist the audience in following and appreciating the music. Skillfully prepared, program notes build and sustain interest in choral concert attendance. The technical level attained and the experiences shared by members of choral groups will be evident in their enjoyment during performances. When involvement is total, enjoyment and pleasure radiate from the performing ensemble; the response of an audience will reflect the spirit. To enhance the pleasure of both choir and audience, a conductor must be skilled in the ability to arrange the order of musical selections in a program. Whether the choir be children or adults, whether it be related to community, school, church, or synagogue, the principles of program building are similar.

Serving Special Occasions

Prior to the nineteenth century, music was not composed for "concert" use. Composers wrote for specific audiences and special occasions: a church service, a court reception, a wedding, a coronation, or a special celebration. In the nineteenth century, composers frequently wrote "salon music" for friends and other musicians. The composer was well aware of both where and when his music would be performed. He understood the acoustics in a particular cathedral, chamber, or theater; knew the number and capabilities of singers; and knew whether or not instruments would be employed. Not until the nineteenth century were public concert halls erected. Before that, audiences were made up of the "privileged" class and the nobility.

The results of planning and awareness, characteristic of pre-twentieth-century composition, were more predictable and the spontaneity more certain when music was composed for performance in smaller, more compact halls or in resonant cathedrals. Although we now have many beautiful performing arts centers, the practice of presenting concerts in available arenas such as gymnasiums, all-purpose rooms, theaters (both indoors and outdoors), and churches with acoustical treatment designed for speech reception rather than for music can make artistic choral performance hazardous. A particular performing arena may constitute an important consideration in determining appropriateness of music composed or selected for performance.

Since today's society finds itself surrounded by music, the element of choice assumes new meaning. To the choral conductor who is planning music for a special occasion or season, the selection process is a challenge and a responsibility. Receptivity of singers and audiences can often be shaped by appropriateness of repertory choices. Whether a conductor works in a church, a public school, a college, or a university, and whether he or she directs a community or a professional chorus, he or she has the opportunity to develop audiences and to help foster a love for and a response to the best in music.

The commissioning of new music by contemporary composers is being encouraged by many choral groups and their sponsors. A premiere performance to celebrate an anniversary or some other special occasion can be an exhilarating experience for performers and audience as well as a stimulus to the composer. When certain components are present, the probability of effective communication is high: The text and the music are appropriate for the occasion; the music is composed for the specific forces to be involved in performance; and the composer is aware of acoustical properties in a particular church or concert hall and of the total musical environment for his or her creation. Performance of a commissioned work provides excitement unique to music as an art form and as a cultural medium.

Developing Community Feeling

Throughout history, churches and synagogues have filled a genuine need for identification and involvement by providing opportunities for singing within their worship services. Choirs have helped familiarize congregations with scriptural and other religious texts and have created an atmosphere for worship. As a result of the church choir conductor's careful planning and selection of appropriate repertory of quality, both musical goals and religious traditions are advanced.

Community chorus conductors who encourage participation and provide singing opportunities that combine ethnic groups can bridge cultural and generation gaps through singing. Under inspired leadership, choral ensembles develop a civic pride in excellence while their members share individual interests and unite their best efforts in performances of great music. Repertory choices affect interest; they have special appeal when they take into account ethnic and community backgrounds of singers and audience.

BUILDING A CONCERT PROGRAM

The term *building* is appropriate to describe the formulating of ideas and the planning for effective sequence that precede a program comprising predominantly shorter compositions. A conductor cannot ensure the desired response if selections are randomly positioned. Program order and content are of vital importance and deserve careful thought. Enjoyment and communication are enhanced by the conductor who keeps in mind certain principles when building a concert program.

A Unifying Theme

A central theme can give purpose and continuity to a concert program. This can be an overall theme or an organizing of text and musical focus for program grouping. Titles such as *Music for Christmas, Songs of Spring, Music for St. Cecilia's Day,* or *Psalm Concert* are a few suggestions for unifying themes. Other titles will result from creative thought. Within a concert, headings for various sections or groups might include *Music from the Renaissance* (or any historical period), *Motets of Heinrich Schütz, Music of German Romanticists, Music from Russia,* or *Madrigals Old and New.*

A special occasion may be celebrated with a concert of appropriate music: a church, school, or national anniversary; a Founder's Day; a composer's birthdate. Within recent years, music devotees have honored Josquin des Prez, Heinrich Schütz, Anton Bruckner, Béla Bartók, Wolfgang Amadeus Mozart, Franz Joseph Haydn, George Frideric Handel, J. S. Bach, and Igor Stravinsky. Recognition has been accorded in festivals and concerts of their music performed in honor of their births or deaths. In 1976 the United States celebrated its 200th birthday with concerts featuring American composers from colonial times to the present.

Living composers are also deserving of recognition through concerts devoted to their choral music. As mentioned earlier, a work commissioned for a particular occasion provides a special point of interest within a concert program.

The Shape of a Concert Program

During examination of a musical work, a conductor becomes aware of its form or shape and identifies its central point of intensity. In a well-conceived concert program, interest will build toward a climax in similar manner. If the concert calls for an intermission, the musical selection providing the highest point of interest may well close the section that precedes the break. This high point of musical interest may be referred to as the "centerpiece" of the program. If no intermission is needed, this climactic selection may still be placed near the center of the program, at a time when the audience's listening powers are most acute. Inclusion of a short concerted work for choir and instruments, such as a Mozart or Haydn *Missa brevis,* can provide a climax. Other possibilities would be a Bach motet, several related compositions by one composer, or a special work chosen or commissioned for the occasion that will bring the program to an aesthetic or emotional height. After selecting music that fulfills this "centerpiece" function, the conductor can proceed to build around or toward it. The "centerpiece" then serves as inspiration for the entire program.

But this central climax should not be the only point of interest. Each group of selections in a well-conceived concert will have its own shape and its arresting moments that may not necessarily be associated with the highest degree of dynamic intensity. A relative point of interest may be provided by a unique avant-garde composition; it may be a selection with unusual rhythmic interest, or a work that displays the choir's particular versatility, skill, or sensitivity.

Just as a floral centerpiece may sometimes be placed at the side or end of a table, a concert centerpiece can serve, upon occasion, as the concluding number in a concert, with preceding groups leading up to the final climactic point.

The Opening Selection

The work chosen to begin a concert should elicit immediate attention from an audience. Listeners need not be expected to give complete concentration at the outset of a program, but their attention will be attracted by a beautiful opening sound and a unified group of singers totally involved in music making. Possible concert beginnings can range from a straightforward Bach chorale, a lively sixteenth-century motet of praise, or a bright, twentieth-century composition. The first selection should be of short to moderate length. It should be relatively simple in its design and demands upon singers. A concert's opening selection elicits the audience's first impression of the choir and sets up a mood of expectation for the remainder of the concert.

An equally important consideration is that the first selection permit singers to accustom themselves to the acoustics of the room or hall in which they are singing; establish their feeling of ensemble; and gain the confidence needed to communicate without overtaxing their voices or the musical concentration of the audience. The opening selection should be a cordial invitation to the concert.

Placement of Music Demanding Intense Concentration

Concert audiences expect "meat and potatoes" as well as "sugar and spice." A listener hopes to be thrilled by the sound of beautiful voices, to hear lovely melodies as well as intricacies of harmonic and rhythmic contrasts. He or she desires to be treated to drama as well as lyricism, and to a variety of tone colors and textures. Juxtaposition of these elements in wise proportion and subtlety can result in a stimulating, satisfying program.

After a notable opening, each section has its own special dynamic impact and potential for development. Intricate and attention-demanding numbers are effectively placed before the midpoint of the program—after the opening numbers have prepared the choir vocally, aurally, and musically. The first and the final sections function as a tension-developer and a tension-relaxer, respectively. A program is said to "flow" when all these elements receive proper attention.

Placement of Serious and Lighter Selections

Of special concern is sensitivity to the juxtaposition of serious or sacred selections and those that are less serious in character. Since the general progression of a program is from music demanding intense concentration toward that which is more relaxing in nature, an audience should not be expected to give deep concentration to music with a sacred or serious text immediately following light or humorous selections. Frequent changes in language within a single group can be distracting and can cause a listener to feel that the program is lacking unity. However, artistic proportioning of contrasts in mood and texture within unifying elements will heighten interest and increase satisfaction.

Contrast within Sections

Each section of the program has its special climax as well as its own variety and contrast. Similar to a classical symphony, the several movements (or selections in a group) alternate fast and slow tempos, key relationships, and changes in meter. Differing moods are contrasted and projected through texture, dynamics, tonalities, and text.

Textures are contrasted through polyphony and homophony, female and male voices, solo and tutti sections, *a cappella* and accompanied singing. Voices in combination with instrumental timbres provide additional variety. Many contrasts are within music itself, or they may be affected by juxtaposing forms from within a single historical period. For example, contrast

> A homophonic chanson with a polyphonic madrigal.
> A Venetian polychoral motet with an English verse anthem.
> A Mendelssohn part song (unaccompanied) with a Brahms lied (accompanied).
> Britten's "Flower Songs" with a Harrison Birthwhistle avant-garde composition.
> Daniel Pinkham's *Wedding Cantata* (with instruments) with the same composer's "In the Beginning of Creation" (with prepared tape).

Each composition has its own basic dynamic. Contemplative moods contrast with lively ones; songs of praise with songs of prayer and adoration; clever texts with serious ones. Contrasting moods and dynamics afford infinite variety and serve as another important criterion for the selection of music within each group of a program.

Contrasts in key, modality, and tonality are also considerations that ensure variety. Key relationships are important within each group of selections. Conductors who program a succession of numbers in the same key will invite pitch difficulties for the singers and monotony for the audience. A change of key, particularly to one that is related harmonically, adds subtle interest and gives welcome variety to the choir's sonorities. A conductor may be guided by principles similar to those applicable to key relationships within movements of a sonata.

Text contrasts are related to mood, but they can also serve to vary a program in other ways. Latin texts encourage lyricism and legato expression because of the nature of the language. Other languages also have distinguishing characteristics. French is recognizable by its resonance and fluidity, German by its rhythmic and percussive qualities. Spanish and Italian, being vowel-oriented, retain many similarities to Latin, while their syllabic natures encourage rhythmic subtleties.

English can vary from folk dialect to the standardized diction advocated by Madeline Marshall[4] or Dorothy Uris.[5] Poetry may be lyric or dramatic. The mood, the subject, and the poet's choice of words all may provide beautiful and exciting contrasts. Reading the poetry aloud in preparation for rehearsal, a conductor will more clearly reveal the language of the poet and the moods conveyed through accentuation, subtle stresses, and elongations.

In striving to ensure an appropriate degree of contrast at any point within a concert program, a conductor is well advised to avoid extremes. He must exercise care that the contrasts do not repeatedly shock or jolt the audience; attention to the "flow" of the concert is essential. A feeling of musical satisfaction is the result of creative planning and consideration of alternative sequences and relationships.

[4]Madeleine Marshall, *The Singer's Manual of English Diction* (New York: G. Schirmer, Inc., 1953).
[5]Dorothy Uris, *To Sing in English* (New York: Boosey & Hawkes, 1971).

Audience Participation

Concert planners increasingly sense the importance of involving the audience in a concert program. In a church service the worshiper becomes involved in congregational hymns and responses. An anthem may also include congregational participation at some point. At a folk-music concert, the pleasure of the audience is often increased if they are encouraged to clap with the choir in response to the rhythm, a practice that is common when traditional gospel music is sung.

In Philadelphia, where the Singing City Choir successfully fulfills objectives of artistic excellence combined with the promotion of human relations through music, an audience is frequently involved in singing folk music. Both Elaine Brown and Sonya Garfinkle, conductors highly skilled in teaching folksongs by rote, heighten noticeably the enjoyment of audiences through such participation during informal concerts. In formal performances of Bach Passions, audiences are frequently invited to sing the chorales; listeners actually become a part of the drama. The popular *Messiah* "sing-alongs" are extreme examples of this practice.

Conductors of high school or college choirs often choose one special selection that is included on each year's program. This heightens esprit de corps and a feeling of belonging. When choir alumni present at a concert are invited to join with the choir in singing this traditional music as the program's final selection or encore, a sense of continuity is developed.

Active involvement of an audience is not always advisable, however. Careful consideration of the prospective audience, the choice of music, and the tasteful manner in which it might be woven into the fabric of a concert program will help the conductor assess its appropriateness and possible effect.

The Program Ending

A pleasing and fulfilling ending for a concert depends on music that has been performed earlier on the program, musical sophistication of the audience, and the particular occasion.

After hearing music that has fulfilled aesthetic needs, that has required careful attention to its complexities, the audience may be ready to respond to music that is lighter, even humorous, in nature. There are degrees of lightness of mood and style appropriate within programs. The nature of a particular program's content and the conductor's innate good taste are guides in determining any selection's appropriateness. Possibilities for selections following intermission include a group of contemporary compositions, music for choir with vocal or instrumental solos, an instrumental or vocal ensemble, a guest soloist, a group of male or treble chorus selections, or any music of transitional character.

The closing group of a program, depending on the focus of the music that precedes it, may include music of a lighter nature, such as appealing folksong arrangements or, at the opposite end of the spectrum, a climactic, uplifting finale. Above all other considerations, the music chosen to end a concert should be so well performed that singers and listeners alike wish the concert had not come to an end.

Types of Concerts

Informal concerts may include a planned demonstration of musical learning that has taken place in choral rehearsals or an attempt to share with an audience some outstanding musical characteristics to be heard in a selection or group of selections. They may also take the form of a madrigal dinner or a Renaissance festival. The educating of audiences can contribute to their enjoyment and increased support for choral music.

Festival programs and concerts may include a variety of choral ensembles representing varying stages of maturity and development. When several choirs or small ensembles are included, special care must be taken in the order and unification of program content. Interest and concentration should be increased gradually; less experienced groups should not be permitted to suffer by comparison with those composed of more advanced singers. The following guides in programming may prove helpful.

Alternate vocal textures (mixed choruses, male and female glee clubs, children's voices, small ensembles, solo voices).

If small ensembles are included, alternate their performances with those of larger groups.

Permit weaker or beginning groups to sing early in the program and place them between small ensembles, not immediately following or preceding more advanced choirs.

Begin the program with a performance by the "second best" rather than the least experienced ensemble.

Plan for contrast by considering tempos, moods, keys, tonality, or modality in each section of the concert.

Alternate a group of a cappella selections with music utilizing accompaniment by a single instrument or by an instrumental ensemble.

Consider the possibility of achieving unity in the program by giving it a central theme, such as Spring Concert, Fall Concert, Christmas Concert, Thanksgiving Concert, A Festival of Sacred Music.

For a choral festival where several choirs sing in succession, arrange the individual performances in order of appropriate contrast in repertory interest, keeping moods and tempos in mind.

Conclude the program with a performance by the most accomplished choir or a combined work with all choirs participating.

Contrast and a fitting climax can be ensured when instrumental and choral groups join forces in concert.

EXAMPLES OF PROGRAM BUILDING

Choral concert programs have been formulated traditionally along historical lines: from sixteenth-century motets and madrigals to music of the twentieth century. A more imaginative and creative approach is possible. Developing a program that flows, that stimulates aesthetic response and provides both unity and contrast, presents a challenge to conductors at every level. The selection of a "centerpiece," as illustrated in the sample programs that follow, leads to other choices that form textual and musical relationships. Combined, they provide a variety of moods and textures for an audience.

When works of a single composer or compositions in honor of a special occasion serve as a central theme or unifying element in a program, a helpful procedure to follow is to select the centerpiece; arrange preceding and succeeding parts of the program in logical sequences (build toward and away from the centerpiece, offering changes of mood between selections); and keep in mind contrasts in tempo and textures as well as unity of subject matter within each group.

Although the type of audience, the ability level of the singers, and the occasion are all important considerations in program selection, interest is maintained and communication is most likely to be enhanced when elements of unity and variety are present. The possibilities for effective and stimulating programming are expanded by a conductor's awareness of the vast choral repertory as well as his or her creativity, imagination, sensitivity, and good taste. Selected examples of creative programming for a variety of choral ensembles follow.

Program 1

ILLINOIS SUMMER YOUTH MUSIC
JUNIOR CHORUS*
Doreen Rao, Conductor

PROGRAM

Mixed Chorus

Music Here .... Eugene Butler

O bone Jesu .... G. P. Palestrina

Vanitas vanitatum .... J. P. Sweelinck

Selections from *Gloria* .... Antonio Vivaldi
    III. *Laudamus te,* Duet
    IV. *Gratias agimus tibi,* Chorus
    V. *Propter magnam gloriam,* Chorus
              (Chorus with String Orchestra)

Girls' Chorus

Kyrie from Mass in G Major .... Franz Schubert

Ticket to Ride .... John Lennon
                               and Paul McCartney
    (Chorus, Double Bass, Drums, and Piano)

Boys' Chorus

Viva tutti .... ed. Ralph Hunter

Bound for Jubilee .... Joyce Eilers

Mixed Chorus

In Stilly Night .... Johannes Brahms

The Fiddler .... Johannes Brahms

The Sally Gardens .... Benjamin Britten

The Circus Band .... Charles Ives

I'm Going Home .... Gospel

I Bought Me a Cat .... Aaron Copland

Amazing Grace .... arr. Coates

*This concert program represents the culmination of two weeks of intensive Summer Youth Music activities for a hundred selected junior high school singers. Included is music for mixed, girls', and boys' voices.

Observations

The concert's opening text by Alfred Lord Tennyson sets the tone for what is to follow. The poem concludes: "Music! Music! Music!—There is sweet music here." This leads directly into two beautiful Renaissance motets by Palestrina and Sweelinck, which are followed by three movements from Vivaldi's *Gloria*.

The flow of the music from subtle motets to the climactic fugue in *Gloria* is smooth, yet contrasting. SA duets are often effective when sung by full sections: This was a perfectly acceptable Baroque practice. "Laudamus te," originally assigned to two singers, is written in polyphonic style with frequent imitation. It is followed by a homophonic choral recitative, "Gratias agimus tibi," leading directly into the contrasting and climactic fugue, "Propter magnam gloriam." Selecting two or three sections from parts of a mass can be effective programming, particularly when the movements chosen bear a relationship to each other and offer contrasts in texture, tempo, or both. A Kyrie and a Gloria, or a Sanctus, Benedictus and Agnus Dei, programmed in sequence are also likely combinations, since a complete mass can be too lengthy to program in its entirety.

Selections for the Girls' and Boys' Choruses provide contrast in this program by their inherent textures as well as changes in mood. Consideration for the ages of singers and the atmosphere of a summer concert are apparent and justifiable. The final mixed chorus choices include music by some of our finest composers and serve to illustrate an important educational truth that excellent music need not be the most difficult or complicated. The group includes a four-part folksong arrangement by Brahms and two unison folksong settings by Britten and Ives. A gospel song and a folksong arranged by Aaron Copland give credence to indigenous American music.

Program 2

The University of Texas, San Antonio CHAMBER CHORALE
John Silantien, Conductor
Presents
LIEDERABEND: An Evening of Viennese Classical Music

PROGRAM

Christ ist erstanden .... Franz Schubert

Psalm 23, Op. 132, for Women's Voices .... Franz Schubert

Abendlied zu Gott .... Franz Joseph Haydn

Mass in C, Op. 48 .... Franz Schubert
      (Soprano, Mezzo Soprano, Tenor, Baritone, Chorus, and Organ)

INTERMISSION

Two Nocturnes .... Wolfgang Amadeus Mozart
    Ecco quel fiero istante
    Mi lagnero tacendo

        (SAB and three Clarinets)

Two Irish Airs .... arr. Ludwig van Beethoven
    I Dreamed I Lay Where Flow'rs (Soprano and Baritone soloists)
    Oh! Would I Were but That Sweet Linnet (Soprano and Tenor soloists)
    (Duets, with Strings and Piano)

Der Tanz .... Franz Schubert

Ständchen .... Franz Schubert
              (Chorus with Tenor solo)

Trinklied .... Franz Schubert

Nachtgesang im Walde .... Franz Schubert
         (Chorus with four French Horns)

Das Wandern .... Franz Schubert
            (Chorus with Tenor Solo)

Lebenslust .... Franz Schubert

Observations

Schubert's Mass in C, a concerted work for chorus, four soloists, and small orchestra (or organ), forms a nucleus around which the entire program is built. Both sacred and secular texts are set by nineteenth-century Viennese composers. The three sacred pieces that open the program project contrasting textures and moods and lead smoothly into Schubert's Mass in C. After an intermission, small instrumental ensembles and soloists are introduced: The clarinet trio, the string ensemble, and the tenor solo provide changes in texture and sonority. The final Schubert selection brings the concert to a bright, joyful conclusion.

Program 3

The University of Santa Clara CHAMBER SINGERS
Stephen Rosolack, Director
Presents a
SPRING CONCERT: "Now Is the Month of Maying"

PROGRAM

Motet and Parody Mass on *Dixit Maria* .... Hans Leo Hassler
    Motet
    Parody Mass
        Kyrie
        Gloria
        Sanctus-Benedictus
        Agnus Dei

Choral Dances from *Gloriana* .... Benjamin Britten
    Time
    Concord
    Country Girls
    Rustics and Fishermen
    Final Dance of Homage

Selections from *New Lovesong* Waltzes, Op. 65 .... Johannes Brahms
    1.   Renounce, O Heart, all rescue
    2.   Perilous darkness of night
    3.   On either hand with pledges
    7.   From the mountain, wave on wave
    8.   Sheltered softly midst the grass
   13. No, beloved, sit not near

INTERMISSION

Renaissance Spring
    Now Is the Month of Maying .... Thomas Morley
    I Know a Young Maiden .... Orlando di Lasso
    Now Is the Gentle Season .... Thomas Morley
    The Cricket... Josquin des Prés
    The Big Fat Goose .... Orlando di Lasso
    Fine Knacks for Ladies ....John Dowland

Observations

This spring choral concert appears to be fashioned around Brahms's *Neue Liebeslieder,* Opus 65. Although this work was originally composed for a solo quartet, it is frequently performed by a well-trained choir. It serves as an effective centerpiece on a choral concert program. The composition from which this group was selected consists of fifteen brief, contrasting movements in which vocal parts are interwoven exquisitely with textures of a four-hand piano accompaniment.

The *Neue Liebeslieder* extols love. Contemplating its inclusion in a program, the conductor apparently thought of other love relationships in musical composition: In the opening group, man's adoration of the Virgin Mary is expressed in music by a composer of the sixteenth century; in the second group he combines five lighthearted expressions of love set to music by Benjamin Britten to honor Queen Elizabeth II on the occasion of her coronation. Reference to "Gloriana" was made frequently in the sixteenth century to honor the first Queen Elizabeth. Both unity and contrast are apparent in this program, which concludes with a selection of madrigals from the sixteenth century.

Program 4

The University of Illinois CONCERT CHOIR
Harold A. Decker, Conductor
Presents
"A Program of Contemporary American Music"

PROGRAM

Wedding Cantata .... Daniel Pinkham
    Rise Up, My Love
    Many Waters
    Awake, O North Wind
    Epilogue: Set Me As a Seal

In the Beginning .... Aaron Copland
                (Choir with Mezzo Soprano Solo

Mass for Choir, Trombones, and Rhythm Section............................. Ben Johnston
    Kyrie-Gloria-Credo-Sanctus/Benedictus-Agnus Dei

INTERMISSION

Folk music from the American scene
    (for audience, choir, and small mixed ensemble)

Babel (Genesis 2:1–9)... Gregg Smith
           (Small Choir, Five Speaking Groups, and Piano)

The Vision... Dale Jergenson
            (Choir and Seven Soloists)

Dirge for Two Veterans .... Normand Lockwood
          (Choir with Soprano Solo)

"Stomp Your Foot" from *The Tender Land* ....Aaron Copland
         (Choir with Piano, four hands)

Observations

Although the Pinkham cantata is a possible centerpiece (it could serve that function if an orchestra were present), the Mass by Ben Johnston is a more appropriate focal point. Its unique jazz accompaniment provides a decided change of pace. The *Wedding Cantata* is an excellent opening number because of its melodic and harmonic simplicity as well as its immediate appeal to an audience. Copland's "In the Beginning" offers another contrast in texture, since it is unaccompanied and is dominated by a soprano solo. The biblical texts from Genesis and Song of Solomon provide a unifying element that moves logically into the Mass.

The fostering of audience participation within the program offers another texture and a further means of communicating with listeners. Sonya Garfinkle of Philadelphia's Singing City was present to lead American folksongs that were both familiar and unfamiliar. Those unfamiliar to the audience consisted of rounds and canons that were quickly taught and rehearsed so that the musical result was genuinely appreciated and enjoyed by all. The concluding selections range from speech dramatically united with song in "Babel" to the lyricism and poignancy of "Dirge for Two Veterans." The concert closes with the folklike energy and jubilance of "Stomp Your Foot" from Copland's *The Tender Land.*

Program 5

The University of Illinois UNIVERSITY CHORALE
Harold A. Decker, Conductor
presents
"The Genius of Heinrich Schütz"

PROGRAM

Psalms from the *Becker Psalter* (1661)
    Psalm 100, *Jauchzet dem Herren*
    Psalm 150, *Lobt Gott in seinem Heiligtum*

Motets from the *Geistliche Chormusik* (1648)
> *Die mit tränen säen*
> *Das ist je gewisslich wahr*

Musicalische Exequien (1648)
> Part I, Concerti in the form of a German Funeral Mass
> Part II, Motet: *Herr, wenn ich nur dich habe*
> Part III, Song of Simeon: *Herr, nun lasset du deinen Diener (Nunc Dimittis)*

INTERMISSION

Concerti for Solo Voices and Instruments

> *Symphoniae Sacrae II* (1647)
>> *Ich werde nicht sterben*
>> (for tenor, strings, and continuo)

> *Symphoniae Sacrae I* (1629)
>> *Paratum cor meum Deus*
>> (for soprano solo, two flutes, and continuo)
>> *O quam tu pulchra es*
>> (for tenor and bass duet, two violins, and continuo)

Psalms of David
> Psalm 100, *Jauchzet dem Herren*
> (for echo choirs, SATB soli, instruments, continuo)
> Psalm 150, *Lobt Gott in seinem Heiligtum*
> (for double choir, SATB soli, instruments, and continuo)

Observations

This concert, in honor of the great German Baroque composer on the 300th anniversary of his death, featured his *German Requiem,* composed for the funeral of his patron and good friend, Prince Heinrich Posthumus von Reiss. The work was written for various combinations of solo voices, quartets, single and double chorus, and instruments *colla parte* with *basso continuo.* Although fundamentally a somber composition, a variety of textural contrasts gives the work an appeal that merits a centerpiece assignment.

To prepare an audience for the major work, the concert opens with short, congregational-type homophonic psalm-settings taken from the *Becker Psalter* and then proceeds with two beautiful polyphonic motets. After intermission, three works for solo voices and instruments are followed by two elaborate polychoral settings taken from Schütz's *Psalms of David.* These final selections lend variety and opulence to the concert and, in addition, serve to unify the program by repeating the biblical texts found in the opening group.

Program 6

The University of Illinois CONCERT CHOIR
Harold A. Decker, Conductor
Presents
A Christmas Concert

I

Vom Himmel hoch, da komm ich her ....Johann Schein

In dulci jubilo .... Samuel Scheidt
(Choir with Trumpets)

Stellam quam viderant Magi .... Philippe de Monte

Jubilate Deo .... Guillaume Bouzignac

Cantata No. 1: *Wie schön leuchtet der Morgenstern* ....J. S. Bach

    Chorus: *Wie schöen leuchtet der Morgenstern*
    Recit. (Tenor): *Du wahrer Gottes und Mariensohn*
    Aria (Soprano): *Erfüllet, ihr himmlischen, göttlichen Flammen*
    Recit. (Bass): *Ein irdischer Glanz*
    Aria (Tenor): *Unser Mund und Ton der Saiten*
    Chorus: Chorale—*Wie bin ich doch so herzlich froh*
       Soprano, Tenor and Bass soloists, Violins, French Horns, Oboes da Caccia,
       Harpsichord, Organ, Bassoon, 'Cello, Double Bass and Chorus

INTERMISSION

III

Singet frisch und wohlgemuth ....Hugo Distler
    I. *Singet frisch, lobet Gott*
    II. *Kinder singet alle gleich*
    III. *Schaut die liebe Engel an*

Maria durch den Dornwald ging ....Johann Nepomuk David

O Sing unto the Lord (1961)..................................... Heinz Werner Zimmermann
(Choir with Double Bass)

The Shepherds' Christmas Songs .... Béla Bartók

Observations

Traditional Christmas concerts are formed around carols, cantatas, and motets that center attention on the story of the Christ-child, shepherds, angels, and wise men. The content of this program focuses on the biblical elements of Christmas, with emphasis on European (particularly German) carols and composers. A broad span of music, from the sixteenth century to the present, is included.

The Bach cantata is a central point of interest. The chorale melody is familiar and accessible to the listener; it serves as a unifying element within the work. Contrast is evident in the cantata, which presents a variety of textures: solo voices, tutti choir with instruments, and homophonic versus polyphonic writing within the music itself.

The opening group presents two well-known Christmas chorale melodies accompanied by brass. There follows a lovely antiphonal setting of a text concerned with the visit of the Magi to the stable in Bethlehem. The group concludes with a fascinating *a cappella* motet by a little-known French composer of the seventeenth century. (Unfortunately eclipsed by his contemporaries Lully and Charpentier, Bouzignac was not associated with Louis XIV's court at Versailles.)

The concluding section of the program includes Christmas music by twentieth-century composers. Interesting contrast is afforded by the Zimmermann work for solo string bass and chorus, and the rhythmic Christmas folk carols from Hungary arranged by Bartók.

Program 7

THE GLEN ELLYN CHILDREN'S CHORUS*
Doreen Rao, Conductor

I

Aesop of Phrygia—Prologue .... Sheldon Elias
Choir with Strings

II

Ave Maria .... Daniel Pinkham

Ave verum corpus .... Wolfgang A. Mozart

Chorale and Duet from Cantata No. 37:
   Wer da glaubet und getanst wird .... J. S. Bach

O Lovely Peace .... George F. Handel

"Prayer" from *Hänsel and Gretel* .... Engelbert Humperdinck

III

Litanie a la vierge noire .... Francis Poulenc

Psalm 150 .... Benjamin Britten

*The GLEN ELLYN CHILDREN'S CHORUS performs frequently with the Chicago Symphony Orchestra whenever children's voices are needed. In addition, Conductor Rao's concert programs are well organized and contain sophisticated music literature.

Observations

This program, sung by boys and girls eight to fourteen years old, is truly an amazing one for this age group. It bears testimony to the adage that children can learn anything that a teacher (conductor) can teach them. Children have the capability not only to sing beautifully but also to express musical ideas emotionally and aesthetically. This concert begins with a first performance of a commissioned work by Sheldon Elias. Although the choral setting is with strings, the content is whimsical and easy to attend. The second group is varied in scope and ranges from a lyrical *a cappella* setting of "Ave Maria" by Pinkham, through works by Mozart, Bach, and Handel, to the familiar "Prayer" from *Hänsel and Gretel*.

This concert illustrates the placing of a centerpiece near the close of the program. The Poulenc "Litanie" is a major undertaking. It is challenging and, at the same time, satisfying in all ways: sonorities, rhythmic interest, and true aesthetic beauty. Britten's "Psalm 150" leaves the audience on a high peak of musical excitement.

EXAMPLES OF CENTERPIECES FOR CONCERT PROGRAMS

Choral Compositions with Strings or Chamber Orchestra

Carl Philipp Emanuel Bach	Magnificat
Johann Sebastian Bach	Cantatas No. 1, 4, 6, 11, 21, 26, 38, 61, 68, 71, 80, 106, 131, 140, 142, 150, 191[6]
	Magnificat in D
	Missa Brevis in g minor
Ludwig van Beethoven	Eligischer Gesang
John Blow	Welcome Song
William Boyce	Two Anthems for the Georgian Court
	"The Souls of the Righteous"
	"The King Shall Rejoice"
Benjamin Britten	Cantata Academica
	Cantata Misericordium
	Rejoice in the Lamb
	St. Nicholas
Dietrich Buxtehude	Alles was ihr tut
	In dulci jubilo
	Jesu, meine Freude
	Neugebornes Kindelein
Antonio Caldara	Magnificat
Giacomo Carissimi	Jephte
Marc-Antoine Charpentier	Messe de minuit de Noel
Luigi Cherubini	Magnificat
Michel-Richard Delalande	Te Deum
Lukas Foss	Behold! I Build Thee an House
George Frideric Handel	Chandos Anthems
	Coronation Anthems
	Dettingen Te Deum
	Dixit Dominus
	Funeral Anthem on the Death of Queen Caroline
	Psalm CXII—Laudate pueri
Joseph Haydn	Missa brevis St. Joannis de Deo
	Missa St. Nikolai
	Seven Last Words
	Stabat Mater
	Te Deum
Pelham Humfrey	By the Waters of Babylon
Niccolo Jomelli	Te Deum in D
Johann Kuhnau	Magnificat
Padre Martini	Domine, ad adjuvandum me festina
	Magnificat
Salvatore Martirano	O,O,O,O,That Shakespeherian Rag
Gian Carlo Menotti	The Unicorn, the Gorgon, and the Manticore
Wolfgang Amadeus Mozart	Coronation Mass
	Missae breves in F and C
	Regina coeli in C
	Venite populi
	Vesperae solemnes de confessore
Johann Pachelbel	Christ lag in Todesbanden
Giovanni Pergolesi	Magnificat
Michael Praetorius	Puer natus in Bethlehem
Henry Purcell	Behold, I Bring You Glad Tidings
	Come Ye Sons of Art Away

[6]These cantatas are primarily choral and are from fifteen to thirty minutes long.

	O Sing unto the Lord
	Welcome to All the Pleasures
Alessandro Scarlatti	Laudate Dominum, omnes gentes
Franz Schubert	Masses in C and G
	Stabat Mater
Heinrich Schütz	The Christmas Oratorio
	German and Latin Magnificats
	Musikalische Exequien
	The Seven Last Words
Roger Sessions	Three Biblical Choruses
John Tavener	Introit for March 27
Georg Philipp Telemann	Nun komm der Heiden Heiland
Edgar Varèse	Magnificat
Ralph Vaughan Williams	Five Mystical Songs
Antonio Vivaldi	Gloria in D
	Psalm 109: Dixit Dominus (double chorus)
	Psalm 111: Beatus vir (double chorus)
	Psalm 121: Laetatus sum
	Magnificat
Anton Webern	Das Augenlicht
	Cantatas: Op. 29 and Op. 31

Short Choral Compositions with Full Orchestra

Béla Bartók	Cantata Profana
Leonard Bernstein	Chichester Psalms
Lili Boulanger	Psaume 29
Johannes Brahms	Alto Rhapsodie
	Nänie
	Schicksalslied
	Triumphlied
Anton Bruckner	Te Deum
Anton Dvořák	Te Deum
Lukas Foss	A Parable of Death
Alberto Ginastera	Psalm 150
Gustav Holst	Christmas Day
	Hymn of Jesus
Alan Hovhaness	Magnificat
Zoltán Kodály	Psalmus Hungaricus
	Te Deum
Leos Janáček	M'sa Glagolskaja (*Festival* Mass)
Felix Mendelssohn	Da Israel aus Aegypten zog
	Lauda Sion
Carl Orff	Carmina Burana
	Catulli Carmina
Sergei Rachmaninoff	The Bells
Franz Schubert	Magnificat in C
	Miriams Siegesgesang
Matyas Seiber	Ulysses
Igor Stravinsky	Canticum sacrum
	Requiem Canticles
	Symphony of Psalms
Ralph Vaughan Williams	Benedicite
	Dona nobis pacem
	Flos campi
	Hodie
	Serenade to Music

Choral Compositions with Solo Instrument or Small Group of Instruments

Johann Sebastian Bach	Six Motets with instruments *colla parte*
Leslie Bassett	Collect, with organ, prepared tape
	Moon Canticles, with cello
Jan Bender	Psalm 150, with brass ensemble
John Biggs	Paul Revere's Ride, with horn, percussion
Gordon Binkerd	Dakota Day, with flute, oboe, clarinet, harp
	Nocturne, with cello solo
Johannes Brahms	Liebeslieder, Op. 52, with piano, four hands
	Five Songs, Op. 104, with piano
	Neue Liebeslieder, Op. 65, with piano, four hands
	Quartets, Op. 31, Op. 64, Op. 92, Op. 112, with piano
	Zigeunerlieder, Op. 103, with piano
Benjamin Britten	Ceremony of Carols, with harp
Paul Chihara	Ninetieth Psalm, with brass
Luigi Dallapiccola	Canti di Prigionia, with two pianos, percussion
Norman Dello Joio	Song of the Open Road, with trumpet, piano
Cecil Effinger	Pastorales, with oboe, piano
	Set of Three, with brass
Irving Fine	Choral New Yorker Suite, with piano
	Mother Goose Suite, with piano
Giovanni Gabrieli	In Ecclesiis, with brass, organ, continuo
	Jubilate Deo, with brass, organ, continuo
Paul Hindemith	Apparebit in repentina dies, with woodwinds, brass
Charles Ives	Psalm XC, with organ, bells, chimes
	Harvest Home Chorales, with brass, double bass, organ
Carolyn Jennings	Two Songs on Chinese Texts, with piano
Ben Johnston	Mass, with trombones (or organ), drum set, double bass
Billy Jim Layton	Three Dillon Poems, with brass
Franz Liszt	Missa Choralis, with organ
Normand Lockwood	Rejoice in the Lord, with brass, timpani
Edwin London	Sacred Hair, with organ, 4 combs
Witold Lutoslowski	Trois poemes d'Henri Michaux, with winds, percussion, 2 pianos, harp
Gian Carlo Menotti	The Unicorn, the Gorgon, and the Manticore, with 9 instruments, dancers
Daniel Moe	Magnificat, with brass
	Psalm Concertato, with brass, double bass
Wolfgang Amadeus Mozart	Misericordias Domini, with 2 violins, cello, organ
Krzysztof Penderecki	Psalms of David, with 2 pianos, celesta, harp, 4 double bass, percussion
Vincent Persichetti	Celebrations, with wind ensemble
Brent Pierce	Eight Japanese Haiku, with flute, violin, percussion
Daniel Pinkham	Christmas Cantata, with brass
	Easter Cantata, with brass, percussion
	Festival Magnificat and Nunc Dimittis, with brass
	Songs of Peaceful Departure, with guitar
	Three Lenten Poems (Robert Crashaw), with strings, handbells
	Wedding Cantata, with strings
Ariel Ramirez	Misa Criolla, with harpsichord, string bass, percussion
Gioacchino Rossini	I gondolieri, with piano
	Le passeggiata, with piano
John Rutter	Gloria, with brass, organ, percussion
Robert Schumann	Zigeunerleben, with piano
Henirich Schütz	Magnificats (German, Latin), with strings, winds, brass, organ, continuo

	Psalm 150 (4 choirs), with winds, brass, strings, organ, continuo
	Saget den Gästen, with 2 violins, bassoon, strings, winds, organ, continuo
	Saul, Saul, was verfolgst du mich?, with strings, winds, organ, continuo
Halsey Stevens	Magnificat, with trumpet, strings
	Te Deum, with brass, timpani, organ
Igor Stravinsky	Les Noces, with 4 pianos, percussion
	Mass, with octet of winds
William Walton	Missa Brevis, with organ
Heinz Werner Zimmermann	Psalmkonzert, with 3 trumpets, vibraphone, double bass

Unaccompanied Choral Compositions with Related Movements

Samuel Barber	Reincarnations
Béla Bartók	Four Hungarian Folksongs
Jean Berger	Brazilian Psalm
	Five Canzonets
	In a Time of Pestilence
Gordon Binkerd	Requiem for Soldiers Lost on Ocean Transports
	Three Institutional Canons
	To Electra
Johannes Brahms	Deutsche Fest- und Gedenksprüche (two choirs), Op. 109
	German Folksongs
	Lieder und Romanzen, Op. 93
	Marienlieder, Op. 22
	Motets, Op. 29, Op. 74, Op. 110
	Partsongs, Op. 104
Benjamin Britten	Choral Dances from *Gloriana*
	Five Flower Songs
	Hymn to St. Cecilia
	Sacred and Profane
William Byrd	Mass for Four Voices
	Mass for Five Voices
Aaron Copland	Choruses from *The Tender Land*
	In the Beginning
	Three Motets
Luigi Dallapiccola	Cori di Michelangelo
Claude Debussy	Trois Chansons de Charles d'Orleans
Emma Lou Diemer	Three Madrigals
Hugo Distler	Selections from *Mörike Chorlieder*
	Der Totentanz
	Weinachtsgeschichte
Maurice Duruflé	Three Motets
Anton Dvořák	Songs of Nature
Cecil Effinger	Three Contemporary Madrigals
Ross Lee Finney	Spherical Madrigals
Irving Fine	The Hour-Glass Suite
Thomas Frederickson	Impressions
Alberto Ginastera	Lamentations of Jeremiah
Eskil Hemberg	Five Nonsense Songs
	Signposts
	Zoo
Paul Hindemith	Five Songs on Old Texts
	Madrigals
	Six Chansons

Andre Jolivet	Epithalome
Zoltán Kodály	Matra Pictures
Edwin London	Three Songs on Hebrew Texts
Frank Martin	Mass for Double Choir
Nicholas Maw	Five Epigrams
Olivier Messiaen	Cinq Rechants
Darius Milhaud	Les deux cités
Thea Musgrave	Four Madrigals
	Rorate coeli
Knut Nystedt	De profundis
Pierluigi de Palestrina	Pope Marcellus Mass
	Stabat Mater (double choir)
Krzysztof Penderecki	Agnus Dei
	Stabat Mater (three choirs)
Vincent Persichetti	Mass
Goffredo Petrassi	Motetti per la Passione
Francis Poulenc	Selected Chansons
	Christmas Motets
	Lenten Motets
	Mass
Sergei Rachmaninoff	Liturgy of St. John Chrysostom
Maurice Ravel	Trois Chansons
Ned Rorem	From an Unknown Past (7 madrigals)
John Rutter	The Falcon
Arnold Schoenberg	Friede auf Erden
William Schuman	Carols of Death
Williametta Spencer	Four Madrigals to Poems by James Joyce
Thomas Tallis	Spem in alium non habui (eight choirs)
Randall Thompson	Five Odes of Horace
	Frostiana
	The Peaceable Kingdom
Ralph Vaughan Williams	Mass in g minor (double choirs)
	Three Choruses from Shakespeare
Robert Wykes	Four American Indian Lyrics

Epilogue

The Prologue and the chapters of this book have focused upon aspects of communication. Responsibilities of the conductor have been outlined and guidelines have been suggested for the development of communication skills needed by the conductor and the choral musicians who constitute the performing instrument.

There is another dimension of the choral art that demands sensitivity: communication with an audience. To communicate effectively, the conveyor of a message must be empathic with the receiver. When this essential sensitivity to the audience is lacking, a choral ensemble may perform *at* or *toward* an audience, with minimal communication.

Audiences are capable of growth in receptivity and understanding. The gap between levels of responsiveness expected and previous experience in listening must not be too wide. If an audience has had no previous experience with the music of J. S. Bach, for instance, that audience will scarcely be ready for an extended Bach work without benefit of clear verbal guides or program notes.

Frequently a concertgoer may notice that little is done to educate an audience in the beauty and other elements that may be sensed or observed aurally in a musical work. Interest and understanding are broadened and deepened when musical responses are elicited from a particular audience. With the help of program notes or carefully devised brief verbal comments, those listening may be enlightened about the composers' intentions. Directed listening can cause an audience to feel truly a part of the artistic process.

By planning programs with the listeners in mind, the conductor encourages receptive attitudes. He or she recognizes the fact that audiences find satisfaction in discovery; concerts need not be planned merely to entertain. Choral musicians grow in their respect and love for repertory through careful selection by the conductor. So also do audiences respond to careful selection of repertory that appropriately challenges their interests and responsiveness. As people become aware that they can listen for specific musical ideas and their development, timbre or color, texture, elements contributing to the feeling of movement, formal design, and patterns of tension-release, their pleasure will increase. Audiences will be motivated to explore composers' communication of expressive nuances through choral performance. The conductor who cares about audiences and their pleasure will share facts about the music and unfold interesting aspects of works being performed. Receptive attitudes are the result of warm, pleasant, enlightening experiences with music.

The preceding chapters and the appendixes that follow are intended to help choral conductors further their understanding and develop necessary habits and skills. Some suggestions may be new to the reader; some may reinforce previous knowledge. Throughout the treatise, three concepts have emerged that provide a key to continuous development: sensitivity, proportion, and relationship.

SENSITIVITY

A conductor will discover an increasing personal sensitivity to musical nuance, to the composer's intention, to choir members, to the direction that learning takes, and to the aesthetic responses of audiences. As sensitivity becomes more acute, a conductor responds in various ways:

1. The conducting gesture *pictures* the music—its character, form, phrasing, shape, and continuity—more clearly and eloquently.
2. The rehearsal improves in efficiency and effectiveness.
3. The planning of concert programs reflects heightened imagination and creativity.

PROPORTION

As a recipe is important to one who would delight palates of those who sample gourmet fare, so proportions indicated by a musical score are essential to the interpreter. The comparison can be carried one step further. As the gourmet cook alters a basic recipe and thereby enhances flavor to taste, so a conductor experiments in an effort to discover the most satisfying musical proportions for

Exact distance of intervals between pitches.
Voices in balance with each other and with instruments.
Degrees of intensity, strength, or quality assigned to particular chord members as determined by chord position or function.
Clarity, emotional quality, and integrity of expression through text.
Contrasts and gradations in dynamic intensity.
Tempos within a musical work.
Accelerandos, rallentandos, ritards, timing of fermatas, and length of final chords.
Contrasts of horizontal and vertical movement.

Proportion is also critical in planning for use of time in a rehearsal. Thinking of sonata-allegro form may be helpful. The introduction and *exposition* section of a rehearsal can comprise physical readying, voice building, ear sharpening, mind and imagination stimulating, and music reading. The *development* section of a rehearsal can be considered that portion of time utilized for clarifying rhythms, pitches, phrasing, balance. The *recapitulation* can include the polishing process. Proportions of rehearsal time devoted to any of these will vary with each rehearsal and can determine the outcome or effectiveness of the rehearsal with respect to advancing the preparation of music to be performed and developing singers' musical skills and understanding.

Proportion must also be considered with respect to program planning. Music that necessitates deep concentration must be balanced with selections that can be enjoyed with ease.

RELATIONSHIP

In creating and re-creating choral music, nothing is in isolation; every aspect is related to all others in some way. Sound is related to silence; melody, rhythm, and harmony are related within themselves, to each other, and to the text; phrasing is related to larger and smaller units that make up the form; an individual voice and personality relates to a group of singers; each section of the choir relates to the choral ensemble as a whole; a conductor relates to performers; performers relate to an audience; and on and on *ad infinitum*.

Appendix A

Projects for Students of Conducting

Chapters of this text are addressed to students of conducting. The projects in Appendix A are intended as helpful and enlightening assignments. Used in close conjunction with the text, these projects can reveal to the student an awareness of his or her abilities and can provide appropriate synthesis for learning.

Projects may be undertaken in the order in which they occur. Those that are designed to result in *continuing* behavior and habitual acquisition of music resource material are presented first, even though the chapter reference occurs later in the text.

Reference to Music for Class Study and Conducting will be abbreviated MCSC.

PROJECT I   Search for Repertory Information

Reference: Chapter 7

Objective: The student engages in an extensive search for repertory. He or she accumulates and organizes information that can be a valuable resource for personal use in all future choral activity.

Tasks: A.   On 5 × 8 cards, duplicate forms for repertory information (general and church choir) similar to the ones that appear in Appendix B. Use different colors for the two cards.

B.   Complete one card for each selection encountered in performance participation, concert attendance, and laboratory study.

C.   Develop the habit of searching for repertory of quality in choral libraries, workshops, convention exhibits, music stores, concert programs and conversations with colleagues.

D. Consult *Choral Music in Print* for relevant information needed to complete index cards.

E. Whenever you encounter music that would be especially appropriate for a service of worship, record the information on the form designed for that purpose.

F. Decide on a practical organizational scheme for filing repertory information. Alphabetize cards according to title; place in categories denoting sacred or secular, and beneath subheadings for voicings (Unison, Treble, Male, Mixed). Sub-subheadings might separate music of the several historical periods, or a color tab attached to a card might identify the appropriate style period.

G. Continue this practice of collecting information. An alternative to the card file may be a personal computer.

PROJECT II   Laboratory Conducting Preparation

Reference: Chapters 1, 2, 3

Objective: The student prepares thoroughly for each conducting experience by studying the score, marking it carefully, practicing gestures, and planning for efficient use of time in rehearsal (class or choral laboratory).

Tasks: A.   Practice conducting gestures as guided in Chapter 1.

B.   Conduct appropriate patterns for the following meters in succession: five times each pattern, then (on repeat) one time each pattern.

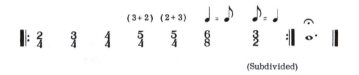

(Subdivided)

Following fermata release, execute the sequence of patterns in reverse order.

C.   Practice conducting music in basic meters:
   Triple (MCSC, pp. 247, 297, 304, 278, 358)
   Duple (MCSC, pp. 268, 269, 311, 324, 248, 253, 286, 316, 289)

D.   Mark the score and practice conducting each selection you choose or are assigned for a laboratory conducting experience.

E.   Keeping length of measure constant, practice alternating duple and triple divisions of meter:

and

F.   Practice conducting compositions that incorporate meter changes. Rest Sweet Nymphs—Pilkington (MCSC, p. 265)

The Lord to Me a Shepherd Is—Alwes (MCSC, p.346)

Deck the Halls (in $\frac{7}{8}$)—arr. McKelvy (MCSC, p. 362)

Sanctus-Benedictus—Johnston (MCSC, p. 358; see analysis in Chapter 3.)

G. Identify, mark in score, and practice conducting hemiole found in

But As for His People—Handel (MCSC, p. 278)

Peace Today Descends from Heaven—Grandi (MCSC, p. 271)

H. Identify, mark in score, and practice conducting syncopation found in

Sanctus-Benedictus—Johnston (MCSC, p. 358; see analysis in Chapter 3.)

I. Practice indicating expressive nuance with left hand only.

Agnus Dei—Haydn (MCSC, p. 304)

Let Nothing Cause You Anguish—Brahms (MCSC, p. 316; see analysis in Chapter 3.)

J. When secure with left hand indication of expressive nuance, combine the two hands.

K. Practice conducting with facial expression only.

L. Combine use of facial expression with right hand and left hand gesture practice.

M. Utilizing study guides in Chapters 2 and 3, mark score for "How Excellent Thy Name/Hallelujah" (MCSC, p. 289). Compare your marked score with that found on page 75.

N. Utilizing study guides and procedures suggested in Chapters 2 and 3, practice conducting each selection you plan to present in the choral laboratory. Whenever appropriate, practice conducting instrumental as well as vocal lines.

PROJECT III Exercises to Encourage Rehearsal Readiness

Reference: Chapters 2, 3, 4

Objective: The student formulates objectives and devises exercises to prepare singers for rehearsals. Encourage physical readiness, mental alertness, aural keenness, and vocal preparedness.

Tasks: A. Keeping in mind that the goal of vocalization is to fulfill objectives of beautiful singing, design exercises that will result in habitual good posture; proper breath management; a sound that is free from tension; unified, resonant vowel sounds; rhythmic, clear articulation of consonants; careful listening for intonation and chordal balance; and artistic phrase shaping.

B. Design exercises that can satisfy more than one of the stated objectives. Keep in mind that a single routine set of exercises can become boring and ineffective. Also, exercises devised from a musical selection to be rehearsed can be particularly effective in fulfilling objectives and in readying singers for work on that specific composition.

C. Examining the composition that you will conduct during your next choral laboratory experience, identify a potential problem that is likely to occur while singers are performing that selection under your direction. Design an exercise that you can incorporate to help singers solve that problem immediately before you conduct the selection.

PROJECT IV   Exercises to Develop Musicianship

Reference: Chapter 6

Objective: The student formulates objectives and designs exercises through which singers improve musicianship. Objectives and exercises reflect special concern for ear training.

Tasks: A.   Notate and practice solfeggio syllables for a chromatic scale beginning on each of the following pitches: D, E♭, E, F, G, A♭.

B.   Consider this statement: *Sing with your ears.* Describe as objectives specific student behaviors that you consider important that will demonstrate students' aural acuity.

C.   Design exercises that can be utilized in a rehearsal to foster or encourage behaviors described in Task B.

D.   Design exercises to develop interval security.

E.   Design exercises to develop rhythmic security.

F.   Design exercises that may be used to develop harmonic security.

G.   Utilizing two or more recorded examples of the same composition performed by different vocal ensembles and conductors, follow the score for that composition. Notice and analyze differences in interpretation. What factors contribute to a feeling of increased satisfaction?

H.   Repeat this task using selected recorded examples representing different styles and periods of musical composition.

PROJECT V   Exercises to Develop Sight-Reading Ability

Reference: Chapters 3, 4, 6

Objective: The student recognizes the importance of daily practice that increases facility in sight singing.

Tasks: A.   Design exercises that associate ear and eye in a meaningful way for children, adolescents, or church choir members who cannot read music fluently.

B.   Outline steps for a high school choir's reading of "Agnus Dei" from *Missa Brevis Sancti Joannis De Deo* (MCSC, page 304).

PROJECT VI   Rehearsal Planning

Reference: Chapters 3, 4

Objective: The student plans rehearsals that are interesting, enlightening, and well timed. They reflect careful study and preparation of the musical score, awareness of singers' attention span, concern for variety and reinforcement of previous learning, and a realistic sense of proportion and timing.

Tasks: A.   Focusing attention on the selection you will conduct in the choral laboratory, plan for wise use of allotted time. Write a brief outline of your plan.

B. Suppose that you are responsible for a chorus of adolescents. You wish to present and rehearse *Musica vivat aeterna* (MCSC, page 247). Describe the group's membership and outline plans for *three* sequential ten-minute rehearsals of this selection.

C. Plan a rehearsal fifty minutes long.

1. Describe the choral ensemble, including number of singers and maturity level: children, middle or junior high school, senior high school, adult church choir, or community chorus.

2. Include in your plan appropriate vocalises; at least three music selections (a composition not previously rehearsed, a composition previously introduced and currently in "working stage," and a composition in "polishing" stage); sight reading; a rehearsal closing selection that the group sings well and enjoys thoroughly.

3. Outline the order of the rehearsal with succinct indications of your planned procedure.

D. From repertory in MSCS, find two sections of music that you might rehearse in logical order for

1. Clarity of diction that can project text and mood of music.

2. Vowel color appropriate to the mood of the text.

3. Baroque rhythm affected by diction.

4. A legato line that can be improved through proper attention to vowels and consonants.

E. Outline two possible rehearsal approaches for each section chosen. An exercise may be used if appropriate. Remember to keep instructions clear and concise.

PROJECT VII   Seating–Standing Arrangements for Singers

Objective: The student places singers advantageously for blend of voices and accommodation of requirements for performance of particular musical styles.

Diagrams for basic seating/standing arrangements for groups of mixed voices in sections include:

1. B   T
   S   A
2. S   A   T   B
3. S   B   T   A
4. BI   BII   TI   TII
   SII   SI   AII   AI

Singers may also be placed in quartets or "mixed" arrangement of parts to facilitate hearing other parts:

S A T B S A T B
B T A S B T A S

Tasks: A. Practice listening carefully to each singer in a section. Select a phrase from a familiar selection; permit each person to sing individually. Rearrange singers' standing (seating) order until the blend of voices is pleasing and singers are comfortable singing next to their neighbors. Repeat procedure for each of the remaining sections.

B. Recognizing that a choice of basic seating/standing arrangements may be determined for a specified group of singers on the basis of sectional sound balance or for effectiveness in performing music from a particular historical style period, suggest an arrangement (or arrangements) for each of the following:

1. A church choir of forty mixed voices (balanced sound)
2. A large oratorio chorus performing Mozart's Requiem
3. Sixty mixed voices with balanced sectional sound performing each of the following:

    How Excellent Thy Name/Hallelujah (MCSC, p. 289)

    Let Nothing Cause You Anguish (MCSC, p. 316)

    Agnus Dei (MCSC, p. 304)
4. A junior high school choir of mixed voices (unbalanced sound) including 30 sopranos, 12 altos, 4 tenors, 8 basses

PROJECT VIII   Auditioning

Objective: The student listens carefully to voices; he or she assesses vocal and musical achievement, range, tessitura, and individual problems.

Tasks: A.   Study the audition form in Appendix B. Think of yourself in the role of either a church choir director or a director of a high school choir. How might you modify and use this form advantageously?

B.   Plan a short audition procedure that can be used to obtain information you will need to work effectively with singers.

C.   Write short musical patterns that you might use during the audition to determine tonal and rhythmic memory capabilities.

D.   If possible, assemble necessary materials and practice using your form to audition a classmate (or classmates).

E.   Revise your audition form if necessary.

PROJECT IX   Concert Program Planning

Reference: Chapter 7

Objective: The student plans concert programs that take into account capabilities of singers, unity and contrast in selections to be performed, increase of interest, feeling of satisfaction for audience and singers.

Tasks: A.   Consider music selections listed under Classic-Romantic period in MCSC. Arrange three or four of these selections in an order of performance that would form an interesting group representing music of that historical period. Consider unity and contrast, tempos, key relationships, text, and all other relevant matters.

B.   Utilizing selections found in MCSC and choral music from your school library (or other source), construct a choral concert that is fifty to seventy-five minutes long. Describe the choral ensemble (or ensembles) performing on the concert. Build the program around a "centerpiece" chosen from those mentioned in Chapter 7. Assess your proposed program carefully for compliance with suggestions for program building presented in Chapter 7.

PROJECT X   Review of Music History

Reference: Chapter 2

Objective: The student demonstrates understanding of music history, composers, and style characteristics through teaching aids.

Tasks: A.   Describe a choral group you hope to conduct (children's chorus, junior high school chorus, senior high school chorus, church choir, or community chorus). Envision a rehearsal room in which this group will meet for rehearsals.

B.   Design for your chorus(es) and rehearsal room a visual aid that can assist in introducing or reinforcing concepts and relationships leading to understanding music history. These may include dates, composers, countries, music of stature, pictures, and pertinent occurrences in the political or artistic life of the Western world. Be careful to make your visual aid large enough to be effective in a classroom.

C.   Think of a way to associate with your visual depiction selected music examples in sound.

PROJECT XI   Developing Musical Security

Reference: Chapter 6

Objective: The student plans exercises that assist singers in their understanding of essential relationships in music.

Tasks: A.   With a specific group of singers in mind, devise exercises to develop aural and visual interval relationship security.

B.   Notate and practice solfeggio syllables for ascending and descending chromatic scales beginning on each of the following pitches:
$$D\ E^\flat\ E\ F\ F^\sharp\ G\ A^\flat\ A\ B^\flat$$

C.   Devise exercises for
   1.   Familiarizing students with various key relationships, including relative major and minor diatonic scales.
   2.   Developing rhythmic accuracy.
   3.   Improving intervallic accuracy.
   4.   Developing awareness of intonation accuracy.

D.   If possible, incorporate one or more of these exercises during one of your laboratory conducting experiences.

PROJECT XII   Stating Objectives

Reference: Robert F. Mager, *Preparing Instructional Objectives* (Belmont, Calif.: Fearon, 1962).

Objective: The student articulates learning objectives in behavioral terms.

Tasks: A.   Describe a group of singers you hope to conduct. They may represent your choice of advancement level.

B.   For the group you have described, formulate learning objectives stated in behavioral terms. Each objective should specify succinctly what the student does to indicate (demonstrate) his or her accumulation of knowledge or development of understanding. The statements should present a clear profile of the student you expect to emerge from the experiences under your direction.

C. Keep in mind that a statement of objectives can guide your choice of repertoire and rehearsal planning.

PROJECT XIII   Conductor Profile

Objective: The student demonstrates awareness of skills and knowledge essential for success as a choral conductor.

Tasks: A. Review the following list of qualifications for a choral conductor:
Ability to communicate a love for music
Ability to hear
Knowledge of the voice
Conducting technique
Rehearsal technique and flexibility
Organizational ability
Understanding of group dynamics and human relations
Knowledge of choral literature and language
Sensitivity to text

B. Add to the list any further qualifications you consider important.

C. Rank all qualifications in order of their importance.

Appendix B

Guides for Teachers of Conducting Classes

A college or university teacher of conducting classes may find the following explanations and suggestions beneficial. These guides are by no means exhaustive; they are intended to stimulate, rather than to limit, a teacher's creativity.

The book can be most helpful when its use spans at least two semesters. This allows time for essential reinforcement and thorough understanding of its contents. Students may be encouraged first to familiarize themselves with the rationale presented in the Prologue.

Perceptive use of the Bibliography can accommodate students who are more advanced musically, and permit assignment of additional readings for which extra credit is awarded. It can also assist students who exhibit particular deficiencies: They may be assigned specific readings and projects.

Projects suggested in Appendix A may be assigned appropriately in relation to textbook study, classroom discussion, and leadership experience. Portions of projects may be selected for class sharing. Projects III–XII are particularly appropriate. Class sharing of student responses to selected projects can be effective in stimulating critical thought.

Excellence in communication through gesture is the result of sharpened perceptions. Conducting communication is a skill that proceeds from crudeness to precision through careful and repeated practice. It begins with conveying meter and tempo through pattern; it can become increasingly clear and effective in depicting nuance.

Two guiding principles for teachers of conducting are these: *Doing* is more important than talking excessively about what should be done; and classroom interaction should reinforce learning that is gained from reading and practice assignments.

Initial progress can be made through practice of meter patterns, timing of breath preparation, releases of sound, shaping of phrases with attention to increase and decrease of intensity, changes in tempo, subtleties of nuance, and treatment of the fermata. Exercises suggested in Chapter 1 may be practiced individually or by the class as a whole. In class, the conducting teacher can serve as a model while standing and conducting with his or her back to the class.

To facilitate maximum class progress, use of a large mirror across the front of the room permits students to observe their own movements as well as those of the teacher; the mirror can also permit the teacher to monitor individual students' posture and gestures. When a mirror is not available, the teacher should glance over his or her shoulder frequently to monitor students' progress.

As soon as possible, conducting gesture practice should be associated with music—either from the keyboard or from recordings that represent expressive interpretation, various meters, and different tempos. Practice partners may be assigned to assist each other during out-of-class practice. (See Figure B-1.) The response of a person to a conductor's indications for intake of breath, beginning of sound, phrase shaping, dynamic contrasts, and release of sound can be extraordinarily helpful.

Effective growth is possible in a laboratory environment. Ideally, conducting students should be in a choral ensemble to be used for practical experience. Whenever more than one conducting class is offered concurrently, students from all classes may be combined to provide more voices for each student to conduct and rehearse. When leadership in the laboratory situation is carefully planned and time is utilized efficiently, all students can learn through their own experience, other students' conducting, and comments or suggestions offered by the teacher(s). (See Figure B-2.)

Laboratory conducting experiences are more valuable when they are videotaped on a VCR and subsequently studied carefully. (See Figure B-3.) Critiquing their own performance recorded on tape, with guidance from a teacher, students grow in skill and confidence. (See Figure B-4.) Each student may have his or her own tape; ownership permits greater flexibility of time for

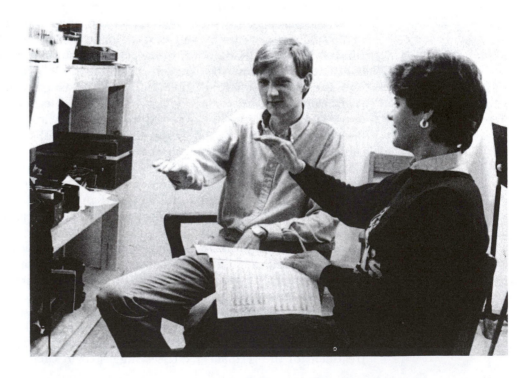

Figure B-1   Students offering help to each other.

Figure B-2   Student conducting laboratory singers.

Figure B-3   Video camera setup: Instructors observing and offering written suggestions.

playing back the recorded experience. When previous conducting experiences are preserved on tape, a student can review his or her progress. An alternative plan is the recording of conductors in succession on a single cassette tape. Students may then schedule individual playbacks following each laboratory experience.

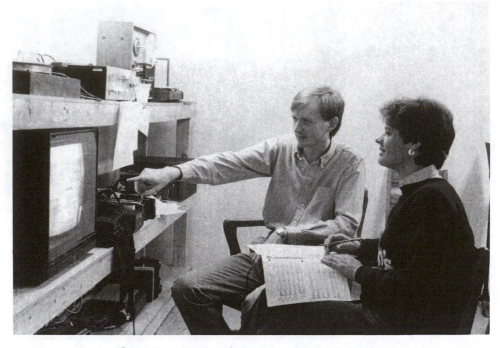

Figure B-4   Students observing video playbacks.

Organization of Laboratory Experience

Established seating (including parts *divisi*) conserves time and facilitates cuing.

Rotation of conductors in alphabetical order helps to ensure equitable portions of time allotted to all. The rotational scheme permits conductors to anticipate precisely when each will conduct and encourages more careful preparation.

A time limit for each conducting experience results in greater progress for all. Frequent experience permits students to profit from previous conducting performance and observations. Five minutes of conducting, videotaped and critiqued, can provide a more effective learning experience than thirty minutes during which the teacher and students offer "on-the-spot" suggestions and discussion. Time allotments can be lengthened gradually as students become more experienced. As they gain confidence in gesture management, student conductors can be encouraged to listen more intently; as they hear more, they will be ready to practice rehearsing.

Brief outlines written by conductors for use of their time can ensure more effective time utilization and develop a necessary habit.

Identification of the accompanist(s) for the choral laboratory allows further preparation and communication. The students can apprise the accompanist of a selection and the procedure well in advance of the class. Valuable rehearsal time can be conserved when an accompanist knows what he or she is expected to play. If the accompaniment calls for sensitivity or presents technical difficulties, its practice prior to the laboratory experience can assist the conductor in achieving the desired musical result. Whenever possible, the conductor will find it beneficial to practice conducting the selection with the accompanist.

If two or more instruments are used in accompaniment, the conductor will find it helpful to rehearse with the instrumental ensemble prior to the choral rehearsal. The conductor's preparation for rehearsal with instruments entails careful study of the capabilities of specific instruments and the requirements placed upon them by the musical score.

Students' utilization of conducting evaluation forms during each video playback time can provide a basis for learning in the student-teacher conference. (See page **199** .)

Caution: There are two extremes of teacher behavior that can result in lessened effectiveness of teaching-learning in conducting classes and laboratories. These are insufficient generalization and positive reinforcement of essential points; and too much time spent talking about specifics with one conductor. Written comments can often replace or augment spoken commentary in the choral laboratory.

Selection of Conducting Materials
from Music For Class Study and Conducting

Predictable stages of development in conducting skill may be accommodated through selection of repertory that presents and limits appropriate challenges. When conducting his or her first musical selection in the choral laboratory, the beginning conductor's attention is devoted almost entirely to gesture. He or she will find the following challenges sufficient: posture, timing of breath preparation and beginning of sound, gesture pattern placement and style portrayal, timing of final cadence and release of sound. Phrase shaping, dynamics, and voice-part cuing can be given attention in subsequent laboratory experiences as control of gesture is developed.

As a conductor becomes increasingly comfortable with gesture, he or she can be encouraged to devote more careful attention to listening while conducting. Ability to rehearse effectively can be developed gradually and consistently in a pattern similar to that employed for development of gesture clarity and control.

Although teaching skills are being developed gradually and carefully through laboratory experience, the most advanced concern of the emerging conductor is the learning and enjoyment of students during the choral rehearsal. The ultimate task is to plan rehearsals that are both aesthetically satisfying and intellectually enlightening.

To assist the teacher of conducting, specific challenges have been identified for each composition included in Music for Class Study and Conducting. Beginning conductors will experience greater success if their first assigned compositions are from Group I. As progress is made, individual students may be encouraged to study and conduct selections from Group II. More advanced conductors will be ready for challenges presented in Group III and Group IV. Eleven compositions have been the focus of guided scrutiny (score analysis and observations) within the text (Chapters 2 and 3). These can serve as models for conductors' study of scores. Procedures learned through this guided study may be applied to preparation of all other scores.

CONDUCTING CHALLENGES GROUPED IN ORDER OF DIFFICULTY

Group I

Musica est Dei donum optimi (Orlando di Lasso)   In $\frac{4}{4}$

    Challenges for the conductor:

      Andante
      Legato gesture pattern
      Phrasing
      Entrances of each part
      Final fermata
      Release
    (See analysis in Chapter 3.)

Musica vivat aeterna (Anonymous)   In $\frac{3}{4}$

    Challenges for the conductor:

Flowing tempo.
Legato gesture pattern.
Breathing in relation to phrases.
Follow rise and fall of dynamics that outline the music.
Entrance of parts on successive beats.
Fermata and final release
(See analysis in Chapter 3.)

Jesu, Priceless Treasure (J. S. Bach)   In $\frac{4}{4}$

Challenges for the conductor:
Andante; dignified; sincere.
Think in terms of the form: AAB. Note variation in length of fermatas in order
   to keep movement within phrases.
Observe ritardando in final phrase.
Give attention to moving eighth notes throughout.
Follow rising and falling melodic lines with appropriate dynamics.

Wake, Awake, for Night Is Flying (J. S. Bach)   In $\frac{4}{4}$

Challenges for the conductor:
Dignified, but not too slow. Expectant!
Observe form and melodic contour.
Give particular attention to bass line. Sing each vocal line separately.
Note suspensions and passing tones that give vitality to the interpretation.
See that consonants at ends of phrases are placed on the rest that follows.

Christ Jesus Lay in Death's Strong Bands (J. S. Bach)   In $\frac{4}{4}$

Challenges for the conductor:
Observe form and melodic contour as they relate to text.
Notice that all but two phrase entrances require a preparatory beat on 3.
After reading remarks in Chapter 3, set an appropriate tempo.
(See analysis in Chapter 3.)

Luci care, luci belle (W. A. Mozart)   In $\frac{4}{4}$

Challenges for the conductor:
Set a tempo that is graceful and animated.
Compare the bass line of the accompaniment with that of the comparable
   voice part.
If sung in Italian, observe the relationships between text syllables and music.
   (Where divisions are not indicated, divide note values evenly.)
If sung in English, approximate the same smoothness of execution as would
   be possible in the original language.
Bring out the frequent "duet" passages between SA and SB.
Check phrasing of instrumental parts so that they agree with those of the vocal
   parts.
(See analysis in Chapter 3.)

Herbstlied (Autumn Song) (Felix Mendelssohn)   In $\frac{6}{8}$

Challenges for the conductor:
Spirited, with agitation.
Graceful, rather long phrases.
Check the formal design and discover where the opening melody is repeated.
   Divide into sections for rehearsal.
Observe special dynamic markings. Let each accent reflect the *meaning* of
   the word it modifies.
If German is preferred, practice speaking the German text so that you can
   model phrases with every consonant articulated distinctly.
If in English, approximate the same precision and clarity.
Indicate in your score where rests will be necessary to clarify ends of phrases
   and prepare a breath for the phrase that follows.
Check dynamics and changes of tempo carefully.

Group II

I Know Where I'm Goin' (arr. William D. Hall)   SA or TB in $\frac{4}{4}$, $\frac{3}{4}$

Challenges for the conductor:

Moderate tempo; flowing; obbligato instrument; sustained.

Observe an instrumentalist playing the obbligato part: Compare parts where notes are played legato, without tonguing, with those that indicate tonguing every two notes. Approximate the same effects with voices: legato, with eighth notes sung clearly on each pitch.

Observe how essential it is to prolong the vowels in each word or syllable as a legato line is sung. Also, no sliding to pitches!

In $\frac{3}{4}$ section, conduct a graceful 3 pattern without increasing the tempo. Be aware that the pianist has an accented second beat.

Rest Sweet Nymphs (Frances Pilkington)   In $\frac{4}{4}$, $\frac{3}{2}$, $\frac{3}{4}$

Challenges for the conductor:

Andante; legato; independent movement of inner parts.

After reading each verse aloud, determine how you will achieve contrast in performance (solo quartet or small group on one verse, a verse sung *a cappella*, dynamic contrast with one verse *pp*, or instruments doubling voices).

Think of the refrain as a lullaby, the $\frac{3}{4}$ in a rocking motion.

Find and mark all parts that move independently.

Observe suspensions at cadence points.

Anthem of Thanksgiving (C.P.E. Bach)   In $\frac{3}{4}$

Challenges for the conductor:

Allegro; sixteenth notes in accompaniment.

Consider evenness and clarity of the sixteenth notes in accompaniment when setting tempo, especially since the first three measures of the introduction contain only quarter notes and rests.

Apportion ♩. ♪ figure in vocal parts precisely in order that it correspond with accompaniment.

Study structure and phrasing that lead toward climactic peaks.

Consider dynamic relationships.

Experiment with timing of *poco ritard* and *a tempo*.

You Lovers That Have Loves Astray (John Hilton)   In $\frac{2}{2}$

Challenges for the conductor:

Tactus circa 65–70; spritely; "with a twinkle in the eye."

To select the proper tempo, repeat several times in succession, as rapidly as possible: "Quick music's best, quick music's best." Now sing the alto and the second and first soprano parts to see how clearly and distinctly they can be sung.

Check the tempo and try the entire madrigal at this speed.

Exaggerate the consonants in *fa, la, la* refrains.

Relate the beginning $\frac{2}{2}$ measures to the $\frac{3}{4}$ as 3:2.

Place more stress on each first beat of the measure in the $\frac{3}{4}$.

Check all dynamic markings and reveal them in your gestures.

He Sent a Thick Darkness from *Israel in Egypt* (G. F. Handel)   In $\frac{4}{4}$

Challenges for the conductor:

Largo; sustained; mystical night.

Prolonged vowels; consonants placed on rests.

Use appoggiaturas as a means of expression. (Bring out the dissonances.)

Keep a sense of continuity from one melodic line to another.

Establish a "dark" tone quality in keeping with the text.

Agnus Dei from *Missa Brevis Sancti Joannis De Deo* (Joseph Haydn)   In $\frac{3}{4}$

Challenges for the conductor:

Adagio; reverent; expressive; string accompaniment, organ.

Be familiar with the other parts of a Mass. Know the function of the final "Agnus Dei." Make a translation of the Latin text.

Notice how skillfully Haydn shaped the words and phrases to the music.

Find the musical climax of this repeated text.

Be aware of the continuous eighth-note pattern of the accompaniment as the choir sings legato.

Look for dynamic markings in the orchestral accompaniment that are also appropriate to the singing.

Group III

Peace Today Descends from Heaven (Hodie, nobis de caelo)
(Alessandro Grandi)   TB or SA; In $\frac{2}{2}$, $\frac{3}{2}$

Challenges for the conductor:

Circa 76; a joyful alleluia; important bass line.

Sing *alleluias* at bottom of page 273 to get feeling of a joyful tempo. Establish this at the beginning.

Play the keyboard part, giving special attention to the bass line.

Find the hemiole in the $\frac{3}{2}$ sections. Relate the $\frac{2}{2}$ sections to the $\frac{3}{2}$ so that measure equals measure (3:2).

Keep rhythm crisp and steady, yet buoyant.

But As for His People from *Israel in Egypt* (G. F. Handel)   In $\frac{3}{4}$

Challenges for the conductor:

Andante; confident; pastoral theme.

Compare the following: a four-measure introductory phrase, which appears three times during the chorus; a pastoral theme introduced twice (observe the dotted rhythms in the oboe part and maintain them in the voice parts); a contrapuntal theme, which is developed extensively the first time and then repeated later, just briefly; a Coda, which contains a strong final statement with four hemiole (including one in the orchestra only).

(See analysis in Chapter 2.)

Let Nothing Cause You Anguish (Lass dich nur nichts nicht dauren)
(J. Brahms)   In $\frac{4}{4}$

Challenges for the conductor:

Lento; legato, sostenuto; espressivo.

Observe the flowing lines in the piano introduction; let this be a clue!

Find *A B A* form plus Coda. Observe relationships between ST and AB throughout. What is the canonic relationship? Compare to the Coda.

Check dynamic treatment of each phrase and motif. Keep long lines in mind throughout. How do the text and the flowing phrase lines affect the tone-color of the voices?

(See analysis in Chapter 3.)

How Excellent Thy Name / Hallelujah! from *Saul* (G. F. Handel)   In $\frac{4}{4}$

Challenge for the conductor:

Maestoso; regal; a song of praise and admiration

(See analysis in Chapter 3.)

Sanctus - Benedictus from *Mass* (Ben Johnston)   In $\frac{3}{4}$

Challenge for the conductor:

Moderately, with a beat (as in jazz); with trombones or organ, string bass, traps

(See analysis in Chapter 3.)

Group IV

"Gratias agimus tibi" and "Propter magnam gloriam" from *Gloria*
(Antonio Vivaldi)   In $\frac{4}{4}$, $\frac{2}{2}$

Challenges for the conductor:

Adagio–Allegro. Recitative for Chorus–Fugue.
Broad, dignified opening statements. Keep continuity and feeling of movement by increasing the intensity as first fermata is sustained.
Conduct the Allegro in 4, at a tempo that will accommodate clearly enunciated eighth notes.
Breathe with entrances of each part.
Observe the TB pairing in thirds (mm. 6–7) and the SB (mm. 8–9).
Note the stretto in m. 12, where there is an entrance on the first three beats of the bar.
Keep intensity until the release at the conclusion.

Tenebrae factae sunt (Darkness Descended) (Marc Antonio Ingegneri)   In $\frac{3}{2}$, $\frac{4}{4}$

Challenges for the conductor:

Awesome introduction. This is a Renaissance painting of Christ's crucifixion in music.
Don't exaggerate: Let the music portray the scene.

(See analysis in Chapter 2.)

Agnus Dei (Lamb of God) (Giovanni Pierluigi da Palestrina)
Plainchant setting and motet in $\frac{4}{4}$ (or $\frac{2}{2}$)

Challenges for the conductor:

Smoothly and calmly; legato 4-beats at first, then in broad 2.
Singing the chant in a flowing, graceful manner creates a proper model for the motet, which follows immediately.
Divide into three phrases, with barely perceptible breaths.
Conduct with horizontal pattern from side to side in front.
Ritard final five notes gradually.

(With chant in mind, see analysis in Chapter 3.)

Duetto buffo di due gatti (Comic Duet for Two Cats)
(Gioacchino Rossini)   For two voices SA or TB in $\frac{4}{4}$, $\frac{6}{8}$

Challenges for the conductor:

With humor. (Don't be afraid to imitate the cat's me-ow!)
To be sung with a straight face. Exaggerate the dynamic markings.
Conduct "animal gait" in 6; quarter notes at approximately 76 at "Cat-like."
   Your release of the first fermata is the preparation for the chorus entrance.
Have fun!

The Lord to Me a Shepherd Is (Chester Alwes)   In $\frac{5}{8}$, $\frac{6}{8}$, $\frac{9}{8}$, $\frac{3}{4}$, $\frac{2}{4}$, $\frac{3}{8}$

Challenges for the conductor:

Flowing eighths in the rhythm of the text; graceful; meaningful.
This is not a difficult piece to conduct if the following guides are heeded:
Reading the rhythm of the music, speak the text quietly.
After feeling comfortable reading in this manner, conduct as you read, with two beats in $\frac{5}{8}$ (long-short), two beats in $\frac{6}{8}$ (equal), three beats in $\frac{9}{8}$.
Divide into five or six beats at all measures of *rit.* and wherever a fermata occurs.
Conduct 3 in $\frac{3}{4}$ measure (m. 16) where TB are singing in $\frac{6}{8}$.
Conduct divided 3 at *molto rit. e dim.* (m. 24).
After the pause (m. 25) conduct 2 (short-long) for one measure, then long-short (m. 26).
Conduct the $\frac{3}{8}$ measure in one beat (m. 27), then continue as at first.
After climax (mm. 41–43) conduct quarter–eighth, quarter–eighth in m. 44, and final three measures in 6.

Keep the gestures small and concise for the most part. Rehearse a number of times in front of a mirror, speaking the text, before attempting to conduct a choir.

Go, Lovely Rose (Halsey Stevens)   In $\frac{2}{2}$, $\frac{3}{2}$, $\frac{4}{2}$, $\frac{5}{4}$, $\frac{7}{4}$

Challenges for the conductor:

Andante; espressando; legato.
Read the text thoughtfully. Conduct as read, using the smallest number of beats possible.

Keep in mind the following:

m. 2—Phrase gently, without disturbing the line, after "Rose."
m. 3—*Subito piano* after *me* (use left hand gesture).
m. 8—Cue TB, then SA.
m. 9—Conduct $\frac{7}{4}$ as a measure of *3* (short-short-long).
m. 12—Conduct $\frac{5}{4}$ in *2* (short-long).
m. 16—Conduct $\frac{7}{4}$ in *3* (long-short-short).
m. 21—Phrase after *admired,* continue with upbeat.
m. 28—Phrase after *tenuto* ever so slightly.

Deck the Halls (in $\frac{7}{8}$) (arr. James McKelvy)   In $\frac{7}{8}$, $\frac{4}{8}$

Challenges for the conductor:

Spirited; joyful; shifting rhythms.
Read composer's note at the beginning. Examine the groupings of 2 and 3 (they shift from "long-short-short" to short-short-long).
Conduct with crisp, precise gestures. Exaggerate tongue movement singing the *fa-la-la*s.
Examine the dynamic development from *mp* at the beginning to *forte* in the second phrase after "C"; *subito pianissimo* at "D"; then, *forte* to the conclusion of the piece (no ritard!).
Practice conducting while speaking the text many times before conducting the choir.

Following are samples of forms to assist developing conductors. The teacher may use them as guides for his or her own forms, which may be duplicated and made available in quantity. Samples included here are for

Repertory Information (General; Church Choir).
Evaluation of Conducting.
Audition Information.

The repertory information forms can be most useful when duplicated on both sides of 5 × 8-inch cards.

Appendix B concludes with suggested models for conducting course syllabi.

Repertory Information—General

(Side One)   Solo _____

Title _____   Unison SA SSA SSAA

Composer/Arranger/Editor _____   TB TTB TBB TTBB

_____   SAB SATB SSAATTBB

Publisher _____   Other _____

Edition number _____   Year of publication _____

Language _____   Source of Text _____

Type of Accompaniment _____   Instrumentation _____

Range and Tessitura:

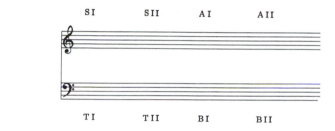

Specific
Difficulty
(Difficulties):

(Side Two)

Dates Performed   _____   _____

                                                 Renaissance _____
                                                 Baroque _____
                                                 Classical _____
Period/Style of Composition: Romantic _____
                                                 20th Century _____
                                                 Folk _____
                                                 Popular/Jazz _____
                                                 Novelty _____

                                                 Large Ensemble _____
                                                 Small Ensemble _____

Possible uses: Program "Opener" _____
                                                 Program "Ending" _____

                                                 Special Occasion (specify) _____
                                                 _____
                                                 Church Service _____

                                                 Teaching/Learning _____
                                                   Sight Singing _____
                                                   Expression/Text _____
                                                   Period/Composer _____
COMMENTS: Other _____

Repertory Information—Church Choir

(Side One)

1. Text: (Source and Treatment)

   _____

   _____

   _____

2. Composer: _____

3. Title: _____

4. Voice Combination: _____

5. Accompaniment: _____

6. Comments: (period, style, type, etc.)

   _____

   _____

7. Form or Movements: _____

8. Rhythmic Treatment: _____

9. Harmonic Treatment: _____

(Side Two)

10. Vocal Treatment: (Density, Range, Color, etc.)

    _____

    _____

11. Special Features, Uses, and Comments:

    _____

    _____

12. Difficulties Presented:

    _____

    Editor: _____ Publisher: _____

    Address: _____

    Price: (Score/Parts) _____

    Date Published: _____ Recording: _____

Dates Performed:

Conducting Evaluation

Assess this conductor's achievement by placing a checkmark at the appropriate point on each line. (10 represents the highest possible attainment.)

Selection conducted: _____

Conductor's Preparation

1. Knowledge of the musical score

   1 2 3 4 5 6 7 8 9 10

2. Understanding of character and style of the music

   1 2 3 4 5 6 7 8 9 10

3. Familiarity with each individual part

   1 2 3 4 5 6 7 8 9 10

4. Appropriateness of rehearsal plan

   1 2 3 4 5 6 7 8 9 10

Conductor's Presentation

1. Clarity of verbal instruction

   1 2 3 4 5 6 7 8 9 10

2. Projection of speaking voice

   1 2 3 4 5 6 7 8 9 10

3. Avoidance of excessive talking/unnecessary remarks

   1 2 3 4 5 6 7 8 9 10

4. Posture and placement of conducting pattern

   1 2 3 4 5 6 7 8 9 10

5. Clarity of conducting pattern

   1 2 3 4 5 6 7 8 9 10

6. Gesture communication of appropriate musical style and character

   1 2 3 4 5 6 7 8 9 10

7. Effectiveness of left hand indications

   1 2 3 4 5 6 7 8 9 10

8. Timing and clarity of cues

   1 2 3 4 5 6 7 8 9 10

9. Confidence communicated through eye contact

   1 2 3 4 5 6 7 8 9 10

10. Enthusiastic participation encouraged through positive approach

    1 2 3 4 5 6 7 8 9 10

11. Musicianship exhibited in presentation

    1 2 3 4 5 6 7 8 9 10

12. Improvement in musicality demonstrated by singers

    1 2 3 4 5 6 7 8 9 10

Conductor's Rehearsal Technique

1. Identification of musical problems

   1 2 3 4 5 6 7 8 9 10

2. Indicate with a + or − the conductor's effectiveness in solving problems related to:

intonation _____	tone quality _____
blend _____	balance _____
tempo _____	dynamics _____
rhythm _____	phrasing _____
consonants _____	posture _____
breathing _____	vowels _____
ensemble _____	

3. Comfortable pacing of the rehearsal

   1 2 3 4 5 6 7 8 9 10

Additional comments or suggestions for the conductor:

_____

_____

_____

Evaluator _____ Date _____

Audition Information

Name _____ Part _____

School (Class) _____

Quality 5   4   3   2   1   *Smoothness* 5   4   3   2   1

Blending Potential 5   4   3   2   1   *Sight Reading*   − 0 +

Melodic Memory 5   4   3   2   1   *Rhythmic Memory* 5   4   3   2   1

Range:

Ensemble Recommendation   5   4   3   2   1

Choral Literature and Conducting I & II
Credit: 2 semester hours

At the conclusion of this two-semester sequence, each student will demonstrate the ability to

  I. Recognize a broad repertoire of choral music appropriate for groups of varying levels of capability and maturity. This repertoire will represent all styles and periods of choral composition. Evidence of this acquaintance will be revealed in each student's card file.
 II. Study and prepare a choral score for rehearsal purposes.
III. Interpret with stylistic understanding choral music of the various styles and periods of choral composition.
 IV. Achieve a unified choral sound appropriate for the work being performed.
  V. Give verbal directions clearly and concisely.
 VI. Indicate interpretive and stylistic ideas in gesture.
VII. *Hear* what a choral group is actually producing; diagnose vocal difficulties and offer effective help toward improvement; and recognize and correct inaccuracies in pitches and rhythms.
VIII. Change a choral sound appropriately through work on breathing, diction (vowels and consonants), balance, blend, and phrasing.
 IX. Encourage participation and a desire for improvement in members of a choral group.

ORGANIZATION AND CLASS PROCEDURE

These course offerings are primarily laboratory situations. Classes should be small (twelve to sixteen students) so that frequent conducting experience is possible. All students should register concurrently in a repertory chorus—a larger choral group that will afford the experiences of conducting and rehearsing a larger choral group; reading of literature appropriate for choral groups of various types; and acquaintance with methods and materials for use in choral music instruction. The repertory chorus will meet for two hours each week. It will carry 1 unit of credit. The conducting classes will meet two hours per week and carry 2 units of credit.

It is anticipated that during the two-semester sequence in *Choral Literature and Conducting*, steady progress will be made toward poise and effectiveness in the conducting role. Students will be supplied with packets of supplementary choral works, and care will be taken to ensure a lack of duplication of specific works being studied in the various classes in any two successive quarters.

Choral Literature and Conducting I will provide practice in the development of basic hearing and conducting skills. Actual choral music will be used. Skill in score study will be emphasized.

Choral Literature and Conducting II will provide further practice as a means to the achievement of confidence in the conducting leadership role. Knowledge of repertoire will be expanded.

Extensive use will be made of the video recorder as a means of self-analysis and self-evaluation.

Students will be evaluated on the basis of assignments covering skill development and growth in leadership capabilities, as well as pertinent outside reading.

SUPPLEMENTARY MUSIC FOR CHORAL LITERATURE
AND CONDUCTING I AND II

Five Centuries of Choral Music (New York: G. Schirmer, Inc.).
The Choral Repertory (Blue Book) (New York: G. Schirmer, Inc.).

Choral Techniques
Credit: 4 semester hours

Prerequisite: Choral Literature, and Conducting I and II.

At the conclusion of this semester each student will demonstrate the ability to

I. Utilize choral leadership skills as outlined for the prerequisite courses, *Choral Literature and Conducting I and II.*
II. Test voices and "seat" choir members advantageously.
III. Select appropriate and helpful vocalises; articulate and conduct these effectively.
IV. Plan for an aesthetically satisfying rehearsal.
V. "Pace" a rehearsal.
VI. Plan a program for public performance with attention to variety, contrast and aesthetic satisfaction.

TOPICAL OUTLINE

   I. Characteristics of the adolescent voice
      A. Range
      B. Quality
  II. Voice classification procedures
      A. Testing
      B. Matching
      C. Grouping for ensemble
 III. Seating arrangements for choral groups
 IV. Vocalises
      A. Development of range
      B. Development of breath control
      C. Clarification and unification of vowel sounds
      D. Rhythmic precision (clarity and timing of consonants)
      E. Hearing chords in tune
      F. Developing awareness of chord members and their function
      G. Singing dissonances in tune
      H. Exercises that fulfill more than one objective
  V. Range criteria for selection of materials
 VI. Music criteria for selection of materials
VII. Rehearsal management
      A. Instructional objectives
      B. Planning the order of the rehearsal
      C. Use of audiovisual techniques, such as tape recorder, overhead projector, and stereo, for increased effectiveness
VIII. Planning for a concert
      A. Music to be performed
      B. Order of program
      C. Dress rehearsals including stage deportment, logistics, and timing
      D. Administrative details such as publicity, tickets, ushers, risers, dress, and curtain.
 IX. Materials for music reading
  X. Training accompanists
 XI. The operetta or musical production
XII. The choral library system
XIII. Choral equipment and storage organization
XIV. Evaluation of the choral music curricular offerings

ORGANIZATION AND CLASS PROCEDURE

The course will be organized as a laboratory situation. There will be some lecture and discussion. All students should register concurrently in a repertory chorus—a larger choral group that will afford the experiences of conducting and rehearsing a larger choral group; reading of literature appropriate for choral groups of various types; and acquaintance with methods and materials for use in choral music instruction. The repertory chorus will meet for two hours each week and carry 1 unit of credit. The Choral Techniques class will meet four hours per week and carry 4 units of credit.

Extensive use will be made of the video recorder as a means of self-analysis and self-evaluation.

Students will be evaluated on the basis of assignments covering skill development and growth in leadership capabilities as well as pertinent outside reading.

Appendix C

Capitalization of Titles and Pronunciation Guides

English

1. Capitalize first and last words, nouns, pronouns, adjectives, verbs, adverbs, proper names, the Deity, and subordinate conjunctions.
2. Do not capitalize articles, coordinate conjunctions, and prepositions.
3. If the title is extracted from a large work or collection, (a) place it in quotation marks (optional) and underline (italicize) the major work, or (b) underline the title (italicize) and place the major work in all capital letters within parentheses.
4. Capitalize the voice classification or name of instrument if it is included on the program.

Examples:
   a. A Dirge for Two Veterans—Gustav Holst
        John Brown, Baritone
        Mary Jones, Percussionist
        Emma Niemeyer, Pianist
   b. The Unicorn, the Gorgan, and the Manticore—Gian Carlo Menotti
   c. Selections from *Gloria*—Antonio Vivaldi
        Laudamus te
        Gratias agimus tibi
        Propter magnam gloriam
   d. ''He That Shall Endure to the End'' from *Elijah*—Felix Mendelssohn
        He That Shall Endure to the End (from ELIJAH)—F. Mendelssohn

Latin, Italian, and French

1. Latin: Capitalize only proper names, references to the Deity, and the initial word.

Examples:
   a. Magnificat in anima mea—Giovanni Pierluigi da Palestrina
   b. Ave Maria, gratia plena—Josquin des Prés
   c. Ave verum corpus—William Byrd

    d. "Plorate filii Israel" from *Jephte*—Giacomo Carissimi
    e. "Agnus Dei" from *Mass for Four Voices*—William Byrd

2. If singing various sections from liturgy, capitalize the beginning words of each.
  Example: "Magnificat," "Et exultavit," and "Et misericordia" from *Magnificat*—Antonio Vivaldi

3. Italian: Follow the same rules as in Latin.
  Examples:
    a. Il bianco e dolce cigno—Jacob Arcadelt
    b. "Improperium" from *Motetti per la Passione*—Goffredo Petrassi
    c. Ecco mormorar l'onde—Claudio Monteverdi

4. French: Capitalize the same as in Latin or Italian.
  Examples:
    a. Cantique de Jean Racine—Gabriel Fauré
    b. Ainsi qu'on oit le cerf bruire—Claude Goudimel
    c. Chantez à Dieu chanson nouvelle—Jan Pieterszoon Sweelinck

German

Capitalize initial word, all nouns, proper names, and Deity.
Examples:
    a. "Nach dir, Herr, verlangete mich" from Cantata 150—J. S. Bach
    b. "O Haupt voll Blut und Wunden" from *Passion According to St. Matthew*—J. S. Bach.
    c. "Gloria" from *Missa brevis St. Joannes de Deo* (Kleine Orgelmesse)—Joseph Haydn
    d. "Vollendet ist das grosse Werk" from *Die Schöpfung*—Joseph Haydn
    e. "Schaffe in mir, Gott, ein reines Herz," Op. 29, No. 2—Johannes Brahms

PHONETIC SPELLING AND PRONUNCIATION IN FOREIGN LANGUAGES

Choral conductors whose repertory includes music in foreign languages will find it helpful to pursue in-depth language study or rely on the assistance of diction coaches. In college and high school choirs, many of the students have studied or are currently studying a language. With their interest and assistance, the conductor will be encouraged to widen the choir's musical horizons. For those who have limited study of foreign languages, the following references will provide some understanding and a background for pronunciation of French and German. This is not a substitute for the choir's hearing the text spoken by someone who speaks the language fluently, or by a diction coach.

Phonetic Equivalent Chart

IPA	Word Application	English Equivalent (Phonetic) where applicable
[æ̃]	nasal, as in jar**din** (Fr.)	no equivalent
[æ]	short, as in l**a**d, **a**nd	ĂA
[ɑ]	long, as in c**a**lm, g**o**d, B**ah**n (Ger.)	AH
[ã]	nasal "Ah" as in d**an**s (Fr.)	no equivalent
[b]	as in **b**oy	b
[ç]	as in ho**ch** (Ger.): forward over the tongue	no equivalent
[d]	as in **d**ough	d
[ɛ]	short, as in m**e**t	EH
[ɛ̃]	nasal EH, as in b**ain** (Fr.)	no equivalent
[e]	long, as in sp**ä**t, b**e**ten (Ger.); m**e**s, l**e**s (Fr.)	no equivalent
[eɪ]	long, as in l**a**te, b**ai**t	AY pronounced with diphthong

[ə]	rounded UH, as in **le** (Fr.); Lie**be** (Ger.); fa**ther**, **heard**, **urge**, **firm**, **term**, **word**	(referred to as *schwa* sound)
[f]	as in **f**it	f
[g]	as in **g**uard	g
[h]	as in **h**ome	h
[hw]	as in **wh**ite	wh
[i]	long, as in m**ee**t; **die**, **mir** (Ger.)	EE
[ɪ]	short, as in l**i**t	IH
[j]	like the *y* in **y**es	y
[ʤ]	like *j* in **j**ust; sometimes *g*, as in **g**orge	j
[k]	as in **k**eep, **c**oo**k**, **qui**ck	k
[l]	as in **l**ight, ba**ll**	l
[m]	as in **M**ay, su**mm**er	m
[n]	as in **n**ow, cu**nn**ing	n
[ɲ]	as in o**ni**on, se**ñ**or (Sp.)	ñ
[o]	long, as in h**ô**tel, **o**deur (Fr.)	OH (no diphthong)
[ou]	b**oa**t, t**oe**	OHoo (most common in English)
[ɔ]	"open *o*," as in f**a**ll, n**au**ght, b**ou**ght	AU
[ɔ̃]	nasal, as in n**on** (Fr.)	no equivalent
[œ]	as EH with rounded lips for AW: c**oeu**r (Fr.); Gl**ö**cken (Ger.)	no equivalent
[œ̃]	nasal, as in **un**, parf**um** (Fr.)	no equivalent
[ø][1]	as AY with rounded lips for OH: sch**ö**n (Ger.)	no equivalent
[p]	as in **p**o**p**	p
[r]	as in bo**rr**ow; Ky**r**ie (Lat.)	r
[s]	as in **s**un, ma**ss**	s
[ʃ]	as in **sh**ow, **sh**ip; sometimes *ch*, as in **ch**ef	sh (unvoiced)
[t]	as in **t**ell, be**tt**ing	t
[θ]	unvoiced, as in **th**in	th
[ð]	voiced, as in **th**en, mo**th**er	th
[u]	as in p**oo**l, d**o**, m**o**ve, s**ui**t, l**u**te	OO
[ʊ]	as in p**u**ll, b**oo**k	OO
[ʌ]	as in f**u**n	UH
[v]	as in **v**ery	v
[w]	as in **w**as	w
[z]	as in **z**ip	z
[ʒ]	as in plea**s**ure, vi**s**ion	*sh* (voiced)
[x]	as the *ch* in a**ch** (Ger.)	no equivalent
[tʃ]	as in **ch**ur**ch**	ch

Liturgical Latin

Languages derived from Classical Latin, known as Romance languages, include Italian, French, and Spanish; liturgical Latin is technically "Italianized" Latin. English is rooted in both the Latin and the Germanic, or Teutonic, languages; many French and German words have been absorbed into our language and anglicized. In the outline that follows, vowels, semivowels, diphthongs, and consonants used in liturgical Latin will be examined and compared with English pronunciations. A knowledge of the International Phonetic Symbols will be helpful in establishing exact pronunciations; the conductor will find that several of these symbols should be mastered by the choir members themselves.

Liturgical language pronunciation is based on its employment in the Ro-

[1]See German chart for pronunciation of umlaut vowels.

man Catholic church, in contrast to Classical Latin learned in the study of Julius Caesar and Cicero. Ecclesiastical Latin is based on rules set up in a decree by Pope Pius X in 1903 for "the singing of liturgical works according to Roman usage." A slightly different pronunciation is used today in performances of Austrian and German music by Classic-Romantic composers such as Haydn, Mozart, Beethoven, and Schubert. The following rules are applicable to the vast majority of music in the Renaissance.

Vowels.   Each vowel has a single sound; good Latin pronunciation has no mixture of sounds, no diphthongs. When two vowels appear together, each maintains its own integrity (with two exceptions).

There are only six vowels in Latin.

IPA	English Equivalent	Latin Word	Phonetic Spelling
[ɑ]	**a** is pronounced as in f**a**ther (AH)	**a**lleluia	AH-lEH-lÓO-yAH
[ɛ]	**e** is pronounced as in m**e**t (EH)	ex**ce**lsis	EHk-shEHl-sEEs
[i]	**i** is pronounced as in m**ee**t (EE)	Christe	krÉE-stEH
[ɔ]	**o** is pronounced as in t**au**ght (AU)	Dominum	dAÚ-mEE-nOOm
[u]	**u** is pronounced as in b**oo**t (OO)	adora**mus**	AH-dAU-rAH́-mOOs
[i]	**y** is pronounced as **i** (EE)	Kyrie	kÉE-rEE-EH

When two or more vowels appear together, both are pronounced: la**u**de (lAH́-OO-dEH), **ai**t (AH́-EEt), fil**ii** (fEÉ-lEE-EE), D**iei** (dEE-EH́-EE).

Exceptions are **ae** and **oe**. They are pronounced the same as the vowel *e* (EH): chEH́-lEE (c**ae**li), chEH́-lOOm (c**oe**lum).

When preceded by *q* or *ng* and followed by another vowel, **u** keeps its normal sound but is uttered as a semivowel (like English *w*) before the vowel that follows: **qui** (kwEE), **quae** (kwEH), san**gu**ine (sÁHn-gwEE-nEH).

Consonants.   The consonants **c, ch, cc,** and **q** are all pronounced as **k** when they precede the vowels *a, o,* and *u.* Before *i, e, ae, oe,* or *y,* **c** and **cc** are sounded like **ch** in *church.* As **k** in **Ch**riste, **c**antus (KÁHn-tOOs), **c**oncentus (kAUn-chÉHn-tOOs), **c**um (kOOm); as **ch** in **c**irca (chÉEr-kAH), **C**ecilia (chEH-chÉE-lEE-AH), **c**ithara (chÉE-tAH-rAH).

The consonants **xc** and **sc** are pronounced **sh** before *i, e, ae, oe,* and *y:* de**sc**endit (dEH-shÉHn-dEEt), e**xc**elsis (EHk-shÉHl-sEEs), su**sc**ipe (sOÓ-shEE-pEH).

The consonant **g,** before *i, e, ae, oe,* or *y,* is pronounced as the *g* in **G**eorge (**j**): Ma**g**i (mÁH-jEE), re**g**ina (rEH-jÉE-nAH); before *a, o,* or *u,* it sounds like the *g* in **g**o: e**g**o (ÉH-gAU), **g**audem (gÁH-OO-dEHm).

The consonant **gn** is pronounced like the *n* in o**n**ion: Ma**gn**ificat (mAH-nyÉE-fEE-kAHt), A**gn**us (ÁH-nyOOs), ma**gn**um (mÁH-nyOOm).

The consonant **h** is always silent, except in the words *nihil* and *mihi,* when it is pronounced as **k**: **H**osanna (AU-zAH́-nAH), **h**odie (AÚ-dEE-EH); mi**h**i (mEÉ-kEE), ni**h**il (nEÉ-kEEl).

The consonant **j** is treated as *y* and is often written as *i:* **e**jus or e**i**us (EH́-yOOs), **j**ubilate or **i**ubilate (yOO-bEE-lAH́-tEH), **j**usti or **i**usti (yOÓ-stEE).

The consonant **r** is always flipped; there are no American *r*'s in Latin.

The consonant **s** is pronounced like the *s* in **s**ea, except when it occurs between two vowels. It then sounds like a soft *z*: Ho**s**anna (AU-zAH́-nAH), mi**s**erere (mEE-zEH-rEH́-rEH); **s**uper (sOÓ-pEHr), re**s**piro (rEH-spEÉ-rAU), re**s**urgo (rEH-zOÓr-gAU).

The syllable **ti** before another vowel and following any consonant except another *t*, *x*, or *s* is pronounced **tsEE:** laetitia (lEH-tEÉ-tsEE-AH), gratia (grAH́-tsEE-AH).

The consonants **t** and **th** are both pronounced as **t:** tibi (tEÉ-bEE), catholicam (kAH-tAÚ-lEE-kAHm).

The consonants **ph** are pronounced as **f:** Phillipi (feé-lEE-pEE).

The consonant **x** is pronounced **ks** but is softened to **gz** when it appears between two vowels: excussorum (EH-kskOO-sAÚ-rOOm), exercitus (EH-gzEH́-rchEE-tOOs).

The consonant **z** is pronounced as **dz:** Lazarus (lAH́-dzAH-rOOs).

The consonants **b, d, f, k, l, m, n, p,** and **v** are all pronounced as in English.

German-Austrian pronunciation of Latin differs from Roman usage as follows:

The vowels **ae, oe, y** have German umlaut sounds: **ä, ö, ü** as in saeculi (sä′-kOO-lEE), coelum (chö′-lOOm), and Kyrie (kü′-rEE-EH).

The consonant **c** is pronounced as **ts** when it occurs before *i*, *e*, *ae*, or *oe*: benedicimus (bEH-nEH-dEÉ-tsEE-mOOs), pacem (pAH́-tsEHm), Caesar (tsä′-zAHr), coeli (tsö′-lEE).

The consonant **g** is always pronounced hard, as in God: magnum (mAH́g-nOOm), Agnus (AH́g-nOOs). The consonant **qu** is pronounced **kv:** quorum (kvAÚ-rOOm), qui (kvEE).

The consonant **s** sounds like **z** before a vowel: solus (zAÚ-lOOs), excelsis (EHk-tsEH́l-zEEs), Osanna (AU-zAH́-nAH).

The consonant **xc** is pronounced **kts:** excelsis (EHk-tsEH́l-sEEs).

German

Athough the German language has many similarities to English, the pronunciations are not identical. German is characteristically a more consonant-oriented language and, whether spoken or sung, requires a clarity of enunciation. When singing English, one usually elides the final consonant of a word with the consonant or vowel that follows. In German, however, all words beginning with a vowel are enunciated separately. As in French and in Latin, each vowel has its own integrity, and there is no glide or diphthong associated with them as there is in English (OHoo, AY, yOO). There are three diphthongs in German: (1) **ei** and **ai,** which sound alike as *eye* (AHɪ) in English; (2) *eu* and *äu,* also sounding alike, as the OY in *boy* (AUɪ); and (3) **au,** which sounds like the OW in *cow* (AHoo). In each case, when singing legato the primary sound is prolonged in the German as it is in English.

There are several consonants and vowel sounds in German that are spelled differently from the way they are spelled in English and some that have no English equivalent in sound. For this reason the International Phonetic Alphabet will again prove helpful.

Word Accents. The principal accent in German words is usually on the first syllable, unless it is preceded by a prefix such as *ur*, as in *Urtext*. Prefixes that exist as separate words for a particular emphasis (such as *über-, her-, mit-*) receive the principal stress: *überfliegen* (fly *over*), *herkommen* (come *here*), *mitgehen* (go *with*); if the prefix has only a literal connotation, it is not stressed: *überall* (everywhere), and the stress goes to the final syllable. In compound words, the main emphasis usually comes on the first word, with secondary stress falling on the succeeding syllable that would normally receive stress: *Wissenschaftslehre* (vIH́-sUHn-shAHfts-lAÝ-rə). Words consisting of an adverb plus a preposition place emphasis on the latter: *herab* (hEHr-AH́p), *hinaus* (hIHn-OẂs).

Vowel Stress.   A stressed vowel is pronounced short if it precedes a double consonant or more than one consonant: brennen (brEH́n-nUHn), offen (AÚf-fUHn), Felsen (fÉHl-zUHn). A stressed vowel is usually long if it precedes the consonant **h** or any single consonant; it is also long if the vowel is doubled: bohlen (bOH́-lUHn), Ehre (AÝ-rə), Blume (blOÓ-mə), Haar (hAHr).

Unstressed vowels are usually pronounced short, except when the vowels appear in endings like -**at** (AHt), -**bar** (bAHr), -**sal** (zAHl), -**sam** (zAHm), and -**tum** (tOOm), as in *Héimat, wúnderbar, lángsam.*

General Rules

1. A long vowel or diphthong is separated from the sound of a single consonant: tr**a**gen (trAH́-gUHn), T**au**be (tÓW-bUH), r**ei**sen (rAH́ɪ-zUHn).
2. After a short vowel, a double consonant or two or more consonants sounding as one are pronounced with both the preceding vowel and the one that follows: Hi**mm**el (hIH́m-mUHl), Be**ch**er (bÉHch-chUHr), si**ng**en (zIH́ng-ngUHn), we**ck**en vÉHch-chUHn), Fi**sch**er (fIH́sh-shUHr).
3. In compound words and in those with prefixes or suffixes, each element retains its own pronunciation: *Winterreise* (vIH́n-tUHr-rAH́ɪ-zə), *Mutterliebe* (mOÓ-tUHr-lEÉ-bə), *Gottesdienst* (gAÚt-tUHs-dEÉnst).
4. Two different consonants are separated, and more than two together divide as they most easily combine: *Liebestod* (lEÉ-bUHs-tOH́t), *lieblich* (lEÉb-lIHch), *Himmelsfahrt* (hIH́m-mUHls-fÁHrt).

Vowels

IPA	English Equivalent	German Word	Phonetic Spelling
[ɑ]	AH, long as in f**a**ther	V**a**ter, M**a**nn	fAH́-tUHr, mAHn
[e]	AY, long as in bl**a**de (without diphthong)	S**ee**le, s**e**lig	zAÝ-lə, zAÝ-lIHch
[ɛ]	EH, short as in m**e**t	B**e**tt, t**ä**glich	bEHt, tÉH-glIHch
[ə]	*s̩chwa*, no spelling equivalent	m**ei**ne, h**au**se	mAH́ɪ-nə, hOẂ-zə
[i]	EE, long as in m**ee**t	**i**hm, L**ie**der	EEm, lEÉ-dUHr
[ɪ]	IH, short as in h**i**t	**i**st, K**i**nd	IHst, kIHnt
[o]	OH, long as in h**o**me	B**o**hne, Kr**o**ne, h**o**ch	bOH́-nə, krÓH-nə, hOHch
[ɔ]	AU, as in t**au**ght	h**o**ffe, W**o**rt	hAÚf-fə, vAUrt
[u]	OO, long as in b**oo**t	g**u**t, J**u**gend	gOOt, YÓO-gUHnt
[v]	OŎ, short as in p**u**t	**u**nd, **u**nter, L**u**st	OŎnt, OŎń-tUHr, lOŎst
[ʌ]	UH as in p**u**tt	ri**ng**en, Bau**er**	rIH́ng-ngUHn, bOẂ-UHr

Consonants.   Although most consonants in German are pronounced similarly in English, there are exceptions.

The consonant **b** is pronounced as **p** when it comes at the end of a syllable or before *t:* Gra**b**, ha**b**t (grAHp, hAHpt).

The consonant **d** is pronounced as **t** when it comes at the end of a syllable or before *t:* Ba**d**, Sta**d**t (bAHt, shtAHt).

The consonant **g** is pronounced as **k** when it comes at the end of a syllable and follows a long vowel, after a short vowel and an *r* or an *l*, or in *ieg:* Zu**g**, Bur**g**, fol**g**t, Krie**g** (tsOOk, bOŎrk, fÁUlkt, krEEk). It is pronounced as **ch** in a word or syllable ending in *ig:* mächti**g** (mÉHch-tich). It is pronounced as a lightly voiced *g* when it is followed by another syllable containing a *ch:* ewi**g**, (AÝ-vIHch), but ewi**g**lich (AÝ-vIHg-lIHch).

The consonant **ch** is pronounced *forward* over the tongue when following *ä, e, i, ö, ü, ai, eu, äu, l, v,* or *n*: lächeln, sprechen, nicht, höchste, feucht (lÉHch-UHln, shprÉHch-UHn, nIHcht, höch-stə, fOYcht). It is pronounced gutturally over the back of the tongue when following *a, o, u,* or *au*: macht, hoch, Buch, rauchen (mAHcht, hAUch, bOOch, rOWch-UHn).

The consonant and vowel **qu** is pronounced as **kv**: Quelle (kvÉhl-lUH).

The consonant **r** is always flipped.

The consonant **s** is voiceless, as in **s**ee (English), when it appears at the end of a syllable, or in the middle of a word after all consonants except *r, l, m,* or *n*; **ss** is always voiceless: was, Wüsten, gabst, wissen (vAHs, vü′st-UHn, gAHpst, vIH́-sUHn). But after *n:* Sehnsucht (ZAÝn-zOOcht), after *l:* Fels (fEHlz).

The consonant **s** is voiced as in **z**oom (English) (1) when it appears between two vowels: Rosen, Esel (rÓH-zUHn, AÝ-zUHl); (2) when it is the initial sound of a word: sagen, so, sieben (zÁH-gUHn, zOH, zÉE-bUHn); (3) when it is preceded by *m, n, l,* or *r* and followed by a vowel, or after a prefix: Balsam, einsam, hinsinken (bÁHl-zAHm, AH́ın-zAHm, hÍHn-zIHnk-UHn); (4) words ending with *-sal* or *-sam*: grausam, Schicksal (grOẂ-zAHm, ShIH́k-zAHl).

The consonant **sch** sounds like the **sh** in **sh**out (English): Schiff, Fischer (shIHf, fÍH-shUHr).

The consonants **st** and **sp** are pronounced as **sht** and **shp** when they begin a word, but when they appear in the middle of a word or at the end, they are pronounced as in English: stehen, sprach, besten, Brust, Raspeln (shtAÝ-UHn, shprAHch, bÉH-stUHn, brŎOst, rAH́-spUHln).

The consonant **th** is always pronounced as **t** in **t**one (English): Thema, Muth (tÁY-mAH, mOOt).

The combination **tion** is pronounced **tsyOHn**: Nation (nÁH-tsyOHn).

The consonant **v** is pronounced as **f**: voll, Vogel (fAU1, fÓH-gUHl).

The consonant **w** is pronounced like **v**: wer, Wangen (vAYr, VÁHng-ngUHn).

The consonants **z, tz** are always pronounced **tz**: Holz, sitze (hΛUltz, zIH́t-tzə).

Umlaut.   In German the two dots placed over *ä, ö,* and *ü* are called *umlaut.* They are sometimes spelled *ae, oe,* and *ue,* particularly in names, like *Schuetz* and *Goethe.* The German umlaut may be pronounced both long or short; they have no English equivalent.

Umlaut **ä** is pronounced long (as AY) in Käse (KÁY-zə) or short (as EH) in mächtig (mEH́ch-tIHch).

Umlaut **ö** is pronounced long, as AY in English, with rounded lips forming OH: schön (shø), or short when pronounced EH with rounded lips forming AW: Glöcken (glǿck-UHn).

Umlaut **ü** is pronounced long when it sounds like the French **u** (ʏ), by singing EE with rounded lips forming OO: Blüte (blʏːtə); when it is short, it is formed by singing IH (I) with rounded lips forming OO: Früchte (frü′ch-chtə).

Diphthongs.   The diphthongs **ei** and **ai** are both pronounced as long **i** (ai) in might (English): reisen, Mai (rAHı-zUHn, mAHı).

The diphthongs **eu** and **äu** also sound alike and are pronounced as OY in toy (English) [ɔɪ]: Bäumen, leuchtend (bOÝ-mUHn, lOÝch-tUHnt).

The diphthong **au** sounds like OW in *how* (English) [au]: Haus, lauschen (hOWs, lÓW-shUHn).

Note: The German **ei** is pronounced **i** (ai), and **ie** is pronounced EE (i).

French

English-speaking conductors find it especially helpful to become familiar with the International Phonetic Alphabet symbols before attempting choral literature in modern foreign languages. Exact equivalents of French in the English language are only approximate, while the phonetic symbols are exact. As in Latin, there are no diphthongs in French, and it is important that singers maintain the integrity of the vowel throughout the time-value of any given note or series of notes.

The following pronunciation requires an understanding of phonetic symbols, but, where possible, the English equivalents are also given. A brief explanation of how to form certain unique French vowels is also presented. Nasals are indicated by the marking (˜) above the appropriate vowel sound. Many French sounds have a different spelling, but their similarity is apparent when spelled phonetically.

Vowels

IPA	English Equivalent	French Words	Phonetic Spelling
[æ]	mat	la, femme, moi	la, fam, mwa
[ɑ]	father	passer, hélas, pas	pɑ-se, e-lɑs, pɑ
[ã]	(nasal)	chant, champs, enfant	ʃã, ʃã, ã-fã'
[e]	late	et, étage, chez	e, etá:ʒ, ʃe
[ə]	(*schwa*-vowel)	me, que, lever	mə, kə, lə-ve
[ɛ]	met	mais, près, mets, sel	mɛ, prɛ, mɛ, sɛl
[ɛ̃]	(nasal)	rien, main, fin, besoin	rjæ, mæ, fæ, bəzwǽ
[i]	seen	sinistre, chic, inimitié	si-ni'-str, ʃik, i-ni-mi-tje
[o]	boat	trop, beau, autant, hôte	tro, bo, otã, o:t
[ɔ]	cloth	bonne, cote, possible	bɔn, kɔt, pɔsíbl
[ɔ̃]	(nasal)	pont, comparer, mons	pɔ̃, kɔ̃-pɑ-re, mɔ̃
[œ]	(Pronounce EH [ɛ], then round lips for AW and keep singing EH.)	boeuf, cueillir, seul	bœf, kœ-ji:r, sœl
[œ̃]	(nasal)	lundi, humble, parfum	lœ̃-di, œ̃:bl, pɑr-fœ̃
[ø]	(Pronounce AY [e], then round lips for OH [o] and keep singing AY.)	peu, mieu, voeux	pø, mjø, vø
[u]	(boot)	tous, aout, coucou, roue	tu, u, ku-ku, ru
[y]	(Pronounce EE [i], then round lips for OO [u] and keep singing EE.)	du, plus, lune, fut	dy, ply, lyn, fy

Consonants

IPA	French Words	Phonetic Spelling
[p]	près, absent	prɛ, ap-sã
[b]	bon, beau, abbé	bɔ̃, bo, a-bé
[m]	mon, madame, femme	mɔ̃, ma-dam, fam
[f]	chef, phrase, fut	ʃɛf, frɑ:z, fy
[v]	voix, vivant, wagon	vwɑ, vi-vã', vɑ-gɔ̃'
[t]	ton, theatre, tête	tɔ̃, te-ɑ:tr, tɛt
[d]	douce, sud, adieu	dus, syd, ɑ-djø
[n]	nouveau, bonne, automne	nu-vó, bɔn, o-tóń
[s]	si, centime, ceci, rébus, scène, faction	si, sã-tím, səsi, re-bys, sɛn, fak-sjɔ̃'

[z]	magazin, **z**èle, deuxième	ma-ga-zɛ̃, zɛl, dø-zjɛ́m
[l]	**l**aisser, aig**l**e, ge**l**	lɛsé, ɛgl, ʒɛl
[ʃ]	dou**ch**e, **ch**ose, pe**ch**e	duʃ, ʃos, pɛʃ
[ʒ]	**j**oie, **g**i**g**ue, **j**u**g**e	ʒwa, ʒig, ʒyʒ
[k]	**k**a**k**i, **c**orps, **qu**el**qu**e, é**ch**o	ka-ki, kɔr, kɛlk, éko
[g]	**g**arçon, **g**uerre, se**c**ond	gar-sõ, gɛ:r, sə-gɔ̃'
[ɲ]	li**gn**e, co**gn**ac, **gn**ole	liɲ, kɔ-ɲak, ɲo:l
[r]	**r**obin, biza**rr**e, **rh**ythme	rɔ-bɛ̃', bi-za:r, ritm
[ks]	a**cc**ent, e**x**pert	ak-sã, ɛk-spɛr
[gz]	e**x**il, e**x**act	ɛg-zil, ɛg-zakt

Semiconsonants

IPA	French Words	Phonetic Spelling
[j]	a**y**ant, p**i**ano, nat**i**on, vo**y**age, ca**h**ier, ta**ill**e	ɛ-jã', pja-nó, na-sjõ, vwa-ja:ʒ, ka-jé, ta:j
[w]	**ou**est, s**oi**r, bes**oi**n	wɛst, swa:r, bə-zwɛ̃
[y]	fr**u**it, m**u**et, h**u**ile, l**u**i	fryi, mye, yil, lyi

Diphthongs

IPA	French Words	Phonetic Spelling
[i:j]	f**ille**, m**ille**	fi:j, mi:j
[ɛ:j]	pa**ye**, sol**eil**, v**eille**	pɛ:j, sɔ-lɛ:j, vɛ:j
[a:j]	trav**ail**	tra-va:j
[ɑ:j]	bat**aille**, p**aille**	ba-tɑ:j, pa:j
[œ:j]	f**euille**, **oeil**	fœ:j, œ:j

Orthographical Signs

Accents:

1. *Acute* accent (é) gives the sound of e, similar to the *ay* in English word *say*, without the diphthong y.
2. *Grave* accent (è, à) gives short vowel sounds (ɛ and a) as in mĕt, măt.
3. *Circumflex* accent (ê) gives the same sound as è (ɛ); when placed over â or ô, the vowels are pronounced long (ɑ, o); when placed over î or û, it indicates the omission of an s in a former spelling; *île* was *isle*, *fût* was *fust*; there is no change in pronunciation.

Other signs:

1. An *apostrophe* (') indicates that a final vowel is omitted before an initial vowel sound: *le enfant* becomes *l'enfant*.
2. A *cedilla* (ç), when placed under a c before a, o, or u, sounds like **s** in **s**o: garçon, façade, reçu.
3. A *diaeresis* (ë), placed over the second of two vowels, indicates that the second vowel is pronounced separately: Noël, naïf.

Liaison.   In conversation, French words are seldom elided but they are quite frequently connected in song to create a stronger legato line. The mute *e*, or *schwa*, requires special attention due to its frequent use in poetry and song, whereas it is *not* sounded in conversational French. It is often referred to as a *neutral* vowel. There are instances when it is silent, however, even in singing.

1. When it is final, or immediately precedes a final *s*: *école, écoles* (singular and plural sound alike).

2. In the verb endings of the third person plural: *ils donnent*.
3. In the body of a word between two consonants: *boulevard*.
4. When a word ending with a mute e (ə) is elided with a word beginning with a vowel: *notre amour, belle âme*. The composer will sometimes write a note for this sound if he or she wants it to be sung.

Rules for applying liaison in singing:

1. When two words are related in thought and the first ends with a consonant and the second begins with a vowel or mute *h*, the consonant of the first word is pronounced as though it were the beginning consonant of the second word.
2. After a pronoun, a preposition, an adjective, an article, a conjunction (except *et*), or an adverb.
3. With endings *rd, rs, rt,* elide the *r* but not the final consonant *except*
    a. Where a pronoun follows a verb: *part-on*.
    b. With the words *toujours, plusieurs—toujours est-il que, plusieurs hommes*—carry the *s*.
    c. When the word is plural: *mortes-eaux*, carry the *s*.
4. Nasal sounds sometimes lose their nasality:
    a. When *-ain* or *-ein* (ɛ̃) are elided: *train est, plein air*.
    b. When the word *bon* (bō) is combined with a vowel: *bon ami*.
    c. The sounds ã and œ̃ always remain nasal when eliding.
5. There are a few consonants that change sounds in liaison:
    a. A final *f* becomes *v*: *neuf ans* (neuv ans).
    b. A final *s* or *x* sounds as *z*: *vous avez* (vou-zah-vay), *jeux heure* (jeu-zeure).
    c. The final *d* in *quand* becomes *t*: *quand-il* (quan-til).
6. Do *not* elide.
    a. If there is a punctuation of any kind.
    b. If the words are not linked in meaning.
    c. Proper names.
    d. Before the aspirate *h*.
    e. After a singular noun.
    f. After the conjunction *et*.
    g. If it prevents a clear phrase meaning.

Appendix D

Selected Repertory

CHORUSES OF CHILDREN, ADOLESCENTS, TREBLE AND MALE VOICES; CHURCH CHOIRS

Selected repertory for children's, adolescents', and treble and male choruses and for church choirs has been assembled by outstanding choral directors with expertise in these areas. Publishers of the music listed may be found in the current edition or supplement of *Choral Music in Print* (Sacred/Secular). In general, the music of nineteenth-century masters that is readily accessible from publishers is not included. Less-familiar works that are not in general publication, especially from the Renaissance, may be found in collected works *(Opera Omnia)* or in such volumes as *CMM (Corpus Mensurabilis Musicae)*. Certain contemporary music for male voices may be secured from IMC (Intercollegiate Music Council). In the listing of material selected for male and treble choruses, SSA and TTBB unaccompanied are considered standard unless otherwise specified. Individual solo assignments are placed in parentheses.

Selected Music for Children's Chorus
(assembled and annotated by Doreen Rao)

Composer	Title	Voicing
J. S. Bach	With Loudest Rejoicing	SA
	Duet from Cantata No. 15, "Denn du wirst meine Seele nicht in der Hölle lassen." German text available in piano/vocal score (Breitkopf #7015). May be performed with violin I and II, viola, and *continuo* (or keyboard only). A rhythmic, expressive composition.	
J. S. Bach	Rejoice, O My Spirit	Unison
	An aria from Cantata No. 15. Like the duets, original performance practice included small groups of treble	

	(boys) voices as well as solos; melismatic, but not difficult.	
J. S. Bach	We Hasten with Eager, yet Faltering Footsteps	SA
	Duet from Cantata No. 78, "Jesu der du meine Seele." May be performed with cello, *continuo* or keyboard only. Effective also with bassoon *continuo*.	
J. S. Bach	O Death, None Could Conquer Thee	SA
	Duet from Cantata No. 4, "Christ lag in Todesbanden." German and English text available in piano/vocal score (Breitkopf-Härtel #7004). Can be accompanied with cornet, trombone, and *continuo* (or keyboard only). A fuller keyboard realization can be found in the G. Schirmer edition.	
J. S. Bach	Domine Deus	SA
	Duet from Mass in G Major. May be performed with violin and continuo or keyboard only. Recorded by the Tapiola Children's Choir on DG 2530-812.	
Ernst Bacon	Bennington's Rifleman	SA
	Among many other wonderful works for children's voices written by this composer, this composition provides for significant musical learning in context of much fun. Piano accompaniment.	
Béla Bartók	Three Hungarian Folk Songs	SSA
	"In the Village"	
	"Boatman! Boatman!"	
	"See the Roses"	
	English version and choral transcription by Benjamin Suchoff. Movements can be done individually or as a delightful experience of contrast in this short but extended work. Piano accompaniment.	
Béla Bartók	Six Children's Songs	
	"Don't Leave Me"	SA
	"Breadbaking"	SA
	"Only Tell Me"	SSA
	"Loafer"	SSA
	"Teasing Song"	SSA
	"Hussar"	SA
	To be sung *a cappella* or with orchestra (parts available on rental from Boosey & Hawkes). Challenging, but logically composed. English text will inspire good diction practice. Changing meter, rhythmic and harmonic interest give this group ample reason for musical study.	
Leslie Bassett	Hear My Prayer, O Lord	SA
	For voices and organ; piano may be used. Some dissonance; much logic. An effective and introspective contemporary choral statement.	
Arthur Baynon	Mrs. Jenny Wren	AB
	Melodic, simple; AB with piano accompaniment.	
Gordon Binkerd	Song of Praise and Prayer	Unison
	In $\frac{5}{8}$ meter; a chantlike melody with prayerful text. More dramatic, rhythmically augmented middle section provides a satisfying musical experience. Piano accompaniment.	
Gordon Binkerd	Sorrow Hath a Double Voice	Unison
	Unison or solo. Moving, introspective poetry. Piano accompaniment.	

Gordon Binkerd	Sung under the Silver Umbrella	
	"The Christ-Child" (piano or harp)	SA
	"Song of Innocence" *(a cappella)*	SSA
	"An Evening Falls" (blues piano)	Unison
	"The Merry Man of Paris" (piano)	SSA
	"Child's Song" (piano)	SSA
	"White Fields" (piano)	SA
	Sensitivity to text and the young voice characterize the writing of these melodically beautiful compositions. This music will challenge, stretch, satisfy, and inspire the best from children's voices. Each piece may be programmed individually.	
John Boda	Before the Paling of the Stars	SA/SSA
	Lilting melody in $\frac{6}{8}$, accompanied by piano. A Christmas text.	
Benjamin Britten	Corpus Christi Carol	Unison
	A subtle composition to be performed by ensemble or solo voice. A medium range with melodic refrain. Piano accompaniment.	
Benjamin Britten	Friday Afternoons, Op. 7	Unison
	A collection of imaginative songs including "A New Year Carol" and "Old Abram Brown" (published separately). This collection should be a basic part of every children's chorus library. Piano accompaniment.	
Benjamin Britten	Oliver Cromwell	Unison
	Performed with piano; repeated patterns make this short piece easy and fun. Dynamic contrast and "Hee-Haw" refrain add comic drama.	
Benjamin Britten	The Sally Gardens	Unison
	An Irish folksong with perfectly shaped phrases for which Britten composed a supportive and harmonically interesting piano accompaniment.	
Benjamin Britten	Three Two-Part Songs	SA
	Short compositions with contrasting tempo, meter, rhythm, and text. Piano accompaniment.	
Antonio Caldara (arr. Rodby)	Sebben, crudele	SSA
	An Italian art song, *Thy Heart Unbending*, carefully arranged, with English translation available. Four-bar phrases invite musical phrasing. Piano accompaniment.	
Mary E. Caldwell	Shine, Lovely Christmas Star *(A Gift of Song)*	SA/SSA
	A well-known, simple, romantic choral piece. Traditional harmony. Piano accompaniment.	
Carolee Curtright	Listen Shepherds, Listen	Unison
	A bright, happy, tuneful song, especially suited for church choir.	
Pierre Certon	French Chansons of the Sixteenth Century	SA
	A cappella, polyphrase part songs. Melismatic, rhythmic, light. In French.	
Blanche Chass, arr.	Hanerot Halalu	SA
	An enjoyable, festive Hanukkah song with repeated pattern on the text *Bim Bom* under a simple melody sung in Hebrew to enhance, followed by a melodically contrasting *B* section.	

Derna Stellati Cotton	Mio bambino	SA

A lilting $\frac{6}{8}$, melodic piece. An Italian lullaby with English text optional. Piano accompaniment is supportive, yet distinct.

Katherine Davis	Little Drummer Boy	SA

A traditional, always beautiful holiday song. The harmonic pattern in thirds and sixths repeats in each verse. Piano accompaniment, snare drum.

Emma Lou Diemer	Alleluia	SSA

An imaginative setting. Sung *a cappella;* very rhythmic.

Emma Lou Diemer	The Magnificat	Unison

The Magnificat is performed with piano or organ. Very simple, with contrasting sections.

English Folksong (arr. Benjamin Britten)	The Golden Vanity	Unison

Traditional English folk melody appropriate for children's voices. Piano accompaniment.

Gabriel Fauré	Ave verum, Op. 65, No.1	SA

An accessible work; melodic. Treble voices and organ (or piano). Without fanfare, a subtle and distinguished composition that is similar in nature to parts of the Requiem.

Richard Felciano	Cosmic Festival	Unison
	Lullaby on a Christmas Chorale	Unison
	O He Did Whistle and She Did Sing	Unison

Use of stage speech, electronic tape with the traditional elements of chorale melody and folksong. Piano accompaniment.

Christian Gregor (arr. Trusler)	Hosanna	SA

An antiphonal piece in G major, effective in any setting—church or concert. Constructed sequentially. Piano or organ.

Clare Grundman	Zoo Illogical	SA

An imaginative and musically rewarding group of zoo songs with piano or optional orchestral accompaniment. Orchestra parts available for purchase.

Philip Hageman	An Easy Song *(a cappella)*	SA
	Say Yes to the Music, or Else *(piano)*	Unison
	Echoes of Gladness *(a cappella)*	SSA
	The Mysterious Pineapple *(piano)*	SA

Delightful texts, accessible, with solid rhythmic development; a sense of shape and proportion in all of the elements.

G. F. Handel (arr. Robert W. Gibb)	Verdant Meadows	SSA

Pastoral; a classic art song, tastefully arranged.

G. F. Handel	Where'er You Walk *(Semele)*	SA

E. C. Schirmer also has a unison version.

Ruth Wason Henderson	Animal Tales (Set IV)	SA
	"The Boar and the Dromedary"	
	"Don't Even Squeeze a Weasel"	
	Animal Tales (Set I)	SA
	"A Tree Toad"	
	"A Lone Dog"	

Clear, clever writing makes text settings unusually appealing

Michael Hennagin	Five Children's Songs Imaginative texts by fifth- and sixth-grade children; rhythmic and melodic. A challenging piano accompaniment is developed independently of the vocal parts.	Unison
Gustav Holst	The Corn Song Two independent melodies, lyrical in quality, sung together. A good exercise in part singing. Piano accompaniment.	SA
Engelbert Humperdinck	Prayer *(Hansel and Gretel)* A simple, romantic piece arranged in thirds and sixths. This well-known piece may be accompanied by piano or orchestra.	SA
Charles Ives	from *114 Songs* "Religion" "Remembrance" "Duty" Songs suited in text and style to children's voices. Young voices hear these intervals readily. Piano accompaniment.	Unison Unison Unison
Charles Ives	Serenity A subtle, plainsong-like melody with rhythmic variation created by duple meter amidst a triple figure. Piano accompaniment.	Unison
Orlando di Lasso (ed. James McKelvy)	Serve bone An equal voice motet of seven motives, ending in unison. *A cappella.*	SA
W. A. Mozart (arr. Thomas Dunn)	Ave verum corpus A pleasing two-part arrangement provides a suitable vehicle for beautiful choral singing. One of many masterworks for treble voices published by E. C. Schirmer. Optional piano accompaniment.	SA
Ron Nelson	The Moon Does Not Sleep Autumn Lullaby for the Moon Ask for the Moon Available with Orff instruments or instrumental ensemble.	SA SA SA
G. P. da Palestrina (arr. Norman Greyson)	Gloria Patri Antiphonal. A piece well suited for concert opening. *A cappella.*	SSA
Vincent Persichetti	Sam Was a Man Imaginative, independent piano accompaniment and rhythmic variety give this short composition interest.	SA
Brent Pierce	Hymn to the Night Contemporary composition using a combination of traditional elements along with twentieth-century devices. Written for voices, piano, and wind chimes, this short piece uses speaking and whispering as well as singing. A simple and satisfying introduction to avant-garde techniques.	SA
Daniel Pinkham	Ave Maria Chantlike in character with contrary motion, meter change, and long melismatic passages. An exquisitely beautiful *a cappella* composition.	SA
Daniel Pinkham	Evergreen A twentieth-century plainsong, with electronic tape.	Unison

A variety of optional instruments provides an effective ostinato.

Daniel Pinkham	Five Canzonets	SA
	A cappella, light, short compositions of contrasting character. Clear, tuneful writing with significant text interest. Well suited for the child's voice.	
Daniel Pinkham	Listen to Me	SA
	Five motets written for the Chicago Children's Choir. Biblical texts with oboe and English horn doubling, if desired. Difficult but beautiful.	
Francis Poulenc	Petites Voix	SA
	"The Good Little Girl"	
	"The Lost Dog"	
	"Coming Home from School"	
	"The Little Sick Boy"	
	"The Hedge-Hog"	
	A well-known group of short songs sung *a cappella*.	
Michael Praetorius (arr. Dr. Theodore Baker)	Lo, How a Rose E'er Blooming	SA
	A transparent, uncluttered setting with piano accompaniment.	
Henry Purcell (arr. Arnold Goldsbrough)	A Trumpet Song	SA
	A short Baroque piece appropriate for concert opening.	
Henry Purcell (arr. C. F. Manney)	Shepherd, Shepherd, Leave Decoying	SSA
	Sound the Trumpet	SA
	Melismatic, but not overly embellished; a good introduction to Baroque-style singing. Piano accompaniment.	
Donald Roach	Kum Ba Yah	Unison
John Rutter	Shepherd's Pipe Carol	Unison
	Rhythmically interesting, with much use of syncopation and changing meter, yet melodically satisfying scalelike patterns. Piano accompaniment.	
Franz Schubert	Nine Two-Three Part Choruses for Children's Voices	SA/SSA
	Familiar, tuneful Schubert melodies in their original two- and three-voice part arrangements. Edition in English only. *A cappella*.	
Franz Schubert (ed. Paul Boepple)	Serenade (Ständchen)	SSAA
	With mezzo-soprano solo and piano accompaniment. Vienna Boys Choir standard repertory.	
Franz Schubert	To Music	SSA
	A melody children should sing. Long phrases, exquisite text with piano accompaniment. Try lots of Schubert songs!	
Robert Schumann	Were I a Tiny Bird	SA
	With German and English texts and piano accompaniment. Many other German lieder two-part arrangements available from National Music Publishers.	
Natalie Sleeth	Love One Another	SA
	Spread Joy	SSA
	Good music for young voices, with texts, rhythms, and melodies readily accessible and immediately pleasing. Piano accompaniment.	

Natalie Sleeth	O Come, O Come, Immanuel	SA
	Dedicated to the Glen Ellyn Children's Chorus; a majestic tune in a very singable tessitura. Piano accompaniment.	
Gregg Smith, arr.	Now I Walk in Beauty (Navajo Indian Prayer)	Canon
	A chantlike canon with haunting melodic repetition. Arranged in SATB setting, but may be done in any voicing. *A cappella.*	
David Stone	Space Travellers	Unison
	Rhythmic text and imaginative contrasting piano accompaniment.	
Eric Thiman	The Path to the Moon	Unison
	A lovely melody; piano accompaniment.	
Jacob Van Vleck	I Will Rejoice in the Lord	SSAA
	Antiphonal; rich harmonically with lilting triple meter. Moravian music; piano accompaniment.	
Grace Williams	The Gentle Dove	Unison
	A lilting, melodic line; contemplative; piano accompaniment.	
R. Vaughn Williams	She's like a Swallow	Unison
	A particularly beautiful English folk melody with a wide range. Piano accompaniment.	
R. Vaughn Williams	Three Children's Songs "Spring" "The Singers" "An Invitation"	Unison
	Clear, melodic, and delightfully singable English choral music written perfectly for the young voice. Piano accompaniment.	
R. Vaughn Williams	Orpheus with His Lute	Unison
	Based on a Shakespeare text, a classic composition with independent yet supportive piano accompaniment. Check the Oxford catalog for other excellent Vaughn Williams pieces.	
John F. Wilson, arr.	O Who's That Yonder?	SA
	A hauntingly beautiful spiritual, tastefully arranged to enhance its melodic integrity. Light, supportive piano accompaniment.	
Luigi Zaninelli	American Folk Song Suite	SSA
	A well-known arrangement of familiar American tunes, including "Shenandoah" and "Skip to My Lou." Piano accompaniment.	

Selected Music for Adolescent Voices
(assembled by Colleen Kirk)

Composer	Title	Special Information
Anonymous, 18th century	Viva tutti (Here's to Women)	TTB
Australian Song	Waltzing Matilda	SAB, piano
Marshall Bartholomew, arr.	De Animals a-Comin'	TTBB
	Gaudeamus	TTBB
Béla Bartók	Three Hungarian Folk Songs	SSA, piano
		SATB, piano
Paolo Bellasio	Love Brings a Little Sadness	SSA, English and Italian

John Bennet	Weep, O Mine Eyes	SATB
Jean Berger	Five Canzonets	S(S)ATB
	My True Love Hath My Heart	SATB
William Billings	Chester	SATB
	Modern Music	SATB
	When Jesus Wept	Four voices, canon
Gordon Binkerd	An Evening Falls	Unison with blues piano
Johannes Brahms	My Beloved	SA; piano, four-hands
	Six Folk Songs	SATB
	Wondrous Cool, Thou Woodland Quiet	SATB(B)
William Byrd	Sacerdotes Domini	SATB
Gwyneth Cooper, arr.	He's Got the Whole World	SA(B)
Aaron Copland	The Nightingale	SAT
	At the River	TTBB, piano
	Ching-a-Ring-Chaw	SATB, piano
	Simple Gifts	SA/TB, piano
	Younger Generation	SATB
Norman Dello Joio	The Holy Infant's Lullaby	SSA, piano
		SATB, piano
Emma Lou Diemer	Four Carols	SA, SSA, SSAA
	Three Madrigals	SATB, piano
Baldassare Donato	All Ye Who Music Love	SATB
John Dowland	Flow My Tears	TB, lute obbligato
	Sweet Love Doth Now Invite	TTBB SATB
Irving Fine	Father William	SSA, piano
		SATB, piano
	The Lobster Quadrille	SSA, piano
		SATB, piano
Giovanni Gabrieli	Agnus Dei	SAAB
Orlando Gibbons	The Silver Swan	SSATTB
George F. Handel	Music, Spread Thy Voice Around (Solomon)	S(S)ATB, piano/organ
	Swell the Full Chorus (Solomon)	SATB, piano
	Thanks Be to Thee	Unison, piano/organ
Hans Leo Hassler	Come, Let Us Start a Joyful Song	SSA SATB
Franz Joseph Haydn	Gloria (Heiligmesse)	SATB, piano/organ
Heinrich Isaac	Innsbruck, I Now Must Leave Thee	SATB
Theron Kirk	Little Wheel a-Turnin'	SATB
Orlando di Lasso	I Know a Young Maiden	SATB
	My Heart Is Offered Still to You	SATB
	O Eyes of My Beloved	SATB
	Serve bone	SA
Antonio Lotti	Miserere mei	SATB
	Vere languores nostros	SSA
Norman Luboff, arr.	Night Herding Song (Cowboy)	TTBB
	Poor Lonesome Cowboy	TTBB
George Mead, arr.	Down in the Valley	TTBB, piano
Wolfgang A. Mozart	Ave verum corpus	SATB, orchestra/piano
G. P. da Palestrina	Gloria Patri	SATB/SATB
	O bone Jesu	SATB
Alice Parker & Robert	Aura Lee	TTBB

Shaw, arr.	Blow the Man Down	TTBB
	Marianina	TTBB
	O Tannenbaum	TTBB
Frances Pilkington	Rest Sweet Nymphs	SATB
Giuseppe Pitoni	Cantate Domino	SATB
Michael Praetorius	Psallite	SATB
Henry Purcell	In These Delightful Pleasant Groves	SATB
Hugh S. Roberton	Nightfall in Skye	SATB
Johann Hermann Schein	Vom Himmel hoch da kom ich her	SATB, brass
Franz Schubert	Der Tanz	SATB, piano
William Schuman, arr.	The Orchestra Song	SATB, quodlibet
Heinrich Schütz	O All Ye Nations	SATB
Matyas Seiber	Three Hungarian Folk Songs	SATB
Natalie Sleeth	Gaudeamus hodie	SATB
Arthur Sullivan	Finale from *The Gondoliers*	S(S)A(A)T(T)B(B); piano, four-hands
Thomas Tallis	Glory to Thee, My God This Night (Tallis' canon)	Five voices, piano
Ernst Toch	Geographical Fugue	Speaking chorus
	Valse	Speaking chorus, percussion
Christopher Tye	Laudate nomen Domini	SATB
Beryl Vick, Jr.	Mark Well, My Heart	SAAB
Antonio Vivaldi	Gloria in excelsis *(Gloria)*	SATB, piano
	Laudamus te *(Gloria)*	SS, piano
	Propter magnam gloriam tuam *(Gloria)*	SATB, piano
Ralph Vaughan Williams	O Mistress Mine	SATB
	Sweet Day	SATB
	The Turtle Dove	SSATB, baritone solo
	The Willow Song	SATB
Thomas Weelkes	The Nightingale	SSA
John Wilbye	Weep, O Mine Eyes	SST/TTB

Collections for Adolescent Voices

Arranger	**Title**	**Special Information**
H. Clough Leiter	*A Cappella Singer*	Mixed Voices (E. C. Schirmer)
	A Cappella Singer	Treble Voices (E. C. Schirmer)
William Henry Smith	*Spirituals*	SATB (Neil A. Kjos)

Selected Music for Treble Chorus (assembled by Monte Atkinson)[1]

Composer	**Title**	**Special Information**
Samuel Adler, arr.	Blow the Wind Southerly (English Folk Song)	With piano
Dominick Argento	Tria carmina Paschalia (Three Latin Easter lyrics)	With harp, guitar (or harpsichord)
Ernst Bacon	From Emily's Diary (a secular cantata)	SSAA (SA), chamber orch. (or piano)
	Precepts of Angelus Silesius	A cycle using 3–6 voice parts, unaccompanied

[1]For SSA, unless otherwise indicated.

Samuel Barber	The Virgin Martyrs, Op. 8	SSAA, unaccompanied
Béla Bartók	Five Choruses (from 27 2- & 3-part choruses)	SA-SSA, with chamber orch.
	"Hussar"	
	"Don't Leave Me"	
	"Loafer's Song"	
	"Wandering"	
	"Bread-Baking"	
	Two Choruses (frequently combined with above)	SA-SSA, with chamber orch.
	"Don't Leave Here"	
	"Boy's Teasing Song"	
	A Cappella Choruses (from 27 2- & 3-part choruses)	SA-SSA, unaccompanied
Gordon Binkerd	Hope Is the Thing with Feathers	SSAA, unaccompanied
	Infant Joy	SSAA, unaccompanied
Johannes Brahms	Ave Maria, Op. 12	SSAA, with orch. or organ
	Psalm XIII	With organ (or piano), strings ad lib
	Three Motets, Op. 37	SSA; SSAA; and SSAA(SA), unaccompanied
	Vier Gesänge, Op. 17	SSAA, two horns, harp
	Zwölf Lieder und Romanzen, Op. 44	SSAA, with piano (ad lib)
Houston Bright	Four Sacred Songs for the Night	
	Trilogy for Women's Voices	SSAA, unaccompanied
Benjamin Britten	A Ceremony of Carols	SSA with unison processional, harp
	Missa brevis	(SSA) with organ
	O Can Ye Sew Cushions? (folksong arr.)	With piano
	The Oxen (Christmas)	SA, with piano
	Psalm 150, Op. 67	SSAA, with orchestra
	Sweet Was the Song (Christmas)	SSAA
	Three Two-Part Songs	SA, with piano
	A Wealdon Trio (The Song of the Women)	Unaccompanied
William Byrd	Rejoice, Rejoice	SSAA (A); preceded by alto solo with organ or strings
Francesca Caccini	Aure volante	With 3 flutes, continuo
Andre Caplet	Messe a trois voix	
Elliott Carter	The Harmony of Morning	SSAA, chamber orchestra (piano)
Pablo Casals	Nigra sum	With organ
Paul Chihara	Magnificat	SSSAAA, unaccompanied
Aaron Copland	An Immorality	(S), with piano
	The House on the Hill	SSAA, unaccompanied
Paul Csonka	Concierto de Navidad (Christmas Concert)	SSAA(S), harp
François Couperin	"Troisieme leçon de Tenebrae" (Lamentations of Jeremiah)	SS or SA(SS) with continuo, strings (or piano)
Henry Cowell	Spring's at Summer's End	
Peter Maxwell Davies	Five Carols	SA-SSA with various solos
	Shall I Die for Mannis Sake?	SA(S), with piano
Claude Debussy	La demoiselle elue	SSAA(S,A), with orch.
	Salut printemps	SSAA(S), orch. (or piano)
Norman Dello Joio	Song's End	With piano

Josquin des Prés	Ave vera virginitas	SSAA, unaccompanied
Emma Lou Diemer	Alleluia	
	Weep No More	
	Fragments from the Mass	SSAA, unaccompanied
Hugo Distler	Jahrkreis, Op. 5	
	Mörike Chorliederbuch, Op. 10	
Ernst von Dohnanyi	Stabat Mater	SSASSA(SSA), with orch. (or piano)
Guillaume Dufay	Gloria ad modum tubae	SA or TB canon with 2 trumpets
Maurice Duruflé	Tota pulchra es (*Quatre Motets*, Op. 10)	SSA *divisi*
Edward Elgar	Fly, Singing Bird	With 2 violins, piano
	The Snow	With 2 violins, orch. (or piano)
Gabriel Fauré	Ave verum, Op. 65, No. 1	SA with organ
	Maria, mater gratiae, Op. 47, No. 2	SA, with organ
	Messe basse	SA (*divisi*) (S), organ
	Tantum ergo, Op. 65, No. 2	SSA (SSA), organ (or piano)
Irving Fine	Caroline Million (*The Choral New Yorker*, No. 2, *scherzando*)	SSAA(SA), with piano
Roy Harris	The Weeping Willow (*Folk Fantasy for Festivals*)	SSA, folk singer, piano
	They Say That Susan Has No Heart for Loving	SSA with piano
	Whitman Triptych	SSAA-SSA, unaccompanied
Johann A. Hasse	Miserere	SSAA-SSA, strings or piano
Michael Haydn	Effunderunt sanguinem	With organ, strings
	Laudate pueri	With organ
	Tenebrae factae sunt	With organ
Gustav Holst	Ave Maria	SSAA (double chorus)
	Four Old English Carols	SSAA(SA), with piano
	Seven Partsongs, Op. 44	SS(*divisi*) (S), strings or piano
Imogen Holst	Greensleeves (traditional)	Unaccompanied
Arthur Honegger	Cantique de Praques (Easter)	SSA(SSA), orch. (organ, harp reduction)
Alan Hovhaness	Ave Maria (*Triptych*)	SSAA, chamber orch.
Leos Janáček	Hradcany Songs (3 sections)	SSAA(SA), flute, harp
Zoltán Kodály	The Angels and the Shepherds	SSA (*divisi*), unaccompanied
	Ave Maria	
	Cease Your Bitter Weeping	SSA (*divisi*, 7 parts), unaccompanied
	Dancing Song	SSA (*divisi*), unaccompanied
	Fancy	SSA (*divisi*, 8 parts), unaccompanied
	See the Gypsies	SSAA, unaccompanied
Ernst Krenek	Five Prayers for Women's Voices (over Pater Noster)	SSAA, unaccompanied
	In paradisum	
	Three Madrigals	
Orlando di Lasso	Cantiones duarum vocem (12 motets for 2 equal voices)	SS, unaccompanied
James A. Laster	De profundis	SSAA (*divisi*, 7 parts), piano, percussion
Franz Liszt	Hymn to the Children's Awakening	SSA (S or A), piano, harp

	O heilige Nacht	SSA (T solo), organ
	Tantum ergo	SSAA, organ
Normand Lockwood	The Birth of Moses	SSA, piano, flute
Edwin London	A Washington Miscellany	Double chorus (10 parts)
	Five Haiku	SSAA *divisi*
	Four Proverbs (Hebrew texts)	SSAA *divisi*
David Maves	A Bestiary	SSAA, percussion
Kirke Mechem	I Shall Not Cease (*The Winds of May*)	SSAA, unaccompanied
	Seven Joys of Christmas (a carol sequence)	SA-SSA, optional piano
	The Winged Joy (in 7 parts)	SA; SSA(S);SSAA(S), #6 unacc., others with piano acc.
Felix Mendelssohn	Laudate pueri, Op. 39, No. 2	SSA(SSA), organ
	Surrexit pastor, Op. 39, No. 3	SSAA(SSA), organ
	Veni Domine, Op. 39, No. 1	SSA, organ
Darius Milhaud	Cantata from Proverbs	SSA, harp, oboe, cello
	Devant sa main nue	SSAA(SA), unaccompanied
	Two Roman Elegies	SSAA(SA), unaccompanied
Thomas Morley	My Heart Why Hast Thou Taken?	SSAA, unaccompanied
	Though Philomena Lost Her Love	Unaccompanied
	Away, Thou Shalt Not Love Me	Unaccompanied
Vaclav Nelhybel	Peter Gray (*Four Ballads*)	Unaccompanied
Ron Nelson	Autumn Night	SSA *divisi*, optional piano
	Jehovah, Hear Our Prayers	SSAA(S), optional piano
	Three Moutain Ballads	SSA, piano
Kent Newbury	Psalm 150	SSAA, unaccompanied
Knut Nystedt	Suoni	SSAA, flute, marimba
	Hosanna	SSAA, unaccompanied
Giovanni Pergolesi	Stabat Mater	SA(SA), strings
Vincent Persichetti	Hist Whist, Op. 46, No. 2	SA, unaccompanied
	Sam Was a Man	SA, piano
	Spring Cantata, Op. 94	SSA, piano
	This Is the Garden, Op. 46, No. 1	
	Winter Cantata, Op.97	SSAA, flute, marimba
Lloyd Pfautsch	Fanfare for Christmas	SSAA, brass
Daniel Pinkham	Angeles ad pastores ait	SSAA, trombones, tuba
	An Emily Dickinson Mosaic	Unison-SSA, chamber orch. (or piano)
	Magnificat	SA-SSA *divisi*(S), oboe, bassoons, harmonium (or piano)
	Now Let Us Praise Famous Men	SA unacc. (or with opt. insts.)
	Three Motets	SSA, organ (or piano)
Niccola Porpora	Credidi (Psalm 116)	SSAA, strings, organ
	Laetatus sum (Psalm 121)	SSAA(SA), strings, organ
	Lauda Jerusalem (Psalm 147)	SSAA, strings, organ
Francis Poulenc	Ave Maria (*Dialogues of the Carmelites*)	SSA with organ (or piano)
	Ave verum corpus	
	Litanies a la vierge noire	SSA, organ
	Petites voix (5 sections)	

Max Reger	Danksaget dem Vater, Op. 72, No. 2	
	Three Choruses, Op. 111c	SSAA, unaccompanied
	Three Choruses, Op. 111c	Unaccompanied
Luise Reichardt	Sechs geistliche Lieder	SSAA, with piano
Ned Rorem	Five Prayers for the Young	SSA-SSAA, unaccompanied
Gioacchino Rossini	La carita	(S), piano
	La speranza	With piano
Domingo Santa Cruz	Cantares de Pascua, Op. 27 (Christmas)	
Johann Hermann Schein	Der kühle Maien (Waldliederlein)	
	Frau Nachtigal (Waldliederlein)	
William Schuman	Requiescat	SSAA, with piano
	Prelude for Women's Voices	SSAA divisi (S), with piano
Robert Schumann	Three Songs, Op. 43	SA, with piano
	Four Songs, Op. 103	SA, with piano
	Three Songs for Three Women's Voices	With piano
	Romances for Women's Chorus, Op. 69	SSAA, piano (ad lib)
	Romances for Women's Chorus, Op. 91	SSAA-SSSAAA, piano (ad lib)
David Stocker	Festival Response	SSAA divisi, unaccompanied
Alan Stout	O Altitudio	SSAA divisi (S), flute solo, chamber ensemble
Igor Stravinsky	Cantata	SSA-SSAA (ST), 2 flutes, Eng. Hn., Cello (or piano)
	Four Russian Peasant Songs	SA-SSAA(SA), unaccompanied
Louise Talma	Celebration	SSAA, orchestra
Randall Thompson	Come In (Frostiana)	With piano
	The Gate of Heaven	SSAA, unaccompanied
	A Girl's Garden (Frostiana)	With piano
	God's Bottles (Americana)	SSAA, unaccompanied
	A Hymn for Scholars and Pupils	Inst. ens. (or flute, piano)
	The Lord Is My Shepherd	SSAA, piano, organ
	Now I Lay Me Down to Sleep	
	The Place of the Blest (Cantata)	Chamber orch.
	Pueri Hebraeorum (double chorus)	SSAA-SSAA, unaccompanied
	Rosemary (four choruses)	SSA-SSAA, unaccompanied
Virgil Thomson	Seven Choruses from the Medea of Euripides	SSAA, percussion (ad lib)
Jacob van Vleck	I Will Rejoice in the Lord (Moravian)	SA-SA (antiphonal), piano
Ralph Vaughan Williams	Folk Songs of the Four Seasons (Cantata)	SSAA(SA), orchestra
	Magnificat	SSAA(A), orchestra (or fl.,piano)
Giuseppe Verdi	Laudi alla vergine Maria (Quatro Pezzi)	SSAA, unaccompanied
	Nun's Chorus (I Lombardi)	SSAA, organ (or piano)
Hector Villa-Lobos	As Costureiras	
Thomas Weelkes	Aye Me, Alas, Heigh Ho	
	Come, Let's Begin	
	Come, Sirrah Jack, Ho!	

	Ha, Ha, This World Doth Pass	
	The Nightingale	
	Tomorrow Is the Marriage Day	
Healy Willan	Regina coeli laetare	SSAA, unaccompanied

Selected Music for Male Chorus (assembled by Jameson Marvin)[2]

Composer	Title	Special Information
Byron Adams	Go Lovely Rose	(IMC)[3]
Alexander Agricola	Credo: Je ne vis oncques I	TTB-TTBB
Maximilian Albrecht	Exultet sanctus	(IMC)
Alonso (15th century)	La tricotea Samartini la vea	TBB
Anonymous (13th century)	Dolent depart	TTB
Anonymous (16th century)	Rex autem David	
Dominick Argenti	The Revelations of St. John the Divine	(T), brass, percussion, piano
Thomas Armstrong	Tranquillity	
Samuel Barber	A Stopwatch and an Ordnance Map	Piano, timpani
Béla Bartók	Five Slavic Folksongs	
Hector Berlioz	Finale to Part II from *The Damnation of Faust*	Orchestra or piano
Thomas Beveridge	Drop, Drop Slow Tears	
Franz Biebl	Ave Maria	
Gordon Binkerd	A Scotch Mist "Wilt Thou Be My Dearie?" "Clout the Cauldron" "Ay Walkin O"	TTB-TTBB
	Dum medium silentium	With piano
	There Is a Garden in Her Face	TTB
	They Lie at Rest	TTB
	Though Your Strangeness Frets My Heart	With bell, lyra
	Two Salieri Canons "Milton" and "Das Glockenspiel"	
Benjamin Britten	Ballad of Little Musgrave and Lady Barnard	Two pianos
	Rustic Fisherman *(Gloriana)*	
Anton Bruckner	Um Mitternacht Sternschnuppen	
Anton Brummel	Ave ancilla trinitatis	TTB
	Du tout plongiet	
	Fors seulement	
	Mater patris et filia	
Vincent de Bussy	Las il n'a nui mal	
William Byrd	Mass for Three Voices	TTB
Elliott Carter	The Defense of Corynth Emblems	With piano, four-hands
	Tarantella	With piano, four-hands

[2]For TTBB unless otherwise indicated; solo voices in parentheses.
[3]IMC: Intercollegiate Music Council, an association of male glee clubs.

Henry Cowell	Day, Evening, Night, Morning	TTTBBB
	Luther's Carol for His Son	
David Conte	Canticle	TTB-TTBB-TTTBB, piano, four-hands
Archibald Davison	The Foggy Dew	
Claude Debussy	Invocation	Orchestra or piano
Josquin des Prés	Absolon, fili mi	
	Missa Mater Patris	TTBB-TTBBB
	Tu pauperium refugium	
Hugo Distler	Abendlied eihes reisenden Male Choruses (Möricke Chorliederbuch)	
Guillaume Dufay	Anima mea liquefacta est	TBB
John Dunstable	Veni sancte spiritus	TTB
Anton Dvořák	Liebeslied im Garten (Five Songs for Men's Chorus)	
Jonothan Elkus	The Dorodos	
Robert Fayrfax	Kyrie (Missa vous ne l'aurez)	TTBB,TTBBB,TTTBBB
	Ave lumen gratiae	(Fayrfax Works, vol. II)
Alphonso Ferrabosco I	Vocem meam audisti	TTTBB
Alphonso Ferrabosco II	Lamentations of Jeremiah	TTTBB
Heinrich Finck	Petre, amas me?	TTBBB
Irving Fine	McCord's Menagerie	
	"Vulture Gryphus"	
	"Jerboa"	
	"Mole"	
	"Clam"	
Nicholas Gombert	O gloriosa Domina	
Jacob Handl	Ante luciferum genitur	TTBBB
	Haec est dies	
	O magnum mysterium	Double chorus
	Replenti sunt omnes	Double chorus
John Harbison	Nunc dimittis	TB, piano
Hans Leo Hassler	Cantate Domino	
	Laetantur coeli	
Michael Haydn	Abschiedslied	
Paul Hindemith	Der Tod	(ms. Schott)
	Erster Schnee	TTTBB
	The Demon of the Gibbett	
Alan Hoddinott	Hymnus ante somnum (in memorium Benjamin Britten)	TB,TTB,TTBB,TTTBB,TTTBBB, with organ
Gustav Holst	Dirge for Two Veterans	Brass, percussion
Vincent d'Indy	Six chansons (Populaires francaises)	Transcribed by F. Darcieux
Leos Janáček	Tři Mužské Sbory (Osamělá Bez Těchy I)	
	Svatý ted prapor	
	Singselige Dumka	
	Perina	
Zoltán Kodály	A Franciaorszagi valtoza sokra	
	Bordal	
	Esti Dal	
	Fölszällott a páva	
	Hej Büngözsdi Bandi	
	Huszt	
	Jelige	
	Katonadal (Soldier's Song)	TTB, trumpet, drum

	Mulató Gajd	
	Rabhazának Fia	
Karl Kohn	Three Galliard Songs	TBB
Kirke Mechem	English Girls	TTB
	"Jenny Kissed Me"	
	"Julia's Voice"	
	"To Celia"	
	Shadows of the Moon	With piano
Darius Milhaud	Psaume 121	
Claudio Monteverdi	Lamento della Ninfa	TTB(A)
	Crucifixus	(IMC)
Jean Mouton	Peccate mea Domine	TTTBB
Joannes Ockeghem	Intemerata Dei Mater	TTTBB
Francis Poulenc	Chanson a boire	
	La belle si nous etion	TTB
	Laudes de St. Antoine de Padoue	
	Quatre petites prières de St. Francois D'Assise	
Max Reger	Abschied	
	Hochsommernacht	
Nikolai Rimsky-Korsakov	Three Russian Folk Songs	
Arnold Schoenberg	Verbundenheit (Sechs Stücke für Männerchor) (#6)	
William Schuman	Truth Shall Deliver	TTB
John Shepard	Alleluia	
	Confitemini Domino	(Early English Music, vol. XVII)
Jean Sibelius	Natus in curas	
Robert Starer	On the Nature of Things	With flute, clar., trp., trb.
	In Praise of Music	TTB
John Taverner	Dum transisset Sabatum	
	Magnificat I	TTB-TTBB
Thomas Tomkins	Hear My Prayer, O Lord	
	The Heavens Declare the Glory of God	
Orazio Vecchi	Imitatione del Venetiano (La veglie di Sienna)	
Ludovico Viadona	Non turbetur cor vestrum	TTB

MUSIC FOR THE CHURCH CHOIR

Composer	Title	Publisher
Alexander Arkangelsky	Hear My Supplication	M. Whitmark
Johann Christoph Bach	I Will Not Let Thee Go	G. Schirmer
Johann Sebastian Bach	Hear the Joyful News	Galaxy
	Jesu, Joy of Man's Desiring	Oliver Ditson
	O Come, Holy Spirit	Neil A. Kjos
	We Hurry with Tired, Unfaltering Footsteps	Galaxy
	With Loudest Rejoicing	Concordia
Jean Berger	The Eyes of All Wait upon Thee	Augsburg
Ernest Bloch	Silent Devotion and Response	C. C. Birchard
Johannes Brahms	Create in Me, O God, a Pure Heart	G. Schirmer
	Grant unto Me the Joy of Thy Salvation	G. Schirmer
	Let Nothing Ever Grieve Thee	C. F. Peters
	O Cast Me Not Away from Thy Countenance	G. Schirmer

	How Lovely Is Thy Dwelling Place	G. Schirmer
Benjamin Britten	O Be Joyful in the Lord	Oxford
Dietrich Buxtehude	Now Sing We, Now Rejoice (In dulci jubilo)	Concordia
John Carter	Lo, How a Rose E'er Blooming	Somerset Press
Luigi Cherubini	Like As a Father	Summy-Birchard
F. Melius Christiansen, arr.	Lamb of God	Augsburg
Anton Dvořák	Blessed Jesu, Fount of Mercy	G. Schirmer
I. Drozdof	Prayer	Boston Music
L. L. Fleming, arr.	Give Me Jesus (Spiritual)	Augsburg
Cesar Franck	O Praise Ye the Lord	J. Fischer
Orlando Gibbons	Almighty and Everlasting God	Bourne
Alexander Gretchaninoff	Nunc Dimittis (with Gloria)	Neil A. Kjos
	Only Begotten Son	J. Fischer
	The Lord Is Gracious	Neil A. Kjos
George Frideric Handel	Let Their Celestial Concerts Unite (Samson)	E. C. Schirmer
	The Righteous Shall Be Had in Everlasting Remembrance	National Music Publ.
	Swell the Full Chorus	Galaxy
	Thanks Be to Thee	Neil A. Kjos
Thomas Hastings	O Taste and See	Mark Foster
Franz Joseph Haydn	Agnus Dei (Lamb of God)	Mark Foster
	Praise We Sing to Thee	Neil A. Kjos
	The Heavens Are Telling (The Creation)	G. Schirmer
Gustav Holst	Let All Mortal Flesh Keep Silence	Galaxy
	Turn Back, O Man	Galaxy
Alan Hovhaness	Jesus, Lover of My Soul	C. F. Peters
Egil Hovland	The Glory of the Father	Walton Music
John Ireland	Greater Love Hath No Man	Galaxy
Gordon Jacob, arr.	Brother James Air	Oxford
Alexander Kopyloff	Russian Easter Song	Oliver Ditson
	Heavenly Light	Carl Fischer
Gerald R. Mack, arr.	The Moon Shines Bright	Carl Fischer
James McKelvy	O God, Our Help in Ages Past (St. Anne)	Mark Foster
Don Malin	Revival Song (Early American)	B. F. Wood
Paul O. Manz	E'en So, Lord Jesus, Quickly Come	Concordia
Jane Marshall	The Greatest of These	Agape
Felix Mendelssohn	All Ye That Cried unto the Lord	Boosey & Hawkes
	He Watching over Israel (Elijah)	G. Schirmer
	The Lord Is a Mighty God	Neil A. Kjos
	There Shall a Star from Jacob Come Forth	Neil A. Kjos
Daniel Moe	Let Your Eyes Be to the Lord	Augsburg
	Hosanna to the Son of David	Mercury
Thomas Morley	Agnus Dei (Lamb of God)	Neil A. Kjos
Walter L. Pelz	Show Me Thy Ways	Augsburg
Ernst Pepping	Laud Him!	Neil A. Kjos
Michael Praetorius	My Song Forever Shall Record	Willis
	Sing We All Now with One Accord	G. Schirmer
Henry Purcell	Rejoice in the Lord Alway	Belwin Mills
	Thou Knowest, Lord, the Secrets of Our Hearts	E. C. Schirmer
Camille Saint-Saëns	Praise Ye the Lord	Boosey & Hawkes
Franz Schubert	Holy, Holy, Holy	E. C. Schirmer
	Psalm 92	Broude

Heinrich Schütz	Glory Be to the Father	Theodore Presser
	O All Ye Nations	Oliver Ditson
Leo Sowerby	I Will Lift Up Mine Eyes	Boston Music
Arthur Sullivan	Turn Thy Face from My Sins	Novello
Thomas Tallis	If Ye Love Me	Oxford
	Magnificat and Nunc Dimittis	Mercury
Paul Tchesnokoff	Salvation Is Created	J. Fischer
Eric Thiman	A Hymn of Praise to the Creator	H. W. Gray
Ralph Vaughan Williams	At the Name of Jesus	Oxford
	Lord, Thou Hast Been Our Refuge	G. Schirmer
	O Clap Your Hands	Galaxy
	O Taste and See	Oxford
	Sine Nomine	Carl Fischer
Charles Wood	Expectans Expectavi	C. C. Birchard
Gordon Young	Let All the World in Every Corner Sing	Galaxy
Heinz Werner Zimmermann	Psalm 23	Augsburg

Carols for Christmas

Composer	Title	Publisher
William Billings	A Virgin Unspotted	Mercury Music
R. Boughton, arr.	The Holly and the Ivy	G. Schirmer
Olaf C. Christiansen, arr.	Guiding Star Carol	Neil A. Kjos
	Rejoice This Night	Neil A. Kjos
Rene Clausen, arr.	On the Mountain Top Blows the Wind Mild	Mark Foster
R. Elmore & R. B. Reed, arr.	Carol of the Wind	J. Fischer
Arnold Freed	From Out of a Wood	C. F. Peters
Imogen Holst, arr.	Out of Your Sleep Arise and Wake	G. Schirmer
Herbert Howells	A Spotless Rose	Galaxy
C. H. Kitson	Whence Those Sounds Symphonious?	Galaxy
Richard Kountz, arr.	Hushing Carol	G. Schirmer
Norman Luboff, arr.	Still, Still, Still	Walton Music Co.
James McKelvy, arr.	This Enders Night	Mark Foster
Gardner Read	Jesous Ahatonhia (Indian)	Lawson-Gould
Max Reger	The Virgin's Slumber Song	Oliver Ditson
David Stanley Smith, arr.	Three Moorish Kings	Galaxy
	O Thou Lovely Night	Galaxy
Gregg Smith, arr.	Wexford Carol	G. Schirmer
Leo Sowerby, arr.	The Snow Lay on the Ground	H. W. Gray
Williametta Spencer	Welcome Yule	Associated Music Publishers
	There Is No Rose of Such Virtue	Associated Music Publishers
David McK. Williams	The Stork	H. W. Gray

Glossary

A cappella: In church or chapel style, unaccompanied; so called because the music of the Sistine Chapel at the Vatican was traditionally sung unaccompanied.

Acoustics: The science of sound; usually refers to the resonance and listening properties of a room or auditorium such as a concert hall or a rehearsal room; reflection of sound and echo.

Ad lib: Derived from Latin *ad libitum,* meaning "according to one's pleasure." In reference to a rehearsal, the conductor may slow or accelerate the tempo, or even pause, as he or she desires for purposes of careful tuning.

Aesthetics: The rules of good taste; the laws of the beautiful; in the art of music making it relates to sentiment and expression.

Aleatoric music: Sometimes called "chance" music; a composer's indication of pitches, rhythms, or intensity that, in performance, may be left to the performer's decision as to order in which they are played or sung.

Appoggiatura: A dissonant note in a chord that resolves to a consonant one; in the eighteenth century there were two kinds: the short appoggiatura, which is played quickly on the beat before the main note; and the long appoggiatura, which also comes on the beat, but takes away half the value of the main note if it is not dotted. If the main note *is* dotted, it receives two-thirds of its value. In the Classic and Romantic periods the rules varied somewhat.

Arsis-thesis (Gr.): Literally, lifting and lowering; in terms of a musical phrase, it refers to the building to a climax of tension and then relaxing to the resolution.

Articulation: The clear and distinct rendering of tones in singing or playing an instrument; it also refers to devices that assist in defining phrases, such as slurs, staccato marks, and accentuations that lead to a proper performance of the music.

Atonal music: Literally, an absence of tonality; a term identified with the twelve-tone serial music of Arnold Schoenberg and his followers.

Aural acuity: In music, the hearing of pitches accurately, with keenness; recognition of intervals and the ability to relate tones.

Avant-garde music: New music that applies to experimental compositional techniques.

Ayre (also **Air**): A popular English solo song in the sixteenth and early seventeenth centuries that was accompanied by the lute or a bass instrument with keyboard; occasionally with two other singers.

Ballett (Eng.), **Balletto** (It.):   A madrigalian form that combined singing with dancing, with a *fa-la-la* refrain; originally Italian and made popular by Gastoldi, it became even more so with the music of Thomas Morley in Renaissance England.

Bassett horn: An obsolete transposing instrument of the clarinet order, with an appealing soft, rich quality; sounds a fifth lower than written; used by Mozart, most notably in the Requiem.

Basso continuo: A feature of Baroque composition, it refers to the bass part composed for keyboard instruments with numbers that indicate the harmonies for the accompaniment (figured bass) and the part written for bass instruments, including the viola da gamba, cello, bassoon, theorba (bass lute), bass trombone, or violone.

Becker Psalter: A collection of paraphrased psalms set to music by Heinrich Schütz in 1628 that had been "rhymed" by Cornelius Becker; intended for congregational use in the German Lutheran church.

Bel canto (It.):   Meaning "beautiful singing"; a style of singing that places emphasis on beautiful tone and technique rather than on dramatic expression.

Cadential trill: A typical Baroque ornament, preceded by an appoggiatura and nearly always trilled from the note above; considered a convention and often omitted from Baroque scores but played in performance.

Canon: The strictest of all contrapuntal compositional practices, in which each voice imitates exactly the melody sung or played by the first voice or instruments. Besides "strict," there are numerous other versions, such as double canon, inverted, augmented, and diminuted.

Cantata: A choral-solo composition of several movements with instrumental accompaniment; somewhat like an oratorio but without specific characters and shorter in length; originally for solo voice with a mixture of recitatives and airs.

Cantus firmus (Lat.):   A preexisting melody used as a basis for a polyphonic composition; originally the subject was based on Gregorian chant.

Canzona, Canzonetta (It.):   In the sixteenth century, a composition similar to a madrigal. Literally, a "song," the counterpart of the German Lied and the French chanson.

Capella, Kapelle: A term used primarily by Schütz to indicate the choir in contrast to the soloists (*favorita* singers) in polychoral music.

Catullus: A Roman poet of the first century.

Cento concerti: A collection of sacred music for solo voice and organ *continuo* that preceded the sacred works of this type by Monteverdi.

Chamber cantata: A popular seventeenth-century form for two singers with instrumental accompaniment; also referred to as chamber-duets. Handel based several of his most famous choruses on music he had previously composed in this genre.

Chanson (Fr.):   Literally, "song"; also a type of polyphonic music for several voices popular in the fifteenth and sixteenth centuries.

Chapel Royal: A private body of musicians, singers, and instrumentalists, which accompanied English kings wherever they went; they played an important role in the development and cultivation of English music.

Choral blend: The result of vowel unification, rhythmic precision, and pitch accuracy in choral performance.

Chorale: Hymns of the German Protestant Lutheran Church; a prominent feature of the German passion oratorio.

Choric speech: One of numerous avant-garde techniques that incorporates the use of the human voice in a nontraditional manner; a speaking chorus.

Circa (Lat.):   Literally, "around" or "about," in reference to uncertain dates; abbreviated as *c.* or *ca.* (ca. 1400).

Circle of Fifths: A method of modulation from dominant to dominant that leads back, after twelve steps, to the original tone.

Colla parte (It.):   The practice of doubling vocal parts with instruments, used extensively during the Renaissance period and with the polychoral music of the early Baroque.

Color: A word used interchangeably with *timbre;* in reference to voices, used to compare the darker tone quality of male voices with the brighter tones of the female voice; also, the darker quality of the *mezzo* voice with that of a *coloratura* soprano.

Coloration: Blackened notes in Renaissance notation that affected the rhythm; simply stated, in duple measure (imperfect) three blackened notes equal two notes of the white; in triple measure (perfect) two white notes of three beats each equal three black notes, each with two beats (hemiola).

Consort song: A seventeenth-century English form made famous by such composers as John Dowland, Thomas Campion, and Francis Pilkington; music for voice and a few instruments, usually with secular text; later adapted by Henry Purcell to the verse anthem.

Cori spezzati (It.): The separated and alternating choirs of the Venetian polychoral style; literally, "spaced choirs" that were placed in various parts of the church to create a "spatial" effect.

Council of Trent: Held from 1643 to 1663, it played a decisive role in the development of Catholic church music; it abolished the use of secular music that had made inroads into the mass and restored dignity to the service.

Cue: An invitational gesture designed to time singers' intake of breath preparatory to a vocal entrace.

Diaphragm: The muscular, membranous partition separating the abdominal and thoracic cavities, which functions in respiration.

Diaphragmatic-intercostal breathing: A type of breathing in the act of singing that makes use of the lower rib cage in coordination with the diaphragm and the abdominal muscles.

Diction: The enunciation and pronunciation of words in any language.

Diminuendo (It.): Lessening the intensity and power of a sustained tone; gradually getting softer.

Diphthong: Two vowel sounds placed together in a word or a syllable; one is usually stressed and the other performed as a "glide" or "semivowel."

Dissonance: A term that describes the disturbing effect of intervals such as seconds or sevenths as against consonance, associated with normality and repose; an example is found in a suspension where the dissonant interval resolves to consonance at the cadence.

Doctrine of Affections: A term associated with pre-Classic *Empfindsamer Stil*, the North German counterpart of the French rococo: an eighteenth-century aesthetic theory that music portrays typical emotions in a prescribed manner; composers associated rhythmic and melodic patterns with emotions such as joy, sorrow, tenderness, or passion.

Double-dotting: A term used interchangeably with *overdotting* in reference to playing or singing dotted quarters, dotted eighths, or dotted sixteenths in Baroque and Classical music; in particular, the music in French Overture style, where dotted notes are traditionally lengthened and the succeeding note is shortened.

Ducal chapels: Centers of musical development and interest that sponsored the leading composers and performing musicians in the sixteenth to eighteenth centuries. During the Renaissance, princedoms flourished in parts of Europe, particularly in the ducal palaces and manor houses of Italy and England; later, as city-states developed, the chapels of North Germany become more prominent.

Duple and triple meters: Units of measure divisible by 2 ($\frac{2}{4}$, $\frac{2}{2}$, $\frac{2}{8}$) or 3 ($\frac{3}{4}$, $\frac{3}{2}$, $\frac{3}{8}$); also quadruple ($\frac{4}{2}$, $\frac{4}{4}$, $\frac{4}{8}$); in addition, there is compound meter that multiplies each by 3: compound duple ($\frac{6}{2}$, $\frac{6}{4}$, $\frac{6}{8}$), compound triple ($\frac{9}{4}$, $\frac{9}{8}$), and compound quadruple ($\frac{12}{4}$, $\frac{12}{8}$).

Ecclesiastical modes: Diatonic scales that form the basis of Gregorian chant (plainchant) and early music before 1600; these are grouped into six called authentic and six referred to as plagal, giving a total of twelve modes on which chant was based: Dorian, Phrygian, Lydian, Mixolydian, Aeolian, and Ionian; each of these had a corresponding plagal mode: hypo-Dorian, hypo-Phrygian, and so on, that had the same tonic and used the same notes of the scale but started a fourth lower.

Ensalada (Sp.): Term meaning "medley"; used in reference to sixteenth-century Spanish songs of a humorous nature; those composed by Matea Flecha were motets that made fun of the poor intonation of guitar players.

Extended vocal techniques: This term is associated with avant-garde music and its use of extended vocal techniques: extreme range, whispering, yelling, grunting, coughing, or other, similar sounds indicated in this music.

Falsetto (It.): Literally, "false" voice. The male voice in the upper range that has a lighter, less resonant quality than the normal range; highly developed in the Renaissance and an aid to the development of the legitimate high voice in male singers.

Favorita: Term used by Heinrich Schütz to denote a group of solo singers in polychoral music.

Figured bass: A Baroque bass part provided for the *continuo* keyboard player with numerals that indicate harmonies and chord positions in the accompaniment.

French Overture: A standard type modelled after Lully in the French court of Louis XIV; a slow, dotted introduction followed by an *allegro* in imitative style. (*See also* **Double-dotting.**)

Frottola (It.): An Italian secular form popular in the fifteenth and sixteenth centuries, basically homophonic, with melody in the soprano and accompanied by instruments, it was superseded by the madrigal around the middle of the sixteenth century.

Fugato (It.): A passage in fugal style contained in a nonfugal composition.

Fugue: The latest and most mature form of strict, imitative counterpoint, developed in the seventeenth century and perfected in works of J. S. Bach.

Gestalt Theory: A teaching concept whereby the approach is from the larger form or concept to its parts; applied to teaching choral music, the conductor first presents the work as a whole, then phrase by phrase in relation to the whole.

Glide: Term used for the short, transitional sound produced in passing from one articulated sound to another; also called a *semivowel*. Examples: few (fyOO), woe (ooOHoo).

Grace note: A note printed in small type before a main note to indicate that its time value is not counted in the rhythm of the bar and must be subtracted from its adjacent note; Italian term is *acciaccatura*.

Gradual, Graduale (Lat.): Originally called *responsorium graduale,* these are responsorial chants and are the second item of the Proper of the Mass; highly florid, polyphonic settings, usually based on Gregorian chant.

Hemiola (Gr.): Literally, "one and one-half," the relationship of 3:2 in rhythm; frequently appearing in Baroque and Renaissance music in the form of $\frac{6}{8}$ meter shifting suddenly to $\frac{3}{4}$; also occurs in shifting from a measure of $\frac{3}{4}$ to $\frac{3}{2}$ covering two measures.

Homophony: A musical texture in which a melody is supported by harmony; it is the opposite of polyphony, where each voice part has its own melody and several are heard simultaneously.

Ictus (Lat.): Literally, "strike." In conducting gestures it refers to the exact point of each beat, where the pulse of the tempo may be seen; it is clearly seen in the marcato beat and appears only slightly in a legato passage.

Impressionism: A musical school of the late nineteenth and early twentieth centuries that reacted against the effusive music of Richard Wagner; inspired by the French school of painting, it was chiefly represented by Claude Debussy and Maurice Ravel. The style is characterized by unresolved dissonances, triads with added seconds, fourths, sixths, and sevenths, whole-tone scale passages in melodic as well as chordal combinations, chords built on fourths; the result is music that is vague and intangible, that seems to hint rather than state, and creates a succession of colors rather than developing dynamics.

Incipit (Lat.): Literally, "it begins"; originally referred to the opening words of a text sung by the cantor before the chorus entered in liturgical chant; in an edited score, refers to the opening four or five notes taken from the manuscript that indicate original time values and pitches.

International Phonetic Alphabet (IPA): Symbols that provide a pronunciation key for all languages; found in most standard dictionaries.

Intonation: The singing or playing "in tune," especially as related to an ensemble; it is referred to as good or bad; also an alternate term for the opening tones of a chant sung by the cantor or priest.

Just intonation, Mean intonation: Terms that relate to systems of tuning that preceded equal-tempered tuning, which adjusts pitches to accommodate modulations in keyboard music; this tuning is particularly adapted to Renaissance music sung *a cappella,* with its "wide" fifths and slightly lowered thirds, lowered minor sevenths, and raised leading tones.

Kapellmeister (Ger.):   Original title for the music director at German courts; corresponds to *maitre de chapelle* in France, *maestro di cappella* in Italy, and Master of the King's Music in England.

Lied, Lieder (Ger.):   A German choral form corresponding to the French chanson; composed in the vernacular, the polyphonic Lied became a true art form in the hands of Isaac and Senfl; later composers were influenced by the Italian *villanella* and resulted in a more homophonic Lied with Orlando di Lasso, Hans Leo Hassler, and Leonhard Lechner.

Ligatures: Signs combining two or more notes in a group in Renaissance notation.

Lute: An ancient instrument popular in the sixteenth century; pear-shaped, it was played by plucking the strings with the fingers of the right hand, with the left on a fretted keyboard; the number of strings varied from six to thirteen, with as many as six bass strings running alongside the fingerboard that were unalterable in pitch.

Macrorhythm, Microrhythm: Refer to the overall tactus and the inner duple–triple relationships pertaining to text and music in Renaissance polyphony.

Madrigal: Derived from the literary form of the Italian *madriale;* the generic term for secular polyphonic music in the Renaissance; counterpart of the sacred motet.

Madrigale spirituale (It.):   Literally, "sacred madrigals"; a form of madrigal with sacred texts for home "enrichment," to be sung outside the church service; a noted composer was Philippe de Monte, *maestro di cappella* for Maximilian II in Vienna.

Magnificat (Lat.):   Originally a canticle to the Virgin Mary sung at the Vesper Service in the Roman Catholic Church; in the Anglican rite it is sung at Evening Prayer; a text frequently chosen by composers from the fourteenth to the twentieth centuries.

Melisma: Several notes sung on a single vowel in a musical passage than can be of considerable length, found particularly in Baroque music.

Mensural notation: Refers to temporal relationships between note values as established in a period between 1250 and 1600; a common example is the relationship between a measure of two half notes or two whole notes ($\frac{2}{2}$, $\frac{2}{1}$) becoming equal to three of the same ($\frac{3}{2}$, $\frac{3}{1}$); the mensural relationship would be: $\mathbf{o} = \mathbf{o}\cdot$ or $|o| = |o|\cdot$. (*See* **Coloration.**)

Meter: The arrangement of beats and accents in music as they are grouped into measures by bar lines.

Mezzo-soprano (It.):   The female voice with range and tone quality midway between soprano and alto.

Microtonal tuning: A present-day avant-garde technique that asks singers and instrumentalists to alter pitch within a composition by various minute degrees, called *cents;* reminiscent of the "mean" and "just" temperament tuning of Renaissance and medieval music.

Missa Brevis (Lat.):   A "short Mass"; also refers to the Lutheran Mass that consists of only the Kyrie and the Gloria.

Motet: A choral composition that developed from a single melody composed over a melisma from Gregorian chant (clausula) called *motetus* in the Middle Ages to the highly developed polyphonic sacred counterpart of the secular madrigal in the late sixteenth century; the number of voice parts increased from the original two to as many as four, six, and eight (even forty in the hands of Thomas Tallis and others). In England the motet was replaced by the anthem; after 1600, solo voices and instrumental parts were frequently added; in the eighteenth and nineteenth centuries the form was brilliantly treated by J. S. Bach, Mozart, Mendelssohn, and Brahms.

Movable Do system: In contrast to the solfeggio form of solmization, where C is always "do" and sharps and flats are sung without changing the "sol-fa" syllables, this system gives accidentals special names and changes "do" to fit the key-note of each major scale; minor scales begin and end on "la" of its relative major scale.

Musica ficta (Lat.):   The practice of chromatically altering diatonic tones based on the hexichord system in music from the tenth through the sixteenth centuries.

Nasopharynx: The portion of the throat directly behind the nasal cavities and above the soft palate; one of three chief sources of resonance in singing, the others are the oral-pharynx (directly behind the mouth) and the larynx itself.

Neo-Romantic, Neo-Classic, Neo-Impressionist composers: Those whose contemporary writings reflect the compositional practices of these periods.

Neutral syllable: Nonsensical syllable used for sight-reading new music; the choice of syllable is in agreement with mood, tempo, and expressiveness of text and music.

Notes inegales (Fr.): Notes that are written as equal notes but are played or sung in an uneven manner according to the French convention of the seventeenth century.

Oratorio: Originally a form of church drama performed outside the sanctuary in the oratorium; in the eighteenth century it became the sacred counterpart of secular opera but without staging or costumes and was presented in concert form.

Ornamentation: Originally, improvised notes added by performers that were embellishments to the melodic line and not a part of the essential harmony; they include the appoggiatura, grace notes, trills, turns, and mordents; often referred to as graces; there are characteristic ornaments identified with all periods from the Renaissance through the Romantic.

Overdotting: Exaggerating the length of a dotted note and shortening the eighth note or the sixteenth note that follows; particularly adaptable to moderately slow and slow movements in seventeenth- and eighteenth-century music.

Parallel consonants: Those that make use of the same articulators, both with and without pitch. Examples are *t*, spoken or sung without pitch, and its corollary, *d*, that is given pitch when pronounced.

Partbooks: The manuscripts or printed books of the Renaissance that contain music for a single voice-part, rather than all the vocal parts as printed today; the parts were designated for *cantus* (or *discantus*, or *superius*), *altus*, *tenor*, and *bassus*, with additional parts such as *cantus* I, *cantus* II, *quinta vox*, and *sexta vox*.

Part song: A choral composition in homophonic style, in contrast to the polyphonic madrigal; it applies chiefly to music of the nineteenth century by such composers as Haydn, Mendelssohn, Schumann, and Elgar.

Phonation: The beginning of sound; the act of starting a tone in singing.

Picardy third, Tierce de Picardie (Fr.): The raising of the interval of a minor third to major at the conclusion of a modal cadence; prior to the sixteenth century, the final chord contained an "empty" fifth, without the third.

Pillar: An illustrative term applying to the architectural form of a piece of music when a single phrase is repeated verbatim at other designated points within the composition.

Plainchant, Plainsong: Terms used interchangeably in reference to Gregorian chant; general terms for the ancient form of monophonic, rhythmically free music of medieval church liturgy.

Polyphony: Contrapuntal music composed for any combination of voices or parts, with each part having more or less pronounced individuality; most closely identified with music prior to the Baroque period, although elements are identifiable in all subsequent periods of composition.

Polyrhythm: Contrasting rhythms occurring in all parts of a musical fabric; particularly identified with the microrhythms of polyphony, where each part has independent rhythms based on both music and text; also found in avant-garde music and other contemporary composition of the twentieth century.

Portato (It.): A manner of singing or playing that is halfway between legato and staccato: usually indicated by a slur with dots under or over each note.

Positive organ: One of the manuals of the organ; originally a small organ that could be moved about to accompany polychoral groups.

Prima prattica, Secunda prattica (It.): Terms applied to the "new" and "old" styles of musical composition at the time of Monteverdi and the Florentine Camerata at the beginning of the Baroque period in Italy. *Primo* refers to the Renaissance polyphonic style of writing, *secundo* to the new concerted homophonic, *nuovo* style associated with *basso continuo*, recitative, and the independent function of instruments with voices.

Pronunciation: The act of articulating text with proper stress and meaning.

Pulse: Regular or rhythmical beating; relating to the tactus in music.

Quarter tone: Actual pitch that is halfway between a semitone in music; common to music of Eastern cultures; experimented with in avant-garde music of today.

Quodlibet (Lat.): Literally, "what you please," a humorous form that employs two or more familiar melodies together; beginning the the thirteenth century with motets that combined religious music with popular songs, the form persisted up through the time of J. S. Bach.

Recorder: Predecessor of the transverse flute, it is played with a "whistle" mouthpiece; families of recorders were most popular during the sixteenth century and were particularly associated with the playing of madrigals in Elizabethan England; the instrument, still popular in the playing of early music today, is played vertically in front of the performer in contrast to the modern flute.

Resonance, Resonation: In singing, the intensification and enhancement of the quality of sound, produced by sympathetic vibrations.

Rhythmic assimilation: A term associated with Baroque practice of incorporating a basic rhythmic figure into all parts; when triplets occur in the bass line, dotted rhythms in the other parts are also played as triplets; when dotted notes predominate, successive eighth notes in other parts are played as dotted.

Di ripieni, Senza ripieni (It.): Baroque indication for full orchestra *(ripieni)* or solo instrumentalists *(senza ripieni)* only; used to indicate solo-tutti in the concerto grosso and also for playing with full chorus versus playing with solo singers.

Rococo: Eighteenth-century French, highly ornamented style preceding the Classic period; also called *gallant* style.

Rubato (It.): Literally, "robbed" time; an indication to give expression to a passage by performing the music with a free rhythm; that is, it may be taken slightly faster but then slowed down expressively, according to the requirements of the music and good taste.

Schwa vowel (ə): An IPA symbol for a certain vowel sound, in particular the indeterminate one in many unstressed syllables, such as the English words belief (bə-lEEF), problem (prAH-bləm), honor (AH-nər).

Semitone: Alternate term for a half step in a scale; a chromatic scale is composed entirely of semitones.

Semivowel: In phonetics, a letter of a vocal sound having the sound of a vowel but used as a consonant, such as *w, y,* and *r.* (*See* **Glide.**).

Sequence: Repetition of a melody or a repeated progression of chords at different pitches in succession within a composition.

Serialism: Identified with the twelve-tone system of composition devised by Arnold Schoenberg in an attempt to arrive at constructive methods to take the place of chord construction, chord relationship, and tonality; an arbitrary arrangement of a tone row is maintained, with modifications, throughout a composition.

Solfeggio (It.): A system of solmization whereby the pitch C is always "do." (*See* **Movable "Do" system.**) The unchanged syllables are *do, re, mi, fa, sol, la, si, do.*

Solo-tutti (It.): The Baroque *concerto grosso* principle of alternating a solo group *(favorita* singers) with a chorus.

Sonata allegro (It.): Term associated with the classic sonata form composed in three sections: exposition, development, and recapitulation; usually concluding with a coda section.

Sprechstimme (Ger.): In a speaking manner; speaking on approximate pitches; designated by Schoenberg in his *De profundis,* a dramatic choral setting of Psalm CXXX.

Sternum: A long, flat bone that articulates with the cartilages forming the midventral support for the ribs.

Stile concertato (It.): The term used to indicate vocal compositions that were supported by instrumental groups in order to distinguish them from polyphonic music with no independent instrumental parts.

Stretto (It.): Literally, "narrow" or "close"; the place in a fugue where the theme is presented in all voices in close succession near the end of the composition.

Sturm und Drang (Ger.): A nineteenth-century musical concept, espoused by Beethoven and his contemporaries, encouraging exaggerated expressivity ("storm and stress").

Suite: An important instrumental form of Baroque music that consisted of several movements, each in the character of a dance and all in the same key. Although there could be as many as twelve movements, four were basic: allemande (slow), courante (fast), sarabande (slow), and gigue (fast). The characteristic rhythms of these dances were reflected in the sacred works of many composers, one of the most notable examples being the final movement of Bach's *Passion According to St. Matthew,* which has the rhythm of a sarabande.

Suspension: A form of appoggiatura that consists of a dissonance and its resolution, a principal expressional device found in Renaissance music and most frequently occurring at a cadence point; a suspension always falls on a strong beat, whereas its preparation and resolution occur on weak beats.

Syncopation: An unequal division of the time or notes; irregular accent, accented notes occurring on the unaccented part of the beat; an interruption of the natural pulsation of music; prominent in spirituals, jazz, and gospel music.

Tactus (Lat.):   Fifteenth- and sixteenth-century term for "beat"; signified a normal tempo of M.M. 50–60; the time it takes to drop the arm and raise it again; corresponds to the down-up beats of a single $\frac{2}{2}$ measure.

Tempo (It.):   Rate of speed in a composition; the speed of the rhythm, the rapidity with which the natural accents follow each other. Tempo markings range from the slowest *largo* to the fastest *prestissimo;* metronome markings also give indications. A conductor's setting of a tempo is influenced by the character of the music, the acoustical properties of the hall, and the speed at which the fastest passages may be executed with clarity.

Tempo giusto (It.):   A tempo used frequently by Handel indicating moderately fast; a normal proper speed.

Tessitura (It.):   The general "lie" of a vocal part; the average pitch, which may be in high, medium, or low range. The term differs from range in that it does not take into account the notes that lie in the extremities of one's vocal range.

Text rhythm: The grouping of text into the natural stressed and unstressed syllables of speech, not accounted for by the divisions of measures in the music.

Texture: Horizontal and vertical elements in a musical composition; music may be contrapuntal or homophonic. Tonal contrasts in music: male versus female tone quality, voices with accompaniment or singing *a cappella,* solo versus tutti. Another textural contrast is found in the music of the various compositional periods: the Romantic, fullblown Requiems for large chorus and orchestra versus a group of Elizabethan madrigals. Choral directors look for textural contrasts when selecting a concert program.

Thomasschule (Ger.):   A school for boys and young men in Leipzig with a long tradition of teaching musicianship and choral music. Although a number of prominent composers have been connected with this school, the most outstanding one was J. S. Bach, from 1723 until his death in 1750.

Timbre (Fr.):   The quality or "color" of a tone; the difference between tones of the same pitch produced by various voices or instruments, or voices *with* instruments; all have differences in timbre.

Tonality: Associated with the change from the modality of the Renaissance to the major-minor tonality of the Baroque period; closely centered on a relationship to the tonic of a key; a key-center.

Tone cluster: A group of adjacent dissonant notes, such as notes of a diatonic or chromatic scale, sounded together; used frequently by contemporary composers.

Trill: A musical ornament consisting of the rapid alternation of a given note with the diatonic second above it. The Baroque trill nearly always begins from the diatonic note above with an appoggiatura *on* the beat. If it is a dotted note it frequently stops momentarily before the eighth note or the sixteenth note that precedes the concluding note; if there is no dot, the trill is usually concluded with a turn before the succeeding note. The cadential trill is often not indicated in Baroque music.

Triphthong: A compound vowel sound resulting from the combination of three separate vowels that function as a unit. Examples are: **fire** (fAHɪə), and **where** (hooEHə); the final **r** is pronounced as a *schwa* vowel. Such combinations are frequently found in other languages: m**iei** (mEE-EH́-EE) in Italian.

Vibrato (It.):   In singing, a scarcely noticeable wavering of the tone that increases the beauty of the sound without resulting in an objectionable wavering of pitch. A lack of balance and coordination between the breath and the larynx can result in an objectionable "wobble," an undesirable situation in a vocal ensemble.

Vowel folds: An accurate description of the vocal cords. (*See* **Larynx.**)

Vowel unification: A choral or ensemble technique that enables singers to blend their voices by approximating the same pronunciation of vowels; awareness of phonetic sounds, insisting on the "integrity" of vowels, and the "timing" of the pronunciation of diphthongs are the chief ingredients of vowel unification.

Word painting: In vocal music, a term for various ways of portraying the meaning of words through the music; also referred to as *musica reservata* at the time of Josquin. William Byrd is another excellent example of a Renaissance composer who emphasized word painting in his music.

Bibliography

These books and reference materials have been selected to supplement "Books and Other Materials for the Choral Musician: A Selected List" by James G. Smith.[1] Emphasis has been placed on publications after 1973; some earlier books and reference materials recommended by the authors have also been included.

A SELECTED BIBLIOGRAPHY

I. Choral Music: History, Performance Practice, Analysis, and Score Preparation

ADLER, SAMUEL, ed., *Choral Conducting: An Anthology*. New York: Holt, Rinehart & Winston, 1971.

ANDREWS, H. K., *The Technique of Byrd's Vocal Polyphony*. London: Oxford University Press, 1966.

ARNOLD, D., AND N. FORTUNE, *The Monteverdi Companion*. London: Faber & Faber, Ltd., 1968.

BLUME, FRIEDRICH, *Protestant Church Music: A History*. New York: W. W. Norton & Co., Inc., 1974.

BROWN, HOWARD M., *Embellishing Sixteenth Century Music*. London: Oxford University Press, 1976.

———, *Music in the Renaissance*. Englewood Cliffs, N.J.: Prentice-Hall, 1976.

CARSE, ADAM VON AHN, *History of Orchestration: The Orchestra of the XVIII Century*. Cambridge: Cambridge University Press, 1940.

---

[1]Harold A. Decker and Julius Herford, *Choral Conducting Symposium*, 2nd ed. (Englewood Cliffs, N.J.: Prentice-Hall, 1988).

COOPER, GROSVENOR, AND LEONARD MEYER, *The Rhythmic Structure of Music.* Chicago: Chicago University Press, 1976.

DAVID, HANS, AND ARTHUR MENDEL, *The Bach Reader.* New York: W. W. Norton & Co., Inc., 1945.

DONINGTON, ROBERT, *A Performance Guide to Baroque Music.* London: Faber & Faber, Ltd., 1978.

EMERY, WALTER, *Bach's Ornaments.* London: Novello & Co., 1961.

FELLOWES, EDMUND H., *The English Madrigal: A Guide to Its Practical Use.* Stainer & Bell, Ltd., 1925.

GROUT, DONALD J., *A History of Western Music.* New York: W. W. Norton & Co., Inc., 1973.

HITCHCOCK, H. WILEY, *Music in the United States* (2nd ed.). Englewood Cliffs, N.J.: Prentice-Hall, 1974.

HOLST, IMOGEN, ed., *Henry Purcell: Essays on His Music.* London: Oxford University Press, 1959.

KERMAN, JOSEPH, *The Masses and Motets of William Byrd.* Berkeley and Los Angeles: University of California Press, 1983.

LANG, PAUL HENRY, *Music in Western Civilization.* New York: W. W. Norton & Co., Inc., 1968.

LA RUE, JAN, *Guidelines for Style Analysis.* New York: W. W. Norton & Co., Inc., 1970.

LEONARD, RICHARD, *A History of Russian Music.* New York: Macmillan, 1961.

MCCLINTOCK, CAROL, ed., *Readings in the History of Music in Performance.* Bloomington, Ind.: Indiana University Press, 1929.

MACHLIS, JOSEPH, *Introduction to Contemporary Music.* New York: W. W. Norton & Co., Inc., 1961.

MONSAINGEON, BRUNO, *Mademoiselle: Conversations with Nadia Boulanger,* trans. Robyn Marsack. Manchester, England: Carcanet Press, 1985.

MUSSULMAN, J. A., *Dear People—Robert Shaw.* Bloomington, Ind.: Indiana University Press, 1979.

PAINE, GORDON, ed., *Essays on Choral Music in Honor of Howard Swan.* New York: Pendragon Press, 1988.

SMITHER, HOWARD E., *History of Oratorio,* vols. I, II. Chapel Hill, N.C.: University of North Carolina Press, 1977.

STEINITZ, PAUL, *Bach's Passions.* Masterworks of Choral Music, Peter Dodd, general ed. London: Paul Elek, 1979.

TEMPERLEY, NICHOLAS, *The Music of the English Parish Church,* vol. 1: text; vol. 2: music. Cambridge: Cambridge University Press, 1984.

ULRICH, HOMER, *A Survey of Choral Music.* The Harcourt History of Musical Forms. New York: Harcourt Brace Jovanovich, Inc., 1973.

———, AND PAUL A. PISK, *A History of Music and Musical Style.* New York: Harcourt Brace Jovanovich, Inc., 1963.

WIENANDT, E. A., ed., *Opinions on Church Music: Comments and Reports from Four-and-One-Half Centuries.* Waco, Tex.: Baylor University Press, 1974.

———, AND PERCY YOUNG, *The Anthem in England and America.* New York: Free Press, 1975.

II. Vocal/Choral Techniques and Conducting

ADLER, SAMUEL, *Sight Singing, Pitch, Interval, Rhythm.* New York: W. W. Norton & Co., Inc., 1979.

BOYD, JACK, *Rehearsal Guide for the Choral Conductor.* West Nyack, N.Y.: Parker Publishing Co., Inc., 1971.

COFFIN, BURTON, *The Sounds of Singing.* Boulder, Colo.: Pruett Publishing Co., 1976.

DECKER, HAROLD A., AND JULIUS HERFORD, *Choral Conducting Symposium* (2nd ed.). Englewood Cliffs, N.J.: Prentice-Hall, 1988.

EHMANN, WILHELM, AND FRAUKE HAASEMANN, *Voice Building for Choirs,* trans. Brenda Smith. Chapel Hill, N.C.: Hinshaw Music, Inc., 1981.

GARRETSON, ROBERT, *Conducting Choral Music* (6th ed.). Englewood Cliffs, N.J.: Prentice-Hall, 1988.

HABERLEN, JOHN, *Mastering Conducting Techniques*. Champaign, Ill.: Mark Foster Music Co., 1977.

HEFFERNAN, CHARLES W., *Choral Music: Technique and Artistry*. Englewood Cliffs, N.J.: Prentice-Hall, 1982.

HINDEMITH, PAUL, *Elementary Training for Musicians*. London: Schott & Co., 1946.

KIRK, THERON W., *Choral Tone and Technique*. Westbury, N.Y.: Pro-Art Publications, 1956.

KRONE, MAX T., *The Chorus and Its Conductor*. San Diego, Calif.: Neil Kjos Music Co., 1945.

LAMB, GORDON H., *Choral Techniques*. Dubuque, Iowa: Wm. C. Brown, 1974.

MORIARTY, JOHN, *Diction*. Boston: E. C. Schirmer Music Co., 1975.

MUSSULMAN, JOSEPH A., *Dear People—Robert Shaw*. Bloomington, Ind.: Indiana University Press, 1979.

ROBINSON, RAY, AND ALLEN WINOLD, *The Choral Experience*. New York: Harper & Row, Pub., 1976.

RUDOLPH, MAX, *The Grammar of Conducting*. New York: G. Schirmer, Inc., 1950.

SIMONS, HARRIET, *Choral Conducting: A Leadership Teaching Approach*. Champaign, Ill.: Mark Foster Music Co., 1978.

SMALLMAN, JOHN, AND JOHN C. WILCOX, *The Art of A Cappella Singing*. Philadelphia: Oliver Ditson Music Co., 1933.

STANTON, ROYAL, *The Dynamic Choral Conductor*. Delaware Water Gap, Pa.: Shawnee Press, Inc., 1971.

THOMAS, KURT, *The Choral Conductor,* trans. Alfred Mann and Wm. H. Reese. New York: Associated Music Publishers, 1971.

URIS, DOROTHY, *To Sing in English*. New York: Boosey & Hawkes, 1971.

WESTERMAN, KENNETH, *The Emergent Voice*. Ann Arbor, Mich.: Edwards Bros., Inc., 1947.

WILSON, HARRY ROBERT, *A Guide for Choral Conductors*. Morristown, N.J.: Silver Burdette, 1950.

————, *Artistic Choral Singing*. New York: G. Schirmer, Inc., 1959.

III. Articles and Pamphlets

ALDRICH, PUTNAM C., "The Authentic Performance of Baroque Music," in *Essays on Music in Honor of Archibald Davison*. Cambridge, Mass.: Harvard University Press, 1957.

BREWER, RICHARD HARDING, "The Two Oratorios of C.P.E. Bach in Relation to Performance," *The Choral Journal*, XV, no. 8 (April 1975), 23–24.

COX, RICHARD, *Singer's Manual of German and French Diction*. New York: G. Schirmer, Inc., 1970.

DART, THURSTON, WALTER EMERY, AND CHRISTOPHER MORRIS, *Editing Choral Music*. London: Novello & Co., Oxford University Press, and Stainer & Bell, Ltd., 1963.

ELLISON, ROSS WESLEY, "Mendelssohn's *Elijah*: Dramatic Climax of a Creative Career," *American Choral Review*, XXII, no. 1 (January 1980), 3–9.

ERICSON, ERIC, GÖSTA OHLIN, AND LENNART SPANGBERG, *Choral Conducting*. New York: Walton Music Corp., 1976.

FORBES, ELLIOT, "The Choral Music of William Matthias," *American Choral Review*, XXI, no. 4 (October 1979), 3–32.

GARRETSON, ROBERT L., "The Falsettists," *The Choral Journal*, XXIV, no. 1 (September 1983), 5–9.

HABERLEN, JOHN, AND STEVEN ROSOLACK, *Elizabethan Madrigal Dinners: Script with Music for Singers, Players, and Dancers*. Champaign, Ill.: Mark Foster Music Co., 1978.

HALL, WILLIAM D., ed., *Latin Pronunciation According to Roman Usage*. Tustin, Calif.: National Music Publishers, 1971.

HERFORD, JULIUS, "J. S. Bach: *Magnificat*," *The Choral Journal*, III, (May 1963), 6–9.

LANG, PAUL HENRY, "Choral Music in the Twentieth Century," *American Choral Review*, XIX, no. 2 (April 1977), 7–18.

LEMONDS, WILLIAM W., "Benjamin Britten's *War Requiem*," *The Choral Journal*, VIII, no. 1 (September/October 1967), 22–24.

LILLIENSTEIN, SAUL E., "A Choral Director's Guide to Beethoven's *Missa Solemnis*," *The Choral Journal*, VII, no. 3 (January/February 1967), 18–20.

ROUTLEY, ERIC, "The Dilemma of Excellence," *Pastoral Music,* no. 5 (March 1979), pp. 29–33.

SCHULER, R. J., "What Makes Music Sacred?" *Sacred Music*, 112, no. 2 (1985), 7–12.

SLATTERBACK, FLOYD, "Mozart's *Requiem*: History, Structure, and Performance," *American Choral Review*, XXVI, no. 2 (April 1984), 3–31.

STEINITZ, PAUL, "The Church Cantatas of J. S. Bach," *The Choral Journal*, VI, no.6 (July/August 1966), 4–7.

STOLZFUS, FRED, "Beethoven's *Mass* in C: Notes on History, Structure, and Performance Practice," *The Choral Journal*, XXIII, no. 3 (November 1982), 26–30.

TARTINI, GIUSEPPE, "Treatise on Ornamentation," trans., ed. Sol Babitz. *Journal of Research in Music Education*, 4, no. 2 (Fall, 1971).

TEMPERLEY, NICHOLAS, "New Light on the Libretto of *The Creation*," in *Music in Eighteenth Century England: Essays in Memory of Charles Cudworth*, ed. Christopher Hogwood and Richard Luckett, pp. 189–211. Cambridge: Cambridge University Press, 1983.

WESTRUP, JAMES, "Monteverdi and the Orchestra," *Music and Letters*, XII (1940), 230.

IV. References, Dictionaries, Lists

APEL, WILLI, *Harvard Dictionary of Music* (2nd ed.). Cambridge, Mass.: Harvard University Press, 1969.

DAVIDSON, JAMES, *Dictionary of Protestant Church Music*. Metuchen, N.J.: Scarecrow, 1975.

EVANS, PETER, *The Music of Benjamin Britten*. Minneapolis: University of Minnesota Press, 1979.

HARTOG, HOWARD, *European Music in the Twentieth Century*. London: Routledge & Paul, 1957.

HAWKINS, MARGARET B., *An Annotated Inventory of Distinctive Choral Literature for Performance at the High School Level*. ACDA monograph, 1976.

HEYER, ANNA HARRIET, *Historical Sets, Collected Editions, and Monuments of Music: A Guide to Their Contents*. Chicago: American Library Association, 1969.

INGRAM, MADELINE D., AND WILLIAM C. RICE, *Vocal Techniques for Children and Youth*. Nashville, Tenn.: Abingdon, 1962.

JACOBS, RUTH KREHBIEL, *The Successful Children's Choir*. Chicago: FitzSimons, 1984.

LANGER, SUSANNE K., *Feeling and Form*. New York: Scribner's, 1953.

———, *Philosophy in a New Key*. Cambridge, Mass.: Harvard University Press, 1974.

LASTER, J., comp., *Catalogue of Choral Music Arranged in Biblical Order*. Metuchen, N.J.: Scarecrow, 1981.

McKENZIE, DUNCAN, *Training the Boy's Changing Voice*. New Brunswick, N.J.: Rutgers University Press, 1936.

MAY, JAMES D., *Avant-garde Choral Music: An Annotated Selected Bibliography*. Metuchen, N.J.: Scarecrow, 1977.

NORDONE, THOMAS R., JAMES H. NYE, AND MARK RESNICK, *Choral Music in Print,* vol. 1: Sacred Music; vol. 2: Secular Music. Supplements: 1976, 1981, 1982. Philadelphia: Musicdata, Inc., 1974–82.

QUANTZ, JOHANN JOACHIM, *On Playing the Flute,* trans. Edward R. Reilly. New York: G. Schirmer Books, 1966 (paperback, 1975). A primary source for Baroque ornamentation.

RILLING, HELMUTH, *Johann Sebastian Bach's B-Minor Mass,* trans. Gordon Paine. Princeton, N.J.: Prestige Publications, 1984. Foreword by Howard S. Swan.

———, *St. Matthew Passion: Introduction and Instructions for Study,* trans. Kenneth Nafzger. New York: C. F. Peters, 1981.

ROBERTS, KENNETH C., *A Checklist of Twentieth Century Choral Music for Male Voices.* Detroit: Information Coordinators, 1970.

SACHS, CURT, *The History of Musical Instruments.* New York: W. W. Norton & Co., Inc., 1940.

SADIE, STANLEY, ed., *New Grove Dictionary of Music and Musicians.* London: Macmillan & Co., 1980.

SMITHER, HOWARD E., *History of Oratorio,* 2 vols. Chapel Hill, N.C.: University of North Carolina Press, 1977.

STEINITZ, PAUL, *Bach's Passions.* Masterworks of Choral Music, Peter Dodd, general ed. London: Paul Elek, 1979.

TERRY, CHARLES SANFORD, *J. S. Bach Cantata Texts, Sacred and Secular.* London: Constable & Co., 1926.

———, *Bach's Orchestra.* London: Oxford University Press, 1932.

TORTOLANO, WILLIAM, *Original Music for Men's Voices: A Selected Bibliography.* Metuchen, N.J.: Scarecrow, 1981.

TUFTS, NANCY POORE, *The Children's Choir,* vol. 2. Philadelphia: Fortress Press, 1965.

VINQUIST, MARY, AND NEAL ZASLAW, *Performance Practise: A Bibliography.* New York: W. W. Norton & Co., Inc., 1971.

VINTON, JOHN, *Dictionary of Contemporary Music.* New York: Dutton, 1974.

WHITE, J. P., *Twentieth Century Choral Music.* Metuchen, N.J.: Scarecrow, 1984.

Music for Class Study and Conducting

TABLE OF CONTENTS[1]

[1]All selections are for SATB unless otherwise indicated.

Romantic

Brahms, Johannes: Let Nothing Cause You Anguish, *316*
Mendelssohn, Felix: Herbstlied, *324*
Rossini, Gioacchino: Duetto buffo di due gatti (SA), *331*
Schumann, Robert: Schön Blümelein (SA or TB), *336*

Twentieth century

Alwes, Chester Lee: The Lord to Me a Shepherd Is, *346*
Hall, William D. (arr.): I Know Where I'm Goin' (SA), *352*
Johnston, Ben: Sanctus-Benedictus (from *Mass*), *358*
McKelvy, James: Deck the Halls (in $\frac{7}{8}$), *362*
Stevens, Halsey: Go, Lovely Rose, *366*

Musica vivat aeterna

Music Lives Forever

MF 3008

YOU LOVERS THAT HAVE LOVES ASTRAY

For S.S.A. a cappella
(Recorder Consort*)

JOHN HILTON
Arranged and edited by Fredrick Stoufer

Instrumental parts on last pages.

CMS-119

CMS-119

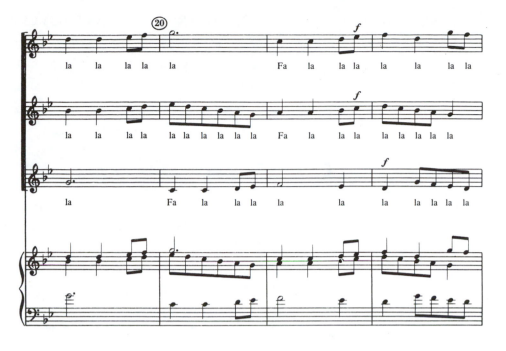

CMS-119

YOU LOVERS THAT HAVE LOVES ASTRAY

YOU LOVERS THAT HAVE LOVES ASTRAY

CMS-119

YOU LOVERS THAT HAVE LOVES ASTRAY

HILTON—STOUFER

"Tenebrae factae sunt"
Marc Antonio Ingegneri

Tenebrae factae sunt,
dum crucifixissent Jesum Judaei:
et circa horam nonam
exclamavit Jesus voce magna:
Deus meus, utquid me dereliquisti?

Exclamans Jesus voce magna, ait:
Pater in manus tuas commendo
spiritum meum.
Et inclinato capite
emisit spiritum.

Darkness fell
when Jesus of Judea was crucified:
And about the ninth hour
Jesus cried out in a loud voice:
My God, why hast Thou forsaken me?

Jesus, crying out in a loud voice, said:
Father, into Thy hands I commend
my spirit.
And inclining his head
he gave up the spirit.

TENEBRAE FACTAE SUNT
For S.A.T.B. A Cappella

Marc Antonio Ingegneri
(1545–1592)
ed. Harold A. Decker

NMP - 140

NMP - 140

tu — as com-men-do spi — ri-tum me — um.

tu — as com-men — do spi — ri-tum me — um.

tu — as com-men — do spi — ri-tum me — um.

Et in-cli — na-to ca — pi-te e-mi-sit spi — ri-tum.

Et in-cli — na-to ca — pi-te e-mi-sit spi — ri-tum.

Et in-cli — na-to ca — pi-te e-mi-sit spi — ri-tum.

Et in-cli — na-to ca — pi-te e-mi-sit spi — ri-tum.

Musica est Dei donum optimi

Orlando di Lasso

MF 3008

MF 3008

AGNUS DEI

(For S. A. A. T. B. A cappella)

GIOVANNI PIERLUIGI DA PALESTRINA (1525-1594)
Edited and Transcribed by Stan Hill

RCS-101

REST SWEET NYMPHS

For S.A.T.B. and Instrumental Consort

Francis Pilkington (C. 1570 - 1638)
ed. Harold A. Decker

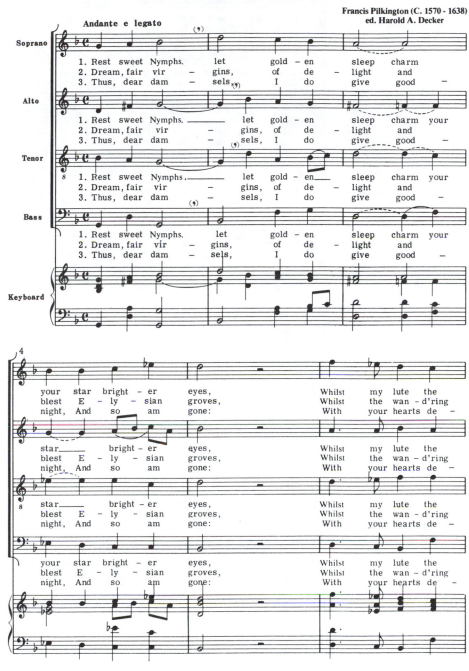

CMS - 121

watch   doth   keep   with   pleas – ing   sym – pa – thies,
shades   of   night   Re –   sem – ble   your   true   loves.   Lul – la,
sites   long   live;   Still   joy   and   ne – ver   moan.

watch   doth   keep   with   pleas – ing   sym – pa – thies,
shades   of   night   Re –   sem – ble   your   true   loves.   Lul – la,
sites   long   live;   Still   joy   and   ne – ver   moan.

watch   doth   keep   with   pleas – ing   sym – pa – thies,
shades   of   night   Re –   sem – ble   your   true   loves.   Lul – la,
sites   long   live;   Still   joy   and   ne – ver   moan.

watch   doth   keep   with   pleas – ing   sym – pa – thies,
shades   of   night   Re –   sem – ble   your   true   loves.
sites   long   live;   Still   joy   and   ne – ver   moan.

1st time **p**
2nd time **pp**

lul – la-by   lul – la, lul – la – by,   Sleep sweet – ly, sleep
                                                          Your   kiss – es, your
                                                          Hath   pleas'd you and

lul – la-by   lul – la-by lul – la – by,   Sleep sweet-ly,   sleep
                                                          Your   kiss – es, your
                                                          Hath   pleas'd you and

lul – la-by   lul – la-by lul – la – by,   Sleep sweet – ly, sleep
                                                          Your   kiss – es, your
                                                          Hath   pleas'd you and

Lul – la,   lul – la-by, lul – la – by   Sleep sweet – ly, sleep
                                                          Your   kiss – es, your
                                                          Hath   pleas'd you and

CMS - 121

Lyrics (soprano, alto, tenor, bass — same text):

Measures 14–16:
- sweet — ly, let no — thing af — fright ye. In
- bliss — es send them by your wish — es, Al —
- eas'd you, and sweet slum — ber seiz'd you, And

Measures 17–end:
- calm con — tent — ments lie. Lul — la lie. (1.2.) / lie. (3.)
- though they be not nigh. nigh. / nigh.
- now to bed I hie. hie. / hie.

CMS - 121

CHRIST JESUS LAY IN DEATH'S STRONG BANDS

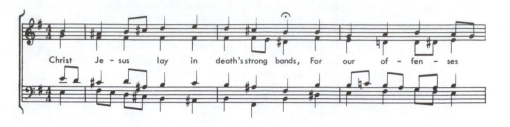

Christ Je - sus lay in death's strong bands, For our of - fen - ses

giv - en; But now at God's right hand He stands, And

brings us life from heav - en; There - fore let us

joy - ful be. And sing to God right thank - ful - ly Loud

songs of al - le - lu - ia! Al - le - lu - ia!

MF 243

JESU, PRICELESS TREASURE

1. Je - su, price - less trea - sure, Source of pur - est plea - sure,
2. Hence, all fear and sad - ness! For the Lord of glad - ness,

Tru - est Friend to me. Ah, how long I've pant - ed, And my heart hath
Je - su, en - ters in. Those who love the Fa - ther, Though the storms may

faint - ed, Thirst - ing, Lord, for Thee. Thine I am, Oh spot - less Lamb!
gath - er, Still have peace with - in; Yea, what - e'er I here must bear,

I will suf - fer nought to hide_____ Thee, Nought I ask be - side_____ Thee.
Thou art still my pur - est plea - sure, Je - su, price - less trea - sure.

WAKE, AWAKE, FOR NIGHT IS FLYING

1. Wake, a - wake, for night is fly - ing, The
   Mid - night hears the wel - come voic - es, And

Wake, a - wake for
Mid - night hears the

MF 243

watch - men on the heights are cry - - ing; A -
at the thrill - ing cry re - joic - - es: Come

wake, Je - ru - sa - lem, at last! The Bride - groom
forth, ye vir - gins, night is past!

comes, a - wake, Your lamps with glad - ness take;

Hal - le - lu - jah! For Him pre - pare a

feast most rare, For ye must go to meet Him there.

2. Now let all the heav'ns adore Thee,
   And men and angels sing before Thee,
   With harp and cymbal's clearest tone;
   Of one pearl each shining portal,
   Where we are with the choir immortal
   Of angels round Thy dazzling throne;

Nor eye hath seen, nor ear
Hath yet attain'd to hear
What there is ours,
But we rejoice, and sing to Thee
Our hymn of joy eternally.

MF 243

Peace Today Descends From Heaven

Hodie, nobis de caelo

Translated and Edited by
DR. WILLIAM TORTOLANO

ALESSANDRO GRANDI

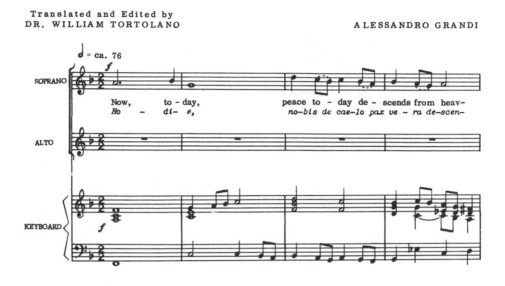

MF 803

MF 803

MF 803

MF 803

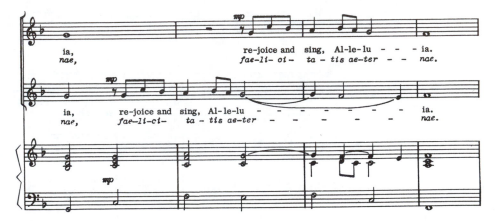

MF 803

MF 803

J. J.

BUT AS FOR HIS PEOPLE

G. F. Handel
ed. by Harold Decker

*This rhythmic pattern should be performed at each
repetition, as in the accompaniment in measure eleven.*

HE SENT A THICK DARKNESS

G. F. Handel
ed. by Harold Decker

HOW EXCELLENT THY NAME/ HALLELUJAH!

For S. A. T. B. and Organ or Piano

G. F. HANDEL

Edited by Hugh Chandler

Attácca

. Hal-le - lu-jah, Hal-le - lu-jah, Hal - le - lu - jah, Hal - le - lu -
. . . Hal-le - lu-jah, Hal-le - lu-jah, Hal - le - lu - jah, Hal - le - lu -
- jah, Hal-le - lu-jah, Hal-le - lu-jah, Hal - le - lu - jah, Hal - le - lu -
Hal-le - lu-jah, Hal-le - lu-jah, Hal - le - lu - jah, Hal - le - lu -
- jah, Hal-le - lu - jah, Hal-le - lu - jah, Hal-le - lu jah, Hal-le - lu -
- jah, Hal-le - lu-jah, Hal-le - lu-jah, Hal-le - lu-jah,
- jah, Hal-le-lu-jah, Hal-le-lu-jah, Hal-le - lu-jah, Hal-le - lu -
- jah, Hal - le - lu - jah, Hal - le - lu - jah, Hal - le - lu - jah, Hal-le - lu -
- jah, ... Hal-le - lu - jah, ... Hal - le - lu -
Hal - le - lu - jah, Hal - le - lu -
- jah, ... Hal-le - lu - jah, ... Hal - le - lu -
- jah,

- jah, Hal-le - lu-jah, Hal-le - lu-jah. Hal - le - lu - jah, Hal - le - lu -
- jah, Hal-le - lu-jah, Hal-le - lu-jah, Hal - le - lu - jah, Hal - le - lu -
- jah, Hal-le - lu-jah, Hal-le - lu-jah, Hal - le - lu - jah, Hal - le - lu -
Hal-le - lu-jah, Hal-le - lu-jah, Hal - le - lu - jah, Hal - le - lu -
- jah, . . . Hal-le - lu - jah, Hal - le - lu - jah, Hal le - lu - jah, . . .
- jah, Hal-le - lu - jah, Hal - le - lu - jah, Hal -
- jah, Hal-le - lu - jah, Hal-le - lu - jah, . . .
- jah, Hal - le - lu - jah,
. . . . . . Hal - le - lu - jah, ... Hal - le - lu - jah, Hal-le - lu -
- le - lu - jah, ... Hal-le-lu -
. . . . . . Hal - le - lu - jah, Hal - le - lu - jah, ... Hal-le - lu -
Hal - le - lu - jah, . . . Hal - le - lu -

GLORIA

ANTONIO VIVALDI

4. Gratias agimus tibi

5. Propter magnam gloriam tuam

ANTHEM OF THANKSGIVING

From *"The Israelites in the Desert"*

For S.A.T.B. and Organ or Instruments*

Paraphrased by Richard H. Brewer

C.P.E. BACH
(1714 - 1788)
Edited and arranged by Richard Brewer

Instrumental parts on sale from publisher (WHC - 74A)

AGNUS DEI

from *Missa Brevis* St. *Joannis de Deo*

Translation by Harold Decker

Franz Josef Haydn
Edited by Harold Decker

Copyright © MCMLXXXVI Fostco Music Press
Sole Selling Agent: Mark Foster Music Company
Box 4012, Champaign, IL 61820

MF 282

MF 282

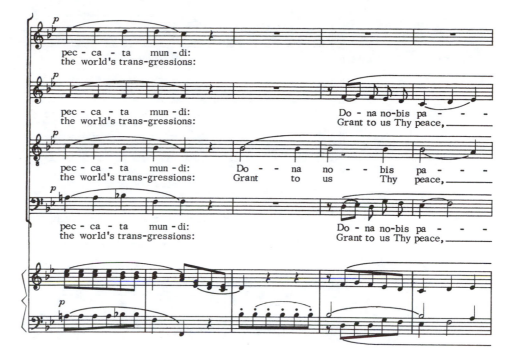

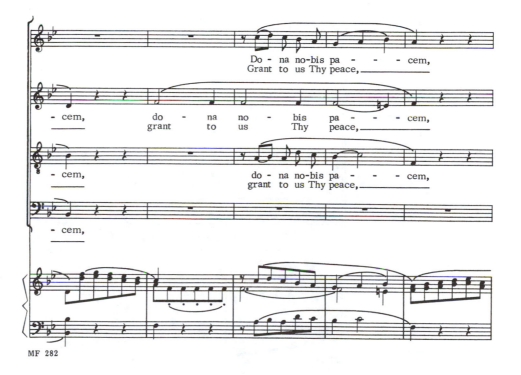

MF 282

MF 282

MF 282

MF 282

> **Phonetic Transcription of "Luci care, luci belle"**
> *W. A. Mozart*
>
> *Lú–ci   cá——re, lú—ci   bel——le,*[2]
> l00-chEE kAH-rEH l00-chEE bEHl-lEH
>
> *cá——ri lú—mi,——a——má——te   stel——le,*
> kAH-rEE l00-mEE AH-mAH-tEH stEHl-lEH
>
> *dá——te cal——ma a qué——sto có——re!*
> dAH-tEH kAH-lmAH- kwEH-stAU kAU-rEH
>
> *Se   per   vó——i so——spí——ro   e   mó——ro,*
> sEH pEHr vAUee sAU-spEE-rAU EH mAU-rAU
>
> *i——dol mí——o bel   te——só——ro,*
> EE-dAU-lmEE-AU bEHl tEH-sAU-rAU
>
> *foŕ——za e sol del   Dí——o d'a——mó——re.*
> fAU-rtsAHEH sAUl dEHl dEE-AU dAH-mAU-rEH

[2]See Latin Pronunciation According to Roman Usage in Appendix C. The rules for Italian pronunciation are similar to those of the Romanized Latin.

LUCI CARE, LUCI BELLE
(Lovely Stars, Beautiful Stars)
For S. A. B. and Three Clarinets*

English Text: Robert Carl
Text Source Unknown

W. A. MOZART, K. 346
Edited by Robert Carl

*Instrumental parts on last page.
**Piano score is an exact reduction of instrumental parts.

co - re, da - te cal - ma a que - sto co - re!
mine, __ calm, __ oh __ calm this __ heart of mine!

co - re, da - te cal - ma a que - sto co - re!
mine, __ calm, oh calm this __ heart __ of mine!

co - re, da - te __ cal - ma a que - sto co - re!
mine, __ calm, __ oh calm this heart of mine! __

Se per voi __ so - spi - ro e mo - ro, i - dol
If I long for you __ and __ die, __ I - dol

Se per voi __ so - spi - ro e mo - ro, i - dol
If I long for you __ and __ die, __ I - dol

Se per voi so - spi - ro e mo - ro, i - dol
If I long __ and __ die, __ I - dol

Luci Care, Luci Belle - 4

Luci Care, Luci Belle - 4

LUCI CARE, LUCI BELLE

1st Bb CLARINET

MOZART - CARL

Luci Care, Luci Belle - 4

LET NOTHING CAUSE YOU ANGUISH
(Lass dich nur nichts nicht dauren)

Paul Fleming (1609-1640)   Johannes Brahms, Op. 30
English translation by R. M. H.   Edited by Ronald M. Huntington

CH-13

CH-13

CH-13

CH–13

tran - quil, be tran - quil.
Dei - ne, das Dei - ne.

due. be tran - quil.
dir das Dei - ne.

e'er is due, be tran - quil, be tran - quil.
gibt auch dir das Dei - ne, das Dei - ne.

what-e'er is due, be tran - quil.
der gibt auch dir das Dei - ne.

Have
Sei

CH–13

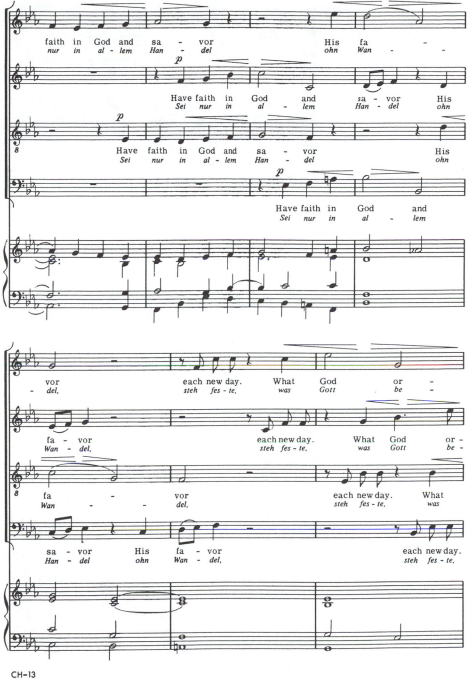

CH-13

CH–13

CH-13

HERBSTLIED
(Autumn Song)
(For S.A. or T.B. & Piano)

Translation:
T. Baker

FELIX MENDELSSOHN
(1809-1847)

NMP-145

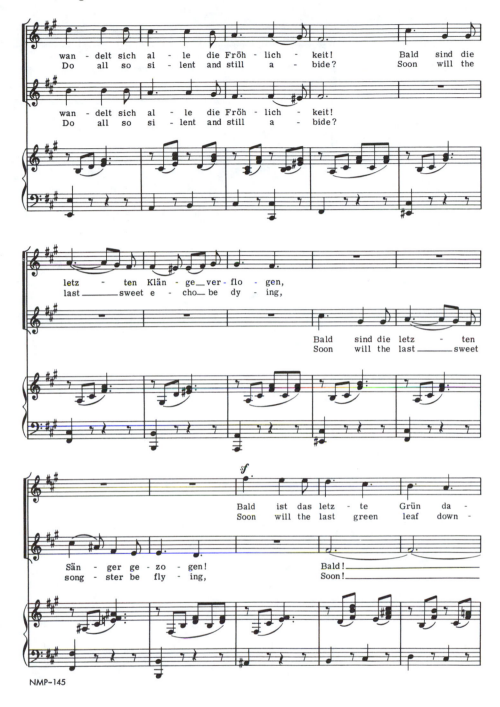

wan - delt sich al - le die Fröh - lich - keit! Bald sind die
Do all so si - lent and still a - bide? Soon will the

wan - delt sich al - le die Fröh - lich - keit!
Do all so si - lent and still a - bide?

letz - ten Klän - ge ver - flo - gen,
last sweet e - cho be dy - ing,

Bald sind die letz - ten
Soon will the last sweet

Bald ist das letz - te Grün da -
Soon will the last green leaf down -

Sän - ger ge - zo - gen! Bald!
song - ster be fly - ing, Soon!

NMP-145

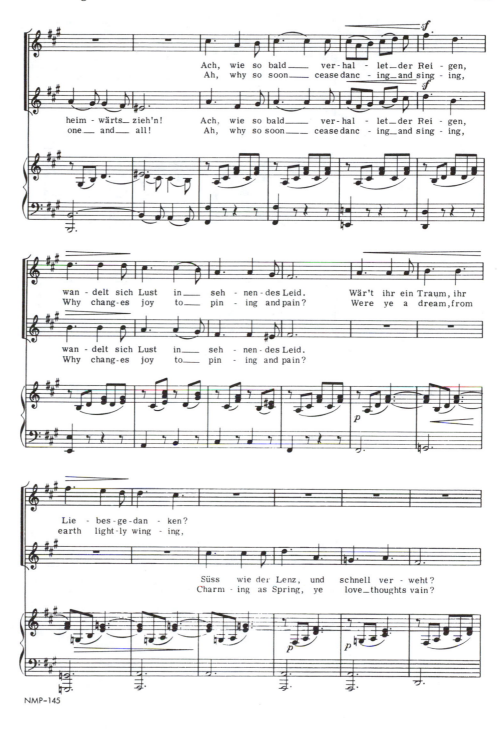

Süss wie der Lenz, und schnell ___ ver-weht?
Charm - ing as Spring, ye love ___ thought's vain?

Ei - nes, nur
One thing, there

Ei - nes, nur Ei - nes will nim - mer wan - ken:
One thing there is that will nev - er leave me

Ei - nes will nim - mer wan - ken, nur Ei - nes will
is that will nev - er leave me, there's one thing will

Es ist das Seh - nen, das nim - mer ver - geht. ___
It is my yearn - ing, 'twill ev - er re - main!___

nim - mer wan - ken: Es ist das Seh - nen, das nim - mer ver - geht.
nev - er leave me It is my yearn - ing, 'twill ev - er re - main!

NMP-145

NMP-145

NMP-145

DUETTO BUFFO DI DUE GATTI
(COMIC DUET FOR TWO CATS)
(or whatever)

For Two-Part Chorus of Treble Voices,
Male Voices or Some Other Kinds of Voices (?),
Dulcimer, Harpsichord, Lyre,
Ophicleide or Piano for Accompaniment

GIOACCHINO ROSSINI
(1792–1868)
Edited by A. Feline

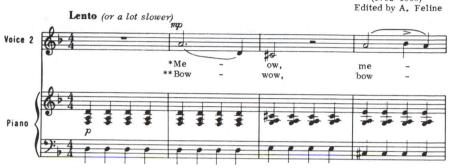

The accompanist may wish to go berserk by playing an extensive two-bar introduction just written by a relative of Rossini. These two bars are kept in the Rossini Gatti Gesellschaft and may be purchased from the publisher for a small fortune.

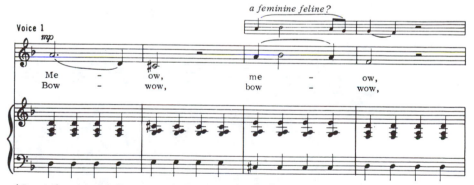

* *Rossini's original Italian was spelled: mi-au. This editor finds either acceptable, or, for that matter, doesn't really care.*

** *The intelligent performer may wish to use some other type of sound generally associated with the domesticated carnivorous mammal. (Heh!)*

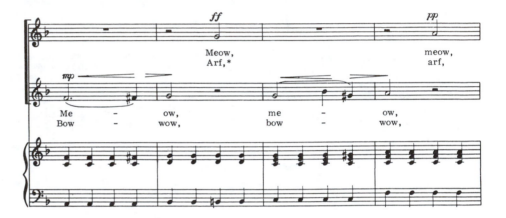

*Notice the 'subtle' change from bowwow to arf. . .

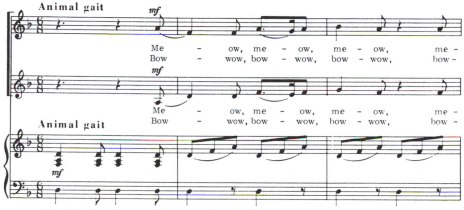

The editor's meticulous dynamic markings don't mean a thing!

me – ow, ow, ow, ow, ow, ow, ow, ow, me – ow.
bow – wow, wow, wow, wow, wow, wow, wow, wow, bow-wow.

me – ow, ow, ow, ow, ow, ow, ow, ow, me – ow.
bow – wow, wow, wow, wow, wow, wow, wow, wow, bow-wow.

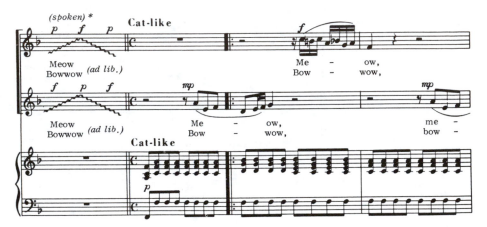

(spoken) *   Cat-like

Meow (ad lib.)   Me – ow,   Me – ow,
Bowwow (ad lib.)   Bow – wow,   bow –

Meow (ad lib.)   Me – ow,   me –
Bowwow (ad lib.)   Bow – wow,   bow –

Cat-like

me – ow,   me –
bow – wow,   bow –

ow,   me – ow,
wow,   bow – wow,

* *Felis catus abandonment*

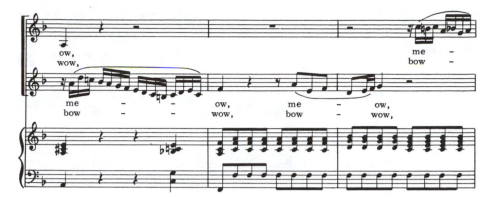

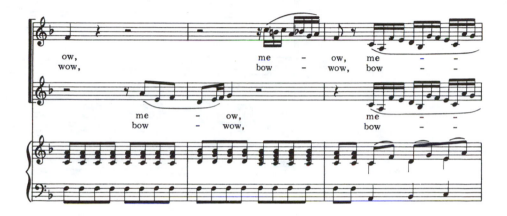

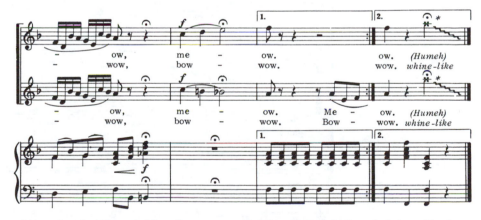

*This editor has discovered through many years of study and research, there is that penultimate moment of ecstatic euphoric finality when all mammals release an "aural offering" created by closing the buccal cavity, and forcing wind pressure to barely escape through the glottal aperture causing an eerie high-pitched sound which makes the hair stand high on any other mammal within that decibelic onslaught. (This can also be achieved by placing your hand over each other's mouths.)

A. Feline

SCHÖN BLÜMELEIN
(Lovely Flower) *

For S.A.T.B. and Piano

English Text:
Anna Maria Jardini

ROBERT SCHUMANN, Op. 43, No. 3
Edited by William D. Hall

* *Source: Drei Zweistimmige Lieder (originally for two voices)*

Die Schmet - ter-ling' und
The but - ter-fly and

Die Schmet - ter-ling' und
The but - ter-fly and

Bie - nen, die_ Kä - fer hell und blank,
small bee, the_ bee - tle bright of shell,

Bie - nen, die Kä - fer hell und blank,
small bee, the bee - tle bright of shell,

die muss - ten all ihm
were met in mer - ry

die muss - ten all ihm
were met in mer - ry

Kä - fer hell und blank, die san - gen mit fro - hen Mie - nen mir
bee - tle bright of shell, turned 'round with their smil - ing fac - es, sang

Kä - fer hell und blank, die san - gen mit fro - hen Mie - nen mir
bee - tle bright of shell, turned 'round with their smil - ing fac - es, sang

Kä - fer hell und blank, die san - gen mit fro - hen Mie - nen mir
bee - tle bright of shell, turned 'round with their smil - ing fac - es, sang

Kä - fer hell und blank, die san - gen mit fro - hen Mie - nen mir
bee - tle bright of shell, turned 'round with their smil - ing fac - es, sang

ei - nen schö - nen Dank, schö - nen Dank!
"Thank you and fare - well, fare thee well!"

ei - nen schö - nen Dank, schö - nen Dank!
"Thank you and fare - well, fare thee well!"

ei - nen schö - nen Dank, schö - nen Dank!
"Thank you and fare - well, fare thee well!"

ei - nen schö - nen Dank, schö - nen Dank!
"Thank you and fare - well, fare thee well!"

For Richard Been and The Hicksville Methodist Church Choir

The Lord to Me a Shepherd Is

Bay Psalm Book, 1640

CHESTER L. ALWES

The setting is reprinted from THE LORD TO ME A SHEPHERD IS by
Charles Alwes, copyright © 1971, assigned to Chantry Music Press, Inc.
Used by permission of Augsburg Fortress. May not be reproduced further.

I KNOW WHERE I'M GOIN'

(Soprano, Alto, Flute, Piano)

FOLKSONG

Arranged by
WILLIAM D. HALL

Flute, Oboe or Melodica

Piano

SOPRANO

I know where I'm go-in'____ and I know who's goin'

ALTO

I know where I'm go-in'____ and I know who's goin'

I Know Where I'm Goin' - 6

John- ny.

John - ny.

I have stock-ings of silk, shoes of fine green

I have stock-ings of silk, shoes of fine green

I Know Where I'm Goin' - 6

lea - ther.   Combs to buck-le my hair   and a
lea - ther.   Combs to buck-le my hair_____ and a

ring for eve - ry fin - ger.
ring for eve - ry fin - ger.

I Know Where I'm Goin' - 6

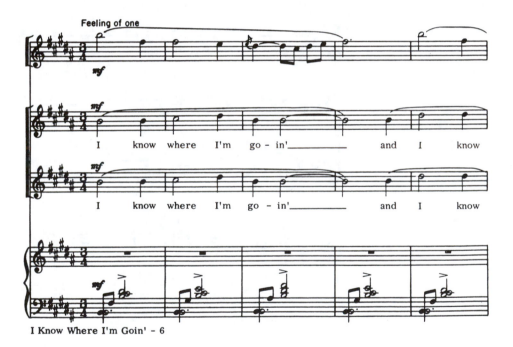

I Know Where I'm Goin' - 6

I Know Where I'm Goin' - 6

MF 141S

SANCTUS

Ben Johnston

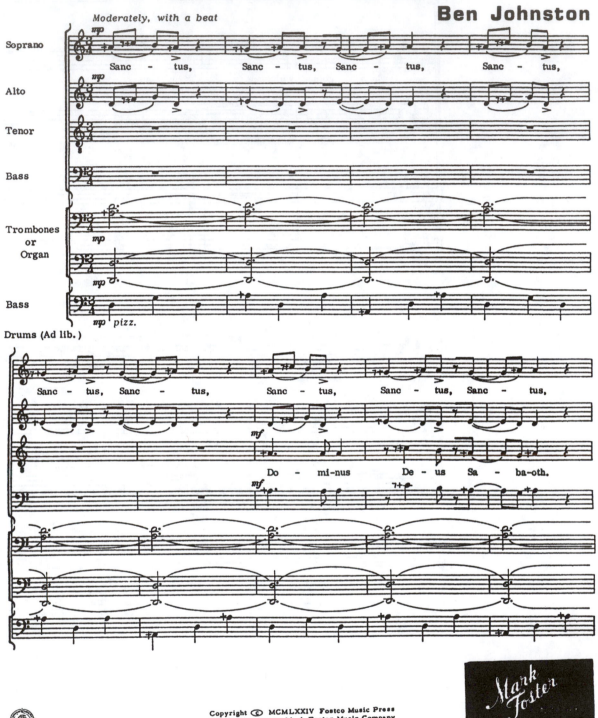

Moderately, with a beat

Soprano — Sanc - tus, Sanc - tus, Sanc - tus, Sanc - tus,

Alto

Tenor

Bass

Trombones or Organ

Bass — pizz.

Drums (Ad lib.)

Sanc - tus, Sanc - tus, Sanc - tus, Sanc - tus, Sanc - tus,

Do - mi-nus De - us Sa - ba-oth.

Copyright © MCMLXXIV Fostco Music Press
Sole Selling Agent: Mark Foster Music Company
Box 4012, Champaign IL, 61820

Mark Foster

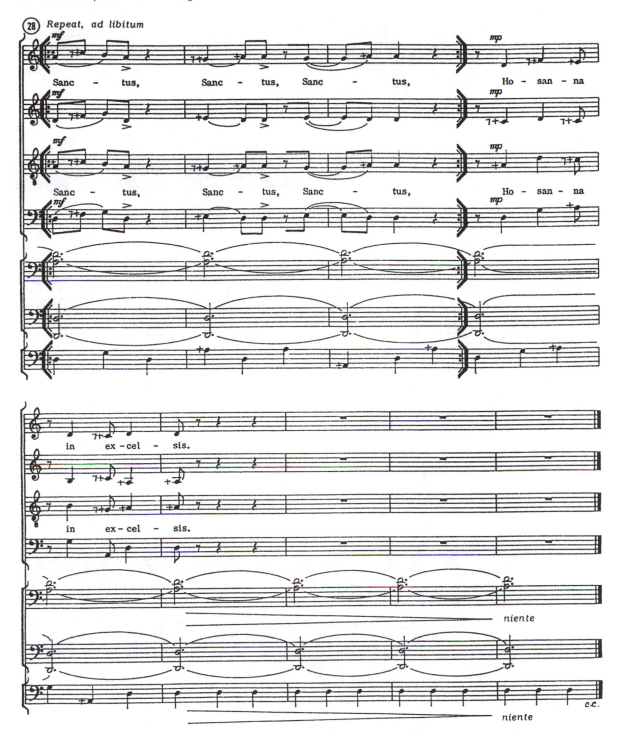

SATB a cappella
MF 605

Box 4012, Champaign IL, 61820

Deck the Halls
(IN 7/8)

Arranged by
JAMES McKELVY

7/8 METER   The eighth note must remain equal in time value whether it is in a group of two (♫) or three (♫♪).
The resulting irregular accents create a fascinating rhythm. It is suggested that the music be learned
with a metronome set at about 152 for an eighth note, gradually increasing the tempo until the singers begin to feel the
lilt. The tempo change indicated for the third stanza may be disregarded, for if the music should begin a little too fast
and/or the tempo gradually increase, a still faster tempo here would destroy the delightful quality of the 7/8 meter.

Also available in 7-8 for SSA, MF 953.

MF 605   Copyright © MCMLXXV Fostco Music Press

International Copyright Secured   Sole Selling Agent: Mark Foster Music Company
                                       Box 4012, Champaign IL, 61820   All Rights Reserved

Don we now our gay ap-par-el,   Fa la la . . . .
Fa la la la,   Fa la la la,

(no rit.)
Troll the an - cient Yule - tide car - ol,   Fa la la . . . . Oh
Fa la la . . . .

See the blaz - ing Yule be - fore us,   Fa la la . . . .

Strike the harp and join the cho - rus,   Fa la la . . . .

MF 605

C Fol – low me in mer - ry meas-ure, Fa la la . . . .

While I tell_ of_ Yule-tide treas-ure, Fa la la . . . .

D *pp* Fa la la . . . .

f Fast a - way the old year pas - ses, Fa la la . . . .
Fast a - way Fa la la . . . .
Fast a - way Fa la la . . . .

MF 605

Hail the new, ye lads and lass-es, Fa la la . . . .
Hail the new, Fa la la . . . .
Hail the new, Fa la la . . . .

Sing we joy-ous all to-geth-er, Fa la la . . . .
Fa la la . . . .
Fa la la la la la la
Fa la la la
Fa la la la

Heed-less of the wind and weath-er, Fa la la . . . .

la la la . . . . Fa la la . . . .

MF 605

for Harriett
Go, Lovely Rose

EDMUND WALLER (1606-87)   HALSEY STEVENS

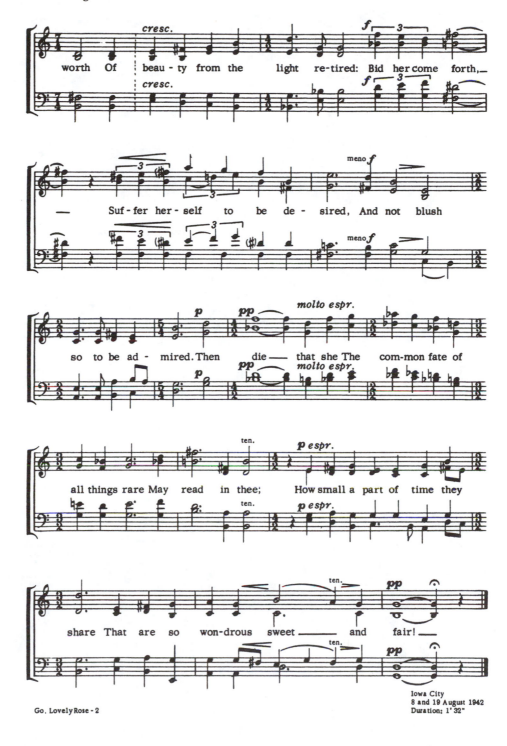

Go, Lovely Rose - 2

Iowa City
8 and 19 August 1942
Duration: 1' 32"

Index